NATION BUILDING PLAN
BETWEEN 2020 & 2064

NATION BUILDING PLAN
BETWEEN 2020 & 2064

*Designing Paradise Cities
to Restore PRIDE through
WEALTH Creation*

FUMENE GEORGE TSIBANI

Nation Building Plan Between 2020 & 2064

Copyright © 2020 by Fumene George Tsibani. All rights reserved.

No part of this publication may be reproduced, stored in a retrieval system or transmitted in any way by any means, electronic, mechanical, photocopy, recording or otherwise without the prior permission of the author except as provided by USA copyright law.

The opinions expressed by the author are not necessarily those of URLink Print and Media.

1603 Capitol Ave., Suite 310 Cheyenne, Wyoming USA 82001
1-888-980-6523 | admin@urlinkpublishing.com

URLink Print and Media is committed to excellence in the publishing industry.

Book design copyright © 2020 by URLink Print and Media. All rights reserved.

Published in the United States of America
ISBN 978-1-64753-247-5 (Paperback)
ISBN 978-1-64753-246-8 (Digital)

Non-Fiction
31.01.20

DEDICATION

The bravest are surely those who have the clearest vision of what is before them, glory and danger alike, and yet notwithstanding go out to meet it.

– Gregory Stock, advisor to former President Bill Clinton of the United States, on the biotechnological challenges of the twenty-first century

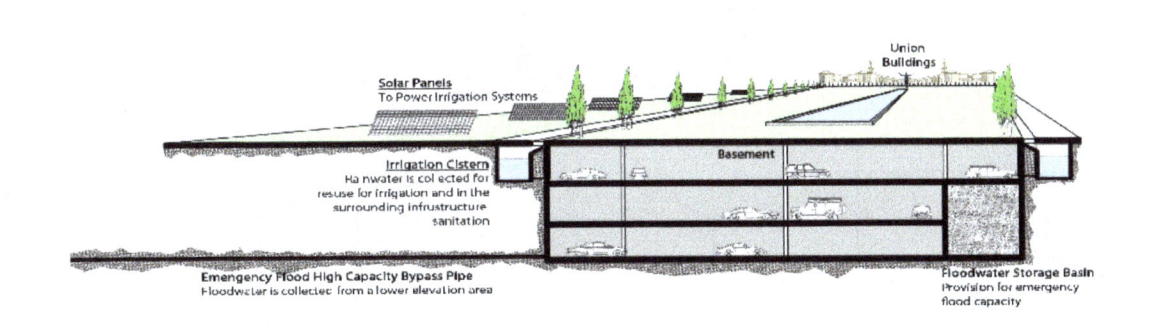

I dedicate this book to the AmaCirha Kingdom, the Imbumba yamaNyama Royal Council, the Congress of Traditional Leaders of South Africa (CONTRALESA), Khoisan Associations in the Southern African Development Community (SADC) region, the institutions of traditional leadership in Africa, and my family members, to encourage them to restore and create Paradise City models as part of the nation-building plan in Africa, without continuing to be held hostage by pseudo-archaeology and related historical distortions of facts for dubious purposes in our beautiful motherland.

DISCLAIMER

This book has been developed and reviewed by Dr. Fumene George Tsibani (founding member of Mthengenya and Associates (Pty) Limited), the Imbumba yamaNyama Royal Council (established in 1882, and launched in 1891 in Port Elizabeth, Nelson Mandela Bay Municipality, by Dr. MWB Rubusana), the Kingdom of Khoekhoen, the Hancumqua Royal House, Khoisan Associations in Southern Africa, and the House of Traditional Leaders in Africa.

Approval does not signify that the contents necessarily reflect the views and policies of Mthengenya and Associates (Pty) Limited, the Imbumba yamaNyama Royal Council, the Kingdom of Khoekhoen, the Hancumqua Royal House, Khoisan Associations in Southern Africa, and the House of Traditional Leaders in Africa; nor does mention of trade names or commercial products constitute endorsement of or recommendation for their use.

The author accepts that the information and views in this book might not be suited to everyone. The author obtained the information contained herein from various sources, but he neither implies nor intends any guarantee of accuracy. He believes that the information is reliable and valid from his personal experience in dealing with sustainable planning and development in the complex contexts described in this book. The author believes that the ideas and views reflected in this book are sound, but readers who are influenced by these ideas and views cannot hold him responsible for either the actions they take or the result of those actions.

FOREWORD

Beauty is in the eye of the beholder.

– Margaret Wolfe Hungerford (date unknown)

Blue and green city models must be rebuilt in the 'Home of Legends'.

The arrival of colonialists (colonial powers) at the southern tip of Africa in 1498 reflects the period of exploration and discovery that came to be known as the European Renaissance, the founding moment of capitalist modernity and Western bourgeois ascendancy in the world.

Simultaneously, it was the start of the wanton destruction of many city civilizations (particularly) throughout Africa. The protracted struggles waged between Africa and Europe had started in antiquity and endured for centuries. They included the famous Punic Wars, which broke out during the years 264 to 146 BC, marking the struggle for power between African Carthage and European Rome. The heroic African general Hannibal nearly defeated the Roman Republic during the Second Punic War, which took place from 218 to 201 BC. The enraged Roman Republic developed a hostility that culminated in the phrase, 'Delenda est Carthago' (Carthage must be destroyed). It was thus during the Third Punic War, or the War of Carthage, in 146 BC, that the Carthaginian Empire was destroyed. This was the destruction of an ancient city civilization that was unequaled in Europe. The ruins of ancient Carthage are today part of Tunis, the capital of Tunisia.

At a meeting of the Organisation of African Unity (OAU) held in Tunis in 1994, the then president of South Africa Nelson Mandela recalled the history of the destruction of Carthage by the generals of the Roman Empire and said:

> In the distant days of antiquity, a Roman sentenced this African city to death, saying that Carthage must be destroyed. In addition, indeed, Carthage was destroyed. Today we wander among its ruins, and only our imagination and historical records enable us to experience its magnificence. Only our African being makes it possible to hear the piteous cries of the victims of the vengeance of the Roman Empire ...

Nelson Mandela reminded the delegates at the summit of how, after the defeat of the African states, their peoples were carted away to foreign lands as slaves; their land became the property of other nations, their resources a source of enrichment for other peoples, and their kings and queens mere servants of foreign powers.

The unbearable conditions to which they were subsequently subjected caused them to vow to reclaim the land of their forefathers, their dignity, and their heritage for the benefit of the generations to come. They vowed to rebuild the city of Carthage.

Africa's challenges have been identified as poor economic performance, poverty, unemployment, poor governance, conflict and war, instability, lack of democracy, poor human rights, gender inequality, lack of cooperation, and tardy development.

The Ntsikana kaGabha Paradise City, or blue and green city models for nation-building, represent the rebuilding of the city of Carthage. They provide a solution to changing society for the better, and develop a vision about the rebuilding of Carthage, as metaphorically expressed by Nelson Mandela.

The decimation of people in the former Cape Colony during the frontier wars after 1820 can be equated to the destruction of the city of Carthage. The challenge is the restoration of the aesthetic relational values that depict bravery, loyalty, patriotism, dignity, courage, commitment, and respect, as demonstrated by the gallant Xhosa warriors of the frontier wars. The monograph, *zemk' iinkomo magwalandini* (Defend thy heritage), by Dr. MWB Rubusana is a clarion call for the restoration of the heritage and the pride that the warriors of the Cape Province (an umbrella term for what is today the Eastern, Northern and Western Cape provinces) sought to defend. The revival of the Cape provinces' aesthetic relational values should be based on the Ubuntu principles of love, respect, and hospitality.

The deeds of our heroes and heroines, such as Sol Plaatje, Chief Autshumato of the Goringhaicoma Khoi group in the Cape (1529-1663) – who was called Harry the Strandloper by Dutch settlers, Queen (Gaos) Krotoa (Eva) of the Goringhaicoma chieftaincy in the Cape Peninsula, Klaas Lukas, Piet Rooi, Jan Kupido among the Khoisan groupings, as well as King Nkosiyamntu, Prophet Gabha, Commander Makhanda, Dr. Rubusana, King Dalindyebo, former ANC President Tambo, former President Mandela, and other extraordinary leaders form part of the former Cape Colony's historical and collective memory. The envisaged city to be raised in these parts should be a reflection of the values epitomized by such heroes and heroines.

Writers, artists, musicians, intellectuals, and workers in ideas should, in their performances, capture the rich history of the struggle, as well as the spirit of commitment to defending their heritage to be passed on to succeeding generations. The museums should not only be a historical reflection, but also have a social conscience. The development of the region's indigenous languages occupies a special place in preserving the memory of the colonized. The knowledge, emotions and intellectual capital must be stored. South Africans must, therefore, develop their own granary and preserve their own memory and intellectual value. The Ntsikana kaGabha Paradise City represents the rebuilding of this envisaged modern world.

The reader of this book will also discover the complexity of some of the archaeological, anthropological and sociological conflicts, as well as the structural and cultural diversity of the Cape provinces (whether the Northern, Eastern or Western Cape) as a Home of Legends. This book seeks to advance an argument for aesthetic relational values in building blue and green city models using the Ubuntu paradigm, through which unique circumstances, values, cultural beliefs, norms, and standards are restored. Although much of the research that went into writing this book relates to aesthetic relational values in planning and development, as well as aesthetic leadership focused on global trends, it includes research on African leaders in the context of the Home of Legends, or any landscape in Africa.

Mziwandile Milance 'Chris' Mandubu
Independent Consultant

PREFACE

First, a disclaimer: I am a practitioner, not an academic. I am a pracademic, a word coined by Professor Erwin Schwella (Stellenbosch University, School of Public Leadership, 2015). I was born in KwaGcisa between the Tsomo and Kei (Nciba) Rivers on Fritz Farm, Stutterheim (Cumakala), in the Eastern Cape as part of the Cape Colony. I started my primary schooling at Lujilo Missionary School before joining Mngqesha Primary School in the early 1980s. I started my secondary schooling at Amantinde High School (1982-1983) and moved to Mzomtsha High School in Keiskammahoek (Qoboqobo) (1984-1985). I then joined Amantinde High School in 1986 for Grade 12 and completed post-matriculation at All Saints Senior College in Bisho in 1987, where I met students from the Southern African Development Community (SADC) countries who were from diverse backgrounds, classes, and races. It is at All Saints Senior College that I tasted multiculturalism before studying for my undergraduate degree at the University of Fort Hare (UFH) from 1988.

I came from a working-class family. My mother, Nongqaqu Nothembile (mamQocwa) Mtshatsheni-kaTsibani, was a traditional medical healer (igqirhakazi). As a woman, my mother had to register her livestock in my uncle's name in terms of farming regulations governed by apartheid laws. When my mother passed on in August 1975, a battle in respect of livestock started between AmaCirha of Phakamile kaTsibani and the Mtshatsheni family, AmaQocwa, from the Gcisa area (between the Tsomo and Kei Rivers near Stutterheim). The battle was due to the fact that the AmaXhosa's relationship with their livestock was (and still is) intimate, emotional, committed and joyous (Mostert, 1992:190). With this emotional attachment, the Tsibani Cirha clan forcefully claimed the livestock from my uncles, Mkhuthukwana, Majwabi, Kolipati, Mtshatsheni, Butsholobentonga, Zikhali-mazembe, Tiyeka and Jojo. The case was then supported from the Cirha side by Sithathu kaPhike (a local businessman in Dikidikana Village, Mngqesha District, which was under the jurisdiction of AmaRharhabe kaSandile). The judgment favored OoZikhali. The Bantu Administration Act was used to justify that my uncle inherits the livestock, while some of the livestock were claimed by the local farmer in payment for grazing on his farm. This was like ukuthelekiswa nguMlungu in 1818-1819 (white provocation) (Opland, 2009:311).

We then moved to Phakamile Tsibani, as my mother had been married to his late first son, Albert Tsibani. Phakamile Tsibani had two wives, and Albert Tsibani was from the Great House. His brother, Dumandile Sileyi Tsibani, who was married to Noleta Nowest Tsibani (MaMkhuma kaRoji), had to take custodianship of my two elder sisters, my younger sister and me after our grandfather passed on in December 1975. As farming and agricultural production were part of our culture as Africans, my roles and responsibilities as a young boy were clearly defined. These duties included looking after livestock at Mangqokwe, near

Magungquza, on the way to Mndingi Village in the district of Mngqesha. My rural background and exposure to master-servant injustice at an early age, along with playing rugby and boxing in the beautiful classroom rings of Mngqesha Primary School (Mr. Luxolo Gqoboshiyana and Ms. Nonceba Makula were my first boxing trainers) and later at Mzomtsha High School in Keiskammahoek (Mr. Letsira Sitengile of Zwelitsha was my boxing trainer) contributed to my appreciation of my upbringing by MaMbathana Nolast Nowest Roji-kaTsibani at Dikidikana Village in the district of Mngqesha in King William's Town. The socio-economic, spiritual, emotional, psychological and cultural influences on my young days flowed from the affirmation and appreciation of Ubuntu principles and the deep valuing of the natural beauty of plants and animals, which were God-given treasures for sustainable planning and development.

Bluebucks did not exist in my life, as European settlers had hunted them. Although they became extinct around 1800, most of the AmaXhosa (Cirha, Jwarha, and Tshawe) clans continued to associate them with their daily living. The bluebuck was the first large African mammal to face extinction in historical times, followed by the quagga or zebra (known as iqwarha by Khoisan communities) in 1883. Only four mounted bluebuck specimens remain, in museums in Leiden, Stockholm, Vienna, and Paris, along with skulls and horns in various museums. The bluebuck was sometimes considered a subspecies of the roan antelope, but a genetic study has confirmed it as a distinct species.

Accordingly, birds like the blue crane; mammals like the blue duiker or bluebuck (iphuthi); the rivers and the wells; the Hoho (named after Queen Hoho), Ntaba kaNdoda and Bhukazana Mountains in the Raymond Mhlaba Local Municipality; the hills, olive trees and Nobhoma forests from Stutterheim (eCumakala) to King William's Town (Qonce), Komga (Qumrha), Keiskammahoek (Qoboqobo), Adelaide (Khobonqaba), Tsitsikamma (Cicikama) Port Alfred (Ndlambe), Uitenhage (Qhagqiwa), Grahamstown (Rhini likaMakhanda), Alice (eDikeni) and so forth all confirm that my life and my environment are inseparable. I have worked in the gardens of King William's Town and sold food for Indian traders during school holidays in suburbs such as Ginsburg (a traditional African area), Schornville and Breidbach (traditional so-called 'colored' human settlements). I know the importance of infrastructure investment from my time as a student at All Saints Senior College near Bisho, from the Iona student accommodation at the University of Fort Hare in Alice, and from the Liesbeeck Student Hostel at the University of Cape Town, which all mean one thing to me: love your neighbor as you love yourself!

Reading Dr. Moshe E Ncilashe Swartz's Ph.D. dissertation, titled 'Restoring and holding on to beauty: The role of aesthetic relational values in sustainable development' (Stellenbosch University, 2010), which focuses on aesthetic relational values in planning and development, inspired me to reflect upon the views on, and principles of, coexistence between human beings and the environment. The dissertation reminded me of the aesthetic relational values and Ubuntu principles that I learned during my upbringing by the Cirha clan and about the role that I had to play after interacting with the Imbumba yamaNyama Royal Council, the

Kingdom of Khoekhoen, the Khoisan Association in the Northern Cape, the Congress of Traditional Leaders of South Africa (CONTRALESA) and the Ntsikana religious life leaders in early 2005 regarding aesthetic leadership, which is required to restore PRIDE through WEALTH creation.

In reality, Swartz's dissertation made me confirm the words written by Imbumba yamaNyama during the Ntsikana Open Day in Thwathwa in 2001, which are very difficult to translate into English, that capture my spiritual, emotional, psychological and mental feelings and reflections. Having read this dissertation, I humbly wish to confirm and confess that ubunzulu bobulungisa yincambu yobom, yintsika yesizwe kwabo baneentliziyo ezingcwele ngokukwazi ukuhlisa ityeya yeZulu nokumisela Imbumba yamaNyama yomthonyama ngomnyaka ka—1882, emva kweminyaka emininzi umthunya kaQamata walishiyayo eli limagada ahlabayo. Umsebenzi kaNtsikana eThwathwa ngumfuziselo wokuhla koMoya oyiNgcwele nozuko lukaQamata kweli lizwe limathumb' ntaka, elihexayo ngenxa yezenzo nemisebenzi yethu. Le ncwadi yimvula mlomo kumathambo alele ukuthula nokubulela uQamata ngokugcukumisa okaNcilashe ngenkozo yetyeya kaQamata nokubuyiswa kozinzo ziinkokheli zeli xesha. It is true that (Liyinyaniso elithi) 'Zemk' iinkomo magwalandini' (loosely translated: cows were stolen under your watch, you cowards!). Dr. Mpilo Walter Benson (Cirha) Rubusana (21 February 1858-19 April 1936) used this analogy and traditional epic poetry to urge his countrymen and -women to defend their heritage and restore their pride, guided by the roadmap provided by Ntsikana kaGabha before him: unity in diversity.

One significant contribution of environmental science is that human beings (abantu), and some clans, regard blue cranes (iindwe), bluebucks (amaphuthi), buffaloes (iinyathi), blue wildebeests (iinkonkoni), kudus (amaqhude), black wildebeests (iinqu), elands (iimpofu), white rhinos (imikhombe), cheetahs (amahlosi) and elephants (iindlovu) as part of their heritage and environmental livelihood. Yet, apart from blue cranes, these exquisite animals have been displaced and no longer exist in their part of South Africa, except on game farms and in nature reserves and zoos. Recognizing and restoring the beautiful relational values of our non-human creatures and their ecosystems may mean restoring and maintaining our heritage, along with an appreciation of God and his creation. The ideas raised in Swartz's dissertation are therefore extremely relevant and call for an urgent intervention by both traditional and elected leaders to *save our fragile world*. As part of avoiding the present pseudoextinction of fauna and flora, we need aesthetic leaders to restore aesthetic relational values in the planning and development of modern paradise cities to ensure a balanced ecosystem so that sustainable planning and development can be managed (Stern, Dietz, Guagnano & Kalof, 1995:611-636).

It is our collective godly business – as stewards, trustees, and custodians – to avoid the extinction of organisms in our beautiful world. For their survival, both the animal and the plant kingdoms are largely dependent on the phylum of vertebrate and Chordata mammals called uNtu or genus Homo. In this fragile world, such an aesthetic relational value or 'business unusual' methodology is critical for incorporation into the planning and development of future communities, villages, cities, provinces and nation states under the conceptual framework of the Ntsikana Paradise City or the future Ntsikana Paradise Cities. This must be guided by nation-building plans, which are unfortunately not available in most African countries. Yet most African countries have adopted, without adjustment, Western and, more recently, Asian programs and projects. These programs and projects do not have the necessary impact on the nation-building plan. Unlike our black ancestors, founding elders and stalwarts who had a nation-building plan, which was institutionalized in 1891 as Imbumba yamaNyama, modern African leaders have national programs and projects that have had relatively little impact on nation-building. A nation-building plan must be based on aesthetic relational values whereby citizens, followers, managers, officials, and leaders acquire dignity, love, peace and Ubuntu principles, and a futuristic vision of various programs and related projects that can feed into the plan.

A nation-building plan guided by aesthetic relational values requires aesthetic leaders with good qualities and traits. These good qualities and traits are linked to leadership strategies for restoring our aesthetic relational values and creating balanced coexistence between human beings and the rest of nature, which makes up our biodiversity. The Kingdom of Khoekhoen, the House of Traditional Leaders, and the Imbumba yamaNyama Royal Council leaders are confronted by various problems. On the one hand, there is a need to guide both traditional and elected leaders to restore aesthetic relational values. On the other hand, this book provides an opportunity to identify what type of leaders are needed to carry out the nation-building plan in such a way that these values are restored and maintained for meeting current and future human needs in harmony with the ecosystem. It aims to offer a thoughtful compilation of the leadership traits and the required strategies for implementing a nation-building plan embedded in aesthetic relational values and Ubuntu philosophy that is worth reading. The focus on leadership is important because

> *[inspiring and aesthetic] leaders are not just born to the role. They are born, then made, and sometimes unmade by their own actions. A leader who is not in tune with the followership will become a leader in limbo.* (Khoza, 2011:3)

In short, technical skills and competencies are not enough to equip leaders. Being able to build aesthetic relational values between nations and ecosystems and to influence other leaders, citizens, community champions, managers and officials are key qualities and traits for aesthetic leaders. Using aesthetic leadership tools, this book will help citizens, community champions, practitioners, officials, managers, executives, and leaders to understand aesthetic relational values and principles, on the one hand. On the other hand, leaders will be able to understand their roles and responsibilities so that they can apply these good qualities and traits to drive aesthetic relational values in the process of sustainable planning and development as part of a nation-building plan, or in the creation of blue and green Paradise Cities as future applicable and appropriate cities for Africa's natural treasures and resources.

Indeed, the book will help readers understand how to make the most of their own leadership styles, build great relationships, and learn how to influence a range of other stakeholders more effectively. It has been written as a practical guide for leaders working in various contexts and settings. As such, one may want to read it from beginning to end, but it is equally useful to dip in and out of when one needs inspiration for advancing human needs without negatively affecting biodiversity. This is particularly true if one considers the fact that

> ... where there is no vision, the people perish. (Proverbs 29:18)

I hope you find this book helpful and of practical value for creating, developing and maintaining effective and influential working relationships in our fragile world. I request that you evaluate the value of everyday statements in your environment against the theme of this book, including your own personal values, in order to drive aesthetic relational values for sustainable planning and development. Above all, I hope you will have the compassion and the zeal to honor God's agape love (Isaiah 65:20-3; Colossians 1:13-15) by actively participating in the implementation of a sustainable action plan for the nation-building plan. In reading this book, I trust you will agree with me that the greater the clarity one has on the inside, the more precise one's actions on the outside will be to restore the aesthetic relational values between God's creatures and their environment in order to save the world from ourselves and restore God's agape love thereof.

It is my humble belief that if we want to restore aesthetic relational values in our families, clans, partnerships, households, communities, municipalities, provinces and countries throughout the beloved continents of our fragile world, we need aesthetic leaders who fear God and hold aesthetic relational values to advance and restore God's will on earth. I invite you to join the Africa House of Traditional Leaders and its counterparts in the rest of the world, the Congress of Traditional Leaders in South Africa (CONTRALESA), the Kingdom of Khoekhoen, the Imbumba yamaNyama Royal Council, the South African Heritage Resources Agency (SAHRA), the National Heritage Council (NHC), and the United Nations Educational, Scientific and Cultural Organization (UNESCO), sectoral departments, state-owned enterprises, development finance institutions (DFIs), international development agencies, private sector companies, research think-tanks and academic institutions to drive this noble vision and incorporate aesthetic relational values into future Ntsikana kaGabha Paradise Cities in our lifetime. Imbumba yamaNyama has been the first voluntary movement to restore and hold aesthetic relational values under the guidance of the Kingdom of God.

Through the collective efforts of TEAM (Together Each Achieves More), we all have a responsibility to:

Fumene George Tsibani

> Breathe light into your body – Breathe light into your heart – Breathe light into your mind – Breathe and OPEN! Breathe and remember that you are all LIGHT – Infinite LIGHT – Blessed LIGHT – open your heart and SHINE ON. (Angie Karan Krezos; 2 Corinthians 4:4-7)

Intelligent life developed over hundreds of millions of years of comparative stability. We have eventually reached the stage where we can study our planet and marvel at it. Scientists have, for instance, achieved a great deal in the field of genetics and related disciplines. Equally, astronomers had already revealed about 2 000 solar systems by 2011, complemented by scientific evidence of a handful of Earth-like planets that make the presence of liquid water a possibility. Perhaps our descendants will achieve some sort of 'immortality' of the species via machines. Yet apocalyptic prophecies predicted that all these scientific findings and results would happen, as intelligence would not give up its hold on the galaxy easily. Furthermore, apocalyptic prophecies indicate that there will be an end of this world. Therefore, a fundamentally new transformational leadership and political will are what is most needed to provide effective responses to these new challenges by implementing scientific solutions, complemented by a nation-building plan and a sustainable action plan, beyond the current narrow interpretation of history, to deliver on a better life for all and deepen an appreciation of God's creation.

While the book is about formulating a nation-building plan and restoring aesthetic relational values in the planning and development of smart cities, post-colonial cities or Paradise City models in Africa (and especially in South Africa), it also emphasizes the need to revisit and review the current distorted historical facts promoted by imperial, colonial and neo-liberal ideologies characterized by years of exclusive political interests in the period from the eighteenth century to the democratic era of South Africa. During this period, 'rich oral histories and facts about African Kingdoms' were replaced by fiction, and a 'winner-takes-all policy of colonial dominance' prevailed (Finnegan, 1988:10). This narrow ethnic-separatist model and its consequences have had widespread negative repercussions for the unification of (South) Africans. This is according to the argument advanced by the Imbumba yamaNyama Royal Council, Khoisan Associations, the Hancumqua Royal Council and House of Traditional Leaders, stalwarts, elders and leaders who attempt to restore aesthetic relational values in planning and development in post-colonial Africa and, in so doing, require more coherent and complex reviewing and revision of the current distorted histories in each country. This clan or kingdom reconciliation, and the restoration of histories lost through a structured imperial, colonial and legislated apartheid public administration and management system, can contribute to a nation-building plan between 2020 and 2064. It is argued that such a plan can lead to growth and development as envisaged in the Agenda for Sustainable Development (AfSD) in African countries up to 2063 and beyond.

EXECUTIVE SUMMARY

The book argues that Ntsikana kaGabha Paradise City models, or blue and green city models, based on an Aesthetic Relational Values in Planning and Development Framework (ARVPDF), will co-create space for governance innovation and partnerships by employing Integrated Rural and Urban Infrastructure Investment Programmes (IR and UIIPs) to feed into a nation-building plan between 2020 and 2064. At the same time, these models will ensure that the needs of the Earth's biodiversity, including humans, are balanced by aesthetic environmental management, leading to good governance for the public good (Musvoto, Nahman, Nortje, De Wet & Mahumani, 2014:7-97; UNEP, 2012a:36). It is argued that, through IR and UIIPs as part of a nation-building plan, collective efforts and co-creating governance partnerships leading to the adoption of a sustainable action plan can significantly unify the world's citizens and Africans, as was recently demonstrated in global bulk infrastructure investment interventions such as the Rugby World Cup in 1995, the Soccer World Cup in 2010 , World Rugby Sevens in 2019, and other world sporting codes are being successfully hosted.

Using North-South and South-South methodologies, this book provides a roadmap whereby the ARVPD Framework is adopted to implement the envisaged infrastructure investment programs as part of a nation-building plan in the Cape provinces (an umbrella term for the present-day Eastern, Northern, and Western Cape provinces), known as the Home of Legends, or at other appropriate sites in towns, cities or countries, as the case may be (Brandy, 2006:279). It is significant that the arrival of European explorers and later settlers at the Cape from the early 1400s onwards led to frontier wars or land dispossession of Africans, with a social Darwinism policy applied against African structures of governance, norms, and standards. The success of social and economic Darwinism was enforced through imperial, colonial and apartheid policies, as well as public administration and management (PAM) systems.

In view of the above, the success and outcomes of a nation-building plan between 2020 and 2064 in the Home of Legends and elsewhere in Africa will be based not only on the success of political leaders and top public servants, but also on the traditional and church leadership structures and leaders who lead institutions towards aesthetic relational values in the planning and development of blue and green city models. This book provides information particularly about the Eastern part of the Cape provinces as an aesthetic landscape – as a good place for global business investment, as a global tourism destination, and as a place rich in cultural heritage and cultural landscapes for growth and development beyond the globalized cities and villages of the twenty-first century. It defines aesthetic relational values in planning and development in the context of a fragile landscape that requires, among others, politicians and international aesthetic leaders to make appropriate decisions for implementing an ARVPD Framework in order to eradicate poverty by means of a blue and green economy, combined with Ntsikana kaGabha's noble advice from the nineteenth century on socio-economic cohesion – implementing Integrated Rural and Urban Infrastructure Investment Programmes (IR and UIIPs) as part of a sustainable action plan to feed into a nation-building plan between 2020 and 2064.

Drawing on material obtained from various meetings, conferences, summits, books, and oral stories, the book provides practical steps for implementing a sustainable action plan for co-creating governance innovation and partnership models as part of a nation-building plan. Such a plan or African roadmap can lead to a new dawn rising over Africa between 2020 and 2064. A new paradigm can be created by subverting and restoring the social, economic, cultural and political histories of African states, leading to a shared vision formulated as 'imbumba yamanyama' by Ntsikana kaGabha and those before him.

The book further argues that the use of pseudo-archaeology, colonial and apartheid-constructed discourse analysis in creating clans and kingdoms is unfair and remains a cancer that obstructs social cohesion as part of a nation-building plan in post-colonial Africa. The complexities of histories require, inter alia, that the authors or writers reconstruct cultural, spiritual, emotional, political, economic, social, technical, legal and environmental knowledge together with historical practices by both the colonialists and colonized people in various landscapes in Africa. This is important to understand that colonial and apartheid historical knowledge and narrative frameworks adopted were subjected power relations between the oppressors and oppressed who used distorted knowledge to justify their imperial and colonial conquests and victories. This unscientific historical discourse in colonial and post-colonial Africa cannot be condoned on any socio-economic, cultural, environmental, spiritual, moral, traditional and political grounds (Nhlapo Commission Terms of Reference and Scope of Work read with Section 25(2)(a)(vi) of the Cooperative Governance and Traditional Affairs (COGTA): Traditional Leadership and Governance Framework Act). It is argued that tensions between the oppressors and oppressed in post-colonial Africa are brought to the fore as a continuation of a Whig concept of history and how South Africa, especially the New South Africa, has tried to deal with the question of state and kingship in terms of such a historiographical inheritance. Therefore, research into the subverting of histories and oral memories under the doctrine of constitutional supremacy (Whig framework) and democratic public administration and management (PAM) systems should be commissioned to unlock Africa's growth and development. Through the proposed inclusive nation-building plan (2020-2064), based on the ARVPD Framework, Africa would move towards becoming a knowledge-based continent with a greater focus on optimal use of its natural resources to re-industrialize and lead manufacturing by means of blue and green economic models. In the context of abject Poverty, systematic Unemployment of youth and women, and increased Inequalities (PUI) among classes and citizens, the proposed nation-building plan means, inter alia, that the poor, who are often unable to operate in the current globalized socio-economic model, must be assisted. The nation-building plan as an inclusive socio-economic model offers leaders a new rethinking of the Agenda for Sustainable Development (AfSD) by African countries.

What is needed under an ARVPD Framework is an inclusive socio-economic compact that rewards employees for a full spectrum of people as the fundamental focus between 2020 and 2064, complemented by advanced fourth industrial revolution skills and competencies using Africa's natural resources and cultural heritage to attract investment and tourism. This means African states must use Integrated Rural and Urban Infrastructure Investment Programmes (IR and UIIPs) to develop new industries and manufacturing plants, acquire new technologies and assets, and set realistic targets. The nation-building plan offers aesthetic leaders the possibility of refining African raw materials at an African source and then exporting the semi- or fully refined products to global markets, leading to more job opportunities. Accordingly, the proposed IR and UIIPs will produce more jobs, reduce poverty more effectively, create more wealth using mega water nexuses, transfer technology to the youth using academic institutions, innovation hubs, and centers of excellence, and create new domestic African businesses linked to our cultural heritage and beautiful landscapes.

The book has five core chapters, followed by Chapter 6 that provides detailed interpretations of the terms used. The six chapters are structured as follows:

Chapter 1: Introduction and background of the Aesthetic Relational Values in Planning and Development Framework in designing Paradise City models in the Home of Legends or other landscapes in Africa.

Chapter 2: Understanding the theoretical framework of Paradise City models and the required aesthetic leaders for a nation-building plan between 2020 and 2064 in the 'Home of Legends' or elsewhere in Africa.

Chapter 3: Motivation for a nation-building plan and social and economic cohesion.

Chapter 4: Application of a nation-building plan using the ARVPD Framework and required leadership traits, qualities and pillars. This chapter provides context for the Cape provinces as a Home of Legends, or any other landscape in Africa.

Chapter 5: This chapter provides a synthesis of the chapters, a conclusion, and recommendations for the implementation of blue and green economic models using IR and UIIPs guided by the ARVPD Framework for the building of post-colonial smart or Paradise City models in terms of the Agenda for Sustainable Development (AfSD) by African states up to and beyond 2063, and in line with the Sustainable Development Goals (SDGs) signed by global leaders on 15 September 2015.

Chapter 6: A section of this chapter defines key terms, which are then interpreted using **c**oncepts (paradigm or ideology), **c**hallenges (problem statement), **c**ontext (country realities or status quo), **c**apabilities (evidence-based analysis in terms of power and potential to use one's resources to advance growth and development) and required **c**ompetencies (scarce and critical skills to have a competitive edge) to understand them. This refers to the **5Cs** framework, which is used to clarify complex terms used in various disciplines or faculties. In addition, the rich historical presupposition of African heritage sites, forts, towns, cities and regions is applied and contextualized. As historiographic, ethnographic, theological and archaeological studies are conducted, academic terminology or jargon is used, but this may become exceedingly abstract for readers. In this book I adopt an interpretation and analysis based on an essay-type approach, so I attempt to simplify terms as far as possible. Given the complexity of our rich heritage from the pre-colonial era to date, there are limited prior scientific studies apart from pseudo-studies written from colonial perspectives.

The first five chapters have the following elements as part of a portable skills assessment and for moderation purposes:

- exit outcomes and objectives
- content using concepts, challenges, contexts, capabilities, and competencies (5Cs)
- required competencies and skills complemented by in-depth reflection on actual leaders
- qualities and traits with a clear vision of social and economic cohesion as part of a nation-building plan
- a conclusion or summary

This book will assist the reader as a guide to draw strength from our rich histories of Africans, such as Ntu, Abantu, Khoi, Kalanga, Nama, Korana, Griqua, Damara, San, and Camissa, including Europeans, Asians, and Indians. The concept of social and economic cohesion as part of economic development linked to blue and green economic models might not be new to readers, but here the focus is on the restoration of human dignity, justice, and unity in diversity in post-colonial Africa. Through these rich social histories we can build a new society based on aesthetic relational values in the planning and development of post-colonial cities or Paradise City models.

ACKNOWLEDGEMENTS

A number of people made inputs and offered comments on the formulation of this book. They highlighted several key factors for the implementation of the proposed Paradise City models using the Aesthetic Relational Values in Planning and Development Framework (ARVPDF) in designing smart blue and green city models in the Home of Legends or elsewhere in Africa. They include the following individuals:

Tracy Murinik and Linde Dietrich for their in-depth inputs and proofreading of the book.

Nkosi Phathekile (Aah! Dilizintaba) kaHolomisa, a leader of AmaHegebe at Mqanduli in the Eastern Cape province, who made his papers on traditional leadership roles and responsibilities available.

Jabu Sindane, former director general of the Department of Human Settlements, Water and Sanitation (DHSWS), and former municipal manager of Thembisile Hani Local Municipality in Mpumalanga, whose scholarly work on corporate governance and traditional leadership models with the Human Sciences Research Council (HSRC) was indispensable.

The Rev. Mbulelo Livingstone Dyibishe (Aah! Ngubesilo).

Dimati (Aah! BhovuleNgwe) kaNgcese.

Zamile (Aah! NgubeNgwe) Ngetu.

Andile (Aah! Zwelibanzi) kaMtiki (May his soul rest in peace: 17 October 1957-21 January 2017).

(u)Miselwa (AmaCirha) Angelina Qwakanisa.

Mutile (Aah! Langalibalele) kaMhlophe.

Welile (Aah! Jongintaba) kaKobe.

Sityebi David (Aah! NgubeNyathi) kaTsibani.

Fumene George Tsibani

Chief Nkosi (Aah! Zweliyandinga) Mthuthuzeli kaMakinana of East London CONTRALESA and various members of Imbumba yamaNyama.

Theko Council (Aah! Bangisizwe) kaGabha, who sadly passed away after an accident in December 2015 without seeing his inputs incorporated in this book.

Lubabalo Dzedze, Eastern Cape National Archives and Records Services of South Africa, for guidance and support.

Professor Erwin Schwella, head of the School of Public Leadership, Stellenbosch University.

Professor Mzo Sirayi, dean of Arts and Culture at Tshwane University of Technology (TUT).

Professor George Mugovhani, dean of Performance Art at Tshwane University of Technology (TUT).

Dr. Charles RE Ruyembe, Tanzanian scholar and lecturer in Creative Arts at Tshwane University of Technology (TUT).

Dr. Moshe Ncilashe Swartz, deputy director general of the Department of Rural Development and Land Reform and originator of the aesthetic relational value application, interpretation and synthesis in planning and development in Mother Africa, based on his Ph.D. dissertation through Stellenbosch University.

Zakhele Mnqayi, former head of Capacity Development of the Municipal Infrastructure Support Agent (MISA).

Mbulelo Ntshngana, Phakamisa Hobongwana and Mchumane Hlazo for supporting the research and its application in the human settlements and water sector in South Africa.

Professor Jeff Peires, University of Fort Hare Archives, with his rich writings on AmaXhosa history.

Dr. Gerhard Backeberg, Water Research Commission, on the water-energy-food nexus.

Siyolo Xotyeni, stakeholder manager, Energy and Water Sector Education and Training Authority (EWSETA).

Dr. Pieter Vermeulen, an independent consultant involved with the Nagaland case study in India.

Nokuhle Mkebe, founding director of EBEMS Consulting and Training Institute, and her inputs on Wildlife Green Economy: Expansion Empowerment and Development Programmes (WREEED).

Sandie Memela, for his paper on xenophobia and social cohesion in South Africa.

Former Councillor of Johannesburg City, Vincent Vena, for metropolitan issues around alternative renewable energy as part of mega water nexuses.

The Rev. Mxolisi Jerome Koom (Tshawe), for preaching about the Kingdom of God with the Cirha Clan at Thwathwa near Fort Beaufort on 24 September 2017, in remembrance of Ntsikana kaGabha's prophetic message in Africa and its relevance in the contemporary history of South Africa.

Ike Motsapi, content developer and communication expert for the Department of Human Settlements, Water and Sanitation (DHSWS).

Musili Mawathe, deputy chair of the Conference on Centre Multiparty Democracy (CMD), Kenya, organized in collaboration with Stellenbosch University's School of Public Leadership on 28-30 November 2015 in Nakuru, Kenya.

Jenipher Otieno, coordinator (consultancy, research, and development) at the Management University of Africa (MUA) in Kenya.

Dr. CFO Onyango, CEO of CMD Kenya, conference on exchange programmes with Stellenbosch University's School of Public Leadership (SU: SPL) in conjunction with the Management University of Africa (MUA) and Jaramogi Oginga Odinga University of Science and Technology (JOOUST), and CMD Institute for Leadership and Governance, on 28-30 November 2015 in Nakuru, Kenya.

John Gibberd and Peter Beukes, Hawks and Hawks Africa Infrastructure Engineers, for co-founding the 17-18 November 2014 workshop at Regent International Hotel, East London, and the presentation of a desktop analysis of existing railway infrastructure systems in the Eastern Cape.

Thato Motedi and Barris Buckley, for graphic designs of the Ntsikana kaGabha Paradise City.

Dr. Clinton Heimann, Service Delivery Coordinator Branch: Rural Infrastructure Development: National Department of Rural Development and Land Reform (DRDLR), for the guidance of Agri-Park and related agribusinesses in South Africa.

Pieter Petrus Venter, program engineer and manager of Hartbeespoort Dam and environmental solutions, in advancing ecosystems and the balancing of human and natural needs.

Dr. Werner Reutter, senior lecturer in the Department of Political Science at the University of Leipzig.

Dr. Mkhululi Ncube, program manager of the Financial and Fiscal Commission.

Phephelaphi Dube, legal officer for the Centre for Constitutional Rights.

Professor Peter E Franks, extraordinary professor of the School of Public Leadership (SPL) at Stellenbosch University.

Skumsa Mancotywa, chief director of Protected Areas Systems Management at the Department of Environmental Affairs (DEA).

Nosipho Ngcaba, director general of the Department of Environmental Affairs (DEA).

Johan Potgieter, managing director of Baadaye Consulting.

Dr. Lebogang Lance Nawa, a research fellow at Tshwane University of Technology (TUT).

Dr. Christina Teichmann, project manager of the Konrad-Adenauer-Stiftung.

Advocate John Welch, legal expert, and constitutional advisor.

Advocate Johan Kruger, director of the Centre for Constitutional Rights.

Nombulelo Hackula, former head of the Department of Local Government and Traditional Affairs, Eastern Cape Provincial Government, and CEO of Africa for African Women (NPC).

Nombasa Nkomana, manager of Special Programmes at the Department of Cooperative Governance and Traditional Affairs, Eastern Cape, situated at Bisho, Eastern Cape.

Thulani Magagula and Jabulani Nkomo for narrating histories of Shaka, Phungashe and Zwide using Mbongiseni Buthelezi's University of KwaZulu-Natal MA thesis (2004): "Kof'Abantu, Kosal' Izibongo?': Contested histories of Shaka, Phungashe, and Zwide in Izibongo and Izithakazelo'.

Office of the Minister of Arts and Culture and the Office of the Deputy President for their strategic guidance.

Prince Dr. B Arends, Prince Dr. Pienaar, Prince JJB Tobias, Prince HF van Staaden, MM Stuart and Marilyn Delaney of the Kingdom of Khoekhoen.

Professor Daniel DW Brown (Aah, Khoebaha!) of the Kingdom of Khoekhoen, the Hancumqua Royal House, an ordained minister of the Independent Congregational Church (founded by Dr. MWB Rubusana in 1884).

Chief of Mwelo Nonkonyana (Aah! Zanemvula) of the Bhala Traditional Council and chairperson of the Eastern Cape House of Traditional Leaders, in his address, 'The strategic role of AmaCirha Kingship in post-colonial South Africa', presented at the Ntsikana kaGabha celebration at Thwathwa, Seymour on the 09 November 2019 funded by Imbumba yamaNyama Royal Council, the National Heritage Council, Eastern Cape Sport, Recreation, Art and Culture, and Raymond Mhlaba Local Municipality, who guided the traditional leaders to optimally utilize the Constitution, Section 83c to support unity in diversity and reconciliation.

I wish to express my appreciation to the following:

The participants from both the East London CONTRALESA and the South African National Civic Organisation (SANCO), as well as the Imbumba yamaNyama Royal Council for their input during the workshops held at the Regent International Hotel in East London on 17-18 November 2014 and 24 March 2017, and comments and policy directives with the National Heritage Council (NHC), whereby the spiritual heritage site at Thwathwa under the Raymond Mhlaba Local Municipality must be seen as part of the Imbumba yamaNyama Royal Council's plan to reconcile families and clans by applying the prophet Ntsikana's message. The celebration of Ntsikana kaGabha's legacy on Heritage Day is set to become an annual event.

The Konrad-Adenauer-Stiftung, EURAC Research, the Centre for Constitutional Rights, the Stellenbosch Good Governance Forum (SGGF), and Stellenbosch University: School of Public Leadership (SU: SPL) for initiating and funding the Conference on Strengthening Constitutional Democracy held at the University of Stellenbosch from 19-21 August 2015, which added greatly to the information contained in this book.

Mthengenya and Associates (Pty) Ltd, a training, consulting and coaching institution whose programs and methodologies are based on working with credible public and private institutions in sustainable development, complemented by socio-economic research with academic institutions since 1994. Headquartered in South Africa's City of Tshwane, Mthengenya and Associates has operated throughout Africa and participated in various international conferences on sustainable development, including in Europe, India and various islands around Africa. Through this North-South and South-South methodology, Mthengenya and Associates funded the interviews with various individuals to uncover aspects of information to compile this book.

Ntombizanele Mabandla and Molefe Mndlankomo for organizing the graduation ceremony for traditional leaders on 10 May 2017, as part of LGSETA's contribution to aesthetic leadership in Africa.

Gugu Dlamini (LGSETA) and Linda Budaza (LGSETA) for funding the training of 350 traditional leaders (in partnership with Eastern Cape Local Government and Traditional Affairs and Dr MWB Rubusana City Municipality); and Dr MWB Rubusana City for spearheading social cohesion on 09 December 2015 and 14 March 2017 together with the Eastern Cape House of Traditional Leaders, the Amathole District Municipality, the Imbumba yamaNyama Royal Council, and their local municipalities.

Advocate Sonwabile Mancotywa, CEO of the South African National Heritage Council (NHC) for contributing to the idea of researching and exploring nation reconciliation from 2018 onwards, leading to the design and construction of the Ntsikana kaGabha Spiritual Heritage Site under the Raymond Mhlaba Local Municipality – 14 March 2017 at Dr MWB Rubusana City (formerly known as East London Municipality and known as Buffalo City post-1994).

Mr. Mlandeli Tengimfene, South African boxing manager, and the best manager of Boxing South Africa in 2017 and 2018 respectively. His explanation of partnership with Imbumba yamaNyama was to identify the raw talent of potential boxers in partnership with traditional leaders in various parts of the Eastern Cape.

Advocate John Ngcebetsha (senior partner: Ngcebetsha Madlanga Attorneys) for his wisdom in guiding and leading as a chairperson of Assemblies of God in Sandton through various local and global experts, and leaders in various aspects of building a morally sound society, rooted in the Ubuntu paradigm and aesthetic relational values in various families and clans, complemented by legal analysis of the future beyond 2063 in Africa. This includes his televised interview on the strategic, tactical and operational role of Assemblies of God in Sandton in embracing modernity and cultural development without compromising the Bible (reference is also made to Sandton Assemblies of God live television interview with Tumi Ramanotsi at 343 TBN in Africa television, Wednesday, 10 January 2018, 28 minutes).

SABC support from a number of managers and experts, including Noma Kunene, Vaylen Kirtley, Sifiso Ramara, Mluleki Ntsabo, and Thokozani Gazo.

Finally, I would like to thank my family for their patience and ongoing support in writing this book.

KEYWORDS

Adaptive behavior
Aesthetic leaders
Aesthetic relational values
Aesthetics
AmaCirha Kingdom
AmaXhosa Kingdom
Anthology
Blue and green cities
Blue and green economic models
Clan
Colonialism
Competencies
Customary norms and standards
Ethnography
Exogamy
Green cities
Green economy
Historiography
Home of Legends
Imperialism
Integrated Rural and Urban Infrastructure Investment Programme
Matrician descent
Paradise
Patrilineal descent
Performance
Pilgrimage
Planning and development
Primogeniture
Pseudo-archaeology
Values

ABBREVIATIONS

3Hs	Head, Heart, Hands
4Cs	Complexity, Context, Change, And Connectedness
4Es	Economy, efficiency, effectiveness and alternative energy
4Hs	Head, Heart, Hands, And Habits
4Ts	Tools, Transfer, Tactics, and Trials
5Cs	Concepts, Challenges, Context, Capabilities and Competencies
ABET	Adult Education and Training
ACES	Analytical, Conceptual, Emotional and Spiritual framework for leaders
ANC	African National Congress
ANC COPE	African National Congress: Congress of the People, 1955
ANCYL	African National Congress Youth League
ARVPDF	Aesthetic Relational Values in Planning and Development Framework
AU	African Union
BBBEE	Broad-Based Black Economic Empowerment
BOTT	Build, Operate, Train and Transfer
BPs	Business plans
BRICS	Brazil, Russia, India, China, South Africa economic bloc
BSA	British Social Attitudes Survey
BVPIs	Best Value Performance Indicators
CAR	Capability, accountability, responsiveness
DBSA	Development Bank of Southern Africa
DIBU	Development Information Business Unit
DEAT	Department of Environmental Affairs and Tourism
DFID	British Agency for International Development
DHETST	Department of Higher Education Training Science and Technology
DHLG	Department of Housing and Local Government at the provincial level
DoE	Department of Education
DoH	Department of Housing
DoL	Department of Labour
ECLGTA	Eastern Cape Local Government and Traditional Affairs
GIZ	German Agency for International Development Cooperation
HIV and AIDS	Human Immunodeficiency Virus/Acquired Immune Deficiency Syndrome

IDP	Individual Development Plan (personal career path development)
IDP	Integrated Development Plan (municipal strategic planning)
IGBP	International Geosphere-Biosphere Programme
IEC	Independent Electoral Commission
IIIPSA	Integrated Infrastructure Investment Programme
IPAP	Industrial Policy Action Plan
IWRM	Integrated Water Resources Management
KFAs	Key focus areas
ME&R	Monitoring, Evaluation, and Reporting
NDP	National Development Plan
NDF	National Development Forum
NPC	National Planning Commission
NPM	New Public Management system of local government
NEC	National Executive Committee
NEC	National Executive Council for a political party
NEPAD	New Partnership for Africa's Development
NGO	Non-governmental organization
NGP	National Growth Path framework by the economic cluster of the South African Cabinet
O&M	Operation and Maintenance
OBE	Outcomes-based Education
OD	Organizational Development
ODA	British Overseas Development Administration
PAC	Pan Africanist Congress of Azania
PAM	Public Administration and Management
PGDP	Provincial Growth and Development Plan
PMU	Program Management Unit
PPP	Private-Public Partnership
PRIDE	Production/Productivity, Re-industrialisation, Innovation, Domestication and Enterprise
PUI	Abject Poverty, systemic Unemployment, and increased Inequality
QCTO	Quality Council for Trades and Occupations
RDP	Reconstruction and Development Programme
RPL	Recognition of Prior Learning
SADC	Southern African Development Community
SALGA	South African Local Government Association
SANNC	South African Native National Congress
SAQA	South African Qualifications Authority

SETAs	Sector Education and Training Authorities
SGB	Standard Generating Bodies
SIP	Strategic Infrastructure Project
SLA	Sustainable Livelihoods Approach
SONA	State of the Nation Address
SOPA	State of the Province Address
SPACE	Situational awareness, Presence, Authenticity, Clarity, and Empathy
SSP	Sector Skills Plan
STEEPLE	Social, technological, economic, ecological, political, legal and environmental factors
SU: SPL	Stellenbosch University: School of Public Leadership
SWOT	Strengths, weaknesses, opportunities, and threats
TA	Technical assistance
TEAM	Together Each Achieves More
TNA	Training needs assessment
UNEP	United Nations Environment Programme
UNESCO	United Nations Educational, Scientific and Cultural Organization
WEALTH	Water, Energy, Environment, Agriculture, Land, Legalities, Technology and Health
WREED	Wildlife Green Economy: Expansion Empowerment and Development Programmes
WSDP	Water Services Development Plan
WSP	Water Services Provider
WSSD	World Summit on Sustainable Development
WSUA	Water Services Users Association
YALI	Young African Leaders Initiative

TABLE OF CONTENTS

DEDICATION v
DISCLAIMER vii
FOREWORD ix
PREFACE xiii
EXECUTIVE SUMMARY xix
ACKNOWLEDGEMENTS xxiii
KEYWORDS xxxi
ABBREVIATIONS xxxiii

CHAPTER 1 1
   1 INTRODUCTION AND BACKGROUND 1
      1.1 Purpose of the blue and green city models in the Home of Legends 1
      1.2 Unity in diversity and formation of Ingqungquthela yabantu (Congress of the People) 2
      1.3 Meaning of unity in diversity in contemporary Africa 6
      1.4 Subverting histories and restoring joint heritage 7
         1.4.1 Sons of Xhosa kaMnguni, kaNtu, kaMentu and kaMentuhotep I 7
         1.4.2 We are from the Cradle of African Civilization before exoduses 10
         1.4.3 We belong to the Garden of Eden as people of God in Heaven 12
         1.4.4. Mentuhotep I is our Great Ancestor for Abantu 19
         1.4.5. Ntsikana's teachings are from God 20
         1.4.6. Khoi, San, and Abantu are Africans of ancient Egypt and the Garden of Eden 20
         1.4.6. 1. Africans come from ancient Egypt before sedimentation and great floods 20
         1.4.6. 2 Hunting skills of AmaXhosa, Khoi, and San 22
         1.4.6.3 African governance and code of conduct systems are based on Order in Heaven 23
      1.5 Reconciliation of clans and kingdoms through nation-building plans 25
      1.6 Need for Paradise City models as part of the Nation-Building Plan 29
         1.6.1 Outcomes for Paradise City models as part of a nation-building plan 30
      1.7 Investment and attraction of investors to Paradise City models in post-colonial Africa 38
         11.7.1 Rich heritage and footprint 38
         1.7.2 WEALTH creation as part of the AU Agenda 2063 48
         1.7.3 Pillars for the Agenda for Sustainable Development (AfSD) 51

1.8 Conclusion 54
Chapter 1: Endnotes 58

CHAPTER 2 69
2 UNDERSTANDING PARADISE CITY MODELS AND AESTHETIC LEADERSHIP 69
2.1 Objectives and outcomes 69
2.2 Beauty is simply in the eye of the beholder 70
2.3 Ntsikana kaGabha – a brief family background 73
2.4 Leadership qualities 76
2.4.1 Ability to restore human dignity and pride 76
2.4.2 Ability to promote hope 77
2.4.3 Visionary and prophetic abilities 79
2.4.4 The Gospel Hymn and the Garden of Eden and Paradise of God 85
2.4.4.1 Geographical location of the Garden of Eden 86
2.4.4.2 Biblical interpretation of the Garden of Eden 88
2.4.4.3 Proposed Paradise City in the Home of Legends 92
2.5 Leading beautifully and aesthetically through a nation-building plan 96
2.6 Difference between moral and aesthetic leaders 97
2.7 A need for aesthetic leaders to build social cohesion 99
2.8 Differences between managers, politicians, and leaders 111
2.9 Conclusion 117
Chapter 2: Endnotes 118

CHAPTER 3 120
3 MOTIVATION FOR A NATION-BUILDING PLAN AND SOCIAL COHESION 120
3.1 Objectives and outcomes 120
3.2 African countries need aesthetic nation-building plans (2020-2064) 120
3.3 Development in conflict with biodiversity 130
3.4 Historical transformation to a blue and green economy 131
3.5 The roles and responsibilities of traditional leaders 132
3.6 Designing Paradise Cities and landscapes 134
3.7 Conclusion 140

CHAPTER 4 142
4 APPLICATION OF A NATION-BUILDING PLAN USING AN AESTHETIC RELATIONAL VALUES IN PLANNING AND DEVELOPMENT FRAMEWORK 142
4.1 Objectives and outcomes 142
4.2 The concept of the Home of Legends 142
4.3 Paradise City models require SPACE competencies 148
4.4 The theoretical framework of African life 149
4.5 Five pillars of an ARVPDF by Swartz (2010) 149
4.6 Interpretation and analysis of ARVPDF 150
4.7 Conclusion 165
Chapter 4: Endnotes 167

CHAPTER 5 168
5 SYNTHESIS, CONCLUSION AND RECOMMENDATIONS 168
5.1 Conclusion 168
5.2 Recommendations 179

CHAPTER 6 187
6 DEFINITION OF TERMS 187
6.1 Vision 188
6.2 State building and nation-building plan 189
6.3 Innovation 192
6.4 Capability 192
6.5 Competencies 193
6.6 Change management 193
6.7 Leadership 193
6.8 Learning organizations 195
6.9 Strategy 195
6.10 Pilgrimage 195
6.11 The similarity between pilgrimage and paradise 196
6.12 Ntsikana Paradise City landscape 196
6.13 Clan 197
6.14 Pseudo-archaeology and pseudo-history 220

REFERENCES 237
APPENDICES 251
    Appendix: Message of Support for the Nation-Building Plan 251
    Appendix: Message From Imbumba Yamanyama Royal Council 253

ABOUT THE AUTHOR 255

LIST OF FIGURES

Figure 1.1: 1400s Thwathwa Road 32
Figure 1.2: Graphic Design of the Paradise City 33
Figure 1.3: Cape footprint with some selected towns of the Eastern Cape 39
Figure 1.4: Aesthetic Relational Values in Planning and Development Framework (ARVPDF) 53
Figure 2.2.1 Ntsikana Paradise City 71
Figure 4.1:4 Cs in advancing WEALTH creation.. 158
Figure 4.2: Population growth in Northern Africa 160
Figure 6.1: Three key areas of leadership 194
Figure 6.2: The history of Abantu 199
Figure 6.3: The sub-clans that form the Ntu clan 201
Figure 6.4A: The History of AmaCirha 202
Figure 6.4B Lineage of Tsibani Family 203
Figure 6.5. Transitional Governance of AmaXhosa Kingdom (2020-2064) 204

LIST OF TABLES

Table 2.1: Difference between managers and aesthetic leaders................................ 111
Table 2.2: Difference between managers, politicians and leaders 113
Table 4.1: Governance and good-enough governance... 144

CHAPTER 1

1 INTRODUCTION AND BACKGROUND

1.1 Purpose of the blue and green city models in the Home of Legends

We see beauty now where we could not see it before.

– C Preston & W Ouderkirk (2006)

This book[1] covers, among others, a theoretical framework for the Aesthetic Relational Values in Planning and Development Framework (ARVPDF) coined by Swartz[2] (2010) and its application to South Africa's Eastern, Northern and Western Cape provinces, formerly known as the Cape Colony or Cape Province before 1994, or the new dawn in democratic South Africa. These three provinces are collectively seen as a Home of Legends within the global context of a fragile world. To this end, the book defines key concepts such as Paradise City models, blue and green city designs, and a nation-building plan to inform a sustainable action plan to co-nurture and co-create local SPACE for good-enough governance and partnerships using Ntsikana kaGabha's philosophy and a prophetic message from the nineteenth century. In this book, SPACE is an acronym that refers to **S**ituational awareness, **P**resence in decision-making, **A**uthenticity in making policy statements, **C**larity when communicating so that people understand the vision and the roadmap, and **E**mpathy with others.

In defining the concept of Home of Legends, it appears that our cultural identity and unique selling points are an attempt by Africans to transcend the excessive suffering under imperialism and colonialism, and to find a new energy in nation-building plans between 2020 and 2064, with greater emphasis on integrated rural and urban infrastructure investment programmes (IR and UIIPs) informed by Swartzism or the ARVPDF (2010). The basic reason why urban poverty is consistently underestimated in South Africa is that it is almost always contrasted with rural poverty.[3] Fortunately, based on the memory of oral narratives and public debates with elders of the Imbumba yamaNyama Royal Council and House of Traditional Leaders between 1992 and 2018, there is a growing recognition that meeting national and international targets for poverty reduction requires an urban as well as a rural focus. Owing to the South African history of migrant labor, poor people's lives often straddle rural and urban boundaries. It is thus a case of needing both an urban and a rural poverty reduction strategy, rather than seeing the problems of poverty in rural versus urban poverty terms, as is too often the case (Parnell, 2004). Africa needs a nation-building plan that uses IR and UIIPs to restore PRIDE using aesthetic relational values to drive reconstruction and development by advancing unity in diversity. The resulting energy emanating from these newly formed program guides will generate solutions for current micro, meso, macro and global governance and leadership problems. Accordingly, Andile (Aah! Zwelibanzi) Mtiki kaNobhoma summed up the lofty advice Ntsikana kaGabha gave before his death in 1821 when he said:

> Zenibe yimbumba yamanyama! Pass the message to Lwaganda kaMlawu, then he must pass it to Ndabanduna, and in turn he must pass it to Zanzolo who must pass it to AbaThembu, and they must be Imbumba yamaNyama. (2 May 2014, Great Place, traditional poem by Andile Mtiki kaNobhoma, Imvo ZabaNtsundu, 26 August 1961, and Imibengo, 10 January 2011)

1.2 Unity in diversity and formation of Ingqungquthela yabantu (Congress of the People)

The true sign of intelligence is not knowledge but imagination.
– Albert Einstein

It is significant that the notion of unity in diversity as part of a nation-building plan has long been the vision of African leaders. 'Zenibe yimbumba yamanyama' calls for a nation-building plan and unity based on aesthetic relational values to be found in Africa's new and unique civilization, conceptualized within the Ubuntu philosophy,[4] to advance socio-economic and developmental interests and meet the needs of citizens without conflict with the environment. Imbumba yamaNyama members saw themselves as black people rooted in their African socio-economic, cultural and political past and present, and seeking a state of equilibrium from the nineteenth century onwards. It meant associations of clans and kingdoms were formed, leading to the unity of the black people in the Cape Colony, and later in South Africa, in the nineteenth century. Unity in diversity was a concept of unity without uniformity of values and norms or social, economic, political and cultural background of the people in the Cape Colony, especially between the blacks (AmaXhosa, Griquas, Khoi and San people) and European settlers from various countries, such as Portugal, the Netherlands, Britain and Germany. It meant unity based on a need for tolerance of ideological differences between black and white inhabitants, on the one hand, and among clans and kingdoms of AmaXhosa and Khoisan groupings (both black peoples) on the other hand. Ideologically, white people were colonizers and black people were being colonized on the basis of socio-economic and political Darwinism. In this context, Ntsikana kaGabha used 'zenibe yimbumba yamanyama' as a religious slogan or motto to unite the people. He used the Word of God to emphasize that God had created humanity. Through unity in diversity (imbumba yamanyama), he referred to the oneness of humanity under one God, the creator of heaven and the stars. Politically, after his death in 1821, imbumba yamanyama was changed from a Pentecostal movement to a congress of the people in 1882 and 1891, whereby black middle-class people using an interdisciplinary approach adopted the concept of launching their own self-determination, freedom and political will.

Through imperialism and colonialism, unity in diversity meant an interaction of African, European and Asian people primarily for economic processes whereby dominant cultures and leadership practices were used to suppress weaker nations, leading to frontier wars in the case of the Cape Colony. In modern democratic countries in Africa and elsewhere in the world, unity in diversity refers to mutual respect characterized by principles of forgiveness without forgetting history, reconciliation, and acceptance of global diversity (Matthew 6:14-16; Luke 23:24). In the context of the developing countries of Africa, it refers to common efforts and strategies to defeat challenges of poverty, crime, corruption, greed, diseases, and underdevelopment. BB Myataza (2012), influenced by Psalm 90:1-17, wrote the poem 'Mzi wase-Afrika' (House of Africa) in which he emphasized the need for social cohesion and nation-building plans:

> Ngoko masimanyane
> Simanyane,
> Sibambane ngezandla
> Sibeke phantsi ubuzwe Nobuhlanga
> Zonk' intshaba Zingawa phantsi kwethu
> Zonk' intshaba
> zonk' intshaba
>
> Zingawa phantsi phambi kwethu
> Ukuba singabayimbumba Yamanyama
> Umanyano lungamandla Angummangaliso
>
> Ngoko masibemoya mnye
> Sonke maAfrika AbaNtsundu nabaMhlophe
> Zonk' izizwe neentlanga Masibhekise kuSomandla
> Asinik' ubulumko Asinike noxolo
> Ukuze iAfrika ibenakho Ukubambana njengebhola
> Mayibuye iAfrika mayibuye

Fumene George Tsibani

ngothando Mayibuye iAfrika mayibuye ngoxolo

His poem, which has been used in various choral music festivals, is loosely translated to mean:

> Then let us be united
> United, united holding hands
> Put down all nationalism and racism
> So all enemies will fall down in front of us
> Fall down in front of us
> If we can be a bundle of unity
> Unity is strength, wonderful strength
> Therefore, we should be in one spirit, all of us Africans
> Black and white
> All nations and tribes, let us ask God to give us wisdom
> And give us peace so that Africa can be united as a ball
> Let Africa come back, come back through love
> Come back to Africa, come back by peace

Like Ntsikana kaGabha before him, Chief Albert Luthuli, in his autobiography, *Let my people go*, predicted that

> somewhere ahead there beckons a civilization, a culture, which will take its place in the parade of God's history beside other great human syntheses: Chinese, Egyptian, Jewish, and European. It will not necessarily be all black: but it will be African.

In the same vein, Isaac William Citashe (incorrectly known as Wauchope in various social anthropology and history books)[5] called for unity, human dignity, and pride. It is true that (Liyinyaniso elithi) 'zemk' iinkomo magwalandini' (loosely translated: cows were stolen under your watch, you cowards). Like Ntsikana kaGabha before him, Dr Mpilo Walter Benson (Cirha) Rubusana (1858-1936), supported by the foundational principles created by Isaac William Citashe, used this analogy and traditional epic poetry to appeal to his countrymen (heroes) and countrywomen (heroines) and urged them to defend their heritage and pride in the Home of Legends. Citashe used the cattle symbol figuratively to appeal to his people, and exhorted them to recover their lost land, national heritage, human rights, and national pride. He encouraged his countrymen and

-women to use education for political emancipation and for restoring lost African histories and land (Opland, 2009:478; Gribble & Scott, 2017:126-127). He stated:

Zimkile! Mfo wohlanga,	Your herds are gone, my countrymen!
Phuthuma, phuthuma;	To the rescue! To the rescue!
Yishiy'imfakadolo,	Abandon the breechloader,
Phuthuma ngosiba;	Go rescue with your pen;
Thabath'iphepha neinki,	So grab your paper and grab your ink,
Likhaka lakho elo.	For that, in truth, is your shield.
Ayemk'amalungelo,	Your rights are going!
Qubula usiba,	Pick up your pen!
Ngxasha, ngxasha, ngeinki,	Load it! Load it with ink!
Hlala esitulweni;	Settle down in your chair,
Ungangeni kwaHoho;	Repair not to Hoho,
Dubula ngosiba.	But fire away with it.

It is clear from Ntsikana kaGabha, Isaac William Citashe, and later Chief Albert Luthuli, that Imbumba yamaNyama[6] was conceptualized to deal with new challenges and the problems of the eighteenth and nineteenth centuries without compromising the generational needs of the next century. This includes dealing with distorted histories and pseudo-archaeology in terms of the rich heritage of African kingdoms and societal structures. In this context – the transformation agenda to ensure justice and righteousness – there is a need to subvert histories to create a state of equilibrium envisaged by African intellectuals in the Home of Legends, such as N kaGabha, T Soga, JT Jabavu, MWB Rubusana, JJR Jolobe, AC Jordan, SEK Mqhayi, DF Jafta, SC Satyo, GV Mona, T Makipela, D Dwanya and others. The transformational agenda for a nation-building plan means that current leaders must develop appropriate responses to current complex capacity constraints characterized by a dual economic system and the negative consequences thereof. As depicted in Figure 4.2, the complex challenges need to be contextualized in the real life of people in our beautiful landscape in order to ensure required change to connect the citizens, i.e. approximately 1.4 billion potential citizens to benefit from a state of equilibrium or post-colonial city models (Matthew 18:3).

1.3 Meaning of unity in diversity in contemporary Africa

> *We must either learn to live together as brothers or we are all going to perish together as fools ... It really boils down to this; that all life is interrelated. We are all caught in an inescapable network of mutuality, tied into a single garment of destiny.*
>
> – Martin Luther King Jr ('A Christmas sermon on peace', 1967)

Imbumba yamanyama refers to a need to identify and reflect on our humanity and commonalities, and to challenge ourselves to restore a sense of building a collective future in our Paradise Cities and communities. The meaning of imbumba yamanyama as part of a nation-building plan between 2020 and 2064 should proactively respond to current realities in Africa, guided by Africa's visionary leaders, such as Sol Plaatje, Chief Autshumato of the Goringhaicoma Khoi group in the Cape, Queen Hoho, Queen Eva (Gaos) Krotoa of the Goringhaicoma Khoi group in the Cape, Ntsikana kaGabha, John Tengo Jabavu, Patrice Lumumba, Amílcar Cabral, Dr Eduardo Mondlane, Samora Moisés Machel (Mashele), Malcolm X, Onkgopotse Tiro, Robert Mangaliso Sobukwe, Stephen Bantu (Steve) Biko, Chris Thembisile Hani, Cheikh Anta Diop, Kwame Nkrumah, Sekou Toure, Henry Sylvester Williams, George Patmore, Edward Wilmot Blyden, Marie-Joseph Angélique, Nolefi Kete Asante, Martin Delany, Walter Rodney, Oliver Reginald Kaizana Tambo, Walter Max Ulyate Sisulu, Chief Albert John Mvumbi Luthuli, Nelson Rolihlahla Mandela, Steve Vukile Tshwete, Ben (Ta-Ben) Tengimfene, Thabo Mbeki, Malcomess Mgabela, Alfred Toto Matele, Thokzamile Gqwetha, Matthew Goniwe, Sparrow Mkhonto, Sicelo Mhlauli, Patrick Lock Otieno Lumumba, Stephen Pandula Gawe, Lilian Ngoyi, Helen Joseph, Frances Baard, Rahima Moosa, Sophia Williams-de Bruyn, Nontsikelelo Mashalaba-Biko, Zondeni Veronica Sobukwe, Ruth First, Albertina Nontsikelelo Sisulu and Nomzamo Winifred (Winnie) Madikizela-Mandela, to mention but a few. These responses include:

- Adjusting and adopting global economic models that can be used for inclusive socio-economic growth and development by implementing integrated rural and urban infrastructure investment programs (IR and UIIPs);
- Strengthening industrial plans in Africa by restoring our rich heritage using aesthetic relational values in planning and development;
- Promoting partnerships through trade agreements between African countries and other investors;
- Promoting match-making and twinning arrangements to re-industrialize and use new technology for transferring skills to new leaders, business entrepreneurs, and ideapreneurs;
- Expanding alternative energy and technology solutions and innovation to adapt and adjust to climate change and global competitiveness in terms of fourth industrial revolution issues and solutions;

- Encouraging private investors to serve as a catalyst for IR and UIIPs based on blue and green economic models in accordance with the COP21 Paris resolutions;
- Utilizing the impact of equity plans, such as Broad-Based Black Economic Empowerment (BBBEE), affirmative action and the industrialization program, as defined by the Department of Trade and Industry (DTI): Industrial Policy Action Plan (IPAP);
- Taking into account the diversity of Africans with unique socio-economic, cultural and ethnic backgrounds, using strengths, weaknesses, opportunities, and threats (SWOT) analysis undertaken in early 2018 in Africa by various Development Finance Institutions (DFIs);
- Relieving the systemic unemployment of youth, abject poverty, and increased inequality, where only a few of the previously oppressed have been promoted onto higher socio-economic rungs;
- Avoiding corruption and tenderpreneurship arising within the state;
- Increasing the satisfaction of citizens by improving services;
- Discouraging current leaders in various sectors and portfolios in African society from having lavish lifestyles;
- Facilitating general cooperation with the United Nations Industrial Development Organization (UNIDO); and
- Restoring our ancient rich histories and values characterized by Heavenly Order from God.

1.4 Subverting histories and restoring joint heritage

1.4.1 Sons of Xhosa kaMnguni, kaNtu, kaMentu and kaMentuhotep I

It is necessary to restore our pre-colonial histories and kingdoms in a context where former colonialists and beneficiaries of colonialism and apartheid have used pseudo-archaeology to erase our true histories, culture and achievements by means of colonial and apartheid-sponsored research programs and projects[7] (Childs & Williams, 1997:123). Pseudo-archaeology, or pseudo-history, is an unscientific methodology to justify imperialism, colonialism and apartheid, whereby African families and clans – despite their lands, cultural sites, villages, and kingdoms – were seen to be less than human beings. Through imperial and colonial policies, laws and regulations, new colonial and apartheid kingdoms were established and institutionalized in all aspects of society in Africa. This was done to silence and erase the original histories of families, clans, and kingdoms so as to achieve hegemonic control over the colonized and oppressed. The imperialists and colonialists have used myths, symbols, and divide-and-rule strategies and policies to promote highly selective colonial and apartheid histories in education from early childhood development (ECD) stages onwards.

Consequently, colonized families are supported in promoting the colonial and apartheid discourse until the colonized become interpreters of their distorted histories and pass it on from generation to generation.[8]

In the case of the competing claims about the history of the AmaXhosa Kingdom, a classic mythical explanation for Cirha losing his kingdom role is based on a general hunt by AmaXhosa, known as ingqina. Balfour-Noyi (2017:28-29) argues that Tshawe succeeded in killing a bluebuck antelope (iphuthi) and Cirha was not successful. Tshawe used this opportunity to overthrow Cirha as king of the AmaXhosa. The author continues with a mythical story where the Amangwevu clan (clan with grey hairs) supported Tshawe to defeat Cirha and Jwarha. Interestingly, Balfour-Noyi concludes, 'Cirha had lost the support of the people because traditionally he should not have demanded a portion of small Blue duiker [iphuthi] because that would have been insufficient to satisfy the nation. He [Cirha] committed a further wrong by insisting on his Royal prerogative at the expense of his people' (Balfour-Noyi, 2017:29). Tshawe's story was constructed to create the impression of a strong leader who defeated his elders (Jwarha and Cirha), which was all part of a colonial and apartheid divide-and-rule strategy that included undermining black people by referring to them as primitive. Accordingly, oral African narratives have been rejected and ignored by Western writers as primitive knowledge, and replaced by Western myths and oral stories about Nongqawuse, Shaka, Tshawe, Thuthula and others. Possessed by the Western ideology of seeing African people and their culture as primitive, missionaries and anthropologists rather opted to train Africans to translate Western values and cultural ideologies as part of their imperial and colonial agenda, whereby myths demonstrating the supposed stupidity of African governance and systems were promoted.

Balfour-Noyi (2017) should not have made such a judgment, particularly if he had read JJR Jolobe's novel *Elundini Lothukela* (1958:5-64, 111-113). Jolobe's novel is gentle, but sharp in rejecting labels and myths created by imperial and colonial administrators, such as that there were no forms of traditional governance, discipline and respect among the Nguni in southern Africa (Opland, 2009:311). Balfour-Noyi's packaging of 'imbeleko' of Tshawe using 'iphuthi' would have provided a positive understanding of African society's dignity, discipline, and respect towards elders. Jolobe's novel, which is linked to the African way of life in terms of mountains and the aesthetic landscape of Uthukela, provides an example of pre-imperial and pre-colonial cultural and socio-political administration and management systems and practices, including the pillars of various clans and kingdoms that can be traced back to ancient Egypt (the cradle of African civilization) and the Garden of Eden before the segmentation of the world into continents, great floods and biblical exoduses. From Jolobe's novel, one would have thought that Tshawe brought 'iphuthi' as a sign of dignity (ukundileka), respect (ukuthobeka nokuzeyisa), protocol (ukuthobela umthetho nabakhuluwa) and order of family genealogy and kinship structural arrangements (nomhlahlo nengqubo yakomkhulu kaNkosiyamntu).

JJR Jolobe would have further articulated that Nkosiyamntu's traditional governance is based on the following order of descent:

- Cirha
- Nkosiyamntu
- Malangana
- Xhosa
- Mnguni
- Ntu – the root word 'Ntu' has been traced back by anthropologists to various African kings. It is significant that in 5000 BC King Narmer (Menes) established a united empire and the first great civilization in Africa. Army Generals of MontuHotep – who was a King of the Kemet Kingdom in 4000 BC, and possibly our greatest ancestor – called themselves Generals of Montu or Ntu. It is argued that MontuHotep is the greatest ancestor of Abantu or Ntu. In the African civilization, the Kemet Kingdom was rich and attracted possible invaders in 5000-2500 BC. It is also significant that in 3600 BC Asians invaded the rich Kemet Kingdom, but King Ahmose I restored order and drove the Asians out. In 5000 BC Persians (Asians), followed by Europeans and later Romans, invaded the Kemet Kingdom, which led to a period of African Dark Ages or Great Migrations or Exoduses of Afro-Africans and Jews out of Egypt. Anthropologists and historians argue that by 2000-1500 BC, Abantu were to be found in the Great Lakes Region of Central Africa and the Upper and southern parts of ancient Egypt. Accordingly, most historians acknowledge King Mnguni (1000 BC to 300 AD). The above-mentioned invasions led to a series of expansions by Africans into various parts of Africa that account for a linguistic commonality across much of central and southern Africa;
- Nebhepetre Mentuhotep II – Pharaoh of the 11th Dynasty (2061-2010 BC);
- Sankhkare Mentuhotep III – 11th Dynasty during the Middle Kingdom or Period of Reunification (2050-1710 BC);
- Sankhkare Mentuhotep IV – last King of the Dynasty (1998-1991 BC): History of Kingdoms is unknown. It is believed that ancestors of Africans (Abantu) lived in the Omo River Valley in present-day Ethiopia (200 000 BC). This is a period where cultural identity was found especially in 170 000-40 000 BC – the foundation of culture common among African groups using Imbola (red ochre); and
- Mentuhotep I – Theban monarch (governor) or independent ruler of Upper Egypt (2181-2055 BC) after the Old Kingdom in Egypt (2686-2181 BC) or the Age of the Pyramids.

1.4.2 We are from the Cradle of African Civilization before exoduses

As part of African unity in the pre-colonial period, ancient Egypt is considered the 'cradle of African civilization', as civilization started in Egypt before invasions by Arabs, Asians, and Europeans. Through Egyptian civilization, Africans refer to Africa as a 'mut' or Mother Africa. Egypt is also referred to as Kemet. Kemet means a mother, place, beloved landscape, womb, or place of production or development, land of the black people or Africans. The Bible books of Genesis, Exodus, Numbers, Joshua, and Judges are useful for discovering clues about the pre-colonial histories of Egyptians and Afro-Egyptians, of which Abantu are a sub-group of Africans, during their migrations in parts of Africa and elsewhere. These groups are linked to Exodus or migration and the need for a messianic prophetic communication strategy, which connects very well with Moses, as a prophet, or 'pool of reeds' where the infant Moses was said to have been found. It has been argued that the original name for Moses was an Egyptian name, 'Sah', meaning 'to draw from'. Theologically, it means to draw from the pool of water. Moses took the side of the downtrodden, led them to the worship of one God in Heaven, and gave them laws after the biblical exodus was completed and Abantu migrated east-, west- and southwards.

Although Africans have physical and genetic differences like the Mbuti, or Bambuti, Mthwa (Twa), San, Khoi (Khoekhoe), Pygmies of equatorial Africa and Asia, Nilotic (Egypt, Sudan, South Sudan, Kenya, Tanzania, Maasai and Tukana, Abantu and Ethiopians), they can be traced in Egypt. According to Ezekiel (29:14), it is probably possible to argue that the civilization in Egypt attracted people in southern Egypt such as Nubian and Kush people (Ethiopians). Upper Egypt is referred to as the land of ancestry (Jeremiah 44:1; Isaiah 11:11; and Ezekiel 29:14). These people in Upper Egypt and Nubia had the greatest biological affinity with people of sub-Saharan Africa.

In short, it can be deduced that humanity evolved first from Africa, as Africa is the only continent in the world grounded in theology (major religions such as Judaism, Christianity and Islam can be traced back to ancient Egypt), science and philosophy, long before Greece. It is also significant that in the precolonial period, ancient Egypt was once conquered as one of the provinces of Ethopia or Abyssinia, like the Republic of Sudan or the Nubian Republic. Likewise, it is significant that excavated evidence of ancient Egyptian civilization was discovered along the Nile River, not in Egypt proper, but in central Sudan near the modern capital of Khartoum. Khartoum is located at the confluence of the White Nile, flowing north from Lake Victoria, and the Blue Nile, flowing west from Ethiopia. The White and Blue Nile rivers meet at al-Mogram. The Nile River continues to flow north towards Egypt and the Mediterranean Sea.

It can be inductively and deductively concluded, in terms of archaeology, ancient history, and anthropology, and my travels to Sudan, Ethiopia and Kenya in 2015, that Nubians, AmaNguni, AbaNtu were part of ancient Egypt before exoduses and the sedimentation of Super-world into various continents in the world, that is to say, hundreds of millions of years before the world drifted into new continents as defined by scientists (Habakkuk 3:5-6; Psalm 144: 5-6). In other words, it is believed that the world was one big mass or Pangaea or supercontinent with a beautiful Garden of Eden characterized by beautiful watered fruits, four main rivers, and mountains in hypothetical or theoretical reasoning (see also Judges 5:4-5; Psalm 97:5). Accordingly, the continents were originally part of a large landmass known as Pangaea before a split formed them a million years ago. Scientists hypothesize that the world segmented into two supercontinents, called Laurasia and Gondwana. Laurasia included the present-day areas of Europe, North America, Siberia, and Greenland. Gondwana included present-day Africa, South America, India, Antarctica and Australia.

Scientists have found stegosaurs in Africa and North America. This provides justification for the idea that some species spread in both continents during the Jurassic period (199 million years ago), and water filled the gaps. Antarctica and Australia detached from Gondwana, and various small islands, and a block of land now called India as part of Asia, moved and drifted northward. Africa also drifted from Europe, starting the formation of the Mediterranean Sea, Italy, Greece, Turkey, and Iran as part of North Africa. Equally, North America separated from Gondwana and drifted west, resulting in the formation of the Gulf of Mexico and the widening of the Northern Atlantic Ocean. South America and Africa began separating, which created a long, narrow seaway that formed shallow seas flooding parts of North America and Europe. This can explain similarities between Africans and the Maori of New Zealand and Aboriginal people of Australia, Fiji and other indigenous people in North America and Asia. Equally, scientists on a continuous basis find similar or identical species on continents that are far apart.

At the time of the writing of this book, it is significant that most of the scientific studies around sedimentation are now focusing on Kenya and Tanzania, where there is continental drift, which will allow scientists and geologists opportunities to conduct conclusive, reliable and valid studies about the period of sedimentation. Once more, the split in Kenya and Tanzania shows how old Africa is, and supports the possibility to claim a place of Creation by God before sedimentation (Pangaea or supercontinent) and the great floods. For instance, the remains of prehistoric plants and animals (fossils), such as Lystrosaurus ('shovel lizards', which were plant eaters with five toes) have been found in South Africa, India and Antarctica (the frozen continent at the South Pole). Similarly, freshwater Mosasaurs (reptiles) have been found in only localized regions of the coasts of Brazil and Uruguay in South America and in southern Africa. Equally, freshwater Mosasaurs are also found in Hungary and Canada, all being scientific evidence supporting the theory of Pangaea or a supercontinent in theory (https://www.nationalgeographic.com/science/phenomena/2012/12/19/freshwater-mosasaur-stirs-marine-reptile-relationships/; accessed on 11/01/2019).

1.4.3 We belong to the Garden of Eden as people of God in Heaven

The complexities of the people of God must be analyzed and traced in the large world before Laurasia and Gondwana. The probabilities of the Garden of Eden having been in the area of Sudan, Ethiopia, ancient Egypt, Iraq, Kuwait, South Arabia and Iran before sedimentation are reasonable and justified, albeit not conclusively. It has been argued that after numbers of the stated natural events, such as sedimentation and great floods, the topography of the Garden of Eden changed completely from the description in the Bible (Genesis 2:10-14) to symbolically mean a paradise and God's place created for His people, including the civilization in the Garden of Eden in ancient Sudan, Ethiopia, ancient Egypt and Mesopotamia (Kuwait, Iraq, South Arabia and Iran), and future cities, or the 'new Jerusalem'. As civilization attracted foreigners, ancient Egypt was invaded and colonized, and Afro-Egyptians of Pharaohs (Abantu) migrated east-, west- and southwards, reaching the Great Lakes Region of Africa. Linguistics divides Abantu languages into various categories, such as Nguni, Sotho-Tswana, Venda and Tsonga. It is relatively concluded in this book that words such as Vanhu, Basotho, Kintu, Kuntu, Buntu, Hunhu, Muntu, and Bantu show the similarities that exist among African people. Furthermore, the Khoi and San use 'qua' to mean 'people of God in Heaven'.

It is also significant that a person in ancient Egypt was born 'in the name of destiny' (birth name) and kept a record through their name of who he/she belonged to. People would attach the name of the father (his name of destiny) to the son's name. For instance, Pharaohs would claim destiny from God 'Ra' (destiny), called 'Rah' by Ethiopians and Egyptians. Rah denotes son of 'sa Ra'. Similarly, Abantu of Mentuhotep I used 'ka' (sa=ka) to mean 'son of' or 'child'. In this book, I use 'ka' (IsiXhosa): kaGabha, kaNkosiyamntu, kaMalangana, kaXhosa, kaMnguni, kaNtu, kaMentuhotep I, and so forth. The Igbo people of southern Nigeria as a group of Abantu use the words 'ndu', that means life, and 'ndi' that means people, as in 'ndi mmadu' or 'otutu ndi'. There are close relationships between Abantu and ancient Egypt, as most elders trace their origins to the beginning of the Nile River and the foothills of the Mountains of the Moon, in other words, Kilimanjaro between Kenya, Tanzania and the Rwenzori Mountains in Uganda or the Great Lakes Region. It would be inaccurate to claim that present-day Egypt is ruled by Pharaohs. Rather, it is colonized, controlled and owned by Arabs, as is the case with Tunisia, Algeria, Libya, Morocco and North Sudan (Nubia in ancient history). Sudan is currently divided into North Sudan (Arabs) and South Sudan (ruled by indigenous Sudanese of Abantu groupings). Therefore, the indigenous people who remained behind in ancient Egypt in pre-colonial history are no longer in power, except in the Republic of South Sudan.

During the spread of Islam, west from Arabia to Egypt, there were noticeable pre-colonial states and societies in Africa, such as the Kingdom of Mapungubwe (1075-1220), the Kingdom of Zimbabwe (1220-1450) and the Kingdom of Kush in Sudan (785 BC to AD 350) (formerly a Kemetian colony composed of the Nubian and Nilotic cultures with relatives of Alur, Luo and Maasai of Kenyans, Somalians, Ethiopians and Egyptians). The Kush people were also Pharaohs of the Twenty-fifth Dynasty of Egypt until they were defeated by the Neo-Assyrian Empire under the rule of Esarhaddon (681-669 BC). The Kush Kingdom covered the entire areas presently conquered by Arabs, such as ancient Aethiopia, ancient Libyan deserts and the Western Sahara, including present-day Morocco, Algeria, and Tunisia. Some of the Kush people also invaded various parts of south-eastern tropical Africa, known as Azania in ancient Greek, including the coastal part of Kenya and south of Tanzania.

In Greek, the word 'Arabia' means 'Ajam'. This refers to East African countries, such as Somalia, Ethiopia, Kenya, and Tanzania. During the great exodus from ancient Egypt, Africans moved east of Africa in northern savannahs until they met Khoi and San people of southern Africa, Azanians of East Africa, the Indonesians, Asians and the Arabs of the coast with whom they merged and composed a common language known as Swahili to advance unity and civilization. Etymologically, Swahili adopted the word 'zanj' from a Persian word meaning 'black', and the word 'mzantsi' means 'south' in IsiXhosa. Countries such as Zanzibar, Mozambique, Zambia, Zaire, and Zimbabwe adopted the Swahili phoneme 'za' or 'z', meaning 'south'. In this context, Azania refers to the land of the Black People. Azania refers to a new South African civilization that will restore African and Black consciousness and human values lost during wars of land dispossession or frontier wars. In this context, the word 'Azania' means indigenous people of Africa united to fight foreign intrusion, invasions, and colonialism, i.e. all people, irrespective of their creed, religion, culture, and language, who pay their patriotic allegiance to Africa and its natural resources. It is then expected of blacks in general, and Africans in particular, that they are united by a rich historical heritage to achieve a common civilization and destiny as part of a national duty guided by inclusive social and economic cohesion and a nation-building plan (2020-2064).

It is also significant that due to various invasions by Asians, and integration, some Azanian people with an ancestral background of Afro-Asiatic features were found in the nucleus of Abantu in present-day Mozambique, and they were minorities among 'Abantu' in sub-Saharan Africa. The name 'Azania' was adopted by the Pan Africanist Congress (PAC) to replace 'South Africa' in democratic public administration and management (PAM) systems in the post-apartheid era. It must be remembered that Africa is the world's second-largest and second-most populous continent after Asia. However, endless wars have dislocated her indigenous people, leading to pockets of groups, and historical stories with gaps. Before these invasions and the Berlin Conference in 1884/1885, Africans did not have borders and boundaries. They were guided by the kings and weather conditions to feed their livestock. Consequently, this also justified different people with different features, but with similarities with the place of central origin (being ancient Egypt).

Historians have estimated that in this pre-colonial age, there were more than 10 000 different states and autonomous groupings with distinct languages and customs. This was followed by the African slavery system by Arabs from the 7th century AD. Africans were transported across the Red Sea (its old name was the Erythraean Sea), the Indian Ocean and the Sahara Desert. From the 15th century, Europeans joined the Arabs in the slave trade, leading to imperialism and colonialism through the Atlantic slave trade initially championed by the Portuguese, and all of Europe thereafter. Subsequently, European colonization of Africa developed rapidly from around 10% (1870) to 90% (1914) in the Scramble for Africa (1881-1914).

This epistemological study of African clans, groupings, and kingdoms is challenging because of limited credible written resources and inconclusive findings, particularly given the destruction of many important manuscripts by colonial regimes before the advent of independent African states. Furthermore, in addition to various social and oral histories propagated by former colonizers, governors, administrators and writers, most of the colonized indigenous people were provided with education systems aimed at serving their masters' and conquerors' priorities and goals. Consequently, there are unsubstantiated and inconclusive reports and critically few African elders in a range that can elaborate using credible and reliable evidence of the Abantu of Mentuhotep I.

I must also admit that most of the true histories or oral memories were lost, with colonial historians, administrators, governors and writers having created alternative histories to justify and maintain their political and economic power at all costs, including marketing and propagating myths and promoting them at various levels to the colonized over the years. In the case of some individuals and entities who have a genuine interest in correcting the past histories in order to create a conducive environment for social and economic cohesion, such as Khoisan groupings, AmaNdwandwe, AmaHlubi, AmaCirha and AmaJwarha, their efforts are suppressed through all forms of strategies, tactics and operational plans on the part of former colonizers, and often beneficiaries of the Black Authorities Act 68 of 1951, Section 2(a) (i) (ii). Before 1994, traditional authorities were established according to the Black Authorities Act 68 of 1951. Section 2(a) (i) (ii) of the Act stated clearly that the State President had the responsibility to:

> *Establish a black tribal authority over a specific black tribe; and establish a community authority over a black community or two or more black tribes or communities jointly, or one or more tribes and one or more such communities jointly.*

Undoubtedly, the value system of governance in South Africa is based on the colonial and apartheid values established during their regimes' years of rule. Colonial and apartheid governments detrimentally changed traditional structures, which were based on traditional values and hereditary leadership. Furthermore, the political values and aspirations of the post-1994 system of governance disregarded ethnic traditional structures, especially of AmaXhosa and Khoisan groupings, until 2018. This kind of discrepancy creates a platform for conflict between traditional structures and democratic South Africa. The argument is that there is a need for incorporating the traditional leadership in the new South Africa within a system of governance that is based on democratic principles.

The fact that the majority of traditional leaders are organized on ethnic lines in former independent and self-governing states, implies that the post-1994 government has the task of ensuring that the traditional leadership system of rule is fully incorporated into the democratic values and system of governance. The incorporation of traditional leadership in the new democratic South Africa would be an achievement in reconciling two different paradigmatic communities in one system of government. According to Brynard and Musitha (2011:113) the purpose of the integration of traditional authorities and the democratically elected local government is to promote cooperative and inclusive government in rural communities and contemporary local government systems. Accordingly, defeated nations during colonialism, and colonialism of a special type, such as AmaCirha, AmaJwarha, AmaNdwandwe, AmaHlubi, and various Khoisan Groupings in Southern Africa, were totally ignored and beneficiaries of the Bantu Administration Act used distorted histories and myths to stay and cross over to the democratic administration period. This was done by ensuring and influencing commissions outside Parliamentary approved criteria for bringing fundamental findings. For instance, significant dates of land dispossessions and claims to kingdoms are deliberately not traced back to pre-colonial periods, but to later centuries. In addition, that, indeed, is unfortunate in post-colonial Africa in general, and South Africa in particular. In other words, the real informants, kings, and queens are either replaced by beneficiaries of colonialism, or colonial resources are optimally used as far as possible to make judgments, as was the case with the Nhlapo Commission on traditional leadership disputes and claims (http://www.thepresidency.gov.za/pebble.asp?relid=583; accessed 14 January 2019).

With the formation of the post-apartheid state, the Nhlapo Commission was mandated to deal with all issues of traditional leadership that were outstanding during the negotiations pre-1994. One case that brought the work of the commission into sharp focus in relation to this question of unresolved issues, is that of AmaXhosa and Khoisan Kingdoms who claimed kingship and made representations to the Nhlapo Commission. To understand the AmaMpondomise, AmaXhosa, and Khoisan Kingdoms and their claims, and the Nhlapo Commission debate, one needs to understand the backdrop of the negotiations process. The claim to autonomy and self-determination of kingship in democratic South Africa was put into question in that the commission had to investigate and determine the veracity, authenticity, and truthfulness of the claim to kingship. In the final analysis, after making considerable efforts, and testing the validity of the claim, the commission had the last word, which was to reject the kingship claim of the claimants, in this case of the AmaMpondomise, AmaCirha, AmaTshawe, and so forth. It is argued that through the predetermined rejection of AmaCirha kingship using distorted histories and inaccurate resources, the Nhlapo Commission and government adopted not just a subjective legal argument based on Whig theory, but also employed a governmental repressive apparatus, that is, continuity with the existing status quo. This suggests that the

Nhlapo Commission was deployed post-apartheid with a similar state apparatus strategy of the past inhuman legacy. The latter is due to the observation that the illegitimate kings and queens continue uninterrupted even in the post-apartheid era in South Africa. Such implied continuity of the inhuman system of apartheid being adopted as part of the Constitution compromises the traditional governance system. As a result, the Nhlapo Commission assisted colonial architectural designers to maintain their structures and systems in the new post-apartheid political order beyond the comprehension of legitimate kingship claims by nations such as AmaMpondomise, AmaCirha, Khoisan groupings and so forth. It is also important to note that the Nhlapo Commission follows at least two other independent commissions of inquiry that dealt with the question of traditional leadership under the colonial and apartheid states. In the late nineteenth century, there was the Brownlee Commission of Inquiry into Native Laws and Customs, in 1880-1881. It was set up to investigate customary practices and laws of the indigenous people in the colony with the intention of developing the many customary laws for natives as markers of the subdivisions of subjects to entrench the idea of ethnic pluralism. Ethnic pluralism implied what Brownlee called 'territorial segregation,' that encouraged the racialization of the state through a physical location, linked to a political system that segregated the ruled institutionally. The commission made a comparison between civil colonial laws and indigenous laws, the basis of which was to establish customary laws for the indigenous people on a number of issues. The Brownlee Commission focused on Native Laws and Customs and ensured, inter alia, that Bantustans were careful to achieve the separation of ethnically motivated systems. In this way, ethnic pluralism took root and created the necessary distance between civil law and native law. In other words, the Brownlee Commission assisted the Cape Colonial state to consolidate the structure of European power in South Africa by driving blacks into reserved poor areas in South Africa, and replaced traditional leaders who were not cooperating with the colonial legislative framework.

CB Young followed the Brownlee Commission under the British colony. The apartheid state instituted an independent commission of inquiry that dealt with issues of traditional leadership in the 1950s. In part, the apartheid state solicited the power and influence of traditional leaders to legitimate themselves in the eyes of the South African people staying in rural areas. Through the Young Commission, the apartheid state sought to establish traditional authorities in line with the Native Administration Act of 1927. The State passed the Bantu Authorities Act of 1951 that sought to give traditional authorities more room to exercise power in their localities. The apartheid state established a system of Tribal Authorities: new tiers of segregated local traditional Bantu administration in which government-appointed chiefs took new powers. This moved to the establishment of Bantustans, where traditional leaders were at the head as a means of softening racism in South Africa. Gibbs argues that this system brought along with it a series of disputes and conflicts between those traditional leaders that supported the apartheid state and those that opposed it. For instance, Kaiser Mathanzima's claim of kingship of the AbaThembu. The so-called independent Young Commission was far from being neutral as it supported Kaiser Mathanzima, who was an apartheid supporter. As a result, King Sabatha Dalindyebo of abaThembula was forced into exile or faced death by both apartheid administrations. In other words, the Bronwlee, Young and Nhlapo Commissions were not independent, nor neutral. They all carried a political mandate, rather than addressing issues and claims of traditional leaders. In the case of the Nhlapo Commission, the democratic government adopted continuity to the post-apartheid apparatus and ignored some traditional leaders who had been crushed and dominated under the colonial and apartheid periods respectively. It appears that the Nhlapo Commission, by its legal representativeness, was used by the democratic administration to shift responsibilities when dealing with sensitive traditional leadership claims and counter-claims.

By ensuring that approximately 90% of the Nhlapo commissioners were lawyers, the democratic administration profoundly settled on the position of establishing an authorized and structured legal discourse analysis based on the continuity of existing traditional frameworks, post-apartheid. Like the Brownlee and Young Commissions, the Nhlapo Commission became a structured institutional tool for the democratic administration by finding itself speaking on behalf of the traditional leaders using colonial and apartheid archival sources, i.e., both material and human resources and knowledge, all part of a Whip doctrine or Westminster system of governance. For instance, the AmaCirha, Khoisan groupings, and others were expected to use the Westminster Governance System to bring tangible evidence of their rightful positions before the promulgation of the Native Authorities Act of 1927. They had to show that the implementation of the Act adversely affected their position, and therefore unfairly robbed them of their kingship status. To satisfy the commission and the state, one would have to present convincing evidence before the commission based on some historical evidence. To do so, traditional leaders would have to visit their archives, colonial and apartheid records, and the state archives. In the case of the AmaXhosa Kingdom and Cirha Kingship claim, the Nhlapo Commission appeared to be totally structured and influenced by ideologies of the colonial and apartheid public administration management (PAM) of traditional leaders. The findings of the Nhlapo Commission supported the Bantu Adminitration Act of 1945, which recognizes two kingdoms of AmaXhosa (AmaGcaleka and AmaRharhabe), echoing the findings of the Young Commission in 1950. In other words, the Nhlapo commissioners deliberately ignored AmaCirha and other legitimate informants. It opted to use what they knew better, being the Westminster System and its legal and colonial and apartheid archival records. It can be deduced that the Nhlapo Commission did not invent the wheel. Rather it opted to re-arrange and re-package the colonial and apartheid traditional narrative knowledge about traditional leaders with legal jargon, rather than new truths.

Furthermore, it is possible to argue that, in the post-colonial era, leaders are more interested in leading through popularity and rhetoric, and in being elected, than in being rich in ethical values to drive Africa's socio-economic agenda. Consequently, evidence and clues about social history and ancient civilization in

Egypt that have been reviewed, interpreted and analyzed in this book are inconclusive, with many historical gaps in post-colonial Africa. Yet it is clear from the oral interviews with elders of the Imbumba yamaNyama Royal Council, a review of historical resources, and study tours of Sudan, Kenya, Tanzania and Egypt, to mention but a few historical heritage sites, that there is compelling evidence to suggest that an Abantu group migrated from ancient Egypt and lived in Upper Egypt as Nubians or Sudanese. This group of Abantu, under the strategic stewardship, guidance, and leadership of various kings, including King Mnguni, eventually headed towards southern Africa due to the fall of the Old Kingdom that was plagued by endless wars, as Ancient Egypt was attacked by colonialists such as the Roman Empire, Asians (Persians), Arabs and Europeans. Additionally, there were severe droughts and extreme weather conditions, followed by famine, as colonizers destroyed and plundered Afro-Egyptian assets and livestock. Afro-Egyptians were then left with no option but to migrate in all directions.

When AmaXhosa say 'mzi kaNtu' (referring to King Mentuhotep I), they collectively believe that nature and the mother world, or the cosmic order through Creation by uQamata, has no end. It is also meant that there was an understanding of infinity, and that human beings were part of their environment. In other words, human beings (Abantu) and their immediate environment coexisted and were inseparable from the Abantu of God in Heaven. This led to the conceptualization of the Ubuntu paradigm, because 'uluntu' is a vital force, and 'umntu' is the personification of Ntu, 'son of Mentuhotep I' who is supposedly governed by human and environmental values, or 'isintu'. Accordingly, human beings must have human virtues, norms and standards of coexistence and cohabitation, and live in balance with their immediate environment and their fellow human beings (Ubuntu, or the art of being human, created by Qamata). The language used by the AmaNguni, as part of a Bantu group, has similarities with the language of ancient Egypt. For instance, under the ancient Egyptian 'maat' or 'Ubuntu' philosophy, human beings supposedly have a divine mind (brain), soul (blood or body), spirit (Qamata connection) and eternal life relationship with the Supreme God.

'Maat', as a word in ancient Egyptian, refers to concepts of truth, balance, order, harmony, law, order, morality and justice. It appears that 'maat' is linked to 'Ubuntu' principles of Abantu and 'Ubuntu' (the art and culture of being incorruptible and living a godly life of Qamata or God). Accordingly, 'umntu' (person) is born with divine attributes, namely intellect, wisdom, rationality, creativity, compassion and love, which make him/her distinctly different from other creations or created beings by Qamata or God. God conferred on humankind the power of dominion over all creatures. Therefore, 'umntu', or 'umuntu' kaMentuhotep I consists of the spirit, soul, and body, in other words, the three-fold principle of 'umntu' based on universal humanity. This theological explanation is linked to the Father, Son, and Holy Spirit in terms of the Christian doctrine, or the ancient Egyptian Christian philosophy of the northern tip of Africa, or Kemet, or Egypt. This universal principle of humanness, humanity, commonness, connection and inter-dependence made ancient Egyptians' Pharaoh Kings, such as kaMentuhotep I, understand God's existence and Creation of man (umntu or umuntu) in His image or likeness and His Presence (Omnipresence in us in terms of the soul, body and spirit) or humanness (Ubuntu) in all members of the human race. Theologically, it can inductively and deductively be concluded that the word 'umntu' or 'muntu' refers to 'God-man,' where God is defined as Omnipotence, Omniscience, and Omnipresence.

1.4.4. Mentuhotep I is our Great Ancestor for Abantu

Mentuhotep (MontuHotep) is an ancient Egyptian name, meaning 'Montu is satisfied.' Mentuhotep refers to several Pharaohs in ancient Egypt. 'Montu' also means unity in diversity of the human race with roots in ancient Africa. In other words, in African governance and the traditional ancient system of governance, everything is knitted and united together, forming a clear line of communication, hierarchy and leadership, from King kaMentuhotep I to ordinary citizens or people, with God as a Father of the universe. It can be concluded that there are logical, ontological and ethical arguments to argue that God in Heaven as revealed to Moses, Joshua and Ntsikana kaGabha finds its equivalent already in ancient Egypt as the Religion of the Anointed One, Savior or Redeemer, who later was confirmed as Jesus Christ. He was defined as Supreme Being, Creator of the Universe and Creator of the Heavenly Kingdom, Pre-existent One and Eternal God, or uMvelinqangi or Qamata or Oludumane, King of kings, and Lord of lords.

The leaders of ancient Egypt are ancestors of 'Ntu.' Through this universal concept, Christianity survived suppression and persecution by the Roman Empire. In AD 391, the Roman Empire destroyed all records of the true Egyptian roots of Christianity. The Roman Empire, through Bishop Theophilus, designed and manufactured an alternative political claim of Christianity as having originated in Judaea. Equally, the Europeans during imperialism and colonialism in Africa introduced the values and ethos of a white God or Jesus Christ aligned to Western philosophy. St Augustine further institutionalized that Christianity started with the birth of Jesus, the son of man (Jesus 'sa' or 'kaJoseph' from 'Ntu' groupings of King KaMentuhotep I). God is Oludumane, or unchanging, He is the Great Source of life (the Ibo people of southern Nigeria called Him Chukwu or Chineke), the Source and Sustainer of the World if we pray to Him alone, and He is the Beginning and End. It can be argued, therefore, that the center of Christianity is ancient Egypt (in the soil of Mother Africa) that symbolizes the Garden of Eden or Paradise under the dominion of 'uNtu', or God-man, or Adam.

Undoubtedly, God, as He had done in the case of Moses and Joshua, also revealed Himself in Spirit to Ntsikana kaGabha, son of Nkosiyamntu, kaMalangana, kaXhosa, kaMnguni, kaNtu and King kaMentuhotep I, as Omnipresent God with Supreme Goodness, Master of masters, and Governor of governors to save His people from all forms of prosecution, suppression and inhuman systems perpetrated by European settlers. As revealed to Ntsikana kaGabha, God's message was to remind His people that He is a God of law, order, rule, truth, righteousness, justice, integrity, and ethics. These concepts of the universality of human beings and oneness were communicated during Ntsikana kaGabha's time as 'zenibe yimbumba yamanyama' in terms of God's commandments or order, i.e., umthetho wesintu kaThixo oseZulwini ('the Commandments and Order of God who is in Heaven,' or 'God's Commandments and Order, which are in Heaven'). It is significant that Ntsikana kaGabha urged Cape people (Home of Legends) to embrace the Commandments or the Word or the Bible, rather than evil capitalism that may lead to greediness and corruption, as 'Ntu' is created by Thixo (God in Heaven) as an incorruptible human being.

1.4.5. Ntsikana's teachings are from God

Ethically, Ntsikana kaGabha taught people against committing adultery, murder, theft, lying, cursing God, bearing false witness, hatred of each other as people (abantu bakaNtu), and abandonment of fellow 'Ntu' beings and parents. Rather, human beings or 'Abantu' must be united in diversity guided by those in authority, or kings or queens (zenibe yimbumba yamanyama). Theologically, this was informed by the ancient Egyptian Christianity principle of 'love each other and love your neighbor as you love yourself'.

Even though it is difficult to make convincing conclusions, it appears that Africans such as Abantu and Khoisan in Mother Africa, or elsewhere in the African diaspora as a result of invasions and slavery systems, come from ancient Egypt in terms of the pre-colonial period. This rich history of African clans and kingdoms, and the historical presupposition of Mnguni, needs to be properly investigated and documented to ensure validity and reliability, which is outside the scope of this book. This would help to guide writers in using logical arguments as far as possible.

1.4.6. Khoi, San, and Abantu are Africans of ancient Egypt and the Garden of Eden

1.4.6. 1. Africans come from ancient Egypt before sedimentation and great floods

We also need to be careful that the history of Africans must include the Khoisan groupings from southern Africa, Namibia, Angola, Zambia, Lesotho (Khoekhoe), Botswana (Tshu-Khwe people), Zimbabwe (Tshu-Khwe people), Burkina Faso and Tanzania (Sandawe people). The Khoekhoe language is spoken by various major clans, namely Khoikhoi or Khoekhoe (meaning 'men of men' or people), Nama, Damara (Damaqua) and Haillom. The Khoekhoe language is related to certain dialects spoken by San people of the Kalahari, such as Khwe and Tshwa. The Griqua people are a mixed-race population in South Africa, of partial Khoikhoi and partial European ancestry. It is observed that most clans and kingdoms have dialectical and cultural differences that require special consideration when traditional leadership frameworks are made.

For instance, Damaqua, who are found in Namibia and Angola, have Cimbi (Tjimba groupings are Herero-speaking people), Kwisi (also known as Cuissi, Mbundyu, or Kwandu) and Kwadi (Angola Kwadi-Khoe) clans or ethnic groupings.

The reasons for outlining these Abantu and Khoisan groupings include the ability to demonstrate beyond a reasonable doubt that African people, irrespective of their ethnic features, languages or geographical settlements, have collectively experienced colonial violence, brutality, land dispossession and dislocation over the past imperial and colonial years. The negative impact of imperial and colonial land dispossession, and dislocation of Africans through slavery systems in the past by Roman empires, Persians, Arabs or Europeans, has been inhuman. These injustices must be addressed without distorting our rich and inspiring histories or by replacing them with unfortunate oral myths, as in the case of the AmaCirha Kingdom among the AmaXhosa. Rather, a genuine reconciliation is required in Africa in order to develop a new growth path or roadmap beyond 2063. This socio-economic cohesion model is defined by the Nation-Building Plan (2020-2064) whereby Africans become more conscious of the things they have in common, rather than their differences, entrenched by colonial Acts of Parliament, policies, strategies, and implementation plans. In terms of the nation-building plan envisaged in this book, it is argued that post-colonial Africa and its beautiful landscapes will be informed by the concept of unity in diversity (zenibe yimbumba yamanyama) to achieve blue and green economic models by working together (harambee in Swahili). Based on Ubuntu paradigm values, the future Paradise Cities in post-colonial Africa will have:

- Broad-based knowledge about and support for a set of values shared by all Africans derived from an Ubuntu paradigm, including the values contained in the Constitution per country;
- An inclusive society and economy informed by blue and green economic models. This means, inter alia, that African Paradise Cities need to seize a more prominent position in the world economy by enhancing their accessibility, connectivity, markets and urban attractiveness to uproot abject poverty, unemployment and increased inequalities by addressing wrongs of the past colonial legacy;
- Increased interaction between Africans from different countries and Paradise Cities by adopting blue and green economic models for diversification in order to increase resilience to global economic shocks as far as possible;
- Enhanced knowledge sharing for reindustrialization and industrial growth and development by emphasizing technology-based, environmentally friendly new modes of public transport to reduce pollution and congestion in cities, and more effectively integrate rural and urban mobility with enhanced transportation of goods and services;

- Food security that coincides with investment in technologies, innovation, logistics and sustainable services in the food sector in all African states and cities; and
- Pragmatic, innovative and aesthetic leadership in all African states to ensure, inter alia, those Paradise Cities perform a quintessential role in Africa's evolving structural transformation because of both rural and urban environments. This will allow Paradise Cities to accommodate industries that have already demonstrated sustainable economic growth in the past. This implies that economic diversification should go hand-in-hand with continental and regional specialization and the complementary division of labor across Africa's beautiful landscapes and heritage sites.

This will lead to an inclusive social and economic cohesion in order to utilize the Home of Legends' developmental potential in the context of a structurally transformed South Africa in Africa. This will also further promote internal competition between Paradise Cities. The competition between cities can be around product markets and inward investments, as well as the establishment of firms, tourists attractions and funding.

1.4.6. 2 Hunting skills of AmaXhosa, Khoi, and San

It is crucial to note that African people were also able to learn from each other. For instance, while many writers have created myths around 'iphuthi', one can argue that AmaXhosa at the time were very skillful and sophisticated in respect of hunting, based on various interactions with Khoisan groupings in the Cape Colony. James James Ranisi (JJR) Jolobe defines African clans and kingdoms' use of rich words, such as ukwenda (establishment of family ties and intermarriages between clans and kingdoms), namasoka agqityiweyo (mature bridegrooms-to-be), ukwembesa (exchange of property, assets, clothes, kitchen utensils and so forth, through ilobola or marriage negotiations), and kwamhlamnene (before the imperialists arrived, AmaNguni were able to hunt and slaughter either a beast (inyamakazi or isilwanyana) or a blue duiker or iphuthi, or any other livestock, as it is recorded that AmaNguni kept tens of thousands of cattle. In 1831, Henry Somerset complained that along the Keiskamma River and around the Amatola Mountains, the cattle of AmaXhosa were so numerous that he found it impossible to track any stolen beasts (iinyamkazi or iinkomo or cattle) when white settlers carried out patrols or raids (Mostert, 1992:858)).

It is significant that the words 'cattle' and 'livestock' are used in various history books and oral narratives. Yet the Cape Colony was home to animals such as lion, leopard, rhinoceros (both black and white species), elephant, Cape buffalo, eland, gemsbuck, blesbuck, bontebok, blue duiker (iphuthi), blue wildebeest, impala, bluebucks, and so forth. These indigenous animals were taken away from the people, and the term 'wild game' was coined. As part of the colonial administration system, followed by deforestation as a military tactic, these animals, which are linked to the lives of African people, were contained and conserved on European-occupied land for commercial purposes. Through highly selective farming concepts as part of the colonial discourse, authors refer to livestock such as cattle, sheep and goats, and not to African indigenous animals. For instance, ingqina (hunting) was common among Africans as wild animals were often hunted during dry seasons to supplement food, especially among Nguni clans and kingdoms.

1.4.6.3 African governance and code of conduct systems are based on Order in Heaven

As part of gently rejecting colonial discourse, JJR Jolobe understood that Tshawe had to do 'imbeleko', Jolobe's novel's use of the word 'izilimela', or mathematical counting after traditional circumcision, should be considered in a traditional sense (not age but the lineage order of houses). In this cultural and leadership context, Jolobe (1958:42-50) argues that the AmaXhosa social code is based on the wholeness of the family, and that there is nothing more important than the maintaining of harmonious relationships within the family's social structures and fabric. Kwetana (2000:108-110) adds that the sociocultural and political stratification of African societies determines who must respect whom.

God created man in His own image to distinguish them from all other forms of life, and endowed them with divine attributes that enable them to reason and strive towards an orderly existence. Humankind's entire historical existence has been characterized by order and the creation of societies for coexistence in an orderly manner. Even during the exoduses from ancient Egypt by Jews to Jerusalem, and Afro-Egyptians to the east, west and south of Africa, there was order and a regulated way of life (Exodus 13: 17-22). In other words, kings, queens, empires and traditional governance systems were born of the inherent drive for order. This was complemented by rules, norms and standards, and codes of conduct for individuals (like Tshawe), clans (AmaTshawe, AmaJwarha, and AmaCirha), and the father (kaNkosiyamntu, kaMalangana, kaXhosa, kaMnguni, kaNtu and so forth) in ancient Egypt thereafter being an authoritative figure and decision-maker.

Within this line of communication and structured family, clan and kingdom framework, fixed relationships were established, including behaviors and cultural practices. Accordingly, the Omniscient, Omnipotent and Omnipresent righteous God, long-departed kings, queens, counselors (abacebisi neentlola), and councillors (amaphakathi), diviners, dignitaries, family ancestors, living kings, chiefs and counselors, aged men and women, middle-aged men and women, young men and women, youth newly graduated from boyhood to manhood (amakrwala) and from girlhood to senior girls who have undergone intonjane (female initiation), and children, give and show respect in this order. As Tshawe was growing up, he arrived at this stable social code of conduct and kingship hierarchy, and its demands, bit by bit, until it was imprinted indelibly on his mind (Jolobe, 1958:23). AmaCirha and AmaJwarha, as well as AmaTshawe, grew up respecting this governance and hierarchy, where they saluted each other at all times[9] (Jolobe, 1958:4).

Another misunderstanding and misrepresentation of AmaXhosa democratic processes and systems by scholars contributes to ensuring a permanent mistrust between the descendants of the three brothers, Cirha, Jwarha, and Tshawe. One such misrepresentation is that Tshawe created a strong AmaXhosa monarchy, where AmaXhosa were able to 'wage wars of extermination with the Bushmen and the Hottentots and occupy the land between the Mbashe and the Cape Point' (Balfour-Noyi, 2017:30-32). In other words, it is suggested that Tshawe also conducted 'wars of extermination,' such as were used against Aboriginals and Maori people in southern Australia and New Zealand respectively by imperialists and colonialists. This is highly unlikely. From interviews with the House of Traditional Leaders in the Eastern Cape, a talk by Chief Mwelo Nonkonyana at Thwathwa on the 09 November 2018, Imbumba yamaNyama elders and stalwarts, it appears that Tshawe grew up at his mother's side and had an attachment to his mother and a better comprehension of clans' sociocultural and political codes. Consequently, he had to come to his elder brothers, Cirha and Jwarha, to do 'imbeleko' using blue duiker (iphuthi). 'Imbeleko' is a clan ceremony that is conducted two weeks after the birth of a baby. It is an act of detaching the umbilical connection of Tshawe from his mother's family's side and introducing him to Nkosiyamntu family or clan values and principles. Unfortunately, Balfour-Noyi's (2017) contribution adds to military conquest and psychological war literature in which social cohesion is destroyed.

Furthermore, a similar myth reflects the story of Thuthula as the cause of a war between the Tshawe dynasties, which was waged between Ngqika and his paternal uncle Ndlambe. Historically, it was rather caused by a power struggle between the elder Ndlambe who did not want to relinquish power, and Ngqika, than by the widely known Thuthula case. This Battle of Amalinde in 1818 was fought near Dimbaza township in the area of Mngqesha district in the direction of Keiskammahoek ('Kheis' is a Khoi word referring to a place of living; 'hoek' is an Afrikaans word for corner, and 'kamma' is a castle from south India, and refers to agriculture in medieval history. In other words, Keiskammahoek is a green agricultural valley and landscape in the area, which then had the shape of a castle.) Clans such as AmaGqunukwebe supported Ndlambe. Ngqika formed an alliance with the British forces and white settlers who exploited the differences between Ndlambe and Ngqika. As a result, the AmaXhosa lost their property, land and cattle between Keiskammahoek and the Fish River (Nxuba). Although lofty advice was provided by Ntsikana kaGabha to the chiefs, it was ignored, and they did not want to be advised. Ntsikana kaGabha, from the Cirha clan, knew that without unity and the settling of internal conflicts between the AmaTshawe dynasties, there would be far-reaching negative repercussions for their clans, and for black people generally.

Historically, it appears that this Battle of Amalinde created a platform for the British administrators to control the land previously occupied by AmaXhosa, and use the 1820 British settlers as a buffer force. This led to the Fifth Frontier War, which followed the Fourth Frontier War (where the Zuurland was completely lost to the British forces). (For a more detailed account of the various frontier wars, see Chapter 6.) In some cases, the white settlers institutionalized the counter-hegemonic public administration and management system using fictitious and mythical stories. Some historians used the Battle of Amalinde as a justification for having AmaRharhabe and AmaGcaleka Kingdoms under Phalo as paramount chief. This further justified the design and establishment of the Ciskei and Transkei homelands by apartheid administrators and supporters in the late 1950s.[10] For instance, colonialists and apartheid agencies reconstructed kingdoms using a 'winner-takes-all policy,' subjecting defeated clans and families to severe suffering under colonial and apartheid domination, and possibly leading to bloodier battles than were ever fought among the AmaXhosa themselves (Mostert, 1992:466). Through the repressive colonial and apartheid systems, legitimate African kingdoms that resisted colonialism and apartheid public administration and management (PAM) faced injustices and severe atrocities and were replaced by new kingdoms and chiefs – all part of a pseudo-archaeology to erase the true histories of African kingdoms and cultural values, at all costs.

Notwithstanding the above facts, European writers, anthropologists, experts, governors, and administrators focused on the notion of a 'native framework' of African people, used all types of labels, and distorted histories to justify racism and pseudo-archaeology. The settler-native or Eurocentric discourse in South Africa has a peculiar history, which required Ntsikana kaGabha to provide a 'roadmap' or 'pathfinder' (vulindlela, as coined by GV Mona, 1995). The South African political and cultural geographies were founded on colonial and apartheid notions of a 'native' and 'settler' society, a 'tribalized' and racialized historiography that classified locals as 'natives'. The historical narrative of African societies is presented using the notion of 'traditional societies.' This tradition-driven account is trapped in 'native' politics and a settler-versus-native discourse, of which the latter was used to justify colonial rule. The concept of the 'native' as a colonial state construct and as a political identity was part of a socio-economic Darwinism where history, law, and modernity defined whites, while the indigenous population was defined by geography, tradition, language, dialect and culture.

1.5 Reconciliation of clans and kingdoms through nation-building plans

The proposed nation-building plan, which entails the reconciliation of families and clans, requires urgent attention from the state and the National Heritage Council (NHC). Its purpose would be not only to eliminate the present concerns of transcending narrow ethnic-separatist definitions of 'historical facts' and royal kingdoms, but also to establish a state of equilibrium through Paradise City models in Africa where justice is achieved and current pseudo-archaeology is replaced with true historical facts and kingdoms for socio-economic stability and social cohesion up to and beyond 2063 (Childs & Williams, 1997:12; Cope, 1968:23; Nyembezi, 1982:1; Soyinka, 1999:36).

It appears that Jolobe's novel presents a pre-colonial era where there were economic, social, political, spiritual and moral systems to create harmonious relationships between clans and kingdoms. Jolobe (1958:51-52) adds that AmaNdwandwe, AmaNgwane, AmaZulu, AmaHlubi and others were not war-like people, nor did they seek power over, or the blood of their fellow countrymen and -women; they were rather people of peace, focused on socio-economic and political stability. As white writers and scholars lacked context, they argued that 'Caffers' arrived before Europeans and that they were at war with each other (Brownlee, 1916/1977:179). CP Brownlee (1916/1977), for example, may have lacked context regarding the term 'imfazwe' (war) as used by Jolobe (1958:61). Jolobe's war is not a war of destruction, or a perpetual war, but can be compared to stick playing for strengthening exercises or sparring in boxing (Kwetana, 2000:120-125). These exercises also served to separate one age group from another: the young group could then know that they were not strong enough to play with the older groups. They had to show respect to the older group until they could play with the older group (ukubethe iintonga). This is an exposition of African military strategy rather than warmongering, as defined by Brownlee (1916/1977:179).

Even cattle ostensibly 'taken' by Ngwane were in fact 'given' to support and establish the Mahlaphahlapha Kingdom (or Great Place or Paradise City). 'Amandla ezo zizwe zithanda uxolo alele ekuncedisaneni' (which can be loosely translated to mean the power of the peaceful nation or clans or kingdoms) was (and still is) rooted in restoring and maintaining social, economic, cultural and political peace, order and stability (Jolobe, 1958:54). Additionally, Jolobe's writings from the 1950s inform readers that 'kwakuse kulithutyana iimfazwe yagqityelwayo ngamaHlubu. Isininzi solutsha sasikhule siyiva ngamavo ... AmaHlosi ayevuyela ithuba lokuzibalula azenzele amagama azuze namava aphathekayo kuphele ukuva ngotyelo ngento yemfazwe (1958:55-56). This is translated to mean that the Hlubi Royal Kingdom had experienced no war for quite a long time. The majority of the youth (amatsha ntliziyo or Hlosi regiment) only heard about the war in stories (or oral memories in various ceremonies or events). Amatsha-ntlizo or the Hlozi regiment were excited and keen to go to war, mainly to gain concrete military experience or to prove their manhood and make their names popular in the AmaHlubi Royal Kingdom by displaying skills in the war, and thereby enabling them to put an end to the fact that they had always relied on stories.

This African democratic system is informed by indigenous idiom, which states that it is true that when two brothers fight, strangers reap the property, land or harvest, as was demonstrated in the series of frontier wars in the Cape Colony (see section 6.4 in Chapter 6). As part of the rejection of conflicts among Africans, Mtuze and Matyila (1990:35) composed a song:

Bawo Thixo Somandla
Ndinesingqala entliziyweni yam
Ndisoloko ndisithi mayidlule le Ndebe Bawo,

Thixo Somandla.
(Father, God, Omnipotent,
I have a sob in my heart;
I keep on saying let this cup or battle pass,
Father, God, Omnipotent).

Overcoming socio-historical problems and historical challenges are fundamental for defining a nation-building plan between 2020 and 2064 (read with paragraph 6.14). The overarching vision 'unity in diversity' (zenibe yimbumba yamanyama),[11] as so eloquently articulated by Ntsikana kaGabha, has become so relevant today that it must be part of our daily activities to avoid the outbreak of World War III, or a chaotic and violence-driven revolution in Africa. In the socio-economic, historical, cultural and political era of Ntsikana kaGabha, as an extraordinary lecturer, teacher, counselor,[12] prophet and spiritual and visionary leader, the concept was informed by historical and economic contradictions and imbalances during the imperial and colonial periods, whose hallmarks are still seen today (Childs & Williams, 1997:123-138). This conceptual expression encompasses all differences and is an appeal by him to the leaders to embrace unity in the Kingdom of uQamata or God.

In the context of the Home of Legends, 'unity in diversity' refers to the societal representation of people with different families, clans, tribes, nations, and kingdoms, characterized by different affiliations and by cultural diversity. In short, 'zenibe yimbumba yamanyama' is a quest for an inclusive approach by revering God as the Creator of humankind and the universe, characterized by love, peace, stability, good governance, righteousness and justice. The Nation-Building Plan (2020-2064) proposed in this book is, therefore, an adaptive strategy to overcome new challenges and problems. These stubborn challenges and systemically complex socio-economic constraints, seen in the light of global trends, require, among others, visionary and aesthetic leaders. Through a nation-building plan using integrated rural and urban investment programs (IR and UIIPs), any capacity deficit in governance and leadership in African institutions that have human, material (assets) and institutional dimensions can be appropriately and adequately addressed pro bono publico, or for the public good.

Rather than becoming tangled up in metaphysical theories, I want to consider Ntsikana's lofty advice as more applicable to concepts such as the blue and green city models for co-nurturing and co-creating local space for good-enough governance and a collaboration with Imbumba yamaNyama and credible institutions using multifunctional IR and UIIPs for consolidating Ntsikana kaGabha's philosophy, which is now subsumed under the Mandela legacy (abaThembu) around unity in diversity and harmony with biodiversity. I want to suggest that the blue and green city models, or Paradise City models, covering Coffee Bay, Ixhorha (Hole in the Wall), Mvezo, Hankey and Thwathwa (henceforth referred to as private-public partnerships or PPPs)[13] have been based on the ARVPD framework, as coined by Swartz (2010). These blue and green city models, or post-colonial cities, as the case may be, may restore and maintain our aesthetic relational values, leading to aesthetic leadership for the country's nation-building plan between 2020 and 2064.

Undoubtedly, it can be argued that only by first establishing a comprehensive nation-building plan (Nation-Building Plan 2020-2064), using multifunctional integrated rural and urban infrastructure investment programs (IR and UIIPs), can Ntsikana's Paradise Cities, or blue and green future cities, know what programs (based on existing sectoral-driven programs such as IPAP, NGP, the NDP 2030 vision and the Black Industrialist Programme (BIP) vision, to name but a few) to implement and what interventions to put in place, using aesthetic relational values to ensure growth and development for their citizens and creative industries.

Mogale (2007:10-18), cited in Tsibani (2014a:81), argues that simply developing programs focused on socio-economic growth and developmental visions is not sufficient to eradicate abject poverty, systemic unemployment and increased inequality (Clapham, 1996:273-4). On the other hand, a comprehensive first-hand, multisensory, emotional and imaginative nation-building plan will take into account previously successful global, continental and regional interventions. This includes acknowledgment of the driving factors for growth and development in the pre- and post-industrial eras in the global economy and the impact of these eras on the current three stages of environmental development, and the movement from the 'Holocene' into the 'Anthropocene' (Goudie, 2013:7-8). Three stages regarding Earth's changes in the past 300 years demonstrate, beyond any reasonable doubt, that global warming will affect hydrological systems and fluvial geomorphology in a whole range of ways, especially in former colonies in Africa. In countries that experience a lack of good-enough governance, characterized by complex capability constraints (3Cs) in their adopted PAM systems, aesthetic leaders are required to deliver economically viable, efficient and effective (3Es) developmental services – a situation that will require accelerated integrated rural (IR) and urban infrastructure investment programme (UIIP) partnership initiatives (UNEP, 2011b:548). This refers to an international leadership judgment that is 'aesthetically sensible and right,' where there is a link between aesthetics and ethics in good-enough governance, with aesthetic leadership applying the founding message of Ntsikana in the nineteenth century and that of Nelson Mandela in the twenty-first century.

On the basis of interactions at various meetings and conferences, it can, on the one hand, be concluded that the proposed Nation-Building Plan (2020-2064) allows for synergies between programs. On the other hand, it allows organs of state – in partnership with international development agencies, including UNEP and UNESCO – to develop a forward-looking blue and green economy vision that targets productivity, inclusivity, and resilience using the ARVPD framework for designing Ntsikana Paradise City models, or blue and green city models. Yet, aesthetic leaders and managers in these models also need to ensure that the public administration and management systems, and related internal technological systems, can support meaningful and purposeful multifunctional IR and UIIP interventions for the eradication of poverty, unemployment and inequality. It is concluded that through the IR and UIIPs, supported by appropriate technology for advancing a blue and green economy and the restoration of aesthetic relational values, a nation-building plan can systematically break down the current sectoral-driven silo programs and encourage the formalization of co-nurturing and co-creating governance and partnership models among the various organs of state. In light of the multidisciplinary nature of the nation-building plan and related governance requirements, participants in the above-mentioned meetings indicated a need for aesthetic leaders to drive a country's nation-building plan and the related multifunctional IR and UIIPs, using public-private partnerships (PPP) as well as city-to-city models and networks in order to spread best practices, embrace new creative paradigm thinking and appropriate technological options, and replicate other creative and innovative Paradise City models and solutions adopted elsewhere (Brandy, 2006:182; UNEP, 2012a:36).

Keep a green tree in your heart, and perhaps a singing bird will come. (Chinese proverb)

This book outlines practical step-by-step solutions to implement Ntsikana Paradise City models. It makes recommendations on how these steps can be implemented using the Aesthetic Relational Values in Planning and Development Framework (ARVPDF) in accordance with the blue and green economy and the need for balancing human and biodiversity needs. These solutions are presented as part of an adaptive strategy to new demands for capable, accountable, responsive, innovative and aesthetic leaders in consolidating democracy through sustainable developmental services. The latter is due to my observation, during the Pan-African Parliament (PAP) held in Midrand from 21 to 25 May 2015, where speakers unanimously agreed that Africa's challenges must be radically addressed so that the continent's aesthetic leaders, using co-creating local governance partnerships, can allocate their countries' resources to potential new emerging markets capable of making profits from free trade agreements signed between African states and the free flow of trade in the global economy, now subsumed under a blue and green economy. Following the adoption of free trade agreements by African states and the COP21 Paris resolutions, blue and green city models, or Paradise Cities, are to be human settlement areas empowered to drive sustainable growth and development. In short, blue and green city models in the Home of Legends, will be able to promote, secure and advance socio-economic growth without compromising the needs of future generations.

1.6 Need for Paradise City models as part of the Nation-Building Plan

Isixeko eso sakomkhulu sasibanzi...kufumane kwasisithabazi nje sengqilikazi yomzi owawungalahlekayo lula kuwo. Nomzi ganye wabe unsesawo isibiyelo seengcongolo ezomileyo njengoko kwakunjalo nakwindlu nganye... Kungemva ngamasango macala

... Owakomkhulu umzi wawusesazulwini nakwindlue sesixeko eso uphahlwe macala ngowomphakathi-mkhosi, uNtlabane, ngasekune nangowesanuse sakomkhule, uDlikiza, ngasekhohlo. (Jolobe, 1958:1)

The Paradise City or Great Place occupies a large aesthetic space. It is a big aesthetic and natural architectural design in which a visitor or stranger can be completely lost ... And each homestead has its own fencing of hermetically dry reeds, and within the homestead, each hut has its own fencing of dry reeds. Entry on all sides of the Paradise City or Great Place is through the gates. The King's residence is at the center of the castle, aesthetically flanked on the right by the army commander-in-chief (Ntlabane) and by the Great Place diviner (Dlikiza) on the left. (Jolobe, 1958:1)

1.6.1 Outcomes for Paradise City models as part of a nation-building plan

Through reading this book, readers will be able to:

- Understand the ethnographic importance of Paradise City models (izixeko) as linked to various integrated senses of human dignity, belonging, culture, heritage, history, emotional and spiritual attachment, and so forth (Jolobe, 1958:1-5).
- Understand and interpret blue and green economic models and associated programs and projects in the context of the Home of Legends or the Cape provinces, viewed as a global cultural heritage landscape. The Cape provinces include the Western, Northern and Eastern Cape provinces under the democratic administration. Legends, stalwarts and founding fathers and mothers of our glorious movement came from these provinces, and together faced brutal wars since the arrival of white settlers in the Cape. While the concept has been developed by the Eastern Cape, its roots should be in the Western Cape where Africans, especially the Cape Khoi, San, and AmaXhosa, first encountered European settlers. Therefore, the use of the Cape provinces as a Home of Legends also refers to any other landscape on African soil, and how evil spirits were conquered by moral and ethical values and principles, as now conceptualized in South Africa under the King IV code on corporate governance.
- Apply blue and green economic models in their own context and the Home of Legends in the case of the Cape provinces of South Africa, in southern Africa, and on the entire African continent. It is also significant that the Eastern, Northern, and Western Cape provinces have similar geographical conditions, with the Northern Cape being the driest province.

- Interpret SPACE competencies in global governance, change management, and leadership innovation as the following:
    - ✓ **Situational analysis** of an aesthetic landscape and its uniqueness for socio-economic growth and development of blue and green city programs and models.
    - ✓ **Presence to influence** global developments and decisions on climate change, read in conjunction with the COP21 Paris resolutions, water scarcity, and limited natural resources.
    - ✓ **Authenticity,** trusteeship and integrity by implementing aesthetic leadership and good governance.
    - ✓ **Clarity** on new investment models and plans, such as the Black Industrialist Programme (BIP), the Industrial Policy Action Plan (IPAP), the New Growth Path Framework (NGP), the National Development Plan (NDP 2030) vision, the 2030 Agenda for Sustainable Development by African countries (AfSD) and the African Union's (AU) Agenda 2063.
    - ✓ **Empathy,** or understanding needs and applying visionary leadership: citizens, business investors, traditional leaders, specialists and leaders, by appreciating the Cape provinces' sustainable pillars – different people, scenarios and landscapes all moving towards blue and green economic models. In his *Treatise of Human Nature*, the philosopher David Hume (1740, cited in McNally, 1988:169), supported later on by Plateau (1994:800), advances the notion of self-identity, self-love, and an outward mindset, which all lead to sympathy and empathy in leadership. According to McNally (1988:183) and Young (1992:73-74), empathy – like sympathy – brings about a fellow-citizenship mental frame of reference. Such a mindset is necessary to restore the social fabric and intergenerational equity, and a notion of coexistence or moral capital informed by truth, acceptance, and obligations to families, clans, communities, countries and regions, as depicted in Figure 1.1 hereunder. The road indicates the long walk to freedom and social justice in the Thwathwa landscape from the early 1800s to 2019. This is complemented by the need to build Paradise Cities using blue and green architectural designs.

Fumene George Tsibani

Figure 1.1: 1400s Thwathwa Road

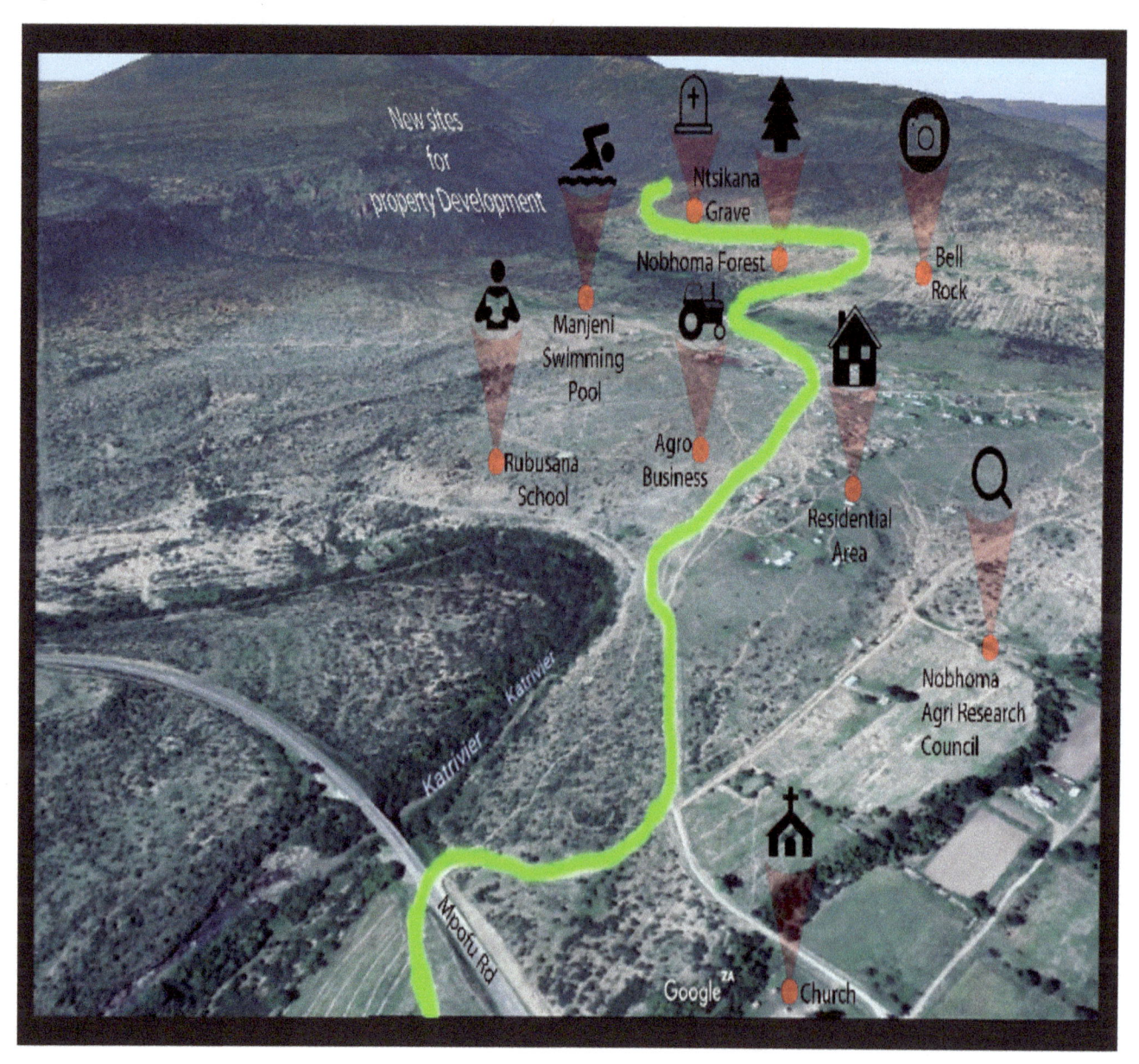

Nation Building Plan Between 2020 & 2064

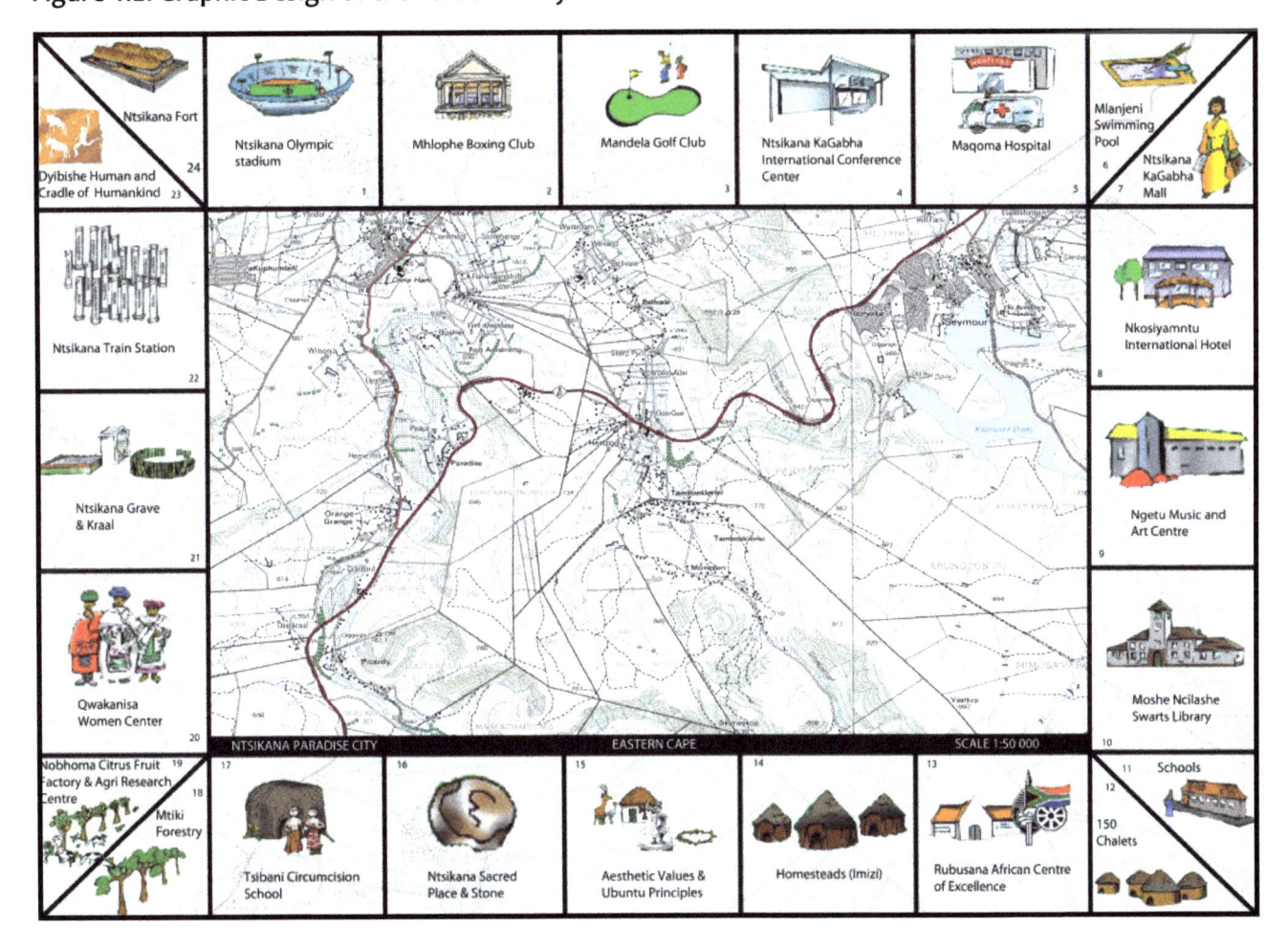

Figure 1.2: Graphic Design of the Paradise City

- Develop and design programmes and projects, as depicted in Figure 1.2, above, to make communities and cities better places, through SPACE, or landscapes for investment, combined with heritage sites in terms of a rich historical genesis of the concept of Home of Legends in Africa, as described in *The end of poverty* authored by Sachs (2002:56-66). In short, readers will be empowered to explore blue and green economic models and related possibilities under the National Development Plan (NDP) 2030 vision and the African Union Agenda 2063, so that the right integrated rural (IR) and urban infrastructure investment programs (UIIPs) can lead to blue and green economic models by exploiting the Western, Eastern and Northern Cape provinces (or former Cape colony). By restoring and maintaining our beauty,[14] it is envisaged that pride will be restored in the Home of Legends, and that business models will be aligned to blue and green economic models required for adaptive strategy in terms of climate change and COP21 Paris resolutions by global leaders. Pride in the context of the Home of Legends refers to planners, decision makers and leaders using aesthetic relational values in planning, and developing post-colony cities, such as Coffee Bay, Mvezo, Ixhorha and Thwathwa near Seymour. It refers to leaders, decision makers and people promoting national pride – a sense of socio-economic, ecological, emotional, environmental, political, legal and spiritual belonging – and history in designing towns and cities, and ensuring alignment of the socio-economic and cultural identity of the plans with people's immediate environment. As defined in detail in this book, such plans based on aesthetic relational values, will make people link the concept of the Home of Legends to the acronym PRIDE to mean the following:

- ✓ **Productivity**, where organs of state, the private sector, civil society, academia and researchers, and development think-tanks are working together to eradicate poverty and institutionalize a nation-building plan (2020-2064), guided by the South African National Development Plan as a chapter of the African Union Agenda 2063.
- ✓ **Reindustrialisation,** where all smart cities have reindustrialized before using blue and green economic models in terms of a climate change adaptation strategy. The Department of Trade and Industry (DTI), through the Industrial Policy Action Plan (IPAP), has considered reindustrialization to address the equity and transformation agenda, whereby the legacy of the past is radically replaced with inclusive social and economic development programs and projects. The DTI's Black Industrialist Programme (BIP) refers to black people being directly involved in the origination, creation, significant ownership, management and operation of industrial enterprises that derive value from the manufacturing of goods and services at a large scale, acting to unlock the productive potential of our country's capital assets for massive employment locally. The following are important elements of being an industrialist:
  - A significant influence in an enterprise or industry
  - Control of an enterprise through shareholding
  - Board and executive management control
  - Production of products (goods and services) with significant, wide use in advancing inclusive economic models and reindustrialization initiatives linked to blue and green economic models.

Some of the immediate benefits of reindustrialization include:

- Diversifying and growing exports
- Improving the trade balance
- Building long-term industrial capability
- Growing domestic technology
- Catalyzing skills development
- Creating millions of indirect and direct jobs over ten years using programs and projects under WEALTH creation components, as discussed further below.

The vision for industrialization must be integrated with overall blue and green economic planning and be based on an understanding of sectoral dynamics and opportunities, taking **w**ater, **e**nergy, **a**griculture, **l**and, **t**echnology, and **h**ealth (WEALTH) into account. The successful industrial policy requires analysis of the challenges and opportunities, design, intervention, and coherence based on IR & UIIP conceptualized under the Aesthetic Relational Values in Planning and Development Framework (ARVPDF). The experience from other countries highlights that this needs to be led politically from the apex of government, and that lessons learned along the way need to be incorporated in an iterative productive process of continuous improvement of policy design and implementation of post-colonial cities or Paradise City models, based on environmental friendly infrastructure investment models in various landscapes in the Home of Legends, or any other aesthetic landscape in Africa. The vision of reindustrialization using blue and green economic models includes a re-shaping of government departments, bringing together those that relate to technology, industry, trade, development finance and regulating markets, and providing for clear aesthetic leadership and coordination with areas including skills development, energy, minerals and agriculture in various Paradise Cities in the Home of Legends, or any landscape in Mother Africa beyond 2063. The new dawn coined as 'thuma mina' by President Cyril Ramaphosa in his State of the Nation Address (SONA, 2018), must set out expectations for large firms for local investment in our rich heritage sites, towns and cities in the Home of Legends. In return, the state must commit to environmentally friendly policies for infrastructure, procurement, skills development, technology, and markets to restore PRIDE through WEALTH creation in our Paradise Cities in mother Africa.

- **Innovation** and creativity in planning new suburbs and towns, with a bias towards integrated rural and urban infrastructure investment programs (IR and UIIPs), rather than the current urban planning programs and designs that lack adaptability to the geographic and topographic nature of African human settlement patterns. Innovation enables the attempt to try out new or improved products, processes or ways to do things and is part of most social, cultural, historical and economic activities. It is also a critical part of industrial development and structural change for heritage sites, small towns and cities, as economic hubs for reindustrialization using blue and green economic models must adapt and adjust to climate change and promote environmentally friendly programs and projects. Industry studies indicate substantial failures in managing the integration of the South African economy with the global economy, as well as failures in developing coherent policies for local and national institutions for technological capabilities. The rapid opening up of the South African economy, which began in the late 1980s, meant exposure to international markets and prices. The challenges involved are exemplified by the metals and machinery industries, in which basic metals prices have fluctuated wildly with global demand and supply, exacerbated by industrial policies in large economies led by China and the USA. The importance of exports to local basic metals producers means they are highly exposed, going from boom to bust. In periods of high international prices, the basic metals producers make substantial profit margins, while in low price periods they lobby for government protection to save jobs. The policy agenda has been preoccupied with the interests of upstream firms, rather than by downstream businesses, which account for much more employment, but which are fragmented. It is significant that basic metals production has undergone global consolidation and, in South Africa, become dominated by TNCs. The government's strategy in the early 2000s in iron and steel was to identify an international company with the technological capabilities to turn around the former state-owned Iscor. Iscor became part of the largest steel company in the world, Arcelor-Mittal, which restructured the business, but failed to make the promised investments. As a result, profits in the boom years were taken out of the business while, following the collapse of prices from 2011, the industry has required support. A similar picture appears in basic chemicals to downstream plastics production, except here the main upstream producer has remained vertically integrated into resource inputs, meaning it has remained profitable, yet has not been subject to effective policies to build broader industry capabilities. The Black Industrial Programme and other progressive policies are putting South Africa on a good manufacturing path whereby the developmental state and its research think-tanks or National Research Councils ensure, inter alia, that companies are shifting to high-value products for global exports.

- **Domestic** consumption, whereby African government institutions and leaders are able to create a conducive environment and implement free trade agreements between African states to benefit the poor and local people (the principle of 'charity begins at home' is relevant in this case). Within manufacturing in South Africa, there has been a structural regression as growth in value added has continued to be biased towards mineral and resource-based sectors. There has been a decrease in manufacturing employment across the board, but the largest losses have been borne by exactly those diversified manufacturing industries where strong growth would create jobs, directly and in related industries. The lack of structural change is reflected in South Africa's undiversified exports. Mineral and resource-based sectors continue to dominate the export basket, and together account for 60% of merchandise exports. South Africa is thus missing out on the gains from international integration from improved competitiveness and 'learning through exporting' in diversified manufacturing industries. Instead, there are 'islands' of export capabilities, such as in mining machinery, which have not been built upon. While financial services have also grown in value added, it has not grown employment. Nor has its growth been associated with higher levels of savings and investment in the real economy. Thus, the increase in the contribution of services to GDP from 60% in 1994 to 68% by 2016 has not been part of a positive structural transformation of the economy. The South African economy continues to be highly concentrated, with some data showing worsening concentration levels, even while ownership has changed with an increase in foreign and local institutional investors. At the same time, average rates of profit have remained high. Firms have been channeling funds towards mergers and acquisitions rather than in expanding and upgrading productive capacity. Monopolistic firms have less of an incentive to invest, since they can earn rents by protecting their market share rather than upgrading their product offering. Furthermore, barriers to entry for smaller firms inhibit investment and thus dynamism. It is significant that a strikingly similar economic structure to South Africa in terms of mining share of GDP, output per head and total factor productivity is present in Malysia. Both South Africa and Malaysia were medium-sized economies with deep racial divides, where the ethnic majority had political power, but economic power lay with the ethnic minority. Over the last three decades, however, Malaysia has continued to industrialize, while South Africa has gone in the opposite direction. Malaysia recorded investment rates averaging 27% of GDP over 1994 to 2015 compared to South Africa's 18%, and high technology manufacturing exports at 43% of the total compared to South Africa's 6%.

- ✓ **Enterprise** development, using blue and green economic models as part of implementing UNEP and UNESCO Sustainable Development Goals (SDGs) beyond 2063. In this context, South Africa's participation in the BRICS bloc provides important opportunities to build its domestic manufacturing base, enhance value added exports, promote technology sharing, support small business development, and expand trade and investment opportunities. It can be argued that the development of complementarities and integrated value chains should be underpinned by an overall approach that puts industrialization at the core of the engagement, as well as designing blue and green city models and complementary projects in the Home of Legends. It is significant that development finance institutions (DFIs) and State Own Enterprises (SOEs) are not only prioritizing developmental state priorities from short-term (NDP 2030 vision) to long-term investment (AU Agenda 2063), but these are also managed and championed by South African managers and leaders in all spheres of government. The latter is due to the fact that DFIs and SOEs have acted as catalysts for accelerated industrialization and economic growth in developed countries, while developmental states such as China, Turkey, India and Brazil show that development finance can play a crucial role in transforming the economy. Successful DFIs and SOEs provide game-changing interventions that alter the growth trajectory of their countries. In South Africa there is a need for 'patient capital', given the time needed to build the scale and reach required to be competitive, and the appetite for risk in financing rivals taking on powerful incumbents. It is regrettable that most DFIs and SOEs in South Africa do not have the appetite for supporting SMME and SME companies, including the Job Fund by National Treasury. Consequently, SMMEs and SMEs in South Africa are lagging behind their counterparts in other emerging economies, and are managed in most instances by foreigners who have no understanding of the contextual realities for South African communities or their needs, except via theoretical and academic frameworks. From a security intelligence perspective, South Africa is the only county in the world where municipalities, DFIs, and SOEs in strategic positions are managed and guided by foreigners. Consequently, they are easily compromised and captured, if the Zondo Commission can be used as a case in point.

1.7 Investment and attraction of investors to Paradise City models in post-colonial Africa

11.7.1 Rich heritage and footprint

The concept of the Home of Legends refers to PRIDE in viewing the Northern, Western and Eastern Cape provinces, which were previously known as the Cape Colony under British rule. Though separated under a democratic administration system, these three provinces and their people have rich shared histories, i.e., one cannot separate their political, environmental, social, technical, legal and economic (PESTLE) factors and needs. In this book, they are collectively referred to as one entity, or Home of Legends, for attracting investors in terms of their rich multicultural heritage sites.[15] Our heritage is associated with the triumph of the human spirit over imperialism, colonialism, neo-colonialism, and pseudo-archaeology,[16] where God (uQamata) revealed himself to us by inspiring, through his Holy Spirit, wisdom among our leaders against evil forces and related rituals.

    The brutality of imperialism and colonialism cannot be forgotten; yet the concept of the Home of Legends is linked to a Paradise City, garden or park where there are harmonious aesthetic relational

Nation Building Plan Between 2020 & 2064

Figure 1.3: Cape footprint with some selected towns of the Eastern Cape

values in the planning and development of smart or Paradise Cities using blue and green economic models, as depicted in Figure 1.3 (five 'toes' or pillars for sustainable cities). This means that through integrated rural and urban planning, and financing of infrastructure to meet human demands and needs, the Paradise Cities must adopt user-friendly policies for investors. As Paradise Cities are expected to be **e**conomically viable, **e**fficient and **ef**fective and to use alternative technology and **e**nergy (4Es), the managers and leaders are expected to invest in research and development as part of global competitiveness. Through the pillars represented as 'toes' in Figure 1.3 (planning, finance, services delivery, policy refinement, and evaluation), Paradise Cities will ensure that citizens are connected by using appropriate technologically advanced planning tools and decisions, whereby the youth acquire appropriate skills and competencies for the industries and can access on-the-job training, advance their career-path development, and grow businesses. Through these pillars, which will bring about connectivity and mobility, the safety, sustainability, and improvement of cities will be ensured, as the state will be investing constantly in infrastructure, technology, research and development.

In the quotation at the start of section 1.6, JJR Jolobe (1958) describes a Paradise City as a 'Great Place' where the king and his subjects stay, or a palace. In terms of engineering, architectural and technical design, a Paradise City may mean a city that seeks to put nature and all its forms at the centre of its design and planning processes to be approved by local and global associations, as well as its executive political and administration systems, guided by a zeal to adjust to climate change as far as possible. Using adopted Swartzism, or the Aesthetic Relational Values in Planning and Development Framework (ARVPDF), a Paradise City refers to a smart city that has adopted WEALTH (Water, (alternative) Energy, Environment, Agriculture, Land, Technology and Health) mega-nexuses to conserve and celebrate its biodiversity (the flora and fauna) and its rich heritage sites and histories by integrating them into new developments and plans.

Furthermore, Paradise City plans and architectural designs are often characterized by an inclusive economic model for a province and region to maximize import and export opportunities through twinning arrangements between cities and countries (Tsibani, 2005). The Paradise City refers to a biophilic city design in terms of which planners, political leaders and administrators take a conscious decision for residents to live, work in and learn from their natural environment, and have interests in and benefit from a coexistence with nature. In short, a smart, paradise or biophilic city also has the necessary dimensions of climate change resilience, i.e., the Paradise City will be able to prepare and plan for disaster management systems and solutions to absorb, recover from and more successfully adapt to adverse events.

The pillars for Paradise Cities shown in Figure 1.3 above include the following:

- Critical infrastructure administration and management using operation and maintenance plans.
- Good-enough public administration and management through using African trade agreements and twinning arrangements between cities, either South-South or North-South.

- Citizen services and immigration control as part of planning and safety measures.
- Law enforcement for the safety and security of citizens.
- Cybersecurity, so that data for citizens and pensions cannot be lost.
- Climate change adaptive capacity to deal with emergencies and disasters as a result of unpredictable weather conditions.
- Inter-city collaboration and partnerships with specific roles and responsibilities through memorandums of understanding (MOUs) and memorandums of agreement (MOAs).

It appears, from Figure 1.3, that the Paradise City models have more sustainability indicators and benefits through using WEALTH creation dimensions. These include:

- Water recycling and a recovery plan for wastewater, for irrigation and gardening projects in various human settlements. The residents are then connected to nature conservation, and money is saved through the use of recycled water.
- Use of alternative energy or solar panels to save electricity.
- An increase in the production of nutritious food for schools and clinics.
- Wastewater recycling, ensuring that diseases are reduced and water is of an acceptable quality that can be released to water sources to advance the economy.
- The land being seen as part of the residents' daily lives. Building and property development agencies, and the mining sector, ensure rehabilitation of land after construction or mining, including the planting of indigenous trees. Such an approach allows for coexistence between human beings and plants, with the city seen as a shared landscape. This leads to the reduction of soil erosion and the return of bird song.
- Residents using technology to support nature and their environment. Given the optimal use of technology, residents will also be curious about various innovative and creative ideas and solutions to address human needs without compromising environmental needs.
- Use of local materials and resources to build city centers, houses, buildings and facilities. The use of local materials can make a city more beautiful and attractive to tourists. Moreover, the health and physical and emotional wellbeing of human beings are influenced by the surroundings in which they live and work. Through Paradise City design, it is envisaged that a sense of ownership, cultural identity, history, spiritual belonging and value will create a harmonious environment.

As can be seen in Figure 1.2, complemented by Figure 1.3, a Paradise City or town in the Home of Legends is envisaged as a spiritual, emotional, social, economic, ecological, environmental, cultural, developmental and political SPACE characterised by peace, prosperity, good-enough governance, accountability, responsibility, integrity, honesty, coherence, stability, responsiveness, beauty and happiness. The concept, Home of Legends, refers to beauty as simply being in the eye of the beholder. From the Cape example in Figure 1.3, it can be seen that the Home of Legends is a footprint – a landscape or architectural design showing integrated planning and support in each site, town, and city in terms of growth and development. This includes walls, zoning and planning practices adopted by engineering, architectural and community designs towards blue and green city models, embedded in aesthetic, spiritual, moral, economic, social, cultural, technical, political and environmental values.

The Home of Legends footprint refers to any landscape that incorporates local and global engineering and architectural plans defined by the demarcation of boundaries and perimeters as per the integrated rural and urban building plans guided by the 2030 Agenda for Sustainable Development (AfSD) framework, which are grounded on inclusive blue and green economy and partnership models. In Figure 1.3, it appears from the five 'toes' at the end of the landscape (planning, finance, sustainable services, appropriate policy guided by 21st century-appropriate technological solutions, and on-going research and development for knowledge management and sharing, as well as new innovation and creativity) that each city in a Home of Legends province, region or country will embrace each other and provide value chains and trade agreements for food security and socio-economic growth and development. These five 'toes' are critical for achieving the AU Agenda of 2063, as adopted by African countries, with the following dimensions of paradise or smart cities:

- Protection of the environment and its unique social, economic, spiritual, cultural, technical, political and environmental values.
- Optimal use of mega-nexuses, such as water, energy, agriculture, land, technology and health facilities, and designs to advance food production and agri-parks.
- Transport infrastructure that is used for the promotion of heritage and culture, attracting tourism and related investment opportunities.
- Adoption of integrated water resources management and water demand management strategies as part of promoting eco-friendly solutions in waterworks and dams.
- Adoption of blue (ocean economy) and green (agri-parks, gardening projects) models that will mean each town or city will have supportive market centers and facilities for free markets, and promote the import and export of products.
- Historical and heritage sites, historical forts and unique centers that are designed for sport, recreation, art, and culture to improve the local economy and create job opportunities.
- Blue and green city models planned as part of the 21st century, using modern technology and answering the question: What type of city is required after 2063?

- Paradise City models that are planned to advance adaptability to climate change by ensuring ecological and environmental designs and plans for the next generation. Besides fostering resilience to climate change, such designs will also mitigate other social and economic shocks.

The Paradise City model is often referred to as the Ntsikana kaGabha Paradise City model, or post-colonial city, as it was expected of aesthetic leaders of Africa to ensure harmony between human and environmental needs, on the one hand and, on the other hand, the theoretical framework of 'zenibe yimbumba yamanyama', formulated as Aesthetic Relational Values in Planning and Development (ARVPD) by Swartz (2010), meant that African leaders would have ensured unity in diversity in post-colonial Africa whereby city models should promote coexistence under the Ubuntu paradigm.

Additional reasons for investing in Paradise Cities or post-colonial cities in the Home of Legends, or other landscapes in Africa include, but are not limited to, the following:

- Africa is one of the continents in the world with a rapidly increasing population that will need industrial products and manufacturing factories.
- The continent's growing middle class and affluent consumers can ensure excellent investment returns.
- Global countries have bilateral and multilateral business relationships in Africa.
- Most African states have mature legal and financial systems characterized by progressive constitutional and judicial systems.
- The African Continental Free Trade Area agreement will boost intra- and extra-Africa trade and related import and export market opportunities.
- The majority of African countries have a sophisticated banking sector and access to global stock exchanges.
- The African Free Trade agreement means that each state must spend billions of Rands on bulk infrastructure to achieve the African Union Agenda 2063.
- African hospitality and tourism areas have rich human values and heritage, which cut across continents and cultures and can be explored by tourists and investors alike.
- African countries have rich natural resources, including mineral resources that offer the potential for more manufacturing and reindustrialization processes.
- African countries have trainable youth for reindustrialization and manufacturing of products, as the current youth are the jewel and future consumers for products, i.e., there is a guarantee of return on investment.

This book argues that by implementing blue and green city models, or Paradise City models, in the Cape provinces as a global pilot study by UNEP and UNESCO, the world would have institutionalized aesthetic relational values for replication in various African countries, using North-South and South-South methodologies. Some of the reasons for adopting blue and green economic models in Africa in general, and the Cape provinces as the Home of Legends in particular, include the literature evidence that such programs and projects in rural Africa may achieve the following:

- Contribute towards job creation and the safety and security of citizens and their families, and particularly the poorest of the poor. Some of the objectives include:
    - ✓ Helping rural and urban communities to exploit opportunities associated with the nation-building plan and the implementation of integrated rural and urban infrastructure investment programs (IR and UIIPs) between the heritage and human settlement towns and three metropolitan cities of the Cape provinces;
    - ✓ Providing enterprise development using IR and UIIPs for socio-economic growth and development to address abject poverty and the systemic unemployment of youth, women, and people living with disabilities, and to decrease inequality in various historical human settlements, among various races and sociocultural classes;
    - ✓ Building robust blue and green economic models for replication in Africa;
    - ✓ Designing green economy enterprises as alternatives, and designing viable local economic drivers in the Home of Legends in accordance with the NDP 2030 vision as a chapter of the African Union Agenda 2063;
    - ✓ Creating sustainable jobs through IR and UIIPs using private-public partnership models; and
    - ✓ Finding investments for funding feasibility studies.

- Help to safeguard existing jobs and skills by moving away from a declining mining-based economy (in the case of South Africa) towards green and blue economic models, whereby local entrepreneurs exploit IR and UIIPs without conflict with the environment.
- Reduce poverty by rehabilitating land and making optimal use of land for green programs, including reducing desertification and deforestation in most parts of the country.
- Grow local investment by using rich historical sites and tourism routes to attract tourists and encourage business investment in property development and hospitality.
- Help to establish an industrial base using tourism programs and twenty-first-century ITC for increasing energy, nutrition, food, and water nexuses.

- Encourage projects that lead to self-reliance and sustainable food security through agribusiness programs.
- Encourage entrepreneurship and creativity in the blue economy, especially aquaculture, and marine and ocean initiatives for coastal rural communities.
- Increase tax revenues through tax payments by small businesses, thereby positively contributing to social networks and developmental state goals and priorities.
- Contribute to social cohesion and national pride, where local people are co-drivers of socio-economic programs and projects for IR and UIIPs envisaged under the Nation-Building Plan between 2020 and 2064.

In addition to the envisaged action plans above, the Cape provinces as the Home of Legends is, both geographically and topographically, a landscape suited to instituting the COP21 Paris resolutions, guided by its rich cultural heritage. Following blue and green city models, global climate pilot programs and projects that can be adapted and adjusted to meet the SDGs and the COP21 Paris resolutions can be implemented. Ideally, the blue and green cities models, such as public-private partnerships (PPPs), will be designed and planned using Swartz's framework (2010) supported by the COP21 Paris resolutions linked to the United Nations Millennium Development Goals (MDGs) and SDGs. The MDGs and SDGs are incorporated into the National Development Plan 2030 vision (South African blueprint) and the African Union Agenda 2063, which was adopted to pursue a people-centered and transformational leadership embedded in the Ubuntu paradigm. In this context, the NDP 2030 vision and Agenda 2063 are strategies adopted in the spirit of Ubuntu principles and values, which demand that leaders be held accountable for their actions to ensure that they abide by their countries' constitutional limitations on power and the avoidance of corrupt activities. These strategies assume that leaders will endeavor to achieve their countries' aspirations and adopt aesthetic relational values.

Like the COP21 Paris resolutions, the MDGs (2000) and SDGs (30 September 2015) were signed in order to achieve, inter alia, meaningful, inclusive and sustainable development goals to create WEALTH. The notion of WEALTH creation to restore PRIDE may mean different things to different countries. As stated earlier, since the proposed Nation-Building Plan between 2020 and 2064 is rooted in the MDGs and SDGs, it is reasonable to argue that WEALTH creation in the envisaged smart Paradise City models refers, among others, to mega-nexuses in their aesthetic planning and development.

In this book, supported by Cloete (2013), WEALTH creation in Paradise City models is an acronym for:

- **W**ater security – infrastructure using the Private Services Provider (PSP) funding model – a global funding model. There is a need for a water master plan complemented by water security and funding models for infrastructure if black industrialization programs and projects are to yield the fruits of an Agenda for Sustainable Development (AfSD) by African states by 2030. It is significant that water security is one of the biggest issues and challenges facing Africa and the world in the twenty-first century. It presents a profound challenge to our social wellbeing and our economic growth. Furthermore, the World Economic Forum's Global Risks Report 2017 reported that in 2017 the environmental concerns were more prominent than ever before. Therefore, urgent measures are required to protect the river systems, as they transfer the lifeblood of the nation around each country in the Southern African Development Community (SADC) region. It appears that inclusive socio-economic growth and development, as well as black industrialization programs, can be effectively implemented beyond the National Development Plan 2030 vision and linked to sustainable development goals (the SDGs succeeded the MDGs as some of the MDGs had not been met).

- **E**nergy solutions – alternative energy solutions for agribusiness processes and for integrating rural communities into modern agricultural services and technology.
- **A**gricultural development – in terms of an ocean economy, also known as a blue economy, and/or a circular economy. (A circular economy is one that is sustainable for future generations without causing harm to the planet.) This refers to the need for smart cities or post-colonial city models whereby aesthetic relational values in planning and development are included in any design or program, not only to accelerate the optimal use of twenty-first-century technology solutions, but also to ensure adaptive capacity to climate change by using blue and green economic models aligned to a sustainable action plan, as per the COP21 Paris resolutions.
- Land – wealth comes from the land. The European physiocrats advised their leaders and politicians that European nations could gain economic wealth by conquering beautiful landscapes and natural resources in Africa. This led to imperialism and colonialism. This mercantilist approach by physiocrats argued that European states should grow their wealth by acquiring diamonds, gold, platinum, and other resources, complemented by colonies producing agricultural products for taxes, subsidies, control and monopoly privileges of European explorers in Africa. The logic of physiocrats was that landowners would collect rent and taxes from farmers and buy goods from farmers and artisans. Those farmers and artisans would then use their money to buy goods from yet more farmers, and mining artisans, manufacturers and industrialists. Consequently, through the colonization of Africa, European farmers, miners, manufacturers, and industrialists were assured of land for a supply chain and an economic model that was sustainable. Therefore, the land is key for social cohesion as part of a nation-building plan. This requires, among others, a proper review and analysis of the negative effects of the 1884/1885 Berlin Demarcation of Africa, which refers to

boundaries created based not on catchment management areas (CMAs), but rather on European countries' socio-economic interests, whereby natural processes were ignored. There is a need for government departments of water and sanitation, and other appropriate departments in Africa, to accelerate licensing of water in partnership with departments such as trade and industry to attract investors.

- **T**echnology – water quality and reporting on water security and availability are key for investors. The South African government initiated an incentive-based monitoring and evaluation municipality-driven program for water quality. This Blue and Green Drop Incentive Programme, whose name was coined by Leonardo Manus and Helgard Muller in 2003 as part of the Department of Human Settlements, Water and Sanitation (DHSWS), created an environment conducive for citizens, water consumers and investors to have confidence in the water quality and to be able to understand and budget for types of investments per locality, region, and so forth, using modern technology for reporting. It is also crucial to mention that Africa has made huge strides in improving its telecommunications, energy and transport infrastructure. The telecommunications made it possible for African people not only to connect, network and trade amongst one another and across borders, but also with the global marketplace. Technology companies are springing up in various African states and cities as African leaders understand that there is a strong relationship between WEALTH creation and internet connectivity and investing in technology. It is concluded that the fourth industrial revolution is bringing the role of technology into sharp focus in moving countries like South Africa towards global competitiveness by restoring PRIDE through WEALTH creation. While the apartheid government heavily supported innovation and industrial development in state-owned enterprises (SOEs) related to its own objectives, post-apartheid democratic administration systems have had more broad-based innovation strategies. Technology is, however, embodied in investment, and the low level of investment in the economy means poor progress in technological upgrading. A strategy for building capabilities must bring together technology policy, investment and industry incentives to present a coherent path for SMMEs and companies to drive socio-economic growth and development, guided by blue and green economic models. Arguably, incentives, technological change from SOEs and development finance institutions (DFIs), therefore, all need to work together, along with cluster initiatives at the local level, in order to achieve IR & UIIP. Bell, Goga, Mondliwa and Roberts (2018:9-10) add that 'incentive programs should include conditionalities to ensure that there are wider benefits to the economy' and care needs to be taken to avoid creating or entrenching firm dominance. Cluster initiatives have a key role to play in linking skills development and shared facilities for technological capabilities, such as design, testing and prototyping, and in supporting firms to pool resources, creating economies of scale and developing supply markets. Understanding how collective action can be supported for private investment in capabilities by groups of firms is central to building dynamic industrial clusters, along with effective institutions of industrial policy. Local and provincial governments have played a leading role in the few cases where clusters have been successful, given the geographical embeddedness of cluster initiatives. The Home of Legends' socio-economic cohesion policy aims to help a heritage site, landscape, town or city to achieve its full potential, and to bring about a convergence of living standards and prosperity across communities in South Africa as far as possible. It is a policy of investment in job creation, competitiveness, economic growth, improved quality of life and sustainable city models grounded on aesthetic relational values in planning and development. These investments support the delivery of a Nation-Building Plan between 2020 and 2064 paradise or smart cities, sustainable and inclusive growth.

- **H**ealth – income and growth, leading to the reduction of malnutrition, are key to the social and economic indicators of a country. The health status linked to food security and nutritional status is a key indicator to measure the socio-economic growth and development of a country where investors can establish their interests. Given the complex nature of the association between socio-economic ties and health, IR & UIIP interventions designed to improve health can occur at multiple levels (e.g., family, clans, group, neighborhood, and kingdoms) and sometimes require cross-sector collaboration (e.g. education, public health, housing) to foster community building and improve health. Further research is needed to better understand how social cohesion affects health, as well as how it can be used to reduce health disparities. This evidence will facilitate public health efforts to address social cohesion as a social determinant of health.

1.7.2 WEALTH creation as part of the AU Agenda 2063

It is clear that the millennium development goals (MDGs) and sustainable development goals (SDGs) briefly summarised under WEALTH creation are linked to a nation-building plan informed by principles of accountability and good governance. According to Russell Loubser, former chief executive of the Johannesburg Stock Exchange, the National Development Plan 2030 vision, read with the African Union's Agenda 2063, is about good-enough governance. Agenda 2063 is a strategic framework for the socio-economic transformation of the continent over the next 50 years. It builds on and seeks to accelerate the implementation of past and existing continental initiatives for growth and sustainable development in accordance with blue and green economic models. Accordingly, good governance is a mindset of doing something about the abject poverty in Africa not because somebody is watching, but simply because it is the right thing to do. South African leaders have seen that the current mechanisms of welfare grants and public spending are not doing enough to confront inequality in the economy. In other words, South African leaders reached an agreement that blue and green inclusive economic models must be explored to resolve the structural colonial and apartheid economic models beyond 2063. There is a need to bridge the gap between the dream of 'zenibe yimbumba yamanyama' and the reality of people. The Reconstruction and Development Programme (RDP) argued that

> *No political democracy can survive and flourish if the mass of our people remains in poverty, without land, without tangible prospects for a better life. Attacking poverty and deprivation must, therefore, be the first priority of a democratic government. (1994 RDP, quoted in 2012 NDP)*

This understanding is also included in the Freedom Charter (1955) and the Preamble to the RSA Constitution. As far back as 1965, Kwame Nkrumah added that

> *We have the blessing of the wealth of our vast resources, the power of our talents and the potentialities of our people. Let us grasp now the opportunities before us and meet the challenge to our survival.*

This statement by Nkrumah read with Freedom Charter, RDP (1994), NDP 2030 Vision, Agenda 2063, the MDGs and SDGs, implicitly and explicitly outlines aesthetic relational values to transform existing institutions in order to implement a new mode of governance, with accountability and responsiveness to climate change.

The African Union stresses that:

> *We recognize that a prosperous, integrated, and united Africa, based on good governance, democracy, social inclusion, and respect for human rights, justice, and the rule of law are the necessary pre-conditions for a peaceful and conflict-free continent.*

By signing up for Agenda 2063, South Africa committed her resources to advance a state of equilibrium in various cities, towns, heritage sites and citizens. It is significant that the Agenda 2063 priorities proactively respond to country blueprints, such as South Africa's National Development Plan 2030 vision and the national development plans of Kenya and Namibia (Khokhoi word for a desert). The socio-political and socio-economic transformation priorities of Agenda 2063 include, among others, the following:

- A prosperous Africa based on inclusive growth and sustainable development.

- An integrated and politically united continent, which should be based on the ideals of Pan-Africanism and the vision of the African Renaissance.
- An Africa of good governance, democracy, and respect for human rights, justice, and the rule of law.
- A peaceful and secure Africa.
- An Africa with a strong cultural identity and a common heritage, values, and ethics.
- An Africa where development is people-driven, unleashing the potential of its women and youth.
- An Africa as a strong, united and influential global player and partner.

Similarly, the COP21 Paris resolutions (2015) aim to achieve the following:

- Restoring aesthetic relational values in promoting blue and green programs and projects.
- Holding the increase in global average temperature to well below 2°C above pre-industrial levels and pursuing efforts to limit the temperature increase to 1.5°C above pre-industrial levels.
- Increasing the ability to adapt to the adverse impacts of climate change and to foster climate resilience and low development of greenhouse gas emissions.
- Meeting the sustainable development goals (SDGs) by reducing poverty in Africa through integrated rural (IR) and urban infrastructure investment programs (UIIPs) using modern and technology-driven water, food and energy nexuses.
- Strengthening the capability, and capacity, accountability and responsiveness (CAR) of parliaments, provincial ordinances, municipal executives and traditional councils in Africa to perform their core functions and to replace outdated and outmoded cultural practices.
- Deepening legal and judicial reforms to ensure executives and leaders are held accountable to citizens.
- Improving public sector management and related infrastructure programs.
- Advancing reindustrialization and enterprise development to support small, medium and micro enterprises (SMMEs).
- Improving health services for the poor.
- Improving transparency and accountability for revenues generated by mineral resources such as gold, platinum, oil, and gas.
- Making financial flows consistent with a pathway towards low greenhouse gas emissions and climate-resilient development.

These millennium development goals (MDGs) have been replaced by the sustainable development goals (SDGs), which are part of a new global development agenda – the 2030 Agenda for Sustainable Development (AfSD), which is a detailed set of aspirations to make the world a better place progressively by 2030 and beyond. The 2030 AfSD should be read with the South African Cabinet's National Development Plan (NDP) 2030 vision, whose battle cry is *'Let local and global leaders support, guide, and lead infrastructure investment programs'*, to eradicate abject poverty, especially in Africa. The SDGs, read with the 2030 AfSD and the African Union Agenda 2063, offer a more profound vision for a nation-building plan aimed at structural change in the Home of Legends and the rest of Africa, the economy and political systems, which would be based on inclusive blue and green economic models. As part of Agenda 2063 and in terms of the Continental Free Trade Agreement (CFTA), African states are expected to invest in infrastructure, which must include high-speed railway networks, roads, shipping lines, sea and air transport, including twenty-first century Information and Communications Technology (ICT), and the digital economy.

At a country level, the South African democratic government has implemented various programs and projects aligned to the MDGs, the SDGs, and the COP21 Paris resolutions. Thus, the adoption of the idea that the Eastern, Northern and Western Cape provinces, as part of the former Cape Province or Cape Colony, should be seen as one province, is in line with these efforts. Collectively, they are referred to as a Home of Legends in an attempt to accelerate sustainable community programs and projects in order to achieve the above-mentioned goals and resolutions. In the same vein, Steve Biko, in *I write what I like*, in the 1970s emphasized the unique value addition that Africa can bring to humanity:

> *The great powers of the world may have done wonders in giving the world an industrial and military look, but the great gift still has to come from Africa – giving the world a more human face. (Steve Biko, cited in Joel Netshitenzhe, 30 October 2013)*

1.7.3 Pillars for the Agenda for Sustainable Development (AfSD)

> *The world's premier cities and architects are competing to design and build highly interconnected smart environments where people, government and business operate in symbiosis with spectacular exponentially improving technologies such as big data, the Internet of Things (IoT), cloud computing, hyperconnectivity, artificial intelligence (AI), robots, drones, autonomous green vehicles, 3D/4D printing, smart materials, and renewable energy. The architectural promise of future smart cities is to harmonize the benefits of these key disruptive technologies for society and provide a high quality of life by design. Some have already implemented smart city architecture and, as the concepts, experiences and success stories spread, the pursuit of*

smart will become a key driver in the evolving future of cities as communities and economic centers. Here we explore some of the critical trends, visions, ideas, and disruptions shaping the rise of smart cities and smart architecture. (Maria Romero, futurist and foresight researcher with Fast Future)

The blue and green city, or Paradise City economic models envisaged by Ntsikana kaGabha, Pixley kaIsaka Seme, Albert kaLuthuli, Steve Biko, Robert Mangaliso Sobukwe, Nelson kaMandela, and others in Africa, are about a true nation-building plan[17] (2020-2064), a sustainable action plan, and long-term strategic thinking informed by the kind of pride in history that acknowledges and draws lessons from positive and negative experiences, as depicted in Figure 1.3 (Footprint), read with the Aesthetic Relational Values in Planning and Development Framework (ARVPDF) adopted from Swartz (2010) and later the Back to Basics (B2B) Campaign by Cooperative Governance and Traditional Affairs (CoGTA, 2014), as depicted in Figure 1.4. It is a mindset that takes pride in the unique contribution that Africa has made to the historical, socio-economic and cultural advancement of humanity, vividly captured in Ntsikana kaGabha's 'Great Hymn', and by other African intellectuals from the nineteenth century onwards. From our new African paradigm, rooted in blue and green economic models using our combined international heritage, culture,[18] and history, it is expected that the Nation-Building Plan (2020 to 2064) must offer 'the great gift' of 'a more human face'.[19] As touched on earlier, some of the pillars for Paradise City models include:

- Planning bulk infrastructure investment programs by using value generated from trade agreements and partnership models with African and international institutions.
- Financing infrastructure programs whereby Build, Operate, Train and Transfer (BOTT) capacity building is adapted to transfer skills to youth and local companies to support socio-economic growth and development.
- Using twenty-first century technological solutions to create WEALTH and adapt to climate change.
- Building knowledge management of programs to deliver on the SDGs targets and performance through strong operation, maintenance and recovery plans, leading to ongoing research and development, and new innovation and creativity.
- Strategizing on maintaining healthy relationships between countries and economic regions for best practices, and implementation of the social cohesion and Nation-Building Plan, as depicted in Figure 1.4 below.

Nation Building Plan Between 2020 & 2064

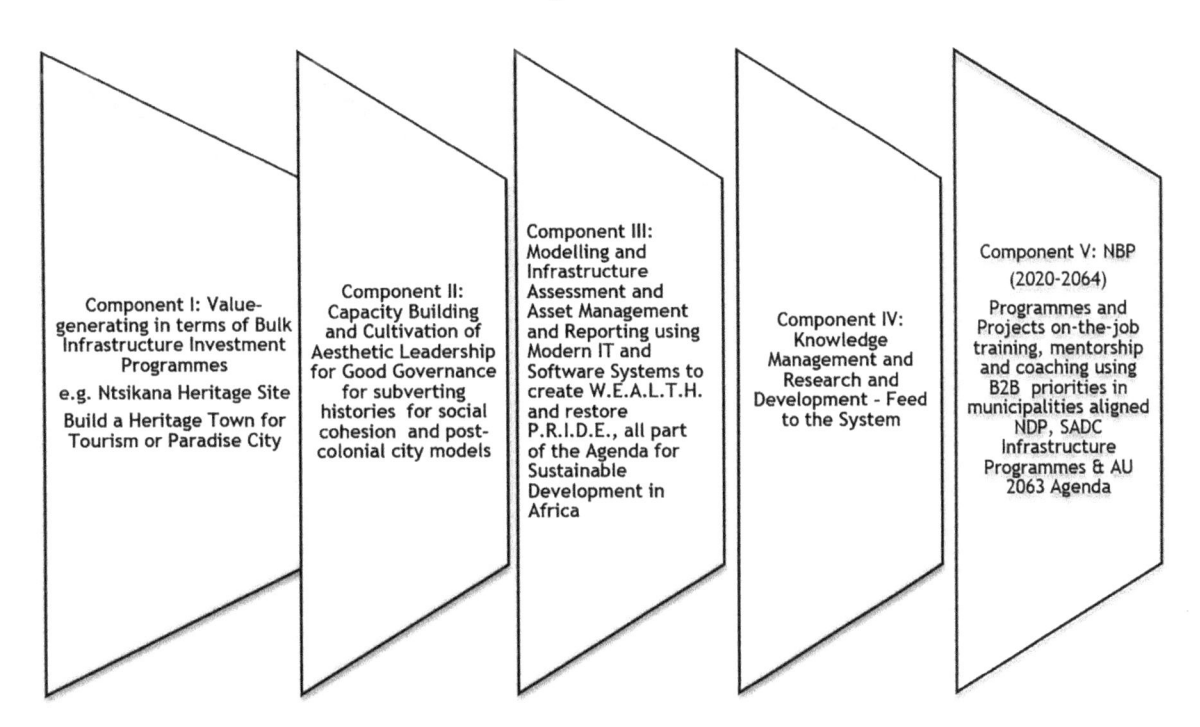

Figure 1.4: Aesthetic Relational Values in Planning and Development Framework (ARVPDF)

Component I: Value-generating in terms of Bulk Infrastructure Investment Programmes
e.g. Ntsikana Heritage Site Build a Heritage Town for Tourism or Paradise City

Component II: Capacity Building and Cultivation of Aesthetic Leadership for Good Governance for subverting histories for social cohesion and post-colonial city models

Component III: Modelling and Infrastructure Assessment and Asset Management and Reporting using Modern IT and Software Systems to create W.E.A.L.T.H. and restore P.R.I.D.E., all part of the Agenda for Sustainable Development in Africa

Component IV: Knowledge Management and Research and Development - Feed to the System

Component V: NBP (2020-2064) Programmes and Projects on-the-job training, mentorship and coaching using B2B priorities in municipalities aligned NDP, SADC Infrastructure Programmes & AU 2063 Agenda

Source: Adapted from Swartz (2010), and later the Back to Basics Campaign by COGTA (2014)

This book has adopted integrated rural and urban infrastructure investment programs (IR and UIIPs) for the Nation-Building Plan (2020-2064) as an implementation tool of the ARVPDF as theorized by Swartz (2010) in order to pursue the following:

- Economic diversification, (re)industrialization and modernization.
- Inclusivity in the conduct of economics and politics.
- Aesthetic relational values and ethics in corporate and political governance.
- Political legitimacy that derives from active citizenship and strategic intellectual discourse as part of a nation-building plan.
- The pooling of continental sovereignties as an indispensable part of the global family of nations embedded in the Ubuntu philosophy and our cultural heritage, branded as a Home of Legends,

which covers Western, Northern and Eastern Cape provinces, to consolidate democracy through sustainable planning and development, and the implementation of the COP21 Paris resolutions as part of the Nation-Building Plan (2020-2064).[20] This is a dream deferred!

1.8 Conclusion

In the literature reviewed looking at three commissions of inquiry dealing with issues of traditional leadership, under colonialism (led by CP Brownlee), apartheid (led by CB Young) and the democratic Government of National Unity (led by Thandabantu Nhlapo), it is inductively and deductively concluded that each Commission ultimately opted to support continuity of the existing status quo of a legally sanctioned pre-apartheid politics of traditional frameworks, rather than providing new truths about legitimate claims and counterclaims in terms of Chapter 12 (sections 211 and 212) of the Constitution of the Republic of South Africa. Instead of uprooting distortions caused by imperialism, colonialism, repressive laws in the Black Administration Act 38 of 1927, and apartheid Laws, which provided for the creation of territorial authorities based on tribalism and ethnicity, self-governing and pseudo-independent Bantustans and leaders, the Nhlapo Commission ignored criteria set out in section 9(1) (b) of the Constitution, and other relevant customs, norms and standards relevant to the establishment of a kingship in an African Governance Framework and Geneology, or principle of male primogeniture of AmaXhosa and Cirha coming from the Great House (indlunkulu) – Jwarha being from the Right Hand House (indlu yasekunene) and Tshawe (Iqadi lendlunkulu) of the Great House. Accordingly, the first-born son of Nkosiyamntu (Cirha) of the Great House would succeed his father, whereas the first-born son of the Right Hand House (Jwarha) may establish a semi-independent separate community, not with equal status to the Great House. Three Commissions failed to properly restore the institution of traditional leadership in South Africa. The Nhlapo Commission failed to provide a good public and moral standing of the democratic administration. Its evaluation and assessment of claims to kingships enforced a continuation with colonial and apartheid structural designs and governance of traditional leaders using a Whig theoretical framework or Westminster system in Africa. Equally, the Congress of Traditional Leaders of South Africa (CONTRLESA) approached the ANC at Kempton Park in the 1990s to change the policies around the House of Traditional Leaders in South Africa, rather than providing the truth about the impact of imperialism, colonialism and apartheid laws and their distortions of histories. The Government of National Unity (GNU) under the ANC used their colonial and apartheid records, archives and distorted histories to write findings on the claims of kingship in South Africa using Westministerial and Roman law. Surely, those laws did not just reflect a rejection of African Governance, but also a lack of political will to listen to suppressed traditional leaders, until AmaCirha and Khoisan Groupings challenged the government of Cyril Ramaphosa to pass legislation on the recognition of Khoisan groupings and other traditional minorities, such as AmaCirha, to claim their kingship. The Cyril Ramaphosa administration approved this legislative framework in early 2020 in order to acknowledge various Khoisan groupings and other traditional leaders, like AmaCirha clan.

President Cyril Ramaphosa's administration realized that it was critical for a democratic government to use its resources to unify South Africans as citizens and restore the dignity of its leaders by implementing an inclusive framework for accelerated social and economic cohesion – one that is not expected to use colonial and apartheid biased archival modes. It is critical to use credible informants and affected people, as they know their history and genealogical background. What is also interesting is that AmaTshawe and other nations are in agreement with the Cirha kingship. It appears that the main problem is that the crossover of colonial and apartheid institutions to the post-colonial democratic administration continued the existing status quo. Unintentionally, these unresolved and politically manufactured traditional institutions in pre- and post-1994 may cause more leaders and servants to lose their benefits and salaries.

It is further concluded that the adopted framework (ARVPDF, Swartz, 2010) to implement integrated rural and urban infrastructure investment programs (IR and UIIPs) calls for new biophilic designs of post-colonial cities in Africa aimed not only at adapting and adjusting to climate change, but also at restoring our balanced coexistence with the environment. This framework (ARVPDF) and its implementation arm (IR and UIIPs) appeal to executive and political leaders in various spheres of government to adopt Paradise City models in order to transform our social-economic ills towards reindustrialization and the manufacturing of products without compromising the sustainable interests of the next generation. The Paradise City model seeks to advance blue and green economic models whereby businesses can flourish using local beneficiation and materials for the construction of cities and related villages. This further calls for the decolonizing of the mind and education so that executive managers and leaders in both private and public entities support environmentally friendly behaviors, activities, plans and solutions. As Paradise Cities are defined as aesthetic and biophilic designs, or multi-faceted environmental designs, they embrace working relationships across cultures and countries – all part of 'unity in diversity,' as was envisaged by Ntsikana kaGabha. This means that post-colonial African executive managers and leaders should be competent enough to appreciate, understand and demonstrate the multi-faceted nature and complexities of African societies and their diverse aesthetic values, norms and standards.

It can be concluded that aesthetic leaders, as informed by the Aesthetic Relational Values in Planning and Development Framework that underlies Figures 1.1 to 1.4, should have the following leadership qualities or traits:

- Integrity to ensure, among others, inclusiveness in creating a sense of active participation by all stakeholders and citizens in Build, Operate, Train and Transfer (BOTT) projects of Paradise Cities for growth and development.
- Accountability to ensure, among others, that the leader accepts co-nurturing, co-facilitation, and co-governance of the shared responsibilities for creating WEALTH and restoring PRIDE through networks and partnerships with credible development institutions. As Ntsikana kaGabha demonstrated in the context of unbearable imperialism, colonialism and uncertainties, present-day aesthetic leaders help people manage anxiety and stress brought about by the economic recession and unemployment.
- Learning means that the aesthetic leader de-emphasizes traditional command and control functions. As demonstrated by Ntsikana kaGabha in the nineteenth century, aesthetic leaders rely on collective intelligence and networking, problem-solving and empowerment when considering creative solutions for the twenty-first century.
- Communication means that through learning and adapting to the changing environment, aesthetic leaders encourage both internal and external communication for sharing information and ideas to advance the notion of 'zenibe yimbumba yamanyama', as Ntsikana kaGabha did.

While the implementation of integrated rural and urban infrastructure investment programs (IR and UIIPs) necessitates shared, distributed and collaborative approaches and techniques on the part of aesthetic leaders, strong centralized aesthetic leadership is still critical. Accordingly, formal structures such as Ingqungquthela kaRubusana are needed to structure the collaborative framework named WEALTH creation to stress the motto: Freedom in our lifetime! The central structure has to ensure, among others, that innovative and shared ideas, including decisions and resolutions, are aligned with the vision and mission statement. This then allows leaders to strike a balance between formal or executive or board members and information dissemination as part of BOTT processes, or to drive the required transformation for meeting the Agenda for Sustainable Development by African states beyond 2063.

In the book, *Extreme Ownership: How US Navy SEALs Lead and Win* by Jocko Willink and Leif Babin (2015), the authors highlight ten pillars for successful leaders, which are applicable in this context:

a) Stay true to the vision of the company or association.
b) Communicate very clearly to all stakeholders using all appropriate resources.
c) Make everybody own the vision of the company or association.
d) Leaders must practice humility.
e) Keep the ego of a leader in check in order to have a profound impact.

f) Through partnership and collaborative efforts, leaders can complement their weaknesses.
g) Keep citizens and followers passionate about the vision and mission statement.
h) Always learn new truths and be flexible.
i) Harness team endeavors.
j) Keep everyone abreast of developments.

These ten pillars will ensure that leaders are able to make informed, difficult decisions considering short-, medium- and long-term strategic goals or targets. The aforementioned qualities linked to leadership tools may lead to creativity, innovation, team building, and effective communication to advance the priorities envisaged when implementing blue and green economic models in various paradise or smart cities between 2020 and 2064.

Ntsikana kaGabha's philosophy of unity in diversity (zenibe yimbumba yamanyama) is what we continue to draw sustenance from in our efforts to chart our roadmap and path to restore our vision embedded in the Ubuntu paradigm. According to this philosophy, African leaders must enter into trade agreements to restore Africa's ancient Egyptian civilization by re-industrializing and manufacturing its natural products using blue and green economic models embedded in Ubuntu principles and the unity in diversity of God's people. 'Zenibe yimbumba yamanyama' means that aesthetic leaders and their public administration and management (PAM) units must relegitimize social and economic development as part of a nation-building plan for Africa's renewal strategy from 2020 to 2064. This social and economic cohesion strategy will simultaneously mobilize Africans, and particularly the youth, for a new inclusive social and economic model by promoting African values and materials in building and architectural designs and the revitalization of post-colonial African Paradise Cities. Therefore, African reindustrialization and manufacturing as part of social and economic cohesion must be informed by a diversity of ideas (cross-pollination) and solutions to achieve the proposed Nation-Building Plan (2020-2064) and a better life for all Africans. This promise of 'a better life for all Africans' requires aesthetic leaders to be united in diversity to improve the living conditions and standards of African people.

In this context, African leaders must identify socio-economic and developmental opportunities that can lead to innovative ideas and solutions from past, current and future realities, and persuade each other to work together to implement social and economic cohesion in each country as part of Africa's renewal strategy from 2020 to 2064. This inclusive social and economic cohesion strategy will ensure the entrenchment of the required social reconciliation between clans and kingdoms in Africa so that their original destinations are intrinsically intertwined, as coined by Ntsikana kaGabha. It can be concluded that we need to reconcile before we can re-industrialize and build a new inclusive Africa. Undoubtedly, the new social and economic cohesion in post-colonial Africa, with her rich heritage and beautiful landscapes, will inspire vulnerable groupings with confidence in the practicality of translating Ntsikana kaGabha's philosophy into a sustainable action plan (SAP) using integrated rural and urban infrastructure investment programs (IR and UIIPs).

In summary, African leaders must understand that they are now carrying serious responsibilities to stand in front of kingdoms, clans, and citizens of Africa to achieve this continental goal. As Ntsikana kaGabha was seen as one of the leaders in the nineteenth century that promoted reconciliation, peace, stability, coexistence, and nation-building, it is also significant that similar African leaders before independence likewise walked extra miles to unify Africans in advancing humanity as created by God. Indeed, Ntsikana kaGabha was different and unique as he advocated social and economic cohesion and nation-building in the context of the brutality and inhuman system of the nineteenth century.

It can be concluded that those who are at the helm of the 55 African states and kingdoms should take heed of Ntsikana kaGabha's vision and prophetic message as part of the roadmap for post-colonial Africa. In the exercise of his extraordinary mentorship and leadership styles, Ntsikana kaGabha has already formulated a vision for the journey of African states. Like his forefathers in ancient Egypt, Ntsikana kaGabha saw his vision to be guided by God in Heaven as part of his African heritage, which is expected to be continued and implemented by post-colonial African leaders. In the next chapter, these qualities of aesthetic leaders will be applied in Paradise City models or post-colonial cities in Africa.

Chapter 1: Endnotes

1. The book has been compiled to summarise the details of Ntsikana Paradise City models, or blue and green city models, for practitioners, managers, leaders, planners, policymakers and decision makers. It is meant to guide practitioners in the planning and development of sustainable city models for Africa's rich heritage resources, beautiful spaces and landscapes for a country's nation-building plan between 2020 and 2064. The notion of Home of Legends refers to any appropriate setting or landscape in Africa which has a rich history, heritage and aesthetic leaders, and may include the entire former Cape Province before 1994, or any human settlement, heritage site, town, city and kingdom in the pre-colonial era in Africa. The concept is adopted as a potential investment model for the Cape provinces in South Africa, or any province or country in Africa, as the concept is used to refer to any aesthetic landscape in Africa. The reference by the author is provided for contextualization and operational purposes as far as possible.

2. Dr. Moshe Ncilashe Swartz's Ph.D. dissertation with the University of Stellenbosch (2010) informs the Nation-Building Plan (2020-2064) in various towns such as Matatiele, Mount Frere, Mount Ayliff, Mzimvubu, Coffee Bay, Umthatha, Butterworth, Kei, Qumrha, Cumakala, Qoboqobo, Dimbaza, Amalinde, Qonce, Rhini, Port Elizabeth, East London, Frankfort, Berlin, Nahoon, Xesi, Dikeni, Queenstown, Alexandra, Kenton-on Sea, Port Alfred, Jansenville, James Town, Aliwal North, Alicedale, Fort Beaufort, Cradock, Hessequa, Tsitsikamma, George, Mossel Bay, Sunday's River, Hankey, Ixhorha, Mvezo, Hessequa, Cape Town, Kimberley, Upington, Thwathwa, and other towns in the Cape in terms of UNEP and UNESCO flagship programs. These towns or areas are used to illustrate possibilities for creating new smart or Paradise Cities as part of restoring our history and destroyed families, clans and kingdoms (such as AmaCirha in the Cape provinces and AmaNdwandwe in the region of KwaZulu-Natal,

Mozambique, Malawi, Zimbabwe and Zambia, Kalanga in Zimbabwe and Botswana, and Khoi and San in most parts of southern Africa, to mention but a few).

3. Parnell (2004) argues that adjudicating urban poverty profiles only in contrast with those of rural poverty has created particular policy distortions in Africa. There are three major explanations for the faulty assessment of urban poverty in South Africa. The first lies in how we define what is 'urban.' Across the world, there is a technical problem when it comes to defining 'urban', which has no easy solution. Typically, countries use both a density and size criterion to indicate the proportion of the population deemed to be urban. South Africa uses neither of these definitions. Nor does it invoke the United Nations' size-based definition of urban (settlements of over 2 000 people). Instead, STATS SA uses variations on the old apartheid definition of urban, which was premised on areas that fell under the political jurisdiction of a municipality elected and run by white people. The South African definition is not only ideologically problematic as it fails to revoke colonial notions that Africans were rural and 'traditional' and not urban and 'civilized', but it is also totally misleading. According to spatial planning experts, it can be argued that huge non-agricultural settlements, sometimes referred to as 'displaced urbanization', characterised by extreme poverty, continue to be named as 'rural' simply because they fell under the former homeland administrations and not under a white local authority. Provinces like the Eastern Cape, KwaZulu-Natal, North West, Mpumalanga and Limpopo are typically seen using the existing definition, as rural and poor would become urban and poor if an alternative, more conventional urban definition were adopted. Parnell (2004) is supported by Imbumba yamaNyama Royal Council elders such as Mbulelo Livingstone Dyibishe and Andile Mtiki (2014). These two stalwarts and elders have argued that the problem is more than semantic – in policy terms it does not matter if an area is classified rural or urban, but rather that it is poor and in need of state assistance. However, in post-apartheid South Africa the designation of rural has been used to target development resources (most notably through the equitable share). Given the limited budget, people in the former homeland administration areas have argued for and defended this distorted definition of poverty without global comparison. Consequently, IR and UIIPs should be adopted to address faulty policy gaps to advance social cohesion as part of the Nation-Building Plan.

4. Ubuntu principles have been incorporated into our Constitution, the National Development Plan 2030 vision, and the African Union Agenda 2063, whereby aesthetic and visionary leaders are expected to practise good-enough governance in their countries, provinces and municipalities (Tsibani, 2014). Some of these principles include spiritual collectiveness, use of scenario planning in decision making (whereby a win-win scenario is always adopted and applied in most cases), humility and helpfulness, reconciliation, coexistence, fairness, morality, optimism (whereby fear is replaced by hope) and inclusiveness during Iimbizos, Iindabas, meetings, or consultation processes. Khoza (2006:xx-xxi) adds that the Ubuntu notion creates 'a common origin,' which 'creates a common bond and destiny for humanity. The individual is absorbed into the collective society, hence I am because you are. And the common idiom umuntu ngumuntu ngabantu (a person is a person because of others).'

5. IW Citashe (1882), cited by De Kock (1996:29), was educated at Lovedale College in Alice where he trained as a teacher. He later returned to Lovedale to be trained as a priest of the Free Presbyterian Church. As a minister of religion, educator, counselor and community developer using literature, history articles and poetry (published through *Imvo zabaNtsundu*), he coined the notion of "Zemk' iinkomo magwalandini' and used Dr MWB Rubusana to organise, coordinate and formulate African democrats to be represented in South African political developments in Port Elizabeth, also known as the Nelson Mandela Bay Municipality. He died with the sinking of the ship SS Mendi during World War I on 20 February 1917. When Advocate Mancotywa (2017) was celebrating the SS Mendi, he mentioned that Chaplain Citashe had appealed to his fellow countrymen to die like heroes by facing their death. Citashe was one of the leading members of the African intelligentsia who in the last quarter of the nineteenth

century used his pen to fight for the rights of Africans. He demonstrated his poetic skills with his poem 'To the rescue', which was published in 1882, and used by Dr MWB Rubusana as the title of an anthology.

6. Imbumba yamaNyama was established in 1882, guided by Ntsikana kaGabha's moral and aesthetic relational values to unite Africans to achieve democracy and freedom from all forms of systemic oppression. Dr MWB Rubusana, reading IW Citashe's articles in *'Zemk' iinkomo magwalandini* in 1882, not only used Citashe's concept to organise unity among Africans, but also launched Imbumba yamanyama (Ingqungquthela ka Dr MWB Rubusana) as a first political movement in 1891 in Port Elizabeth (now Nelson Mandela Bay Municipality). Imbumba yamaNyama led to the formation of the South African Native National Congress (SANNC) and later the African National Congress (ANC). As the National Party (NP) tried to mobilise Africans to accept the homeland system, the notion of 'imbumba yamanyama' was used to promote narrow ethnicity informed by grand apartheid philosophy – especially in the former Transkei in the Eastern Cape, where Homeland leaders, to serve the interests of the apartheid administration, manipulated the meaning of 'imbumba yamanyama'. The AmaCirha Kingdom reviewed and revised this historical context by tracing imbumba yamanyama back to nineteenth-century African intellectuals who were inspired by Ntsikana kaGabha (Dyibishe and Mtiki, 2014; Tsibani, 2017; Tsibani, 2014; Mancotywa, 2017). As part of this restoration of African dignity and unity to advance a nation-building plan, the AmaCirha Kingdom restored the concept to its original meaning from the nineteenth century and revived it to include aesthetic relational values in planning and development of current and future infrastructure investment models to achieve the Agenda for Sustainable Development by 55 countries in Africa.

7. This is a similar argument to that on the trans-Atlantic slave trade. W Soyinka (1999) asked whether reparations for the slave trade could have been sought from former European colonial powers that conducted trade in slaves, without making the same argument about the Islamic slave trade that predated the trans-Atlantic trade. More recently, the Libya slave investigation (2017), which has horrified the world, will not lead to the misuse of forgiveness as witnessed in democratic South Africa, where perpetrators of 'apartheid as a global inhuman system' were neither brought to book nor subjected to self-confirmation, except in prominent cases. In the same argument, the Nhlapo Commission on kingdom claims in South Africa has left historical gaps about 'beneficiaries of Apartheid Bantu Administration', alongside prominent historians who have been party to writing inaccurate histories using oral memories to manage black people and their affairs. Consequently, wrong informants, and authors who lacked context, often caused the misdirecting of findings. For instance, if one consults the book *The House of Phalo* (JB Peires' book about the paramount chief, from 1736 until his death in 1775) as an authentic source of reference without providing informants for the argument in the book, it can be argued that Peires' argument started from the wrong premise of the Tshawe Kingdom (Iqadi). In short, the Tshawe Kingdom, articulated by Professor Jeff Peires, is not only a demonstration of the impact of Western historians trying to write the history of AmaXhosa, but is also a demonstration beyond any reasonable doubt of a lost opportunity by the Nhlapo Commission to engage known, legitimate Royal Councils, such as the AmaCirha Kingdom, Dwandwe, AmaNdebele kaMzilikazi, Khoi and San, including AmaJwarha, to provide a clear historical presupposition of AmaXhosa Kingdoms. All those in authority that 'distorted historical facts' are not just historical hostages, but are also delaying social, economic, cultural, spiritual, ecological, environmental and political cohesion in Africa. In some cases the colonial, and later the apartheid public administration and management systems in Africa, were too modern for narrow ethnic-separatist agendas, which cannot lead to socio-economic growth and development of the democratic administration in Africa. The proposed Nation-Building Plan, using interdisciplinary and multidisciplinary hermeneutics in re-evaluating history, can deconstruct imperial, colonial and apartheid histories in Africa, which would lead to genuine social, economic, cultural, environmental and political cohesion, and a state of equilibrium through Paradise City models. The cases cited are used to illustrate the fact that pseudo-archaeology has been used to reconstruct histories of families, clans, regions and kingdoms for imperial and colonial purposes.

Through scholars, anthropologists, ethnologists, historians, and colonial and apartheid administrators, unjust wars against Africans were redefined as a collective narrative, which reinterpreted histories using moral and ethical terms, as Africans were seen as beasts or animals (Sam Ditshego, *The Sunday Independent*, 21 January 2017:17, earlier supported by Malkki, 1995:54-55). Through the Berlin Conference of 1884/1885, European countries agreed to divide and rule colonised people in order to better rule them, and to co-opt traditional leaders and refashion traditional governance, norms and standards so that these traditional leaders became indirect rulers or administrators of the colonial state in their own lands. If local clans, populations and/or groupings had different cultural features and identities, they were then categorised as either racial or tribal identities. Legitimate kings and queens were transformed into paramount chiefs reporting to a colonial governor and had a defined territory as part of the homeland public administration and management (PAM) system of a tribe. If legitimate kings and queens did not cooperate with the colonial administrators and governors, they were either brutally killed, or replaced with illegitimate kings and queens. Cultural and customary practices were radically changed into political identity, as can be seen among AmaZulu, AmaXhosa, AmaSwazi, AmaNdebele, AmaNdebele kaMzilikazi, and AmaShangana, who belong to Mnguni kaNtu. The clans and local population were further classified into sub-categories, such as 'native' or 'indigenous', to entrench divisions and racism. According to the colonial state PAM system, a 'native' referred to a person who lived in a territorial PAM system or under a paramount chief selected, screened and appointed by a colonial state governor. These 'native' or 'indigenous' people were further classified into 'aboriginal native' and 'colonial native'. 'Aboriginal native' referred to an ethnic group that was defined as belonging to that particular territory and therefore had certain rights of access to land. But a 'colonial native', like AmaMfengu and AmaHlubi in the case of the Cape Province, who lived in a particular territorial PAM system and land, did not belong to the Cape Province at the time. Furthermore, there were also people who were not classified as tribes or ethnic groupings, such as Europeans and Indians. Both Europeans and Indians were classified as 'races' from a colonial perspective. In southern Africa, the descendants of slaves and mixed populations were defined as 'coloreds', and colonial PAM administrators and governors used them as intermediaries between European settlers and those seen as 'natives' or 'indigenous' people. They were elevated above 'natives', tribes, and ethnic groups designed by the colonial PAM system, but kept well below the European settlers' living standards and rights. The colonial PAM strategy ensured popular resentment against 'coloreds' by oppressed indigenous local people, on the one hand, while on the other hand, the colonial PAM system created a mistrust between indigenous people that caused them to fight among themselves, as paramount chiefs were constructed to suit the colonial PAM system. The 'coloreds' were then provided with racist propaganda against indigenous people, and vice versa; indigenous people who happened to be black Africans were provided with racist propaganda against the so-called 'colored people'. All these racist propaganda tools led to stereotypes that supported colonial administration units and systems. In advancing this colonial racist policy, Prime Minister Hertzog (1924) co-opted 'coloreds' to vote to ensure that they would not partner with indigenous people, such as AmaXhosa, Khoi, and San, to mention but a few. The National Party manifesto and strategy aimed to eliminate black Africans from what is now the Western Cape as they were expected to move to the Transkei and Ciskei homelands. This National Party policy ensured that 'coloreds' were co-opted, leading to Influx Control laws and the Coloured Labour Preference Area Policy. These apartheid policies complemented Bantu Administration policies that were implemented through the use of forced removals, apartheid brutality, and propaganda against black Africans. In 1955, Black African Labour Regulations were introduced. Black Africans were not expected to be employed on a permanent basis and had to have scarce labour skills to work in the Western Cape. Employers had to motivate that a job required a black African and obtain a clearance certificate from the Department of Manpower (Department of Labour) that they had not received applications from a suitable 'colored' person for the position. This was followed by the Tricameral Parliament of 1984 to 1994 to entrench the political power of whites under the National Party (NP) and counter the United Democratic Front (UDF) that had managed to undermine the NP's racism and propaganda systems on all levels, supported by OR Tambo's global campaigns and success against apartheid laws and policies. As part of apartheid policy strategy, the Tricameral Parliament for the so-called 'colored' and Indian populations was established in terms of the apartheid Constitution of 1983. It dated back to 1981, when an apartheid Senate was replaced with an apartheid President's Council, which was an advisory body consisting of sixty nominated members from the white, 'colored', Indian and Chinese population groups. This excluded the majority of black Africans, as the NP had created a homeland system for them as part of its social engineering policies and strategies to maintain the oppressive and repressive PAM system. Through the UDF, 'colored' and Indian members of the Tricameral Parliament suffered severely from a crisis of credibility and were rejected by both 'colored' and Indian population groups who then joined the pro-ANC UDF in numbers. This led to a total transformation in South Africa and a negotiated settlement and compromises through the Convention for a Democratic South Africa (CODESA) and its impact on the current and future South Africa thereafter. Chief among the compromises reached at CODESA was the 'sunset clause', which had huge implications for a current and future inclusive South African identity. As part of the Government of National Unity (GNU), the sunset clause referred to an agreement reached mainly by the ANC (representing the revolutionary movement) and the National Party (representative of oppressors and architectural designers of both colonialism and apartheid) whereby a political party that received 10% of the votes would be part of the GNU to avoid a 'winner-takes-all' scenario. Furthermore, the new GNU would accept NP civil servants in the ANC's democratic public administration and management (DPAM) systems for the next five years based on Constitutional laws and rules. The really key issue of the sunset clause that was institutionalized through the Constitution was the protection of private property rights that limits the democratic administration from dealing decisively with the legacy of colonialism in terms of property ownership and land distribution, which up to now has been addressed by using a failed 'willing buyer, willing seller' guideline. Such private property rights accumulated under colonial and apartheid states include land, mines, banks, and a monopoly of industries. In other words, any change in the Constitution to review the status quo of the sunset clause requires a two-thirds majority in the National Assembly. This two-thirds majority is required to address the land question and restore human dignity, finally.

8. Professor Julian Raymond Dennis Cobbing (who taught History at Rhodes University) added that what is referred to as pseudo-archaeology in this book (see definition in Chapter 6) could be observed in the creation of the Mfecane and Shaka (and Nongqawuse Mhlakaza) myths. He described the Mfecane as an alibi or justification for colonialization and apartheid, leading to the formation of British Indirect Rule, and the notion of 'empty spaces or depopulated areas' surrounded by 'horseshoe' areas with African clans and kingdoms, as explained by anthropologists, ethnologists, historians and administrators, which led to the establishment of the former apartheid Bantustans. He further rejected Shaka's unfortunate narrative as the main cause of the Mfecane. According to him, the conflict was caused by Portuguese slave traders and whites who wanted the British government to annex Natal for their economic development. The annexation of the Natal region was motivated by whites in the region based on the fact that there was 'empty land', as Shaka's wars had forced other clans and kingdoms to move away to escape Shaka's violence. As Europeans viewed Africans as less than human, i.e. as animals or beasts, Shaka was re-created as either a beast or a warrior, or both, as justification for the occupation or putting of Natal under British administration. As part of silencing alternative versions, the stories of the Mfecane, Shaka and Nongqawuse Mhlakaza were promoted, popularized and institutionalized through colonial and apartheid public administration and management systems among all societal structures, starting from early childhood development (ECD) onwards, using oral memories (iintsomi), publications, choirs, and so forth (Cobbing, 1988:487-89). In short, the causes of the Mfecane had more to do with the economic interests of whites. Africa, and its regions like Natal, was regarded as a big zoo, which President Donald Trump recently called a 's***hole', thereby justifying imperialism and colonialism (Ditshego, 2018:17). The main reason for this justification, read with the Berlin Conference of 1884/1885 and later justification of apartheid, was that Africa had minerals and other resources that come from the 's***hole,' as defined by the president of the USA. Therefore, the class struggle institutionalized through racism and tribalism must

be replaced by the African mindset based on micro, meso and macro social and economic solidarity programmes and plans embedded under the Ubuntu paradigm (Mtiki & Dyibishe, 2014; Ngcukaitobi, 2018:1-5).

9. Jolobe (1958:4) dramatizes this African, Nguni and AmaXhosa hierarchy respect: 'Ah! Dlomo, Ncobo, Mthimkhulu, Dlamini, Malunga!', which is loosely translated as 'Hail! King Dlomo, son of King Dlomo, grandson of Mthimkhulu, Great-grandson of King Dlamini, and Great-great-grandson of King Malunga!' Probably, Tshawe would have saluted his elders as 'bantwana benkosi Nkosiyamntu (great sons of Nkosiyamntu)'. The logic of salutes is clearly explained by Jolobe (1958:48-49, 56, 59, 61, 71, 101, 107, 111). On arrival, Tshawe would probably have saluted his elder brothers Cirha and Jwarha. He would have greeted a sitting king or wafika wenza izibuliso zesiqhelo kubakhuluwa bakho nakwikumkani ekhoyo (see Jolobe, 1958:47). Furthermore, whenever there is a ceremony among clans and kingdoms, people take their time to greet the king and his counselors (Jolobe, 1958:113). It is unfortunate that African writers could not properly read, interpret and analyse JJR Jolobe's noble themes, which are very gentle, but reject pseudo-archaeology in toto.

10. Unlike what happens in the AmaCirha and AmaJwarha clans, when Tshawe was prepared to create an uncultural snake and frog among the elders, Ngqika and Ndlambe had forgotten about the African wisdom that if two brothers are fighting, the enemy takes property, land and livestock like cattle, goats, sheep, buffalo, elephant, springbuck, and so forth (see Tiyo Soga and JJR Jolobe's poem about Thuthula – 'Hamba Thuthula' or Go Thuthula – as she was dividing the brothers). This directly contradicts the Queen of AmaHlubi in Jolobe's novel *Elundini Lothukela* (1958). Literally, JJR Jolobe was reminding leaders about egoism and greediness that had been totally discouraged by Ntsikana kaGabha's macroeconomic analysis of capitalism and its ills for Africans. Equally, Thuthula symbolised ego-centralism and greediness, which were unacceptable to people on all levels.

11. 'Zenibe yimbumba yamanyama', as defined by Ntsikana kaGabha, refers to unity in diversity of human beings, with God as the omniscient, omnipotent and omnipresent creator. John Tengo Jabavu, as a political activist and editor of South Africa's first newspaper to be written in isiXhosa, used the concept to ensure unity among Africans in the struggle for liberation. In the *Isigidimi samaXhosa* (the Xhosa Messenger) (October 1870 to December 1888), imbumba yamanyama was used to advocate unity that cut across all racial and ethnic divisions. All humanity shares an African socio-economic, cultural and biological heritage. Ntsikana kaGabha's vision and communication strategy was that we are one diverse species across the globe with roots in Africa, and that we are created by God (uQamata). JT Jabavu institutionalized the vision and mission of Ntsikana in his writings. He then outlined the threat of Afrikaner nationalism and the need for unity in diversity whereby everybody has equal rights. He also advocated non-racialism and non-sexism in his writings. As an educated black man, he was approached by prominent politicians, such as William Schreiner, Mpilo Walter Benson Rubusana, and others to stand for election to the Cape Parliament in 1883. He reluctantly joined the Cape's South African Party against Cecil John Rhodes' Progressive Party as they were advancing not only neo-liberalism, but also modernizing racism and colonialism in southern Africa, and demonizing legitimate kings and replacing them with illigimate kings and queens to support Queen Victoria. Cecil John Rhodes' imperial vision, guided by his notion of the superiority of the Englishman as the greatest homo specimen on earth, meant that he believed in extending the British Empire to the whole world for the sake of humanity. At the age of 24, Cecil John Rhodes shared his vision of imperialism and colonialism: 'The object to which I intend to devote my life is the defence and extension of the British Empire. I think that object a worthy one because the British Empire stands for the protection of all the inhabitants of a country in life, liberty, property, fair play and happiness and it is the greatest platform the world has ever seen for these purposes and for human enjoyment.' Olive Schreiner wrote in a letter to her comrades, including John Merriman, that they must fight Cecil John Rhodes because he intended to inflict so much oppression, injustice and moral degradation on southern Africa. According to this early will, Rhodes wanted his

funds to be used for the establishment, promotion and development of a secret society, the true aim and object of which would be 'the extension of British rule throughout the world, the perfecting of a system of emigration from the United Kingdom, and of colonisation by British subjects of all lands where the means of livelihood are attainable by energy, labour and enterprise, and especially the occupation by British settlers of the entire continent of Africa, the Holy Land, the Valley of the Euphrates, the Islands of Cyprus and Candia, the whole of South America, the Islands of the Pacific not heretofore possessed by Great Britain, the whole of the Malay Archipelago, the seaboard of China and Japan, the ultimate recovery of the United States of America as an integral part of the British Empire, the inauguration of a system of Colonial representation in the Imperial Parliament which may tend to weld together the disjointed members of the Empire and, finally, the foundation of so great a Power as to render wars impossible, and promote the best interests of humanity' (Rotberg, 2014:551-567; Rotberg, 1988:856; Ferguson, 1999:45). The aforementioned letter by Olive Schreiner, as well as racist and brutal killings of blacks, convinced JT Jabavu to join the political party to oppose white political parties and Cecil John Rhodes' envisaged secret society under the British Empire. JT Jabavu is further acknowledged for the role played by his anti-racism writings in the establishment of numerous World Conferences Against Racism (WCAR) organized by UNESCO in 1978, 1983, 2001, 2009 and so forth. Through contributions by African intellectuals, UNESCO published a report in 1950 titled 'The Race Question', signed by various internationally renowned scholars. The Race Question report was issued on 18 July 1950, following World War II and Nazi racism, to clarify what was scientifically known about race, and as a moral condemnation of racism. These interventions by UNESCO encouraged political activists to campaign vigorously against racism.

12. As part of highly selective histories of the past, exacerbated by imperial, colonial and apartheid fracturing of indigenous knowledge, intelligence and education, white ethnologists, anthropologists, writers and historians may have neglected to write that Ntsikana kaGabha's father was a counselor, or advisor. The European writers preferred to recall that Ntsikana was born in 1760 of Gabha, a councillor of Ngqika, i.e. an elected member of the Ngqika Royal Kingdom. From my perspective and reading of the influence Ntsikana kaGabha had on people at the time, he was not just a prophet, but also a visionary leader who provided leaders and the community with strategic guidance, advice and support to balance the emotional state of a people who had to survive the atrocities of colonialism. It can be argued that Gabha (Ntsikana's father) was one of the super-genius leaders and a counselor of Ngqika who helped Ntsikana with social, cultural, communal, environmental, ecological, spiritual, emotional and politically complex problems and challenges. As an indigenous counselor, Gabha was able to transfer his aesthetic, social, emotional and cognitive skills to Ntsikana. Consequently, as Ntsikana was nurtured and guided by his father, he was in turn able to advise leaders and people on problems. Gabha had two wives, namely Nonabe (Right Hand) and Noyiki (Great Wife). But, as Noyiki did not have a son, Ntsikana was transferred to the Great House. There he grew up under Noyiki and learned to be emotionally and psychologically fit to assume his father's legacy in Tyume Valley, which led to his encounter with the Holy Spirit at the age of 30, in 1790. Theologically, a prophet was born of the Cirha clan in 1790 with strong *emotional* (self-awareness and self-management of his internal state, preferences and intuitions, including resources), *interpersonal* (social awareness and relationship management as a coach and mentor, inspirational leader, influencer and team worker), *cognitive* (systems thinking and ability to perceive themes and patterns), and *social* skills (the ability to build rapport with others and network successfully with AmaXhosa kingdoms, Khoi and San groups and missionary schools).

13. During various sessions and workshops with delegates of the Imbumba yamaNyama Royal Council, Khoisan Associations and CONTRALESA on 17-18 November 2014 and 23-25 October 2015 at Pirie Mission, delegates requested a guideline or manual on an aesthetic relational values framework and training of traditional leaders on creative arts and performance, as well as on public governance and leadership. As the Nation-Building Plan requires multidisciplinary and interdisciplinary teams, Dr. George Tsibani

engaged institutions of higher education, such as Fort Hare, Walter Sisulu University, Rhodes University, Tshwane University of Technology's (TUT) faculty of Arts and Culture, and Stellenbosch University's School of Public Leadership (SU: SPL). As a nation-building plan has various planning and development programs and projects, a bottom-up community approach with traditional leaders and local governance was highly recommended, with various state organs to coordinate and lead practical programs and projects towards developing a sustainable action plan. These workshops and inclusive consultation meetings with relevant stakeholders, such as the National Heritage Council on 14 March 2017, Dr. MWB Rubusana City and Raymond Mhlaba Local Municipality in September 2017, and potential beneficiaries, especially vulnerable groups and rural poor, will lead to accurate bills of quantities (BOQs) and provide a clear scope of work using mixed methods, with credible institutions and individuals in sustainable planning and development and integrated rural and urban infrastructure investment programmes (IR and UIIPs), as a result of which a bankable business plan can be developed both for funding purposes and for implementation thereafter. The National Heritage Council (NHC) appealed to the Imbumba yamaNyama Royal Council to focus on the reconciliation of clans and kingdoms, whereby Ntsikana kaGabha's prophetic message is interpreted in contemporary Africa and requires a Spiritual Heritage Site in Raymond Mhlaba Local Municipality (National Heritage Council CEO Proposal, 14 March 2017).

14. There is an isiXhosa proverb 'Ilizwe liyintombazana' (The country is a girl), which is a metaphor for 'the sky is clear' or 'natural resources in a country are beautiful'. When a Xhosa girl came of age, she used to be taken to an initiation school to undergo a ritual called 'ukuthonjiswa'. This ritual was an indication that the girl was now ready for marriage. Some African writers even praise God as a Creator when they argue that '… ekhul' emyezweni, phakathi kweziqhamo ezingcwele' (growing in the orchard between holy fruit). This refers to the Garden of Eden, a story found in the biblical book of Genesis. The relationship with God is expressed in this song when Qwesha closes thus: 'Ndiyambong' uMdali ngawe' (I thank the Creator for you), in this case for creating a holy country or world with beautiful resources and aesthetic leaders to drive the socio-economic transformation of Africa beyond 2063. These writers are calling for social cohesion or solidarity in our beautiful landscapes in Africa. Accordingly, from the logic of Creation, social cohesion refers to those factors that have an impact on the ability of a country or society to be united towards the attainment of a common goal. It represents the extent to which kings, queens, leaders, experts, specialists, administrations and ordinary members in a country or society respond collectively in pursuit of these shared strategic, tactical and operational goals, and how they deal with the **p**olitical, **e**conomic, **e**cological, **s**ocial, **t**echnological, **t**echnical, **l**and, **l**egal and **e**nvironmental (PESTLE) challenges and opportunities in their beautiful spaces to pursue growth and development as part of a long walk to freedom, justice and fairness under Section 1 of the Constitution, in the case of South Africa (Department of Arts and Culture, 2010b).

15. Throughout this book, imperialism is understood as a brutal and inhumane project, which refers to the illegitimate acquisition of territories and land, especially in Africa by Europeans. It refers to domination of a colony by more technologically developed colonizers; hence, it is used interchangeably with colonialism. As a form of advanced capitalism, imperialism used military propaganda and military supremacy, whereby countries in Africa and Asia were subjugated to extremely oppressive and unbearable circumstances through which their identities were deliberately destroyed and replaced with imperial or colonial histories, values and discourse. From the fifteenth century onwards, settlers in the colonized territories exploited local indigenous or native people and their natural and economic resources. Imperialists and colonizers used military supremacy to crush any form of resistance from natives or indigenous people, including genocide, mass killing and other inhuman military tactics, like burning habitats and food, and created myths justifying their position – all part of the institutionalization of imperial and colonial public administration and management systems.

16. Throughout this book, the pre-1994 Cape Province (present-day Eastern, Northern and Western Cape provinces) with its rich history and heritage is used as a typical landscape in which to implement integrated rural and urban infrastructure investment programmes (IR and UIIP) towards instituting blue and green economic models. The author uses the Cape provinces as an example of a beautiful landscape with a culturally rich heritage, but also a traumatic history of land dispossession that nevertheless produced legends with aesthetic leadership, traits and qualities. This example can be adopted to enhance and accelerate inclusive economic growth and development using mega water nexuses such as Water, Energy, Environment, Agriculture, Land, Water Licensing, Technology, Technical engineering values, and Health (represented by the acronym WEALTH). It is proposed in this book that these sustainable developmental goals (SDGs) and related water nexuses in various Paradise City models may lead to wealth creation as envisaged under the Agenda for Sustainable Development (AfSD, 2030) by African states.

17. As Cope (1968:23), supported by CLS Nyembezi (1992:1) and Childs & Williams (1997:123), suggests, African histories and their royal kingdoms, such as Zulu, Ndwandwe, AbaThembu, AmaHlubu, AmaMpondo, AmaMpondomise, AmaCirha, Khoi, San, Kalanga, and so forth must be reviewed. White missionaries, historians, ethnologists, ethnographers, anthropologists and literary theorists wrote about the AmaXhosa Kingdoms, as African scholars were limited to those who had attended the few missionary schools. African scholars who had attained a high level of education in history and literary scholarship were often poorly resourced, and their writings were subjected to the approval of white scholars for publication purposes. It is also significant that colonial and apartheid scholarships in African studies and African languages were poorly administered, and favoured international white scholars rather than Africans. In universities such as Fort Hare, Rhodes, Walter Sisulu, Stellenbosch, Cape Town and Western Cape, African languages, histories and literary studies departments were designed and structured to further the aims of Bantu Education and produce African graduates who were largely qualified to become reproducers of colonial and apartheid discourses and distorted histories. Even in 2017, the history of Africans was still written by white scholars, and even if the Nhlapo Commission was managed by African scholars, it is my personal observation that the sources and informants used for the commission's findings were highly selective studies by white scholars, anthropologists and writers, and kings, chiefs and headmen established as beneficiaries of colonial and apartheid regimes. One can argue that the Nhlapo Commission avoided an interaction and consultation with the Imbumba yamaNyama Royal Council or AmaCirha Kingdom, Ndwandwe, Kalanga, Khoi, San, Cape Khoi, Griqua, and a few other kingdoms, despite confirmation by the current traditional leaders, such as King (Aah! Khoebaha) Brown of the Khoekhoen Kingdom, Chief (Aah! Zanemvula) Mwelo Nonkonyana, Chief Ngangomhlaba Mathanzima, Nkosi Phathekile (Ah! Dilizintaba) Holomisa and King Mpisekhaya (Ah! Ngangomhlaba) Sigcawu, who all argue that AmaCirha are legitimate kings of the AmaXhosa. In short, even the famous Home of Legends, informed by Jeff Peires's *House of Phalo* may be subjected to this endless pseudo-archaeology.

18. In the anthropological, archaeological and sociological context of the former Cape Province (Eastern, Northern and Western Cape provinces under the democratic administration) as a Home of Legends, 'culture' refers to the complexity of the rich history of the Cape, including knowledge, belief, art, moral and aesthetic values, law, custom, ritual practices and any other capabilities and habits acquired by both indigenous people and citizens in the pre- and post-colonial history of this blue and green aesthetic landscape. Cabral, in his speech, 'National Liberation and Culture' (1980), defined culture as the result of economic and social relations (rather than the very opposite, or newly demarcated boundaries that indirectly re-affirm colonial and apartheid social engineering Acts, laws and policies in the case of South Africa. For instance, AmaXhosa, Khoi and San were found all over the region that used to be called the Cape Colony. In other words, the Home of Legends is an inclusive landscape of a pre-colonial era, with demarcation boundaries not guided by battles and wars of land dispossession. Africans find themselves in a crisis of identity as they have adopted colonialist modes of production, and even progressive nation-building concepts that are meant to

focus on social cohesion are bounded by institutionalized boundaries rather than the contextual realities of the pre-colonial era, as in the case of the Cape Colony (Swartz, 2010:9).

19. The Nation-Building Plan envisaged in this book refers to a macro socio-economic process linked to integrated rural and urban infrastructure investment models whereby a South African society and its people with diverse origins, histories, languages, cultural values and regions come together within the boundaries of a sovereign state with a unified Constitutional and legal dispensation, a national public education system, integrated national blue and green socio-economic models rooted in the Ubuntu paradigm, shared symbols and values rooted in our diverse and rich heritages in pre- and post-colonial South Africa, and agree to work towards eradicating the divisions and injustices of the past, to foster unity and to promote a countrywide conscious sense of being proudly South African (Department of Arts and Culture, 2012; The Presidency, 2016b; The MTSF 2014-2019, outcome 14). The proposed Nation-Building Plan (2020-2064) should be linked to the true history of Africa. This requires, inter alia, that misuse of forgiveness be revisited by democrats, peace-lovers and aesthetic leaders so as to build a new inclusive South Africa as part of Africa, and that colonial and apartheid historical discourse constructed and institutionalized over more than 400 years be replaced. In the case of the Home of Legends, i.e. the former Cape Province, this subverting of history will ensure that the history of families and clans, such as the AmaCirha, AmaJwarha, AmaNdwandwe, AmaXesibe and Khoisan associations, to name but a few, are rewritten to transcend imperial, colonial and neo-colonial legacies by Western experts and scholars who claim to be experts on these people. I am using the phrase 'subverting history' to empower people about what they think they know, and to make them look again at what current Western- and apartheid-dominated history tells about African people and their kingdoms (Jaggi, 1994:26). In a similar way, we need to view the AmaCirha Kingdom, AmaXhosa Kingdom, Imbumba yamanyama Royal Council, AmaXhosa histories and the notion of Home of Legends as part of the former Cape Province rather than as part of the narrowly defined provincial boundaries of the Demarcation Board. We need to look at comparative histories that are significant to a more nuanced understanding of the AmaXhosa Kingdom, or any other kingdom in Africa, for which highly selective oral memories and histories based on colonial and apartheid accounts are currently used. Such counter-hegemonic analysis, which reverts the colonial and apartheid scholars' writing back to the imperial centre can be objectively set out, using the articulation and reflections of leaders from the defeated and assimilated clans and kingdoms, such as AmaCirha and AmaNdwandwe, to name only a few (Buthelezi, 2004:19-21). It goes without saying that the suppressed histories of defeated and assimilated families, clans and kingdoms, such as AmaCirha, Khoi, San, Cape Xam (Khoi), and Kalanga (Zimbambe and Botswana) may lead to a true reconciliation and social cohesion, which has unfortunately not been prioritized since the dawn of South Africa's democracy. In cases where projects were undertaken by the colonial and apartheid regimes, highly selective oral memories and case studies were used to further suppress the defeated and assimilated families and clans at the expense of taxpayers. It appears that deconstructionist methods should be adopted by the Nation-Building Plan leaders in partnership with the National Heritage Council to remedy this. It is argued that, until the suppressed and colonized families and clans are able to tell, write and co-write their legitimate histories using their mother languages, true histories cannot be revealed. This will take us a long way in our journey towards justice, fairness, reconciliation, peace and unity, and will ensure that confidence is institutionalized to restore our human dignity, and that socio-economic human rights are protected and realized, as envisaged in Section 1 of the RSA Constitution.

20. The National Development Plan 2030 vision is about aesthetic relational values in the planning and development of blue and green city models aligned to the African Union Agenda 2063 priorities and values, as depicted in Figure 1.3. In short, the aforementioned strategies assume that African countries are practising good-enough governance under constitutional democracy. Some of the characteristics of a constitutional democracy include a greater milieu of community participation in the planning and

development of cities and heritage sites, adherence to the rule of law and equality before the law, accountability, transparency, economic freedom, control of abuse of power, human rights, and access to basic services (National Planning Commission, 2011a). The National Development Plan sees a nation-building plan (NBP) as a critical pillar for uniting the nation based on social cohesion. It defines social cohesion as community-based and located at the micro-social level of a city or town, which is a degree of social solidarity similar to the Paradise City, as defined in this book. The period of 2020-2064 will be measured on an ongoing basis based on the NBP goals, which are: to foster Constitutional Values of Traditional Leaders, whereby suppressed legitimate kingdoms in Africa will be restored in a dignified manner, including AmaCirha, Khoi and San groupings in the case of the former Cape Province, and in some parts of southern Africa, such as Namibia, Zambia, Botswana and Zimbabwe; create a conducive environment for equal opportunities through reindustrialization and manufacturing programs and projects, including developing an advanced education, training and development system from early childhood development, with mathematics and science as compulsory subjects to build future engineers and technical experts in terms of fourth industrial revolution requirements. The future leaders are required to have SPACE competencies in order to move towards the super-professionalism that is needed to build social cohesion and solidarity at micro-, meso- and macro-levels. These competencies are required for the execution of various commissioned studies by Parliament and related recommendations in the context of building blue and green smart Paradise City models and architectural designs. Some key recommendations in the context of architectural designs of post-colonial cities may mean that the Pan-African Parliament (PAP) must approve Special Industrial Economic and Development Zones for reindustrialization and manufacturing purposes to exploit our national resources and youthful African human resources beyond 2063. Accordingly, the current Agri-park framework designed by the Department of Rural Development and Land Reform (DRDLR) in South Africa must be funded by Development Finance Institutions (DFIs) and implemented in African countries, as agriculture and farming are intertwined with the living conditions of Africans, and agriculture can create sustainable jobs if the African Continental Free Trade Agreement can be prioritised by PAP and individual African countries, thereby championing blue and green economic models as an African adaptive capacity strategy to accelerate food security and socio-economic growth as part of a NBP in each country. It is also clear that PAP should encourage countries to make budgets available to support informal traders, SMMEs and cooperatives, as is the case with Kenyan small farmers associations. Given our rich heritage and diverse histories, rural tourism using historical and heritage routes must be promoted and funded adequately in order to consolidate social cohesion and make the NBP a very practical exercise. These social and economic reforms must be backed by an appropriate quality education system to respond to new industry needs and opportunities presented by advanced 21st century technology to improve quality of life in order to achieve the Agenda for Sustainable Development (AfSD, 2030) vision, read with the concept of blue and green economic models, to adapt to climate change in building and designing post-colonial cities or Paradise City models in Africa.

CHAPTER 2

2 UNDERSTANDING PARADISE CITY MODELS AND AESTHETIC LEADERSHIP

2.1 Objectives and outcomes

On reaching the end of this chapter, the reader will be able to:

- Understand and explain the integrated rural (IR) and urban infrastructure investment program (UIIP) as part of an Aesthetic Relational Value in Planning and Development (ARVPD) framework to achieve smart cities or Paradise City models using the concept of the Home of Legends, as applicable to any aesthetic landscape in Africa.
- Define and explain the history of Paradise City models and values, as defined in aesthetics or philosophies about art, beauty and taste in landscapes such as the Home of Legends, and the pride of people at leading efforts to defend their land and striving to achieve justice and righteousness. These aesthetic values led to intellectuals and prophets, like Ntsikana Gabha, and African scholars before him, to form associations, such as Imbumba yamaNyama (an early political movement), to overcome the systematic and structural challenges of imperialism, colonialism, and neo-colonialism in South Africa and aesthetic leadership. In other words, the liberation movement envisaged by Ntsikana Gabha and others before him was based on aesthetics, i.e., the philosophical branch of inquiry concerned with beauty, art, and perception or war for justice, equality, reconciliation, fairness and righteousness under guidance by God (uQamata) as a Creator of a beautiful Universe and man in His Divine Image.
- Define tools or policy instruments that can be used by aesthetic leaders to develop a nation-building plan between 2020 and 2064 in Africa using blue and green economic models, guided by an ARVPD framework and its implementation arm, namely IR and UIIPs. It is argued that the ARVPD and its values are centered on unique styles of art and design in planning and development provided by aesthetic leaders in the nineteenth century towards the modern Home of Legends, and South African's long walk to freedom.

- Articulate and explain objectives of blue and green or Paradise City models using various acronyms, such as SPACE, SMART, PRIDE and WEALTH creation in implementing IR and UIIPs as part of the Nation-Building Plan between 2020 and 2064, guided by roadmaps adopted by African countries.
- Provide definitions of concepts such as 'paradise' and 'aesthetic leadership' in the context of sustainable development goals (SDGs) and the rich historical heritage of settlements, settings or landscapes and their sites, such as the Home of Legends.
- Understand and explain the meaning of leading beautifully and aesthetically through a nation-building plan.
- Explain and interpret the qualities and traits of aesthetic leaders.
- Explain and interpret the irrefutable laws of leadership.
- Understand differences between managers, politicians and leaders using various leadership tools and frameworks, such as PAM, PESTLE, DISC, ACES, CAR and SPACE.
- Understand differences between leaders and prophets in leadership theories and management.
- Evaluate and interpret leadership requirements, competencies, and skills in organizations.

2.2 Beauty is simply in the eye of the beholder

The concept of 'paradise' means different things to different people. Hence it is critical to define it within the context of a nation-building plan, whereby local, provincial, national, regional, continental and global governance institutions, such as the United Nations Educational, Scientific and Cultural Organization (UNESCO), can play a vital role in implementing Paradise City models (both blue or green city designs) between 2020 and 2064, as depicted in Figure 2.2.1

Figure 2.2.1 Ntsikana Paradise City

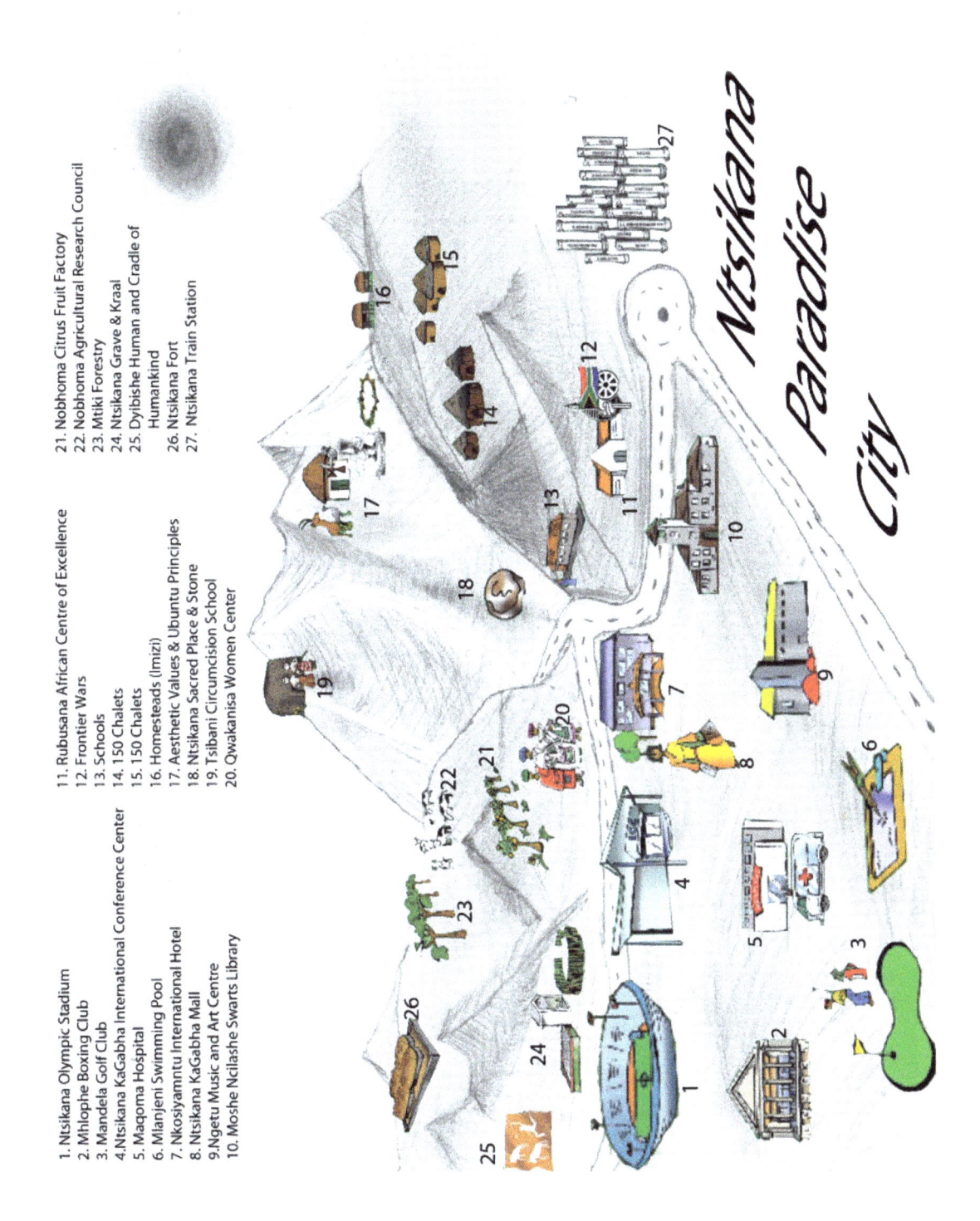

1. Ntsikana Olympic Stadium
2. Mhlophe Boxing Club
3. Mandela Golf Club
4. Ntsikana KaGabha International Conference Center
5. Maqoma Hospital
6. Mlanjeni Swimming Pool
7. Nkosiyamntu International Hotel
8. Ntsikana KaGabha Mall
9. Ngetu Music and Art Centre
10. Moshe Ncilashe Swarts Library
11. Rubusana African Centre of Excellence
12. Frontier Wars
13. Schools
14. 150 Chalets
15. 150 Chalets
16. Homesteads (Imizi)
17. Aesthetic Values & Ubuntu Principles
18. Ntsikana Sacred Place & Stone
19. Tsibani Circumcision School
20. Qwakanisa Women Center
21. Nobhoma Citrus Fruit Factory
22. Nobhoma Agricultural Research Council
23. Mtiki Forestry
24. Ntsikana Grave & Kraal
25. Dyibishe Human and Cradle of Humankind
26. Ntsikana Fort
27. Ntsikana Train Station

Ntsikana Paradise City

This will be done by using Ntsikana kaGabha's nineteenth-century philosophy as a unifying theme towards a common identity, the co-nurturing, and co-creation of inclusive partnership models, and collaboration to eradicate abject poverty, systemic unemployment and increased inequality in Mother Africa, using the former Cape Province, with its rich historical heritage and human settlement sites, serving as a flagship public environment mission.

Under the Aesthetic Relational Values in Planning and Development Framework (ARVPDF), the concept of a Paradise City model, based on Ntsikana's lofty advice, is the best way of conceptualizing and operationalizing not only a bottom-up IR and UIIP approach, but also a multifunctional co-nurturing and co-creating of local governance to exploit the potential opportunities of the landscape in terms of a blue and green economy, so as to yield the required results of African aesthetic leaders from Ntsikana to Mandela's legacy beyond 2064 (Van Wart, 2011:8). As a blue and green landscape, or the Home of Legends, the Cape provinces' blue and green economy strategy and plan aligns with both the national strategy and the African Union (AU) Agenda 2063. This will ensure, inter alia, that aesthetic designing of post-colonial cities, towns, and villages will use integrated rural and urban infrastructure investment programs (IR and UIIPs) to eradicate the chronically high unemployment rate, abject poverty of vulnerable groups (especially in deep rural communities), and the increased inequality between households and families in various human settlements. The Home of Legends' blue and green economy strategy and plan will also identify the diverse risks that threaten human security – examples of which were recently witnessed in South Sudan, the Great Lakes region, and at the time of the so-called Arab Spring uprisings in Egypt and Libya. Furthermore, the social fabric is tearing, with a marked increase in service delivery protests – from an average of 900 a year in South Africa between 1997 and 2013, to 2 000 a year between 2014 and 2017. Moreover, the recent protests appear to have been driven by communities' exclusion from democracy in addition to discontent around lack of delivery of basic services. The highest levels of income inequality in the world are combined with a large proportion of the South African population living below the poverty line – 30.4 million (55.5%) survive on less than R992 per person per month. Meanwhile, all the indications are of an ongoing concentration of wealth.

A Paradise City is a religious or metaphysical term for various cities, towns or landscapes, such as Ixhorha (Hole in the Wall), Mvezo, Coffee Bay, Port Elizabeth, Seymour, Grahamstown, Berlin, Bisho, King William's Town, Keiskammahoek, Alice, Fort Beaufort, Haga-Haga, Komga, Elliot, East London, Peddie, Middledrift, Queenstown, Bedford, Cradock, Addo, Aberdeen, Joubertina, Kenton-on-Sea, Port Alfred, Uitenhage, Nqamakwe, Centane, Lady Frere, Lusikisiki, Ntabankulu, Mount Frere, Port St. Johns, Gatyane, Tsolo, Bizana, Elliotdale, Mthatha, Barkly West, Douglas, Kimberley, Warrenton, Kakamas, Mier, Olifantshoek, Upington, Garies, Okiep, Springbok, De Aar, Richmond, Victoria East, Cape Town, George, Hessequa, Jacobsbaai, Hopefield, Saldanha, Vredenburg, Kayamandi, Paarl, Stellenbosch, Wellington, Saron, Worcester, Caledon,

Fisherhaven, Hermanus, Swellendam, Albertinia, De Rust, Haarlem, Knysna, Mossel Bay, Port Beaufort, Plettenberg Bay, Uniondale, Zoar, Prince Albert, or any other town or city as a holy place in which Ntsikana kaGabha was a prophet or visionary leader, to ensure the establishment of harmonious, aesthetic relational values and the liberation of people to accept salvation for eternal life (John 3:14-17). An Ntsikana Paradise City is a spiritual, emotional, social, economic, developmental and political place characterized by peace, prosperity, good-enough governance, accountability, responsibility, integrity, honesty, coherence, stability, responsiveness, beauty and happiness. The planners and designers of a Paradise City have the ability to create a state of equilibrium whereby there is completion based on God's teachings, as summarized by Ntsikana in his Gospel Hymn, also known as his Great Hymn.

2.3 Ntsikana kaGabha – a brief family background

> *The greatness of a man is not in how much wealth he acquires, but in his integrity and his ability to affect those around him positively.*
>
> – Bob Marley

Ntsikana kaGabha was born from the royal family of AmaCirha (Iikumkani zomthonyama) in a rondavel at iQawuka kaBindi in 1760. His father, Gabha, lived on the iXesi River. He was circumcised at Zinqayi in the early 1800s. Afterwards, Ntsikana traveled to Chief Ndlambe at Mlanjeni (Bushman's River, not necessarily the town of Alexandria). From there he moved to Mankazana, and onwards to Gqorha in the Ngqushwa district. It was at Gqorha that he experienced his revelation in 1790, and became a prophet. By invitation of Chief Ngqika, he settled at Mankazana. JM Vimbe stated: 'Kwafika uNtsikana eGqora, wafika kwa-Mankazana, owakowethu umzi useJadu, umfula ongena kwaMankazana.' In his book titled *Solving Tough Problems*, Adam Kahane tells the story of

> *A man who wanted to change the world. He tried as hard as he could, but he had had no success with that either. Then he tried to change his city and the neighbourhood, still unsuccessfully. Then he thought that he could at least change his family, and he failed again. So he decided to change himself. Then a surprising thing happened. As he changed himself, his family changed too. And as his family changed, his neighborhood changed. As his neighborhood changed, his city changed. As his city changed, his country changed, and as his country changed, the continent changed. As his continent changed, the world changed.* (Kahane, 2011:125)

According to oral history, Ntsikana used to preach under an umQonci tree surrounded by wild olive trees at a place called Nontluto in the neighborhood of Blinkwater, Fort Beaufort, which is now called Argyll Farm. He decided to go to Tyhume because he had heard of a mission station being opened there, according to Professor Jeffrey Peires. Peires (2014) explains that Ntsikana stopped at a place called kwaNdonga, between Seymour and Whittlesea, before reaching Thwathwa. He was buried at Thwathwa in 1821. Wood from indigenous trees was used for his coffin. Ntsikana possessed all the qualities of greatness. He was endowed with the deep Holy Spirit, faith, empathy, and a broad vision of zenibe yimbumba yamanya. In the case of Ntsikana, the words of HG Wells are particularly apt: 'A man's greatness can be measured by what he leaves to grow, and whether he started others to think along fresh lines with a vigour that persisted after him.'

Ntsikana's Gospel Hymn was informed by his exposure to the entire Cape landscape and its affirmation of God's Omniscience, Omnipotence, and Omnipresence in creating the world beautifully. It reflected his aesthetic environmental appreciation. A hymn is a type of song, usually religious, specifically written for the purpose of praise, adoration or prayer, and typically addressed to uQamata (God, the Creator). The Ntsikana kaGabha prophecies and teachings speak of dark times when colonialism, as part of the scramble for Africa, was at its peak, and when evil ruled the hearts and minds of brothers and sisters in the world in general, and and in Africa in particular. Ntsikana, as a prophet, an extraordinary lecturer, preacher, coach, and teacher, saw his nation perishing in front of him, and he then yearned for the coming of God's Kingdom on earth. At the time of the colonial and frontier wars, between 1779 and 1879, African royal dynasties turned their backs on each other and allowed colonialists to divide them. Massacres and human suffering were the order of the day. Ntsikana kaGabha yearned for a time of peace (Philippians 3:18-21). As a prophet, he knew that peace could only come when landowners achieved justice and the colonial legacy was replaced with aesthetic relational values and a future vision of a world without war.

What Ntsikana saw around him might have caused him to experience feelings similar to those expressed by the psalmist in Psalm 140:

> Deliver me, O Lord, from evil men;
> preserve me from violent men,
> who plan evil things in their heart
> and stir up wars continually.
>
> They make their tongue sharp as a serpent's,
> and vipers' venom is under their lips.

Guard me, O Lord, from the hands of the wicked;
preserve me from violent men,
who have planned to trip up my feet.

The arrogant have hidden a trap for me,
and with cords, they have spread a net,
besides the way they have set snares for me.

I say to the Lord, You are my God,
give ear to the voice of my pleas for mercy, O Lord!

O Lord, my Lord, the strength of my salvation,
you have covered my head in the day of battle.

Grant not, O Lord, the desires of the wicked;
do not further their evil plot, or they will be exalted!

As for the head of those who surround me,
let the mischief of their lips overwhelm them!
Let burning coals fall upon them!
Let them be cast into the fire,
into miry pits, no more to rise!

Let not the slanderer be established in the land;
let evil hunt down the violent man speedily!

I know that the Lord will maintain the cause of the afflicted,
and will execute justice for the needy.
Surely the righteous shall give thanks to your name;
the upright shall dwell in your presence.

Against the background of his times, Ntsikana kaGabha started writing his Gospel Hymn, which influenced the foundational principles of Imbumba yamaNyama to restore aesthetic relational values in planning and development (ARVPD). The great writer HG Wells (1866-1946) would have argued that Ntsikana kaGabha's

Gospel Hymn showed that 'the doctrine of the Kingdom of Heaven, which was the main teaching of Jesus, is certainly one of the most revolutionary doctrines that ever stirred and changed human thought'. It is significant that Ntsikana's hymn was composed during the frontier wars and sung not only during that era, but also in other difficult times. As a prophet, he was aware that words are weapons that can hurt, destroy, or build formidable unity (Psalm 58:4; Matthew 12:35). Professor Angie Karan Krezos argues that

> *when we speak from our heart and say the words our soul has only dared to whisper, that's when miracles happen. When we communicate in a heartfelt way, it's dignified and compelling, and it usually evokes support and open-heartedness from others. Words create energy. From the spoken word to the written word, from the DNA messages encoded in cells to nerve impulses connecting our mind and body, words will influence life. Words spoken from the heart bring more inspiration, motivation and good energy into our world ... [M]arinate your heart in your words so that what you speak from your heart will reflect the love you possess inside.*

2.4 Leadership qualities

2.4.1 Ability to restore human dignity and pride

As an aesthetic leader, Ntsikana kaGabha was aware that words could restore dignity and pride in his followers, citizens, and people, including the kings and queens of his time. Ntsikana kaGabha's words and messages communicated hope and an alternative vision to a world sick of endless wars. Ntsikana's Gospel Hymn demonstrates his aesthetic leadership qualities. Such qualities included:

- **Emotional awareness,** by advising his fellow leaders and rulers through positive engagement with them and providing advice to prevent loss of life at all costs. This inspired people to act with consciousness, cultural dignity and pride in the multiracial and multinational political environment of the nineteenth century.
- **Sensory and somatic attentiveness,** by advising people to reject capitalism and appealing to them to accept the Word of God to restore dignity and self-confidence, as all people are created in the image of God.
- **Interest in organizational beauty,** by encouraging every person to be part of Imbumba yamaNyama and spread the Word of God. This also included using the environment to describe God's agape love (the highest form of love and charity). He further encouraged his sons to continue working

for human salvation in partnership with various church leaders during his time at the Mgwalana Missionary Church in Alice.
- **Promotion of moral purpose**, by appealing to rulers and colonizers to stop wars and allow peace to prevail for the good of all. According to Ntsikana, the Creation is a sensuous bonding between uQamata and His people to seek His Kingdom first and to practise a life of respect for each other as children of God.

Further aesthetic leadership qualities can be deduced from Ntsikana's life and work. He began to preach in earnest, and crowds came to listen to his words. As a prophet and spiritual leader, he knew that:

> After the night, we pray for dawn,
> After the war, we pray for peace,
> O Lord, fill our hearts with compassion and love,
> So that we may walk through the darkness
> And emerge into a morning filled with Agape Love.

The word compassion literally means 'to suffer together.' It refers to a feeling that arises when one is confronted with another's suffering and feels motivated to relieve that suffering. Ntsikana kaGabha's choice of words demonstrates that he had the ability to think very deeply about human suffering and his role in guiding people to salvation against evil rulers and colonialists. Ntsikana was motivated to replace the loss of dignity and pride with spiritual power and values of self-confidence, and to replace human suffering with joy and happiness. Through his messages, he improved the wellbeing and interpersonal relationships of people and provided them with survival skills against all colonial strategies and tactics used at the time. To the surprise of the colonial rulers, his Gospel Hymn activated spiritual pleasure circuits in the brain, and rewarded the followers of the Kingdom of God and Imbumba yamaNyama with a sense of strong cultural identity and a zeal to create, through Imbumba yamaNyama, cultural, psychological, emotional, mental and spiritual freedom, a quest for justice and fairness, and self-reported happiness.

2.4.2 Ability to promote hope

It is significant that during Ntsikana's era, there were no major cases of heart disease among Africans. This was because his followers and leaders around him had their vagus nerve function stimulated, which kept their heart rates constant and reduced the chance of heart attacks. His spiritual teaching made people experience a 'transdisciplinary' state of unity of knowledge, an emotional and spiritual feeling of existing in the realm of

God, and a reward of living comforted by the Holy Spirit under multiculturalism. Consequently, his followers demonstrated resilience against British imperialism and colonialism that led to the political formation of Imbumba yamaNyama (1882) and the South African Native National Congress (SANNC) in 1912, guided by Ntsikana kaGabha's Imbumba yamaNyama Association (2 Timothy 3:12; 2 Corinthians 4:8-9). Knowing that they were made in the image of God, he told his followers and leaders that God expected them to spread these views to His Kingdom (2 Corinthians 10:5). He may have inspired his followers by arguing that

> *better a meal of vegetables where there is love, than a fattened calf with hatred.* (Proverbs 15:17)

Ntsikana had the ability to communicate with his followers in such a way that they accepted his messages and analyses. He was able to socially construct reality through framing techniques. He used everyday interactions as strategic encounters in which he attempted to 'sell' a particular self-image. Ntsikana, as an organic scientist, or neuroscientist, might have believed that the mind is in a unique position between the human spirit and body. It is through a paradigm shift of the mind that God's authority or power can be felt (Romans 12:2). Through his approach, he was able to advance God's Kingdom and stimulate the people's brains to think about God's Kingdom and, in this way, the Holy Spirit[21] communicated with them. Paradoxical to the expectations of evil men, Ntsikana's aesthetic leadership style led to the establishment of churches, which in turn led to caring couples and marriages. As people experienced compassion, the neural systems in their brains known to support parental nurturing and other caregiving behaviors were activated. In short, Ntsikana's teachings made people adapt and survive in the face of inhuman systems based on systemic colonialism. Both Imbumba yamaNyama and the SANNC provided people with a vision of a non-racial and non-sexist future with democracy and constitutionalism (1 John 1:9).

Aesthetically, people began to work together to change their environment using Ntsikana's aesthetic relational values. A spirit of prophecy seemed to have taken possession of Ntsikana at this time. At one of the many religious meetings that were held during Ngqika's visit, Ntsikana prophesied about the coming of the Fingoes (AmaMfengu) to the Cape Colony, which at the time included the present-day Northern, Eastern and Western Cape provinces of democratic South Africa (Abantu baseMbo okanye AmaMfengu). Moreover, he prophesied about the land being taken from Ngqika and divided among white settlers or colonialists. He also prophesied about the Battle of Amalinde near Dimbaza Township in 1818, where Ngqika's forces were shamefully defeated. He further envisioned the establishment of Imbumba yamaNyama to shield and unite his people against colonialists and their encouragement of tribalism in pursuit of their divide-and-rule strategy. Ntsikana had a big picture where his wisdom, teachings, messages and prophetic addresses led to the establishment of independent African churches before his death in 1821 at the age of 61. The establishment of these churches led to what can be called a new social, spiritual and political revolution towards the end of the nineteenth century.

2.4.3 Visionary and prophetic abilities

As a spiritual and aesthetic leader, a visionary, an extraordinary preacher and prophet, Ntsikana provided his nation with a clear leadership succession plan to advance God's purpose in Creation. He provided spiritual mentorship and guidance to his two sons, Kobe (the elder), who was his backbone (iintonga yasemhlana yakhe), and Dukwana to lead the followers to the Kingdom of God and obtain inspiration and spiritual strength at a retreat at Mgwalana Mission Station near Alice.

Even though Ntsikana kaGabha died in 1821, his Gospel Hymn was sung from memory in all the churches until it was published by Lovedale College in 1876. As an artist and composer who also wrote other hymns, Ntsikana kaGabha left his followers with the Gospel Hymn and the Imbumba yamaNyama movement or association, which led to the formation of the SANNC, that later became the African National Congress (ANC). Through the artistic message of his Gospel Hymn, his influence has remained in the hearts and minds of peace lovers and Christians to the present time (Matthew, 12:35-36; Proverbs 3:6). His Gospel Hymn is still highly valued and loved by gospel singers across the global village. Ntsikana kaGabha's hymn confirms oneness, humanity, Ubuntu and God's agape love (Psalm 51:10-11). By the end of the nineteenth century, churches were known as independent schools. By the 1950s, the number of independent schools was close to 5 000 as they had begun to provide fertile spiritual and educational guidance, mentorship and coaching to approximately 700 000 learners in the Cape Province, using Ntsikana's vision. In this context, it can be deduced that Ntsikana's church marked the formation of independent African churches, leading to the current status quo of non-racial churches in the democratic states of Africa.

The words of Ntsikana's Gospel Hymn read as follows:

ULO THIXO MKHULU
(arranged and translated by JK Bokwe)

Ulo Thixo omkhulu, ngoseZulwini;
Ungu Wena-wena Khakha lenyaniso.
Ungu Wena-wena Nqaba yenyaniso.
Ungu Wena-wena iHlati lenyaniso.
Ungu Wena-wen' uhlel' enyangwaneni.
Ulo dal' ubomi. wadala nezulu.

Fumene George Tsibani

Hom, hom-na!

Lo Mdal' owadala, wadala izulu.
Lo Menzi wenkwenkwezi nezilimela;
Yabinza inkwenkwezi. isixelela.
Lo Menzi wemfaman' uzenza ngabomi?
Hom, hom-na!
Lathetha ixilongo. lisibizile,
Ulonqin' izingela imiphefumlo.
Ulohlanganis' imihlamb' eyalanayo.
Ulo Mkokeli wasikhokela thina.
Ulengub' inkul' esiyambata thina.
Ozandla Zako zinamanxeba wena.
Onyawo Zako zinamanxeba wena.
U gazi Lako limrolo yinina?
U gazi Lako liphalele thina.
Lemali enkulu-na siyibizile?
Lomzi Wakho-na-na siwubizile?
Hom, hom-na!

THOU GREAT

The Great God, He is in heaven.
Thou art thou, Shield of truth.
Thou art thou, Stronghold of truth.
Thou art thou, Thicket of truth.
Thou art thou, who dwellest in the highest.
Who created life (below) and created life (above).
The Creator, who created, created heaven.
This Maker of the stars, and the Pleiades (seasons).
A star flashed forth, telling us.
The Maker of the blind, does He not make them
on purpose?

> The trumpet sounded, it has called us,
> As for His hunting, He hunteth for souls.
> Who draweth together flocks opposed to each other.
> The Leader, he led us.
>
> Whose great mantle, we put it on.
> Those hands of Thine, they are wounded.
> Those feet of Thine, they are wounded.
> Thy blood, why is it streaming?
> Thy blood, it was shed for us.
> This great price, have we called for it?
> This home of Thine, have we called for it?

Ntsikana kaGabha's Gospel Hymn separated the evil men from God's purpose for the creation of man and the universe (Romans 12:16; Ephesians 4:31-32; John 8:36). The hymn was sung at very sensitive times to give hope to the hopeless people, and to inspire unity among dispossessed indigenous people. Ntsikana's hymn demonstrates, beyond any reasonable doubt, his indigenous knowledge of botany, biology, and the environment as an innocent, meek, religious and studious leader, an agreeable conversationalist, an enthusiastic teacher, and a great favorite with his followers. He was, in addition, an authority on music, and a distinguished physician, becoming an extraordinary lecturer in planning and development using chameleon methodology to overcome conflict-riddled circumstances.

'Hom, hom-na!' is used by Ntsikana kaGabha as a traditional rhythm to promote consistency and rhythm between the stanzas of his hymn. It also creates beautiful structural patterns and some artistic synergy between themes and words of the new Christian movement, and African music, dance and expression. His Gospel Hymn, anchored in his vision: zenibe yimbumba yamanyama, aesthetically articulated critical pillars for God's people and the Congress of the People (Ingqungquthela yenkululeko):

- **Anointed leaders** of God led aesthetically (if the Gospel Hymn is used or seen as a manifesto to lead people to good-enough governance). This refers to the Bible as a manifesto for daily business based on God's agape love (uQamata) (Ruth 3:3; Luke 7:46; 1 Kings 19:16; Psalm 105:15; Exodus 40:15; Numbers 3:3; I Samuel 9:16; 1 Kings 1:34-39). The anointed kings and queens on earth are to introduce the divine influence or presence to the lost sheep of Israel or lead people back to God. Therefore, ceremonial blessings, such as for the coronation of clans, kingdoms and monarchs, are meant as a consecration act to praise God on earth by carrying out God's will or holy orders as summarized in the Ten Commandments (Joshua 3:5; I Corinthians 7:1-6; Psalms 51:2-7; Psalms 77:13-14; and 1 Peter 2:9-10).

- The struggle for decolonization must be based on **faith and patience**. In other words, there is a long walk to freedom, as reflected by Dalibhunga kaMandela of the AbaThembu Royal Kingdom. Faith in God and in His guidance through the Holy Spirit would sustain the people of God in the increasingly more oppressive circumstances of the nineteenth century and beyond. Under unbearable imperial and colonial conditions, Ntsikana focused on the pillar of faith and patience in times of uncertainty and testing. According to Ntsikana kaGabha, people must have trust in God and in His willingness to provide sustainable solutions under difficult conditions. People should obey His guidance and look for spiritual development and growth through agape love. In this regard, Ntsikana said:

> Lathetha ixilongo. Lisibizile,
> Ulonqin' izingela imiphefumlo.
> Ulohlanganis' imihlamb' eyalanayo.
> Ulo Mkokeli wasikhokela thina.
>
> The trumpet sounded, it has called us,
> As for His hunting, He hunteth for souls.
> Who draweth together flocks opposed to each other.
> The Leader, he led us.

- Fighting imperialism and colonialism requires **boldness and bold leaders** (Acts 4:31). The Gospel Hymn of Ntsikana was written at a time of a series of frontier wars in the Eastern Cape. As a bold aesthetic and visionary leader, Ntsikana was courageous and was prepared to go against the tide of popular theory and thinking at the time. He refused to argue about the God of Abantu (Africans) and the God of white settlers. He wrote 'The Maker of the blind, does He not make them on purpose? (Lo Menzi wemfaman' uzenza ngabomi? Hom, hom-na!). As an organic scientist and accounting expert, as divinely revealed to him, the frontier wars were meant to be an opportunity to spread God's news of salvation. The wars between Ndlambe and Ngqika, and between the British settlers and black people (African and Khoisan groupings), filled him with unselfish and committed passion, a burning fire and spirit to achieve the vision of unity in diversity (imbumba yamanyama) as a vision for the post-frontier wars scenario in a democratic, non-racial and non-sexist country guided by God, the Creator of the blind to possibly test our faith in Him. In fact, Ntsikana's boldness grew throughout the entire Cape Colony where churches were established and used as a magnet to lead people to God's agape love in the midst of unjust frontier wars. It is clear that Ntsikana, as a bold leader, had a vision, and his Gospel Hymn was written as a communication strategy or plan of action to restore the loss of dignity among his followers. The Gospel Hymn of this intelligent and extraordinary priest and prophet of God appears to have been guided by divine revelation. The stanzas show beyond any reasonable doubt that God is Emmanuel. Some of the principles from the Gospel Hymn include the following:

- ✓ ***The will of God is made known through the Gospel Hymn (and Bible or Word of God):*** Seek Divine guidance or Emmanuel (Ulo Mkokeli wasikhokela thina). In his hymn, Ntsikana kaGabha defines God as Omniscient, Omnipotent and Omnipresent, a righteous God who is the Creator of Heaven, the maker of the stars, and the Pleiades, who causes the stars to flash forth. As a prophet growing among the AmaXhosa, Ntsikana knew that people take note of visual images before making sense of anything. God's core values become rooted and established in people's socialization, and the Gospel Hymn was used to guide people to the Word of God in their hearts so that they could overcome all forms of oppression and a painful life during the endless frontier wars in the nineteenth century. It is also significant that Ntsikana as a known traditional dancer of his time, used the African rhythm expressed in 'Hom, hom-na!' to draw artistic sense from hearing, feeling and thinking.
- ✓ ***God is confirmed during the bloody nineteenth-century frontier wars and other unbearable circumstances:*** The death of Christ Jesus is a demonstration of God's agape love (Ozandla Zako zinamanxeba wena, Onyawo Zako zinamanxeba wena, Igazi Lakhe esathengwa ngalo yinina?/ Thy blood. Why is it streaming? Thy blood, it was shed for us. This great price, have we called for it?). In the context of the bloody wars of his time, Ntsikana advanced the notion of faith and trust in God whereby he urged his countrymen and countrywomen to ask God to prove Himself as a living God.
- ✓ ***The Holy Spirit speaks from where He dwells:*** Ntsikana's Gospel Hymn states that 'As for His hunting, He hunteth for souls … Thou art thou, who dwellest in the highest.' God does not dwell only in heaven, He uses our bodies as His temple. He dwells in souls. Accordingly, our bodies are temples of Christ. When bodies of Christ join, they form imbumba or rock. Consequently, Ntsikana always provided a gospel of hope and victory in Christ Jesus (Colossians 1:27).
- ✓ ***Divine guidance comes from meeting God's conditions:*** uQamata, the source, and giver of life (uMniki-bomi) must give clans, families and kingdoms based on the conditions stipulated in Isaiah (58:11). This would be followed by peace in the midst of the bloody frontier wars

(James 3:17). In Psalms (25:9) it is wisely declared that 'the meek will He guide in judgment, and the meek He will teach His way'. This is about humility, whereby people of God humble themselves before Him for creating heaven and the stars and for sacrificing His son for people's sins. The principle is that of giving in sincerity, not to win praise. Christ taught that giving should not be done with the motive of self-glorification, or to attract attention and praise, but out of sincerity, for the benefit of the poor (Matthew 6:2).

- As beggars we must **humble ourselves** before Him, the Creator of heaven and earth, the owner of the bread of life (John 6:25-59). Aesthetic leaders put the interests of their followers first. It is in this context that Ntsikana advised clans and kings to take up the Bible rather than choosing capitalism, as capitalism might lead to personal pride, corruption, and greediness. It was revealed by God to Ntsikana that He had chosen His people to have 'compassion, kindness, humility, gentleness and patience' in respect of His kingdom (Colossians 3:12). While spreading the Word of God, Ntsikana knew that racism, colonialism, and egoism are against God's will. The Gospel Hymn was used to empower people by asserting that there is only one God, and to encourage the followers to pray to Him alone as He is the Creator of everything, including them. He then advised clans, families, queens and kings to:
    - ✓ **be open** to a new truth about God, i.e. that an ultimate price was paid by Him, and that they should, therefore, support those in need;
    - ✓ **admit mistakes**, such as the unnecessary wars for power between Ndlambe and Ngqika against cultural norms and standards in terms of African traditional governance, and God's values, principles and Word; and
    - ✓ **self-reflect**, by encouraging followers to build more churches. Through Ntsikana's mentorship and coaching skills, individuals developed personal excellence, created personal game plans for their successes, and advanced collective team efforts to organize churches. Consequently, everyone understood his or her personal contribution and role to restore peace, love, stability, trust, and happiness guided by God's Will or Word as summarized in the Gospel Hymn.

The chosen people of God were supported and empowered to perform their Pentecostal duties and activities in the Cape Colony, and they interacted with families, clans, chiefs, and kings. Spiritually, Thwathwa is regarded by the Imbumba yamaNyama Royal Council (launched in 1891 in Port Elizabeth or Nelson Mandela Bay Municipality) and its potential 1.4 billion spiritual members in Mother Africa, as one of the holiest places where the children of God and the righteous dead hope to spend eternity. The 'holiest place' refers to the appreciation of God's revelation to Ntsikana to support human relationships, living meaningfully in symmetry, balance, and harmony since Jesus Christ has paid the price on the cross. From an Aristotelian perspective, art in living is cathartic and palliative, which then produces contentment or a state of equilibrium or paradise, as existed in the Garden of Eden before the fall of man (Swartz, 2010:48-51).

2.4.4 The Gospel Hymn and the Garden of Eden and Paradise of God

Throughout Ntsikana kaGabha's Gospel Hymn, it appears that he reminded Christians of the Garden of Eden and its location according to the Holy Bible. In this book, the Garden of Eden is interpreted to mean an earthly paradise, or physical city, and a Heavenly paradise or theological and spiritual place of God based on God's Creation as recounted in the First Book of the Bible (Genesis) and Revelation as the Last Book of the Bible.

Fumene George Tsibani

2.4.4.1 Geographical location of the Garden of Eden

Theologians, scholars and archaeologists have long debated the location of the Garden of Eden. It remains debatable, depending on one's perspective, as demonstrated in Map 1 and Map 2 hereunder.

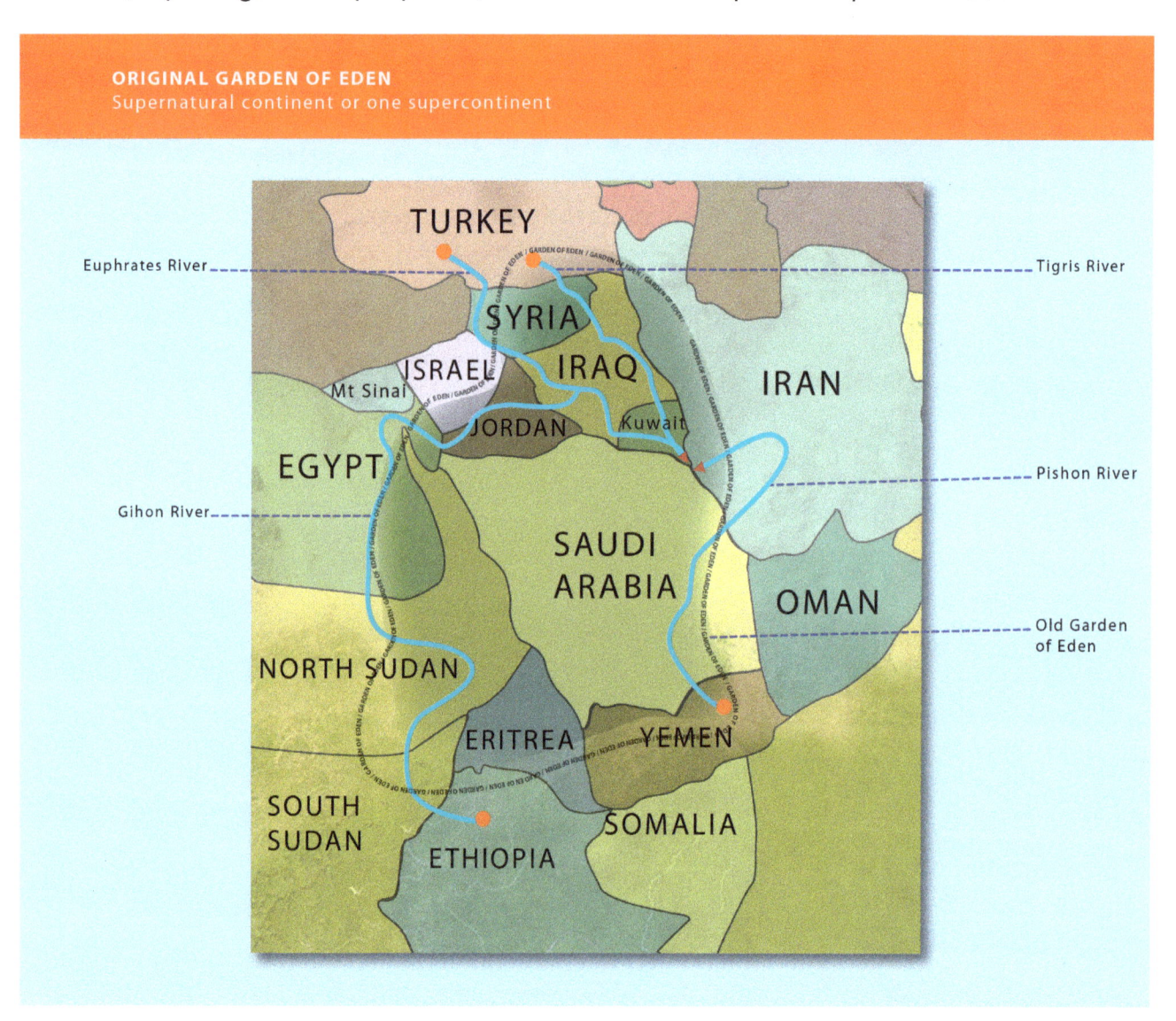

ORIGINAL GARDEN OF EDEN
Supernatural continent or one supercontinent

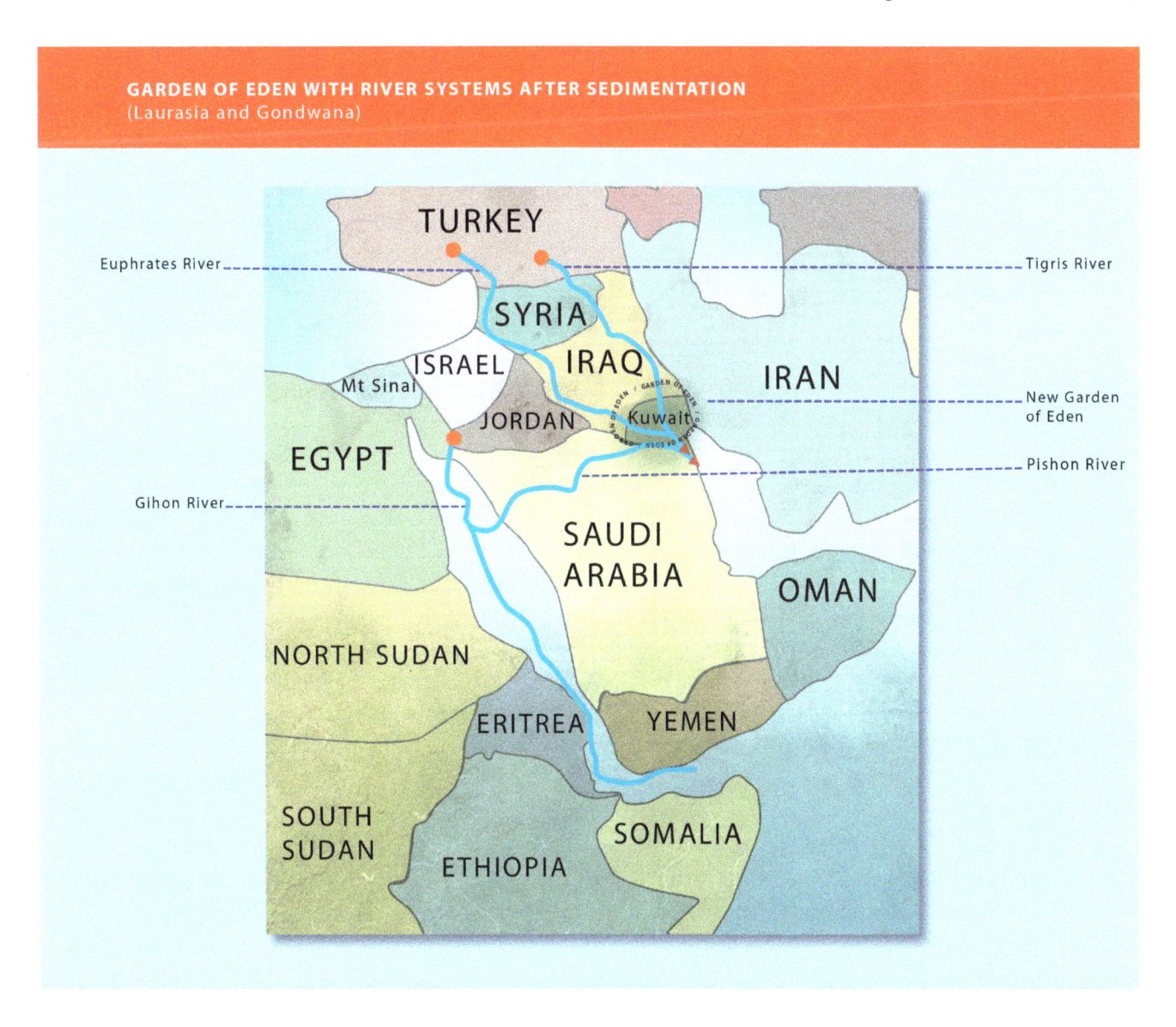

GARDEN OF EDEN WITH RIVER SYSTEMS AFTER SEDIMENTATION
(Laurasia and Gondwana)

According to the description in the Bible (Genesis 2:10-14), the Garden of Eden was created around the following four rivers:

- The first river is the mountainous Pishon (now Wadi al Batin) in the land of Havilah (sandy land), which is east of Egypt towards Assyria, where exceptionally pure and good gold or a cradle of gold (Genesis 2:12) or the source of King Solomon's gold (Genesis 10:29 or 961-922 BC), and the gold of Ophir (1 Kings 9:28; 1 Chronicles 8:19 and Isaiah 13:12), aromatic resin, copper, metals and onyx stone (Genesis 2:12) were found. Other metals came from the land of Ur or present-day Iran. This is the largest sand desert-land of Saudi Arabia and Yemen (the Queen of Sheba came from ancient Mariaba, or part of Yemen, in terms of 1 Kings 10:10), or in the world. Historically, the land of Havilah refers to the whole region rather than one particular place. According to Genesis, Abraham did not go himself, but sent a servant with camels to go and look for a wife for Isaac (Genesis 24:10 and 19).
- The second river is the mountainous Gihon (now Karun or Karkheh, joined by the Kashkan River in the region of Kush, later called Khuzestan). These rivers flow directly to the Persian Gulf at Salaymanan towards the east of the Tigris River. The Wadi system once drained the entire central part of Arabia and is connected to the Tigris and Euphrates rivers in Iraq and Kuwait after they have joined to become Shatt al-Arab. Shatt al-Arab (the river of the Arabs) currently flows into the top of the Persian Gulf. The translation of Cush or Kush (the land encircled by the Gihon according to Genesis) to mean Ethiopia is an error; rather, it should be the land of the Kassites, which was previously known as the land of Elam or Susiana. The Kassites lived in the east of Mesopotamia, or present-day western Iran, in the Old Babylonian period (1800-1600 BC).
- The third river is the Tigris (Hiddekel), which flows east of the land of Asshur or Ashur. The Tigris River rises on the southern slopes of the Taurus Mountains in eastern Turkey and flows for 1 160 miles towards the Persian Gulf. On its way to the sea, it is joined by a number of tributaries flowing from the Zagros Mountains: the Khabur, Great Zab, Little Zab, Nahr al'Uzaym, Diyah, Karkheh, and Karun.
- The fourth river is the Euphrates. The Euphrates River drains the western part of the historical region of Mesopotamia. It starts in the highlands of Turkey, flows south-eastwards over a limestone hill terrain in northern Iraq, and enters its delta at Hit about 80 miles west of Baghdad.
- The Tigris and Euphrates rivers are in Mesopotamia (Iraq) and Kuwait.

2.4.4.2 Biblical interpretation of the Garden of Eden

Biblical scholars, archaeologists, anthropologists, geologists, and scientists relatively agree that the Garden of Eden is in Basra in Iraq. It is located between Kuwait and Iran at the top of the Persian Gulf, and covers parts of Iran, or the modern landscape at the head of the Persian Gulf. The four rivers converged near the head of the Persian Gulf to create a fertile land or paradise fit for the garden. There is also geological evidence that the Dammam formation is the principal aquifer (water-bearing rock) for all of Kuwait, Saudi Arabia and Bahrain. The Dammam formation is composed of sedimentary limestone rock that covers an extensive part of western Iraq, occurring on both the surface and subsurface west of the Euphrates River. These four rivers symbolize the rivers of living water with deposits of precious stones. The biblical description of the Garden of Eden fits the modern landscape of southern Iraq, and this must be read with chapters 21 to 22 of the Book of Revelation that refers to Jerusalem. As people in Mesopotamia used bitumen at Hit, Noah also probably used it in building the ark. The pitch for the ark of Noah was supplied by sedimentary rock.

The United Nations Educational, Scientific and Cultural Organization (UNESCO) declared a wetland in southeast Iraq, which is believed to be the location of the Garden of Eden, as a world heritage site. It is also possible to argue that, instead of the current description of the Garden of Eden as having been in Iraq, it covered the Middle East, Iran, Iraq, Kuwait, Egypt, Ethiopia and Sudan before great sedimentation processes and the drifting of land created new continents (Genesis 2:14). These sedimentation processes and great floods can be justified by the fact that Ethiopia is more than a thousand miles away from Iraq (across the Red Sea). It can be concluded that the Garden of Eden is a paradise or Garden of God before sedimentation or drift of the world into two supercontinents and before the great floods. Theologically, if one can pinpoint the four rivers Pishon, Gihon, Tigris and Euphrates, one can pinpoint a paradise of God on earth. Some Christians place the Garden of Eden in Armenia, in the Zagros Mountains of Iran, and in Bahrain where a lonely tree known as the Tree of Life grows by itself in a waterless desert in the southern Iraqi village of Qurna or Al Qurnah, where Abraham prayed in approximately 2000 BC. Qurna is an Arabic word for connection or joint. The village of Qurna is 74 km northwest of Basra within the town of Nahairat and is located at the confluence of the Tigris and the Euphrates (Genesis 2-3).

The term 'paradise' is associated with the Divine Garden or Garden of Eden, a fruitful well-watered landscape, a paradise of pleasure (Genesis 18:12) or a park-based coexistence with environmental aesthetics – i.e. the perfect state of the world prior to the fall from Grace, and the perfect state that will be restored in the world to come (Colossians 4:6; Luke 23:43; 2 Corinthians 12:4; Revelation 2:7; Genesis 2:8; Jeremiah 22:24). The meaning of Eden and the four rivers may signify the real Jerusalem, the Temple of Solomon, or the Promised Land (Genesis 15:18-21 and Exodus 23:31). It may signify the Divine Garden on Zion, and the mountain of God, which was also Jerusalem. It also means a fruitful and well-watered place of extreme beauty, delight and happiness, a state just prior to Resurrection (Luke 23:43). It is a place where prophetic messages from the Old Testament and the New Restatement are fulfilled in Heaven.

This Orchard, Park or Heavenly Place is also defined as an intermediate place for the departed souls of the righteous men and women waiting for Resurrection. It can be defined as a promised land that signifies Jerusalem, or a beautiful Garden of Eden before sedimentation and great floods, that contained a tree of life, where God intended Adam and Eve to live (Genesis 18:12). This is the City of David, Abraham's Blossomed House of Holiness or Body of Christ or Church for praising the Omniscience, Omnipresence, and Omnipotence of the living and righteous God. As men and women are created in the image of God, the paradise of the Garden of Eden also refers to the Temple of God in us (soul, spirit and body) and the related attributes of man. In the case of the fall of man, or sin, it refers to the whole doctrine of Christianity, or the paradigm shift from being sinners to being sons and daughters of God through Jesus Christ's sacrifice on the Cross (Isaiah 64:1). In short, those who die in faith will be with Christ (Philippians 1:23) or in paradise with Jesus Christ (Luke 23:43). Eschatologically, through Redemption of sin, it is argued that death is now cast out of human beings or children of God if they have faith in Jesus Christ as King of kings, Lord of lords, and Governor of governors. Theologically, the way is now open for the faithful people to return to God's eschatological Garden of Eden or paradise (Revelation 2:7; 2 Corinthians 12:4, 2 Corinthians 5: 1-10; Thessalonians 4:13-14).

Fill the earth and subdue it. (Genesis 1: 28)

In this book, it is accepted that the earth was formed and created to be inhabited by God's people (Isaiah 45:18 and 55:11), whereby people of God were expected to build cities and houses and plant fruits for them to eat (Isaiah 65:21). The book of Proverbs (2:21) states:

For the upright shall dwell in the land, and the perfect shall remain in it (earth).

Theologically, Jesus Christ spoke about an earthly paradise (Revelation 22:1-22). The Garden of Eden was an architectural design of God, and the aesthetic Leader and Builder were God (Hebrews 11:10-16). In this sense, it refers to a Place of Presence of God and an invisible dwelling place of the living God, or a palace Garden of God complete with fruit trees (Genesis 3:8). This refers to God's natural environment. Jesus Christ also promised a Heavenly Paradise (Luke 12:32), as those who are faithful to Him will be in a Heavenly Paradise. He urged people to join Him to rule over the earthly paradise. These co-governors, co-leaders, co-rulers or Christians will ensure that the paradise on earth will be properly governed and maintained according to God's Ten Commandments or standards. Jesus Christ knew that this was God the Father's will on earth. He was with His Father in Heaven when the Garden of Eden was created.

Life in the future earthly paradise is open to all people who practise faith in Jesus Christ (John 3:16; Luke 23:43). In the New Paradise or Jerusalem, gates will be open and no longer closed at night as people will exist in the light of God our Creator (Isaiah 24:23; Isaiah 60:11-19; Revelation 21: 24; 22:15), and the Lamb will be the light as God will shine for His people. It is also significant that all people of God have been blessed through Abraham, as people are expected to live according to the standards of the New Jerusalem. In the

New Jerusalem, John sees a whole avenue of trees of life planted on either side of the river that flows down the middle of the street of the great city of Jerusalem. Inhabitants of the New Jerusalem may freely pick of their fruits of all kinds (Ezekiel 47:12), with twelve Angels standing guard. The guard of twelve Angels will regulate the stream of those who would come in to make their home in the New Jerusalem. One can even think of

Welcome to the Paradise of God, where you may freely pick fruit from the tree of life!

Theologically, it appears from the description of the Garden of Eden in Genesis (2:10-14) that water leaves Eden. Water flows and passes through the paradise garden. From there it splits into the headwaters of the four separate rivers, each with its own name: Pishon, Gihon, Tigris, and Euphrates. In this way, the blessings of Eden in terms of life and fertility are distributed all over the earth. Pishon and Gihon do not exist today. However, from the account in Genesis 2 (the First Book of the Bible) read with Revelation 22 (the Last Book of the Bible), it appears that these four rivers of the world, no matter where we place them geographically, all rise from one and the same source, located upstream of the paradise garden of God. The apocryphal book of Jesus Sirah adds to these four rivers the Jordan and the Nile. In this context, the addition of the Jordan (Israel) and the Nile (ancient Egypt, including the Republic of Sudan and Ethiopia) brings the water supply and distribution systems of paradise very close to ancient Egyptian civilization, and close to God's Creation in the Book of Genesis. This Paradise City is close to John's visionary portrayal of the Great City of Jerusalem (Revelation 21:18-21). The Garden of Eden, or the New Jerusalem as visualized by John, includes streets, mineral resources including pure gold, and the beauty and splendor of precious stones, which are already described in an earlier vision in Revelation (4:3), or the chosen bride and her beauty (Isaiah 54:11-12).

The original Garden of Eden has disappeared and two of the rivers are no longer in existence. Given the sedimentation and great floods of Noah, it appears that the topography and geographical areas drifted and are completely changed from the original description in Genesis 2. In other words, the Old Paradise has been removed from the face of the earth. Yet God's promise of Jerusalem will be fulfilled in the New Garden of Eden or Jerusalem (Isaiah 51:1-3; Ezekiel 36:35). Under the promised New Garden of Eden, Heavenly Paradise and House of God, or New Jerusalem, future life will be different. Some of the paradigm changes will include the following:

- The Garden of Eden will be radically changed into a garden city, the New Jerusalem, a dwelling place for all the nations of the world;
- The architectural design of the New Jerusalem by God will remain forever without death;

- The Light of God will eclipse the light of the sun and the moon, and God's blessing will move to all nations;
- Humanity will exercise responsibility together with God and the Lamb, i.e., the dominion over the world will last forever;
- There will be free access to the tree of life, characterized by welcoming Angels holding all gates open;
- Precious stones and pure gold are not to be found in the Garden of Eden especially in the far-off land of Havilah and major parts of Africa, but are now part and parcel of the New Jerusalem; and
- The ancient dragon-serpent is completely removed, and the paradise curse of Adam and Eve will be changed into an eternal blessing, leading to a dwelling together of God and man in endless and undisturbed bliss.

2.4.4.3 Proposed Paradise City in the Home of Legends

From the perspective of geoscientific and engineering disciplines, the word 'paradise' refers to a state of equilibrium in building cities. The proposed Paradise City models will make use of the blue and green economy in the coastal and inland towns, and the attractive tourism and heritage sites of the former Cape Province. The state of equilibrium refers to co-creating and co-nurturing local space using bottom-up integrated rural and urban infrastructure investment programs (IR and UIIPs) to eradicate poverty without conflict with the local biodiversity (UNEP, 2012a). Under the proposed Paradise Cities, a blue and green economy will achieve a state of equilibrium through the implementation of IR and UIIPs to ensure that the environment can be used sustainably for the benefit of current and future generations. It is envisaged that programs and related projects will be implemented with low carbon emissions and be characterized by resource efficiency, social inclusiveness, and the ability of aesthetic leaders to support the reduction of pollution and waste, the prevention of biodiversity degradation, and the restoration of ecosystems in the beautiful landscape of the Cape provinces (UNEP, 2011b:548).

The individual elements of a Paradise City as a place of attachment, belonging, combined heritage, history, culture, craft, healing, emotional reflection and spiritual retreat are many, and it may take years before such cities are graphically designed in Mother Africa. In the case of the Cape provinces as a Home of Legends, they make up beautiful and coherent landscapes, including prominent or eye-catching features such as Coffee Bay, Ixhorha (Hole in the Wall), Mvezo, George, Hessequa, Cape Town's famous District Six area, the AbaThembu Kingdom valleys and villages, the Bhukazana, Nkonkobe and Table Mountains, the hills, savannahs, wild olive trees (iminquma), the Katberg, the Kat River Dam, Amatola Mountains, large ports, beautiful game reserves, natural caves and parks, rivers and related catchment management areas, forts, academic buildings, and the Thwathwa Road as a link between households and their immediate environment.

One's local environment is a form of identity for members of imbumba yamanyama. According to Swartz (2010:59-60), identity is primary among African people. It is through one's identity that one knows one's lineage, spanning from one generation to the next. One's lineage is important and is recognized at public gatherings and ceremonies. When people meet each other for the first time, for example, in AmaXhosa or AmaNguni communities, they are inclined to inquire about each other's identities by directly asking: 'Ungumni?' or 'Zithuthe?' – that is, 'Declare who you are'. A person's identity gives clues as to patterns of being and therefore the type of behavior that is likely to flow from him or her (Swartz, 2010:60). Additionally, people identify themselves by stating their place or association, as well as where they come from, such as their clan or kingdom.

The Ntsikana Paradise City is a landscape that is characterized by various environmental descriptions and patterns resulting from particular combinations of natural (physical and biological) and cultural (land use) factors, and how people perceive these features as part of the combined global heritage site. On the basis of Ntsikana's Gospel Hymn and prophecy, the most common terms to describe smart cities (or Paradise Cities, or blue and green cities) is the Home of Legends, for a Paradise City includes coherence, variety, diversity, balance, harmony, symmetry, stability, beauty and integrity. From the graphic design of the Ntsikana Paradise City in Figure 1.2, it is clear that the visual dimension of the landscape is a reflection of the way in which these concepts create repetitive groupings and interact so as to create areas that have a specific visual identity and beauty in both inland and coastal areas of the Cape provinces.

The process of landscape character assessment can increase appreciation of what makes the landscape distinctive, and what is important about the Cape provinces as a Home of Legends and as part of a global heritage site recognised by the National Heritage Council (NHC) and the United Nations Educational, Scientific and Cultural Organization (UNESCO), as well as a potential blue and green economy by the United Nations Environment Programme (UNEP). Some critical aspects of the landscape in which to build Paradise City models using modern and aesthetic values are that one should:

- Develop and implement environmentally friendly policies for purposes of sustainability;
- Design a value management guideline and tool to facilitate an ecological approach and aesthetic relational values between human and environmental needs;
- Develop the role of forestry and the planting of trees as part of adaptive capacity to climate change and related consequences;
- Incorporate contextual considerations in the planning and development of Paradise Cities, taking into account rural and urban dimensions and related settings;

- Empower citizens and leaders in respect of aesthetic landscapes and aesthetic management of cities to fulfill the needs of current and future generations; and
- Encourage research and development relating to aesthetic sustainability of the landscape or Paradise Cities. This will lead to aesthetic management and governance of the city where primary production, secondary industries, and tertiary sectors drive blue and green economic models. There is, therefore, an urgent need for a nation-building program on agrarian reform policy that goes beyond distributing land to restructuring production and markets. If land reform is to address poverty concerns in African states, agrarian reforms will require moving towards a mixed farming sector with growing smallholder landholding, supported by twinning arrangements, exchange programs and private sector investment models guided by development finance institutions and regional economic structures.

Although Ntsikana kaGabha was highly respected and greatly loved by many within and outside the era of the frontier wars, he was and is regarded as a 'sell-out' by others. It can be deduced that Ntsikana kaGabha's greatness can be measured by the relevance of his vision and a prophetic message from the 1800s to 2063. His selection of words and messages show inter-generational relevance and a sustained legacy in contemporary contexts, realities, and facts in Mother Africa. He articulated a need for unity in diversity and socio-economic reconciliation to counter social Darwinism using the Word and faith in God in Heaven. When Ntsikana kaGabha died, the nation mourned his death and they did not eat (walila umzi akwatyiwa, xa shashiywa nguNtsikana, Amathambo ento kaGabha alele apho) (Ezekiel 1:28; Ezekiel 2:1-3). This song reminds us that loss is a tragic yet inevitable part of the human experience. When it strikes it leaves despair and misery in its path. Loss can eat away at the very heart and soul of a human being. It leaves a gnawing pain that nothing can heal. It leaves an open wound that tries to heal and yet is re-opened repeatedly by memories and regret.

In Maya Angelou's poem 'When great trees fall', the speaker identifies with all who have felt the deep searing pain of losing someone close to them, like Ntsikana. The speaker is able not only to effectively identify with the feeling of deep loss and anguish, but is also able to offer hope for healing through her powerful words. In the case of Ntsikana, there is a reference to the 'bones of Ntsikana' that referred to life after death and the Christian doctrine of resurrection, as revealed to Ntsikana in 1790. Ezekiel's prophetic vision epitomizes Ntsikana as well when he said:

> *Thus saith the Lord God unto these bones: Behold, I will cause breath to enter into you, and ye shall live ... Also, He said to me, 'Prophesy to the breath, prophesy, son of man, and say to the breath, "Thus says the Lord God: 'Come from the four winds, O breath, and breathe on this*

slain, that they may live'" ... So I prophesied as He commanded me, and breath came into them, and they lived ... and stood upon their feet, an exceedingly great army ... Then He said to me, 'Son of man, these bones are the whole house of Israel' ... Thus says the Lord God: 'Behold, O My people, I will open your graves and cause you to come up from your graves, and bring you into the land of Israel. Then you shall know that I am the Lord ... I will put My [Holy] Spirit in you, and you shall live.' (Ezekiel 37:5-14)

It is significant that physical human beings cannot live without drawing breath – the essence of our fleshly life. Even excellent swimmers, experts at holding their breath, cannot survive long without breathing air. Even if life without Ntsikana kaGabha will never be the same again, and even if there will always be pain and sadness due to colonialism, there is hope for healing and joy in the midst of great loss because of faith and resurrection, as symbolized by the 'bones of Ntsikana'. The 'bones of Ntsikana' symbolize the restoration of the African clans and kingdoms from any form of colonialism and oppression, including greediness and corruption, if they have accepted God in Heaven. Through faith (imagination of unity in diversity or zenibe yimbumba yamanyama), the house of Israel will be saved. These called-out ones, true Christians, will be resurrected to receive everlasting life when Christ returns (1 Corinthians 15:50-54; 1 Thessalonians 4:13-18; Philippians 3:20-21). As God is the Creator of all flesh, Africans will be saved (Jeremiah 32:27) and the righteous will live (Ezekiel 18:32).

It is clear that the bones used in the vision of Ezekiel symbolize the creation of man, as God breathed life into Adam (Genesis 2:7). Ezekiel obeyed, the bones came together, flesh developed, skin covered the flesh, breath entered the bodies, and they stood up in a vast army. This vision symbolized the whole house of Israel that was then in captivity. Like unburied skeletons, the people were in a state of living death, pining away with no end to their judgment in sight. They thought their hope was gone and that they were cut off forever. The surviving Israelites felt that their national hopes had been dashed and that the nation had died in the flames of Babylon's attack with no hope of resurrection. The reviving of the dry bones signified God's plan for Israel's future national restoration. The vision also, and most importantly, showed that Israel's new life depended on God's power and not on the circumstances of the people. Putting 'breath' by God's Spirit into the bones showed that God would not only restore them physically, but also spiritually. The Israelites residing in the Holy Land today are not the fulfillment of this prophecy. It will be fulfilled when God re-gathers believing Israelites to the land (Jeremiah 31:33; 33:14-16) and Christ returns to establish His Millennial Kingdom (Matthew 24:30-31). We can have faith in our God in Heaven as Ntsikana kaGabha was sent by Him to urge us to follow justice, righteousness and the fear of God in our daily business as managers, experts, practitioners, and leaders.

2.5 Leading beautifully and aesthetically through a nation-building plan

Look deep into nature, and then you will understand everything better.

– Albert Einstein

The United Nations Environment Programme (UNEP) created the concept of a green economy. The concept of a blue economy, which relates to marine resources, has emerged as a way of conceptualizing and operationalizing the potential opportunities arising from the current global economic and sustainable development challenges. Like a blue economy, a green economy refers to a type of economy that seeks to improve human wellbeing and social equity while protecting the environment and contributing to sustainable development. In the green economy, agribusinesses and agriculture using twenty-first century technology models are seen as key drivers for socio-economic growth and the eradication of poverty (CSIR, 2014:i).

The United Nations Educational, Scientific and Cultural Organization (UNESCO) and UNEP have stressed the importance of seizing opportunities provided by growth and development solutions that embrace the green economy and the need to articulate conditions that will encourage greater public and private investment in both blue and green opportunities. The main areas targeted by the green stimulus packages are infrastructure in railways and electricity grids, water and waste, energy efficiency, renewable energies, and low-carbon vehicles. In this context, the transition to a blue and green economy in Africa requires supportive enabling environments and aesthetic, inspiring servant leaders who can promote investment, entrepreneurship, development and innovation, in partnership with the organs of civil society, using public-private partnership (PPP) models as far as possible, to eradicate abject poverty, chronic unemployment and increased inequality (UNEP, 2011b:42; Matthew 20:27-28). Therefore, in this book, 'blue' refers to the sea and coastal areas and 'green' to agriculture and land programs, and projects aimed at encouraging the building of sustainable livelihoods without compromising the needs of future generations.

Furthermore, aesthetic relational values are foundational principles for beautiful blue and green city models, which should support a country's nation-building plan. To understand the concept of nation-building and the related plan, one needs to have some definition of what a nation is. A nation refers to a large body of people united by common descent, history, heritage, culture and language, inhabiting a particular state or territory or kingdom. The people of a nation generally share a common national identity, and part of nation-building is the building of that common identity and culture using the landscape. The concepts 'nation' and 'Nation-Building' are defined in more detail in Chapter 6.

Some distinguish between an ethnic nation, based on (the social construction of) race or ethnicity, and a civic nation, based on a common identity and loyalty to a set of political ideas and institutions and the linkage of citizenship to nationality. Today the word *nation* is often used synonymously with the *state*, as in the United Nations. In some cases, the term *state* is more properly used to define the governmental apparatus by which a nation rules itself through a public administration and management system. The term *nation-building* is often used interchangeably with state building, democratization, modernization, political development, post-conflict reconstruction, economic development and growth path frameworks, the balance between human needs and aesthetic relational values, peacebuilding, and living in harmony with the environment. Through the process of globalization of national states and advanced technology in terms of communication networks, business links, and collaboration between countries and regional economic powerhouses, we have a global spiritual, cultural, aesthetic and social culture.

2.6 Difference between moral and aesthetic leaders

> *Good character is not formed in a week or a month. It is created little by little, day by day. Protracted and patient effort is needed to develop good character.*
>
> – Heraclitus, Greek philosopher

It is necessary to explain the difference between moral values and aesthetic relational values. In academic literature, aesthetic leaders have both a spiritual and moral duty to motivate followers, citizens, managers and officials to restore aesthetic relational values and harmony with the environment. These physical, emotional, spiritual, moral, social, economic, mental and political convictions and internal motivations must be based on care and compassion, as demonstrated by Ntsikana kaGabha in the early 1800s. Moral values are limited to the ability of an individual in an organization to practise adherence to the law or to be a law-abiding citizen in his or her daily business and activities. Moral values are about the principles and practices of right and wrong in behavior based on law or doctrine. Moral values are therefore an important, if not the most important, part of our judgment as to whether a matter has aesthetic relational values.

Robert Greenleaf's book *Servant leadership* (1977) provides more insights into ethical leadership than aesthetic leadership. Accordingly, ethical leadership is about ethical responsibilities to citizens and followers, primary and secondary stakeholders, and society (Van Wart, 2011; Matthew 20:27-28; Matthew 4:19). Ethical leadership, as derived from Ubuntu principles and the Constitution of South Africa as the supreme law, builds on socio-economic, cultural, ecological, environmental and political factors, whereby leaders are expected to manifest behavior, actions, and codes of conduct that exemplify caring, respect, honesty, trust, accountability, loyalty, fairness, integrity and responsible citizenship (Dinh et al., 2014; Lu & Guy, 2014). It is often argued that ethical leaders advocate and promote these values in organizations and institutions in order to set their organizations' moral and ethical compass through personal and organizational processes and systems (see *Through the eye of the needle*, ANC, 2001).

Aesthetic relational values are beliefs used to make judgments and decisions to alter outdated social and cultural practices and unjust public administration systems, by empowering or inspiring others to do something. In other words, aesthetic relational values are values that encourage leaders to make personal commitments to their beliefs so that they will sacrifice themselves for their beliefs and be prepared to die for them. For instance, Ntsikana was more focused on inspiring people about the existence of an aesthetic reality, where there is salvation and peace between the colonizers and the colonized, as well as black and white people, as hoped for in a just and democratic South Africa. He then undertook actions to influence people to accept this aesthetic reality towards the vision of a democratic South Africa, in the early 1800s.

Aesthetic leadership, as deduced from Ntsikana kaGabha, highlights a leader who is self-aware, projects a positive vision in a balanced manner, and is guided in the process by moral, ethical and aesthetic values, norms and standards, beyond the thinking capability and capacity of an ordinary person or leader. Related to this, as a visionary and prophetic leader, Ntsikana kaGabha's reflection on his immediate environment and circumstances embraced the notion that a leader embodies a shared vision, practises altruistic love, chooses hope over fear, instills faith under difficult circumstances and, in testing scenarios, shows perseverance in attaining goals, and conveys a vision that is deeply and personally motivating to citizens and followers. This develops a nurturing struggle and cultural identity founded on agape love, care, appreciation, and unconditional support for fellow citizens. Through these aesthetic leadership qualities and traits, Ntsikana kaGabha was able to inspire in his people a sense of dignity, pride, history, culture, and belonging, to God and to the African nation.

Through his inspiration, people of the Home of Legends were organized, faced challenges and problems imposed on them by imperialism and colonialism, and were empowered through Imbumba yamaNyama to challenge inhuman public administration and management systems in later years, such as the Bantu Authorities Act of 1951, which led to the formation of ten ethnic reserves or homelands. Besides being a prophet, Ntsikana kaGabha appears to have been one of the few aesthetic and visionary leaders. The latter is owing to the fact that visionary leaders inspire followers, articulate a compelling vision of 'zenibe yimbumba yamanyama', build pride among followers, and bring out the best in people or get them to pull together, or 'harambee' in the Swahili language. Through this, churches were established and traditional leaders were provided with lofty advice without any reported contradictions.[22] Lovedale Press reports that *Imibengo* and *Imvo ZabaNtsundu* indicated that Ntsikana made his followers excited about God's work, which motivated them as they were guided and led to a vision of 'zenibe yimbumba yamanyama'. From the early foundational principles and inspiring leadership on the part of African intellectuals like Ntsikana kaGabha, it is correct to deduce that 'If you want to be a leader … you must understand yourself first' (Senge et al., 2004:180).

'Zenibe yimbumba yamanyama', or striving for unity in diversity – from the nineteenth century to the National Development Plan 2030 vision in South Africa, Namibia and Kenya, and to the African Union Agenda 2063 – has transcended space, time and culture. In this context, zenibe yimbumba yamanyama means to *know thyself* to aesthetic leaders. It refers to oneness in the varieties of societal matters and country dynamics. Unity in diversity focuses on the existence of unity even after numerous wars and conflicts, and in the face of cultural, social, physical, linguistic, religious, political, ideological and psychological differences, and points towards a more complex unity based on understanding that differences enrich human interactions and coexistence. Theologically, 'love your God with your heart, mind, and soul' and 'love your neighbor as yourself' mean treating others in the same way you want to be treated. Aesthetic values and ethics, combined with emotional intelligence, made Ntsikana kaGabha a unique and distinct visionary leader.

2.7 A need for aesthetic leaders to build social cohesion

Ntsikana kaGabha's vision and his plan of action provided a solid foundation and platform for black cohesion. Black cohesion implies that all black people were committed to working together to achieve the strategic goal of unity in diversity. This social cohesion refers to aesthetic relational values in planning and development by clans and kingdoms, or the bond of Imbumba yamaNyama, which manifested itself on intrapersonal, intragroup and interpersonal levels as follows:

- **Intra**personal cohesion is reflected in members' sense of belonging, acceptance, commitment and loyalty to the Imbumba yamaNyama vision and mission statement beyond the nineteenth century;
- **Intra**group cohesion is reflected in the attractiveness of Imbumba yamaNyama to local and global citizens, as well as the mutual liking, trust, support, caring and commitment to working for Ingqungquthela yabantu (Congress of the People) until the vision and mission statement is achieved; and
- **Inter**personal cohesion focuses on positive and engaging interpersonal exchanges between Imbumba yamaNyama members and other associations or unions guided by the Ubuntu paradigm and 'Nkosi sikelela iAfrika' (Lord Bless Africa) by Enoch Sontonga (1897), which was adopted as the national and pan-African liberation anthem in Zambia, Tanzania, Namibia, Zimbabwe and South Africa.

When one views Ntsikana kaGabha as a strategist, his roadmap and plan of action take into account the social cohesion levels mentioned above, guided by five stages of Imbumba yamaNyama development:

- **Forming**: members address dependency and inclusion needs and expectations whereby the structure or hierarchy is developed using an inclusive approach;
- **Storming**: members are competing for positions, roles and responsibilities, and portfolios agreed upon with executive management, or the queen or king in the case of House of Traditional Leaders;
- **Norming**: members establish a structure of the royal kingdom or representative of the royal kingdom. At this stage, members give feedback, and acknowledge the contributions of all the parties involved;
- **Performing**: members are concerned about task accomplishment using mega water nexuses conceptualized as WEALTH creation; and
- **Adjourning**: short-, medium- and long-term tasks, assignments, and projects are now terminated. While the work is slowing down, it is significant that members acknowledge individual and group contributions and achievements because of the zeal of the people and the championing of democratic freedom by activists. It was in this context that the foundational principles and values of Imbumba yamaNyama were incorporated into liberation movements in Africa.

It appears that aesthetic relational values mean that leaders such as Ntsikana kaGabha, James James Ranisi (affectionately known as JJR) Jolobe, Samuel Edward Krune (affectionately known as SEK) Mqhayi, John Tengo Jabavu, Thomas Mapikela, Mpilo Benson Walter Rubusana, John Langalibalele Dube, Saul Msane, Sol Plaatje, Pixley ka Isaka Seme, Duma Nokwe, Albert Luthuli, Steve Biko, Robert Sobukwe, Potlako Leballo, John Nyathi Pokela, Walter Sisulu, Oliver Tambo, Lillian Ngoyi, Helen Joseph, Dorothy Nyembe, Sophie du Bruyn, Ray Alexander, Francis Baard, Rahima Moosa, Charlotte Maxeke, Winnie Madikizela-Mandela, Albertina Sisulu, Nontsikelelo Biko, Raymond Mhlaba, Chris Hani, Nelson Mandela, Steve Tshwete, Thabo Mbeki, Mosibudi Mangena, Thenjiwe Mtintso, Peter Mokaba and others experienced an exceptional state of mind that was qualitatively different from that taught in *normal* everyday business programs or schedules. In this mental state, these aesthetic leaders were fascinated by a world or national vision whereby racism is replaced by non-racialism, sexism is replaced by non-sexism, and inhuman public administration and management systems are replaced by democracy for the people by the people.

It can be deduced that aesthetic relational values include a winning combination of a strong appetitive (or wish) tendency associated with the experience of natural treasures and environmental aesthetic beauty and a certain intrinsic *liberating* tendency associated with exceptional states of mind by aesthetic leaders (Swartz, 2010:86-7). For instance, Ntsikana's personal experience as captured in his Gospel Hymn and the prophetic message may lead to self-discovery and self-understanding of our individual roles and responsibilities to restore and maintain our beauty using integrated rural and urban infrastructure investment programs (IR and UIIPs) as part of a nation-building plan. In our own era, Ntsikana kaGabha's Gospel Hymn has been supported by Kaschula (1993:vii) when he argued that:

> *The future of African oral literature [or the Gospel Hymn of Ntsikana kaGabha] lies, therefore, in comparative interdisciplinary approaches which enable the study [of a context, space, landscape, heritage site or Paradise City] to come alive and take its rightful place in scholarly circles worldwide.*

To elaborate further, it is critical to analyse Ntsikana kaGabha's interdisciplinary approach in the Gospel Hymn, as it is a combination of literature, socio-economic realities of the nineteenth century, history, music with traditional rhymes, medicine to those who face famine (Isaiah 64:11) and land dispossession, spiritual advancement for the poor, the blind and slaves, and advancement of the individual emotional intelligence of people to help them overcome the scars of imperialism and colonialism. In his Gospel Hymn, Ntsikana kaGabha, using his imagination (zenibe yimbumba yamanyama dream, vision, and mission statement), explicitly elaborated on the need for social cohesion rooted in the Ubuntu paradigm. As an organic intellectual, poet, orator, visionary leader of oppressed black people, Oracle, spiritual leader and prophet, he was able to comprehend the past, the present and the ideal future.

Ntsikana kaGabha, as one of the greatest African orators of all time, advocated unity in diversity among people in the early 1800s while white settlers and colonialists were exploiting clan and tribal differences through divisive campaigns. At the same time his gospel message, rooted in Christian values, was accepted by the black middle class, composed of missionaries, priests, teachers and clerks, in the early 1880s, out of which black associations were formed, such as the embryos of trade unions and African educational associations. Also formed at this time was the general political organisation known as Imbumba yamaNyama as direct forerunner of the South African Native Congress (SANC, 1898), and the South African Native National Congress (SANNC) launched on 8 January 1912 by John Langalibalele Dube in Mangaung, which later became known as the African National Congress (ANC).

It can be argued that from the formation of Imbumba yamaNyama in 1882 onwards, the unity in diversity of all black people continued steadily. Imbumba yamaNyama members included Simon P Sihlali, SN Mvambo, Mesach Pelem and Paul Xiniwe, to mention but a few. From the first black political organization, Imbumba yamaNyama, the Reverend Isaac Williams Citashe (Wauchope) led Ingqungquthela yabantu. Reverend Citashe's writings had a socio-economic and political influence on Dr. Mpilo Walter Benson Rubusana, leading to his collection of poems, *Zemk' iinkomo magwala ndini!*. In June 1914, a SANNC delegation that consisted of Thomas Mapikela, Dr. Rubusana, John Langalibalele Dube, Saul Msane and Sol Plaatje went to England. The delegates demanded that the British prime minister acknowledge the founding principles of the SANNC as the true democratic representation of the African people, established by Pixley ka Isaka Seme, the second South African black attorney, founder, and president of the ANC. The first black advocate in South Africa, Philemon Pearce Dumasile (Duma) Nokwe, was secretary-general of the ANC from 1958 to 1969. Advocate Nokwe was inspired by the first South African black attorney, Alfred Mangena (1879-1924), who had returned from England in 1909. Attorney Alfred Mangena (senior treasurer of the ANC) defended black Africans against Europeans in courts, presented a petition to the British government on behalf of those who faced trials after the 1906 Mbambatha rebellion, and laid charges against the Natal Governor for illegally declaring a state of emergency. Upon Pixley kaSeme's return from England in 1911, he and Alfred Mangena worked together to defend their people in the law courts. This partnership of attorneys was adopted by the African National Congress Youth League (ANCYL) leaders along with the law partnership in southern Johannesburg of two iconic freedom fighters, Nelson Mandela and Oliver Reginald Tambo, who had established one of the first black-owned and -operated firms.

Unfortunately, Ntsikana kaGabha died in 1821 without seeing the establishment of Imbumba yamaNyama (1882), the SANNC (1912) and the All-African Convention (AAC) (by Davidson Don Tengo Jabavu in 1935). He could not witness the formation and establishment of Imbumba Yolutsha (ANCYL in the 1940s) led by leaders such as Dr. Alfred Bathini Xuma, Anton Muziwakhe Lembede (first president of the ANCYL), Attorney Nelson Rolihlahla Mandela, Attorney Oliver Reginald Kaizana Tambo, and others, and Ugxhalaba libanzi (United Democratic Front or UDF of the early 1980s), Imbumba yamazwe wase-Afrika (Organisation of African Unity (OAU) established on 25 May 1963 in Addis Ababa, now the African Union (AU) established on 26 May 2001 in Addis Ababa), the BRICS partnership between Brazil, Russia, India, China and South Africa (a powerful economic bloc in which South Africa was included in 2010), the New United States-Africa Partnership on Trade and Development established by former President Barack Hussein Obama, and more recently the new United Kingdom-Africa partnership announced by the UK Prime Minister Theresa May. The aforementioned organizations exhibited Ntsikana kaGabha's socio-economic, cultural, spiritual, emotional, ecological, environmental, political and philosophical influence to shape a state of equilibrium in Africa and various Paradise City models (Sirayi, 1985:190-195; Karis & Carter, 1973:102-107).

JJR Jolobe further championed Ntsikana kaGabha's notion of Imbumba yamaNyama in his poems. These poems were not included in his anthology, but were published in the *Umteteleli* and *Umthunywa* newspapers in 1952. Professor JJR Jolobe's poems, such as 'Osemboniselweni', 'Abakhululi belizwe' and 'Izwi-laBantu' guided ANCYL and UDF leaders in the 1940s and early 1980s respectively. 'Abakhululi besizwe' reads as follows:

Abakhululi besizwe

Ndalama umfo ezolile
Ondele kumwonyo wekamva,
Ethe cwaka ethungw'umlomo,
Izandla zibotshwe ngobhedu,
Imbonakal'isoyikeka
Ziimpawu zokutshutshiseka,
Uvuyo luvangwe nosizi,
Uxolo luxutywe nentlungu,
Idin' elithozamileyo

Ukuvul' amaty' entliziyo,
Ukuhluphez'otyhafileyo.
Inyembezi sezisuliwe,
Umlomo ukhululekile,
Eqhawulwe namakhamandela
Ijonge kumxokelelwano
Ubomvu ligazi lotyabuko.
Yathi ngelizwi lenzukiso,
'Intyatyambo yenkululeko
Inkcenkceshelwe ngomgudu
Negazi nokubandezelwa
Kwabanjengawe gorhandini!'

This poem, written in the early 1940s to inspire Imbumba Yolutsha (ANCYL) leaders, can be loosely translated as follows:

The ones who will set the nation free

I saw a quiet gentleman
Looking into the deep future,
Being quiet,
His mouth closed,

Hands tied with gold.
He had a fearful outlook,
Signs of oppression,
Happiness mixed with sorrow,
Peace mixed with pain.
A sacrifice that is yielding
To open the rocks of the heart,
To encourage the one who has lost hope.
I saw in the dark background
A healthy young man standing,
Smiling without any fear,
Tears wiped away,
The mouth granted freedom,
The shackles were broken.

Looking at the chain
Which was red with the blood from the scourging,
He said with a voice of exultation,
'The flower of freedom
Has been watered by the efforts,
Struggles, the blood, and the suffering of
persons such as you, courageous one!'

Drawing on the vision of Ntsikana kaGabha, Jolobe saw the ANC Youth League as potential champions to bring democratic freedom, whereby the impact or effects of nine frontier wars would be broken by the unity and sacrifice of the youth. As the youth saw and appreciated the contribution of founding members of Imbumba yamaNyama in 1882 and the SANNC (later known as the ANC) in 1912, they argued that the colonial and apartheid machinery, atrocities, brutal killings of innocent people, and inhuman laws undermined the non-violent tactics and strategy of the ANC.

The notion of Imbumba yamaNyama to alter the chain of oppression had a huge influence on cadres and struggle icons such as Margaret Mcingana, Miriam Makeba (affectionately known as Mama Africa), Vuyisile Mini with his 'Ndodemnyama we Verwoerd' (or 'Watch out, Verwoerd'), Hugh Masekela, Abdullah Ibrahim, Johnny Clegg, Peter Gabriel, Brenda Fassie (affectionately known as MaBrrr, or Queen of Africa), and so forth. GV Mona (2015:69) argues that these subsequent generations of South African activists who were involved in the struggle for liberation used JJR Jolobe's poems. Accordingly, in a song she composed, Miriam Makeba, one of the greatest artists who dedicated their lives to the struggle, sang 'Ndinomqokoz' obomvu, ndawuphiwa ngubawo' (I have this red chain which I inherited from my father). Makeba's red chain symbolizes oppression by the imperial, colonial and apartheid ideologies. Mona maintains that Jolobe's red chain motif, which is in a fixed text, re-emerges in an oral form in the indigenous song of Makeba. Before going to the gallows in 1979, Solomon Kalushi Mahlangu, the young Umkhonto weSizwe (MK) member of the ANC freedom fighters who was executed by the apartheid regime, said:

> Xelela abantu ukuba 'ndiyabathanda
> Mabaqhube nomzabalo wenkululeko
> Igazi lam linkcenkceshele njengomthi okanye iintyatyambo
> ezakukhupha iziqhamo zenkululeko. Bakuqhutyelwe phambili
> singajika maAfrika akantu!

> Tell my people that I love them and that they must continue the fight.
> My blood will nourish the tree that will bear the fruits of freedom,
> Aluta continua!

Mona (2015:66-67) argues that Jolobe's 'flower of freedom … watered by … the blood and suffering' re-emerges in Mahlangu's political oratory. Similarly, Robert Sobukwe, the first president of the Pan Africanist Congress (PAC) and one of the great orators, quoted JJR Jolobe in his speech to the Basutoland Congress Party in 1957 when he said:

> Apho igazi lenu lithe lathontsela khona,
> Komila intyatyambo evumba limnandi,
> Eliya kuthwalwa ngamaphiko empepho,
> Zithi zonk'izizwe zilirogole.

This is loosely translated to mean:

> Wherever your blood has dropped
> Will blossom a flower of exceeding sweetness,
> Whose scent the wings of the air will carry on
> And all the nations will inhale it.

The struggle icons of the 1940s maintained that 'the divine destiny of the African people is national freedom' (Mona, 2015:70; Colossians 1:10; John 13:13-14). It was argued that as a result of educational and industrial color bars, young African men and women were converted into juvenile delinquents, and the negative consequences of the frontier wars, complemented by the Nongqawuse story of the killing of livestock, were still being experienced. Consequently, the youth's vision, influenced by the zenibe yimbumba yamanyama of the elders, made it clear that the call for a national revolution was a 'panacea' for all the ills of imperialism and colonialism.

In his poem 'Imbumba Yolutsha' (The Youth League), Jolobe notes that the youth's vision is for freedom 'exactly in our time' (kanye ngexesha lethu). The closing line of the second stanza is the closing line of the policy document that was presented as the motto of the ANCYL, i.e. the phrase 'Freedom in our lifetime'. At the 53rd National Conference of the ANC (2012) in Mangaung in the Free State, a motto similar to that of the ANCYL was adopted, i.e. 'Economic Freedom in our lifetime,' with an emphasis on radical economic freedom or transformation in order to fundamentally change and restructure Africa's economy by focusing on reindustrialization, manufacturing, and local beneficiation. This theme was used by presidential candidates of the ANC at the 54th National Conference of the ANC held at Nasrec, south of Johannesburg, and was adopted as one of the key resolutions for the ANC Manifesto for the 2019 national elections, representing the ultimate rebirth and renewal of the ANC. The ANC's 5th National Policy Conference, held from 30 June to 5 July 2017 at the Gallagher Convention Centre, Midrand, was organized under the theme 'The year of Oliver Reginald Tambo: Let us deepen unity'. The Economic Transformation Discussion Document that emanated from this conference focused on employment creation, economic growth and structural change in order to strengthen the program of radical economic transformation.

This recurring motto demonstrates the interface between the written text and the socio-political oratory of the generation that followed Jolobe's. It is against this background that Jolobe's poem is interpreted as a contribution to the Africanist discourse of the late 1940s. Jolobe's motif of a freedom that is watered with the blood of martyrs re-emerged in the oratory, the art of speech and persuasion, of political activists of the next generation of Youth Leaguers, such as Nelson Mandela, Walter Sisulu, Oliver Tambo, Anton Lembede, Robert Sobukwe, and later the likes of Steve Biko, Chris Hani, Thabo Mbeki and Peter Mokaba (first ANCYL president after the unbanning of liberation movements, namely the ANC, the PAC and AZAPO, to mention but a few). The poems also demonstrate how Jolobe's fixed poetry text gave birth to oral forms that accelerated the Africanist discourse to restore lost dignity under apartheid public administration and management systems. As British governors and apartheid administrators censored freedom of expression, it is possible to argue that Jolobe's poem was not published in the early 1940s because it was able to mobilize activists, cadres and revolutionaries. JJR Jolobe's poems were probably distributed underground, as the apartheid administrators sought to ensure that ANCYL and ANC leaders were deprived of this poet's rich cultural heritage. Though excluded from his anthology, his political poems referred to above were published in newspapers in 1952, whereafter revolutionaries and cadres of the struggle were able to rehearse the poems with ethnomusicologists and students of oratory (Saunders, 1970:8).

The adopted mottos and conference resolutions call for a deep, complicated progression of mental development, reflection and affirmation of our natural beauty for the benefit of citizens through IR and UIIP designs in our landscapes. As South Africa is a water-stressed country, the use of blue economy models prompts us to protect and conserve our water resources, such as the Katberg Dam, and related green spaces, such as Citrus in Seymour. Inductively, the aesthetic relational values in response to our fragile world, limited natural resources, and the need to eradicate poverty, guide us towards developing a nation-building plan to co-nurture, co-create and co-develop green and blue cities in both Mvezo and Thwathwa in partnership with the National Heritage Council, the South African Heritage Resources Agency (SAHRA), UNEP and UNESCO, to name only a few.

Once again, inductively, Africa does not need politicians and managers, but rather aesthetic leaders like Abraham Lincoln, Ntsikana kaGabha, Nxele kaMakhanda, Martin Luther King Jr, Steve Biko, Robert Sobukwe, OR Tambo, Nelson Mandela and Mahatma Gandhi, who would also address the so-called silent matters in the global scenario. Africa is currently experiencing challenges of leadership and integrity, human and food security, water governance, environmental conservation, climate change, and infrastructure, among others. Therefore, aesthetic leaders are required, bearing in mind the following:

> *The ultimate measure of a man [and woman] is not where he [or she] stands in the moment of comfort and convenience, but where he [or she] stands at times of challenge and controversy.*
> (Martin Luther King Jr)

In supporting Martin Luther King Jr, the State President of the Republic of South Africa, Cyril Ramaphosa (07 February 2019, SONA) cited Theodore Roosevelt, who served as the 26th president of the United States from 1901 to 1909, on the type of leaders to address complex nationhood challenges in South Africa when he said:

> *It is not the critic who counts; not the man who points out how the strong man stumbles, or where the doer of deeds could have done them better ... The credit belongs to the man who is actually in the arena, whose face is marred by dust and sweat and blood; who strives valiantly; who errs, who comes short again and again, because there is no effort without error and shortcoming; but who does actually strive to do the deeds; who knows great enthusiasms, the great devotions; who spends himself in a worthy cause; who at the best knows in the end the*

triumph of high achievement, and who at the worst, if he fails, at least fails while daring greatly, so that his place shall never be with those cold and timid souls who neither know victory nor defeat.

In *The 21 irrefutable laws of leadership*, John Maxwell sums up his definition of leadership as 'leadership is influence'. This moves beyond the position of defining the leader, to looking at the ability of the leader to influence others – both those who would consider themselves followers and those outside that circle. Leadership is about character and having the values to lead, using a leadership charter and ethical principles in relation to people. According to Maxwell, leadership includes the ability to lead, influence, focus on the plan, navigate an implementation plan and strategy, add value in providing solutions to complex scenarios and circumstances, build trust of followers, earn respect from citizens, apply rationality and objectivity using facts and information management systems, connect to citizens and followers through aesthetic relational values and interpersonal skills and competencies, attract support from all citizens irrespective of their demographic background, creed, colour, race, age and gender, empower citizens with new skills and development approaches of the twenty-first century, be humble and act as a role model, sell the vision of unity in diversity, and mentor and advise.

Warren Bennis's definition of leadership focuses much more on the individual capability of the leader. In the literature on the subject there is an academic difference between management and leadership. Management is about doing things right; leadership is about doing the right things. Management is more about routine delivery, about working within set parameters to carry out known tasks, about minimizing risks, and about delivering efficiency and effectiveness. Leadership is more about delivering change, about going beyond set parameters, about managing risks, and about crossing boundaries in terms of the organizational, personal, group, sociocultural and traditional norms in tackling a challenge and the problems of our fragile environment. The form of leadership that seeks to do the right things right is a function of knowing yourself, having a vision that is well communicated, building trust among colleagues, and taking effective action to realize your own leadership potential.

The new trends in modern globalized institutions mean that the right leadership skills are different from those used conventionally. For example, where leaders seek to work in partnership with other organizations, they will need to do the following:

- Understand and respond to the interests of the other stakeholders;
- Move beyond their comfort zone, where they have authority over managing intergovernmental and institutional relationships that are not under their direct control; and
- Depend more on skills of communication, negotiation, and influence than on direction and control.

The leadership skills and practices used for managing and leading learning organizations or institutions, such as the Imbumba yamaNyama Royal Council (established in 1882), the Kingdom of Khoekhoen, and other African kingdoms, are not in themselves enough. They need to be supplemented by the skills and practices necessary for their global and continental roles and responsibilities. In the context of aesthetic relational values in modern or Paradise Cities, these include the following:

- Leading by example in accordance with the core values of the organization, institution or company;
- Building the trust and confidence of the people with whom they work;
- Continually seeking improvement in their methods and effectiveness;
- Keeping people informed;
- Being accountable for their actions and holding others accountable for their decisions and judgments;
- Involving people, seeking their views, listening actively to what they have to say, and representing these views honestly;
- Being clear on what is expected and providing feedback on progress;
- Showing tolerance of people's differences and dealing with their issues fairly;
- Acknowledging and recognizing people for their contributions, performance, and achievements; and
- Weighing alternatives, considering both short- and long-term effects, and then being resolute in decisions made.

The roles and qualities of aesthetic and visionary leaders include:

- Humaneness based on the Ubuntu paradigm and principles;
- Empathy (i.e. displaying acts of kindness);
- Objectivity and the establishment of trust and rapport with people at all levels of an organization;
- Transparency, a method whereby leaders model the desired behaviors and adopt a position of openness regarding their strengths and weaknesses, in terms of:
    - ✓ Capability
    - ✓ Capacity
    - ✓ Accountability
    - ✓ Responsibility
    - ✓ Honesty
    - ✓ Integrity

- ✓ Assertiveness in reacting to new demands, trends and developments
- ✓ Consistency with regard to a country's constitution in their judgment and decisions

With regard to using blue and green economic models in the Home of Legends, the following leadership behaviors are highly recommended. Some of the behaviors in organizations and Paradise Cities include leaders doing the following:

- Openly admitting mistakes and failures so that they can be rectified;
- Not claiming credit for accomplishments that they were not directly involved in;
- Maintaining the highest ethical standards when dealing with customers, suppliers, vendors, communities or citizens;
- Keeping promises to co-workers, management, and customers, or at least offering an explanation of why promises cannot be kept;
- Not manipulating data or information for personal gain or protection;
- Upholding, protecting and defending a country's constitution as the supreme law at all times.

It is clear that aesthetic and visionary leadership is about the articulation and definition of what has previously remained implicit or unsaid. Aesthetic and visionary leaders invent images, metaphors, and Paradise City models that provide a new focus of attention. By so doing, they consolidate or challenge prevailing knowledge and wisdom so that the structural problems and challenges in the Cape provinces as a Home of Legends, including the deep rural areas, are replaced with Paradise City models and aesthetic relational values in the planning and development of blue and green city models, without compromising the needs of future generations. In short, an essential factor in leadership is the capacity to influence and organize meaning for the members of the organization, whereby hope and virtue factors are incorporated in the integrated rural (IR) and urban infrastructure investment program (UIIP). By adopting aesthetic relational values in the planning and development of blue and green city models, aesthetic or visionary leaders are creating new Paradise City models.

It can be argued that aesthetic and visionary leaders are in the privileged position of being able to facilitate sustainable planning and development in their communities by inspiring and allowing their followers opportunities not only to ask questions, but also raise suggestions pertaining to smarter methods of work. A leader's ability to lead in an innovative manner will naturally encourage the communities and institutions, such as Imbumba yamaNyama and the Kingdom of Khoekhoen, to have a desire for new developments using IR and UIIPs, and blue and green city models. Leaders will thereby create an ongoing curiosity and enthusiasm for the most effective manner of promoting the Cape provinces as a beautiful environment and global tourist destination, an international heritage site with a rich archaeological history, and an attraction for investment in terms of a water-energy-food nexus, including the need for industrialization opportunities.

2.8 Differences between managers, politicians, and leaders

It is significant to highlight the difference between leaders and managers, as set out in Table 2.1, which shows that leaders are expected to lead, and managers are expected to manage, as guided by leaders. Leaders cannot escape the responsibility of tomorrow by evading it today. For instance, the behavior of citizens, officials and managers are triggered by rewards and recognition in the workplace. If workers know that there is something to be gained for them by working hard, they will do their utmost to get the rewards and recognition they deserve. Unlike aesthetic leaders (who are always concerned with a future vision and the aesthetic relational values of a nation), citizens, officials and managers are more focused on personal incentives and personal status in communities and institutions, as depicted in Tables 2.1 and 2.2.

Table 2.1: Difference between managers and aesthetic leaders

MANAGERS	AESTHETIC LEADERS
Administer	Innovate and create
Ask how and when	Ask what and why
Focus on systems	Focus on people
Do things right	Do the right things
Maintain	Develop
Motivate and solve problems	Move people in new directions/have a vision
Produce order	Realize a new vision
Rely on control	Inspire trust
Have a short-term perspective	Have a longer-term perspective
Accept the status quo	Challenge the status quo
Have an eye on the bottom line	Have an eye on the horizon
Imitate	Originate
Emulate the classic good soldier	Are their own person
Maintain systems	Identify systems
Produce stability	Disrupt through change
Get people to do things more efficiently	Get people to agree about what things should be done

Source: Tsibani (2014b)

It appears that many of Africa's aesthetic leaders who are or have been visionary in their approaches, have been inspired by and have taken to heart the lofty advice from Ntsikana kaGabha that colonialists and imperialists would never destroy Imbumba yamaNyama, the original kingdoms of Africa before imperialism, and our beautiful heritage with a solid foundation from God. In this context, aesthetic leaders inspire people and citizens to have faith in their institutional leadership and believe in the vision that they have jointly articulated, leading to practical operational strategies and plans to eradicate poverty, unemployment and inequality. In cases where human error or unintended consequences are identified, these leaders listen and act in a way that promotes fairness, trust, equality and integrity. If we falter and lose our purpose on this earth and decide to ignore Ntsikana kaGabha's Gospel Hymn and our national anthems, we need to take responsibility as individuals and as collective cadres of our heavenly kingdom. With reference to his own country, US President Abraham Lincoln (1861) wisely said in his first inaugural address:

> *This country, with its institutions, belongs to the people who inhabit it. Whenever they shall grow weary of the existing government, they can exercise their constitutional right of amending it or exercise their revolutionary right to dismember or overthrow it.*

As explained, managers are enforcers of law, policies and procedures, and are reactionary in terms of their thinking. But leaders are assertive and diplomatic and are seekers of creativity and innovation through providing a conducive environment (Currie, 2006:14-15). As set out in Table 2.2, aesthetic or true leaders have a direct connection with God, or uQamata (1 Timothy 2: 5-7).

Table 2.2: Difference between managers, politicians and leaders

Managers	Politicians	Aesthetic or true leaders

• Control risks
• React
• Enforce organizational rules
• Seek and then follow the direction
• Coordinate effort
• Seek rewards
• Are motivated by salary increases and appraisal by leaders
• Seek economic and political stability
• Look at saving costs
• Produce orders by planning and budgeting
• Provide progress through internal and external reporting systems and related processes
	• Specialize in false promises
	• Are concerned about goals
	• Are concerned about projects
	• Are concerned about the next elections
	• Are propagandists with no souls
	• Promote party interests at the expense of good governance, accountability, and responsiveness
	• Protect their seats
	• Protect power
	• Compromise to survive
	• Sell their souls to survive
	• Are often less concerned about the change
		• Take risks for the benefit of a country and a nation of God. It is argued that leadership is not about comfort, but about discomfort with our desire for ease and complacency. Some of the discomfort factors include:
		  ✓ Trust in finding solutions by asking the right questions, guided by the long-term vision, mission, and strategy adopted for humanity or socio-economic growth and development.
		  ✓ Pull out one's assumptions by opening up to new truths or listening to members of organizations or the community.
		  ✓ Facilitate, reflect on and explore ideas in order to arrive at practical solutions and answers, using participatory methodologies and techniques.
		  ✓ Allow new creative and innovative thinking, as new complex global challenges cannot be solved by the same ideas and opinions we used to create them (as suggested by Albert Einstein). Rather, new ideas are required for our twenty-first century globalized existence.
		  ✓ Success consists of going from failure to failure without loss of enthusiasm (Winston Churchill).
		  ✓ Are concerned about purpose and vision, and that vision is more important than the leader him/herself. In other words, true leaders value innovation, creativity, and ideapreneurship over popularity.
		• Are concerned about a nation-building plan, have a vision as the source of the constitution and destiny; develop a country according to a nation-building plan for the public good and a better life for all.
		• Seek opportunities to restore aesthetic relational values and good governance.
		• Change organizational rules.
		• Turn servants into followers by setting priorities and planning self-imposed parameters and boundaries for ensuring moral ground rules and role models.
		• Provide something to believe in.
		• Inspire achievement and performance.
		• Provide accurate information and are accountable to citizens. A true leader is always trustworthy, just, loving and compassionate (Munroe, 2014: 144-5).
		• Are always concerned about the growth and sustainable development of citizens and a country's plans.
		• Endeavor to drive a Nation-building plan without compromising current and future generational needs and demands.
		• Sacrifice for the next generation.
		• Believe that a national vision will lead to national discipline, pride and investment.
		• Are concerned about values, priorities, unity and having a clear national vision.

Source: Tsibani (2014a)

It is clear from Tables 2.1 and 2.2 that aesthetic leadership requires a balance of characteristics in various organizations. The four quadrants of leadership proposed by Sugerman, Scullard & Wilhelm (2011:8-9) are applicable to the required aesthetic leadership characteristics. This refers to leadership as having four quadrants, or DISCs, namely:

- Dominance
- Influence
- Steadiness
- Conscientiousness

The DISC leadership model is similar to the Analytical, Conceptual, Emotional and Spiritual framework (ACES)[23] and the Situational Awareness, Presence, Authenticity and Empathy (SPACE) model. The DISC leadership styles are further broken down into eight non-hierarchical and non-sequential leadership dimensions:

- **Pioneering**
  - ✓ Finding opportunities
  - ✓ Stretching the boundaries
  - ✓ Promoting bold action

- **Energising**
  - ✓ Showing enthusiasm
  - ✓ Building professional networks
  - ✓ Rallying people to achieve goals

- **Affirming**
  - ✓ Being approachable
  - ✓ Acknowledging contributions
  - ✓ Creating a positive environment

- **Inclusive**
  - ✓ Staying open to input
  - ✓ Showing diplomacy
  - ✓ Facilitating dialogue

- **Humble**
  - ✓ Maintaining composure
  - ✓ Showing modesty
  - ✓ Being fair-minded

- **Deliberate**
  - ✓ Communicating with clarity
  - ✓ Promoting disciplined analysis
  - ✓ Providing a sense of stability

- **Resolute**
  - ✓ Setting high expectations
  - ✓ Speaking up about problems
  - ✓ Improving methods

- **Commanding**
  - ✓ Showing confidence
  - ✓ Taking charge
  - ✓ Focusing on results

Furthermore, aesthetic leadership qualities in modern Paradise Cities include:

- An effective personality
- The art of inducing compliance
- The ability to influence
- A function of a set of acts or behaviors to ensure return on investment and quality of services
- The ability to persuade
- The power of building relationships
- The ability to achieve goals
- The talent to interact effectively
- A differentiated role
- The initiation of structure to develop a roadmap or sustainable action plan (SAP)

A review of exactly what leadership development is could end here, but the development of ideas about leadership and its significance will be continued. Kouzes and Posner (1995:18) explain leadership by listing ten commitments of leadership:

- To search out challenging opportunities to change, grow, innovate and improve.
- To experiment, take risks and learn from the accompanying mistakes.
- To envision an uplifting and enabling future.
- To enlist others in a common vision by appealing to their values, interests, hopes and dreams.
- To foster collaboration by promoting cooperative goals and building trust.
- To strengthen people by giving power away, providing choice, developing competence, assigning critical tasks and offering visible support.
- To set the example by behaving in ways that are consistent with shared values.
- To achieve small wins that promote consistent progress and build commitment.
- To recognize individual contributions to the success of every project.
- To celebrate team accomplishments regularly.

Kouzes and Posner (1995:9) also believe leaders are at their best when they are able to 'challenge the process, inspire a shared vision, enable others to act, model the way and encourage the heart'. Researchers in leadership have addressed many issues, but a better understanding of youth leadership is what is needed to develop a coherent leadership curriculum for the youth in career planning and technical education.

This assessment can be used to determine aesthetic leadership in modern organizations. There are different leadership methods and styles that coincide with each personality type, which could help leaders to be more effective. DISC has also been used to help determine a course of action when dealing with problems as a leadership team (i.e. taking the various aspects of each personality type into account when solving problems or assigning jobs in the organization). Using such tools is crucial for the success and performance of organizations. They can assist leaders in assessing themselves and the human resources qualities and traits in their organizations so that both the leaders and organizations can continue to improve and grow.

This book attempts to provide flexible leadership models and options to help individuals and their organizations expand their capacity to inspire, energize, support, analyze and direct their aesthetic relational values. I suggest that one should first identify one's leadership strengths, and then expand them to include other dimensions as part of improving one's career path development and the organizational performance thereof. It must be noted that the ACES, CAR (capability, accountability, and responsiveness) and DISC leadership models and related tools are provided to ensure that aesthetic leaders have exceptionally strong convictions about their moral correctness and aesthetic relational beliefs, and are kept passionate about their causes and their leadership styles based on future-oriented visions and performance areas. With regard to organizational growth, leadership competencies and innovation are not optional; they are prerequisites in designing environmentally aesthetic solutions within complex and changing metaphysical environments.

It is also significant that this book is unique, in that it demonstrates the following:

- The importance of an aesthetic leadership role in addressing our fragile world.
- The strategic role of aesthetic relational values to restore our beautiful environment as citizens of the Kingdom of Heaven on earth.
- The institutionalization of innovation, creativity, ideapreneurship, aesthetic relational values and Ubuntu principles in the corporate business of organizations in order to derive benefits and increase production for the public good and sustainable planning and development.
- The importance of environmental aesthetics in current and future planning and development programs. Projects must feed into a nation-building plan in order to inspire, energize, support, analyze and direct Paradise Cities. It is a profound and penetrating book that highlights the need for thorough technical infrastructure assessment, environmental impact assessment, and a combination of historiographical and retrospective research on historical sites and their relevance to environmental aesthetics.

2.9 Conclusion

There is no universal definition of leadership. Aesthetic leadership principles and behaviors that are presented in this chapter can be applied in virtually any landscape, plan and situation – especially in countries trying to advance socio-economic growth and development – to help define their city models or social cohesion. In the context of the global village and the need for a nation-building plan to restore aesthetic relational values in the planning and development of new cities in a rapidly changing environment, this chapter defines differences between managers, politicians and leaders. There is a huge difference between moral and aesthetic leaders, as explained in this chapter, which is written in the context of a nation-building plan.

In the chapters that follow, the realities and the need for aesthetic leaders in Mother Africa, rather than managers and politicians, are outlined. Managers and politicians have not changed the status quo in independent African countries. Accordingly, I call on aesthetic leaders to implement inclusive socio-economic growth in aesthetic Mother Africa, with its rich natural resources and heritage. This can alter the current status quo. Unfortunately, managers and politicians who are unable to build Paradise City models have replaced the founding fathers of African revolutions. In this context, managers and politicians need to be empowered in respect of integrated rural (IR) and urban infrastructure investment programs (UIIPs) using blue and green economic models for them to drive aesthetic relational values in planning and development. Managers and politicians must be empowered to be aesthetic leaders with the help of DISC, ACES, SPACE, PRIDE, CAR and other leadership tools and instruments, so that they can respond appropriately to climate change and various other natural and environmental disasters and cater for the service delivery needs of citizens.

As discussed in this chapter, we need aesthetic leaders to deal with the systemic problems of unemployment, crime, housing shortages, lack of and inaccessibility to health facilities, water scarcity for farming, communities and industrialists, general poor basic services, inaccessible transport systems and infrastructure for trade throughout Africa, and inappropriate education systems offered to the majority of poor youth. A poor education system and systemic unemployment are the main causes of poverty. Abject poverty leads to a range of problems in Mother Africa, including homelessness, trading in slaves, hunger, malnutrition, ill-health and related social pathologies such as one-parent families, child-headed families, drug and alcohol abuse, and child mortality. These social pathologies give rise to socio-economic and political instability and corruption, characterized by a disregard for the lofty advice of Ntsikana kaGabha that 'we must avoid greed for money' and rather seek justice and a Paradise City model where there is harmony between human needs and environmental needs.

The chapter concludes that Africa is the only continent in the world that is rich in natural resources but lacks the aesthetic leaders to drive social cohesion and a nation-building plan using available natural resources and a youthful population to its collective advantage. As an example of what may be witnessed in some mature democratic countries, France proactively responds to twenty-first century technology skills requirements to adapt and adjust to an ever-changing metaphysical environment. In other words, as machines begin to replace human intelligence, French leaders and political and economic advisors consider grooming youthful leadership to run the country for global competitiveness, as opposed to Africa's gerontocracy (government by old people and leaders) and its negative consequences for modernity (see Silke, 2011:205-210).

Chapter 3 explains the motivation for and significance of Paradise City models for social cohesion as part of nation-building between 2020 and 2064.

Chapter 2: Endnotes

21. There is a lot of debate between African elders based on unsubstantiated oral memories that Ntsikana kaGabha had never heard about the early preaching of the missionary Van der Kemp at Ngqika's Great Place, as accounted for in Mostert (1992:462). According to Dyibishe & Mtiki (2014), Ntsikana was an organic intellectual, like his brother Nxele kaMakhanda. Because people learnt histories written by colonial and apartheid administrators and scholars, it is also possible that this misunderstanding would have been informed by racism, as Africans were seen as beasts and ungodly barbarians. From this narrative, Nxele kaMakhanda's early black consciousness thinking was countered with unbelievers' arguments, or the 'Caffers" theoretical framework of the

nineteenth century. With the benefit of historical hindsight, Nxele kaMakhanda (Cirha) was considered too influential and critical of the Fifth Frontier War, and had to be banished to Robben Island. During the height of colonial disturbances, Nxele went to live near Ndlambe, who allowed him to set up his own Great Place. Nxele became concerned with finding a way to overpower the evil that motivated the white colonists to drive his people from their land. Thus, as Peires (1980:101) noted, 'he spent much of his time in the new frontier outpost of Grahamstown, carefully observing the military and technical side of the behemoth', but interested in learning about the colonial regime and its 'magical underpinnings'. He was arrested and banished to Robben Island with some leaders of the Khoisan grouping in the area of Grahamstown. In line with colonial justifications, it was reported that he died trying to escape on 9 August 1820. While we cannot compare his death with many justifications of the deaths of activists like Steve Bantubonke Biko, it can be argued that this escape and drowning of Nxele Cirha Makhanda, who grew up in the Grahamstown and Port Alfred areas, was a fictitious cover-up for his assassination. This argument is based on the fact that he grew up in Grahamstown, which is approximately 57.2 km from the sea. As a young African boy he used to travel by horse or donkey (Jolobe, 1958). He knew about the distance of Robben Island from the mainland, and he knew about sea life and the environment surrounding the coast, just as his brother Ntsikana kaGabha did. As one of the genuine and radical leaders, with similar articulation and reflection as Onkgopotse Tiro, David Webster, Sabelo Phama, Robert Sobukwe, Steve Biko and Chris Hani, to mention but a few, he had a balanced emotional intelligence. It is also difficult to assume that he committed suicide.

22. Ntsikana was able to influence most of the kings, chiefs, commanders, traditional and church leaders. He was, however, aware that although isiXhosa was a common language, people shared different fabrics of meaning and understanding of political principles. Even though he communicated in isiXhosa, there was misunderstanding of the strategies and tactics for fighting enemies and restoring the human dignity of African people. Some of the principles in the daily activities of Ntsikana included representative government, equality before the law, freedom of the people and citizens, and freedom of association and the press in a united non-racial and non-sexist South Africa under a Christian society. John Tengo Jabavu, as a political activist, wrote about these principles, stating that the bill of rights, equal administration of justice, and guarantees of opportunities for all people must be assured for all South Africans and not be limited only to educated black people in the Cape.

CHAPTER 3

3 MOTIVATION FOR A NATION-BUILDING PLAN AND SOCIAL COHESION

3.1 Objectives and outcomes

With the definitions of Paradise City models and a required nation-building plan to reconstruct our history and restore our aesthetic relational values having been explained, this chapter will ensure that the reader is able to:

- Motivate the significance of restoring aesthetic relational values in planning and development and set out the role of aesthetic leaders in championing the Nation-Building Plan;
- Define global problems and challenges which may affect social cohesion and a nation-building plan from an environmental management perspective;
- Provide a theoretical framework required for Mother Africa or the Home of Legends or similar landscapes to adapt to the current changing metaphysical environment and climate change consequences;
- Outline tools to design Paradise Cities and landscapes using examples and case studies; and
- Explain fundamental principles of project management in applying and implementing the Aesthetic Relational Values in Planning and Development Framework (ARVPDF), and the need for SPACE competencies for African visionary or aesthetic leaders.

3.2 African countries need aesthetic nation-building plans (2020-2064)

Africa, as part of the fragile world, is faced with near-insurmountable obstacles, from poor infrastructure investment models and ineffective leadership to poor management of its treasures. This desperate state has led to administrative, social, cultural, spiritual, moral, economic and political weaknesses, characterized by dysfunctional infrastructure systems. One sees this logic in the conclusion of the Brundtland Report:

If large parts of the developing world are to avert economic, social, and environmental catastrophes, it is essential that global economic growth is revitalized. (World Commission on Environment and Development, 1987)

It is made clear in the Brundtland Report that the world faces a challenge: countries need to develop economically. To achieve this aim, countries need to use natural resources economically and, simultaneously, they need to preserve the environment using the blue and green economy approach, which provides related job opportunities, so that future generations can succeed (UNEP, 2011b:548).

During the Southern African Young African Leaders Initiative (YALI) Conference held at the Southern Sun International Hotel in Kempton Park, and hosted by the City of Ekurhuleni Metropolitan Municipality, on 17-19 May 2015, speakers acknowledged the existence of the challenge of economic development, which is greater in sub-Saharan Africa. It was noted by YALI speakers that wars and interstate conflicts have defined the contours of the history of the human race. Revolutions, domestic violence, terrorism, crime, and societal turbulence were some of their key terms. Many of the factors that have been responsible for such violence are common to both interstate and intrastate wars and armed conflict. But national revolutions that have taken on different forms, whatever the reasons, are rooted in a set of factors that can be identified reasonably clearly, and present a great deal of commonality among them, even if these revolutions have been separated by space and time, and spread over centuries. Speakers argued that solutions to global problems would require global cooperation, where investment in the youth and infrastructure can yield more positive results than the purchasing of military equipment in sub-Saharan Africa. According to the speakers, the greatest global challenge that faces the international community today is the current transnational revolution in human affairs, which in turn is triggered by the combination of three revolutions:

- A revolution of rising expectations
- The information and communications revolution
- A broader industrial-technological revolution

In addition to the above challenges, further threats and risks were highlighted. These include:

- The communities and citizens in various African countries do not see the fruits of liberation.
- Poor leadership, a crisis of governance, and collapsed administration systems in most African states lead to uncontrolled migration by the victims.
- African leaders tend to promote tribalism, cronyism and factionalism, leading to civil wars and abject poverty, systemic unemployment of youth and increased inequality among citizens.

- Legitimate demands are hijacked by criminal elements, and politicians and leaders adopt cheap politics without addressing the root causes of civil unrest and violent public protests.
- Intergenerational gaps between the youth and current uninspiring leaders are a ticking time bomb for the next uprising, as witnessed in 1976 in South Africa with the Soweto revolt of senior school children, and in the Arab Spring in countries such as Egypt and Libya.
- Human insecurities lead to instability and political chaos.
- Poor infrastructure, poor visa facilitation, poor networks and the lack of connectivity remain challenges for Africa's potential growth.
- Unlike Europe and other continents, Africa is producing managers and politicians instead of leaders of the caliber of Tambo, Mandela, Hani, Biko, Madikizela-Mandela, Tshwete, Skweyiya and Sisulu, to mention but a few (Mancham, 2015).
- The world has undergone dramatic structural change, yet African governance and public administration and management systems have failed to adapt or change.

To exacerbate matters, there is literature evidence that Africa's population will double by 2050 (from 1.4 to 2.4 billion people). South Africa's population will reach 58.1 million in 2019, an increase of 10.9% from 2012. Research by the Institute for Security Studies (2018), complemented by the World Bank South African Report (2018), paints a different picture and predicts a population of 68.8 million by 2030, with rapidly increasing in-migration of 'environmental refugees' from neighboring countries if the effects of climate change are not addressed urgently through blue and green city models.

Furthermore, it is significant that, according to data from Statistics South Africa (STATS SA) since 1990, the numbers of black youth aged 0-24 have increased by 11%, while those of coloreds, Asians and whites have decreased by 1%, 9%, and 15% respectively. The approximately 10 million youth (aged 15-24) currently account for 20% of the total population, while the young (aged 0-14) form 30% of the total population and number about 16 million. Adding these two groups together, it is significant to note that their number comprises 50% of the total population, i.e. about 26 million young people. Thus, we are faced with a ticking time bomb unless the developmental state (both public and private sectors jointly) implements sustainable job opportunities using blue and green economic models. The South African economy needs to grow rapidly, starting now, if it is going to absorb another 26 (or 36) million job seekers over the next 15 years. We cannot export them; we have to create jobs for them!

It is clear that Africa's future economic and development strategies should be based on blue and green economic models to plan new smart, creative and technologically advanced cities. On the one hand, this will help ensure, inter alia, that country plans are in a position to accelerate economic growth to achieve the sustainable development goals (SDGs) and other socio-economic and cultural developments associated with the Home of Legends. On the other hand, blue and green economic models will ensure that planning and development are consistent with the COP21 Paris resolutions and environmental sustainability. This presents UNESCO and UNEP with a historic opportunity, as the Cape provinces have significant heritage sites and routes that can be exploited positively in the context of sustainable development and poverty eradication.

The world is described as being fragile because security and the environment are inextricably linked, and the survival of future generations depends on the current generation of leaders making morally sound decisions about growth, climate change, and desertification – especially in Africa. As may be seen from the stages of environmental destruction, starting from the industrial era until now, the negative consequences of climate change are already felt by the citizens of poor countries. Scientists have discovered that warming trends in South Africa are much higher than the global average. A recent publication predicts a rise of 3°C in temperatures by the end of the century, should the countries of the world greatly reduce their carbon emissions; and 6°C if they do not. The rate of warming in South Africa is near twice the average rise worldwide. A hot and dry South Africa that will get hotter, and in many areas drier, with uncertain and changing weather patterns, would put agricultural production under strain and make South Africa more vulnerable than many other countries in the region, from where a large number of environmental refugees can be expected.

The Council for Scientific and Industrial Research (CSIR) further predicts that winter rainfall in the Southern African Development Community (SADC) countries will decrease by an average of 23% by 2030, while summer rainfall will decrease by an average of 13%. The CSIR predicts that when the rains do come, precipitation will occur in shorter and heavier spells (i.e. rain will damage crops, and will pour down hard onto the ground, creating run-off rather than soaking into the soil – thus negatively affecting planting seasons). In this context, El Niño, droughts, water scarcity, and food insecurity will become the norm in agriculture.

Another major problem in Africa in general, and in South Africa in particular, is desertification. Ban Ki-moon (2007), the former United Nations secretary-general, warns that 'desertification is a phenomenon that ranks among the greatest environmental challenges of our time'. Desertification happens when plant cover (trees and bushes) that binds the soil is removed or stripped away for fuel and timber, or to clear the land for cultivation. This process is known as deforestation. Deforestation contributes to the loss of habitat for millions of animal and bird species. Where trees no longer protect the moist forest soils from the glare of the sun, the soils quickly dry out, which leads to land degradation. Animals eat away grasses, which allows topsoil to erode, while intensive farming depletes the nutrients in the soil. Wind and water erosion aggravate the damage, carrying away topsoil and leaving behind an infertile mix of stones and sand. The combination of these factors transforms degraded land into desert.

It is also significant that land degradation and soil erosion have reduced the grain-producing capability of sub-Saharan Africa by an estimated 8 million tons per year, costing about US$68 billion. Worldwide, 52% of the land used for agriculture is moderately or severely affected by soil degradation, negatively affecting the lives of 1.5 billion people. Each year, 12 million hectares of land are lost (23 hectares per minute) – owing to drought and desertification – where 20 million tons of grain could have been grown. It is critical to consider trees among the most prominent and critical organisms on earth. Trees store huge amounts of carbon, are essential for the cycling of nutrients, for maintenance of water and air quality, and for countless human services. Trees help to perpetuate the water cycle by returning water vapor into the atmosphere. Without trees, the land will become a barren desert. It is significant that the earth is losing about 15 billion trees and 13 million hectares of arable land a year as a result of deforestation. This loss negatively affects nature's ability to mitigate the adverse effects of carbon pollution, which contributes to climate change and land degradation, leading to desertification, and eventually to increased poverty, hunger, and malnutrition.

According to STATS SA (2011), 38% of the population in South Africa reside in rural parts of the country, of which 72% live below the poverty line. Accordingly, the Eastern, Western and Northern Cape provinces – the Home of Legends – are largely rural provinces, with the physical scars of frontier wars and former homeland lifestyles. The Eastern Cape with two former homelands is especially vulnerable, after decades of deforestation during the frontier wars for the building of forts instead of towns, and the implementation of poor farming practices. This overexploitation of the environment (exacerbated by climate change) has resulted in soil erosion and land degradation. Currently, only about 1% of rural households produce crops and only 4% keep livestock, leaving 80% of the population of the rural Eastern Cape between the ages of 16 and 65 unemployed. Therefore, the concept of the Home of Legends must be complemented by a comprehensive approach to land recovery.

The current status quo requires aesthetic leaders to have SPACE competencies to design blue and green city models and programs. This requires, inter alia, a simultaneous blue and green strategy to mitigate the effects of climate change, address land degradation, reverse soil erosion, and enhance soil fertility towards sustainable land management, and towards meeting sustainable development goals (SDGs). This would contribute towards job creation, eradication of poverty, and reduction of hunger, malnutrition, and feelings of hopelessness – allowing populations not only to survive but also to thrive through growth and development undertaken with PRIDE and dignity. In this case, the acronym PRIDE means 'personal responsibility in delivering excellence' in the Home of Legends, or 'personal responsibility in a desirable environment' for restoring and maintaining our beautiful landscape for coexistence. The current state of global warming and economic collapse requires, inter alia, a new model of economics rooted in Africa's aesthetic relational values and the Ubuntu paradigm, as other global models have failed.

The point of departure for this new global model for good-enough governance and leadership is the understanding of aesthetic relational values through the empowerment of leaders and citizens based on SPACE competencies within blue and green city models using Ntsikana kaGabha's prophetic message given before his death in 1821. It can be argued that Ntsikana kaGabha, if one analyses his Gospel Hymn, understood the concept of SPACE in terms of aesthetic relational values. His hymn can best be interpreted in the Home of Legends using SPACE leadership components. Accordingly, we have to base our strategic position and action evaluation of the current global environment on the advice given by former US president Barack Obama (2015):

> *We are the first generation experiencing climate change and the last that can do something about it.*

When one considers SPACE dimensions of social intelligence found in aesthetic leaders such as Ntsikana kaGabha, as conveyed in his hymn, and read with former president Obama's quote cited above, one is tempted to conclude that SPACE competencies refer to the ability of aesthetic leaders to get along well with others and to get them to cooperate in implementing global and country-based solutions, such as a blue and green strategy in the Home of Legends. SPACE competencies are often referred to as 'people skills'. People skills involve a certain amount of self-insight and consciousness of one's own perceptions of and reactions to local and global patterns regarding the environment. Evidence in the literature reveals that Ntsikana kaGabha's leadership style made people feel valued, respected, affirmed, encouraged and competent to join the church of God. As an indigenous counselor, Ntsikana – born of the great leader Gabha – was able to nourish people, using his social upbringing and environment to enable them to have SPACE competencies. In the case of Ntsikana, the term 'competency' referred to an underlying characteristic of an individual that was causally related to criterion-referenced or effective and superior performance in dealing with complex socio-economic, cultural and political situations in the nineteenth century, and how he and his followers worked hard to achieve emotional intelligence in analyzing colonial systems and their related patterns (Goleman, 2013).

From his Gospel Hymn, it would appear that Ntsikana kaGabha had value-based leadership qualities informed by **C**oncepts, **C**hallenges, **C**ontext, **C**apabilities, and **C**ompetencies (**5Cs**) and **O**pportunities in his time. Using the 5Cs and SPACE leadership traits, it is also possible to claim that Ntsikana was an aesthetic, visionary, value-based and authentic leader whose prophetic message and vision is as valuable in the contemporary global village as it was in the nineteenth century (Mancotywa, 2017; Tsibani, 2017). Leaders like Ntsikana are able to motivate citizens, managers and leaders to focus on shared growth and development embedded in the Ubuntu paradigm and related values, principles and behavioral competencies. Aesthetic leaders, like Ntsikana, are able to provide well-researched ideas (concepts) that are informed by local, regional, continental and global realities (challenges) and their consequences for societies and people (contexts). They possess the required leadership abilities and responses (competencies to comprehend the complexity of colonialism and required strategies and tactics to deal with the consequences, without compromising morality and Ubuntu values) and ability (capabilities) to change any situation positively (opportunities), simultaneously restoring human dignity and respecting God's will. Ntsikana's aesthetic, value-based and authentic leadership qualities, which can be described in terms of SPACE and the 5Cs, made him remain steadfast despite the repressive imperial and colonial administration policies and systems of the eighteenth and nineteenth centuries. Literature reveals that Ntsikana kaGabha had the ability to:

- Be reflective in his Gospel Hymn after his personal encounter with the Holy Spirit in 1790 at the age of 30. God spoke to Ntsikana, commanding him to empower others to advance good-enough governance and to restore God's Kingdom in the midst of colonialism, conflicts, human greed and hatred from the colonized and colonizers alike;
- Undergo personal emotional and spiritual transformation in order to ensure that his teachings about God's Kingdom were timeless and his ideas and concepts about capitalism and its effect on people's behaviors could be shared by generations to come. In this context, he had to repent and lead a balanced and healthy life. This practical moral high ground demonstrated by Ntsikana meant that people had to change their minds and actions, as the will to overcome imperial and colonial realities at the time depended on the ability of leaders and people to have the willpower to make persistent efforts towards self-liberation;
- Take on leadership responsibilities and duties to support God's people to fight the evils of imperialism, colonialism and personal greed resulting from a lack of moral grounding and values;
- Display humbleness by serving all people, irrespective of the clans and kingdoms at the time. He advocated that the notion of 'zenibe yimbumba yamanyama' be communicated to all kings and queens, families and clans (Andile Mtiki, 2014). As an authentic leader he was stable, strong, clear and consistent; his prophetic message is still applicable in this century and will be in the next century.

These aesthetic, value-based and authentic leadership qualities of Ntsikana, so beautifully conceptualized in his Gospel Hymn, include, inter alia:

- Self-awareness and genuineness about a cultural and societal upbringing, and use of personal experiences guided by a long-term vision of 'zenibe yimbumba yamanyama';
- The ability to unite people around noble values and ideas by means of a mission statement;
- The wisdom to be an advisor, counselor, educator, coach, mentor, preacher, spiritual teacher and study leader to deal with people's personal challenges, constraints and problems, as well as guiding

established churches as centres of excellence through knowledge sharing and SWOT analyses of prevailing situations to uncover the opportunities these bring (Matthew 4:19);
- Principle-centredness. Ntsikana had followers because they had personal trust in him – this partly because he showed integrity and decisiveness in advising his traditional leaders regarding the Battle of Amalinde and other unrecorded conflicts;
- Technical expertise in networking. This is evident from the way that he established church stakeholders and committees to communicate the vision of 'zenibe yimbumba yamanyama' by working for the restoration of the Kingdom of God on earth.
- A talent for diplomatic and administrative competencies extracted from indigenous knowledge management systems[23]. This talent flowed from an analysis of 'capitalism' and associated greed. Using the complexity of imperialism and colonialism, he constructed a mission of 'zenibe yimbumba yamanyama' as a strategy and opportunity to promote TEAM (Together Each Achieves More) collective efforts, self-defense, and self-protection strategies and tactics, and simultaneously encouraged participative efforts.

In addition, Ntsikana represented qualities of a team leader and a COACH. With reference to the required aesthetic leadership qualities in our own era, the acronym COACH stands for:

- **C**aring, by maintaining time frames in terms of blue and green economy programs and related projects, and assisting people to cope with colonial consequences.
- **O**penness by giving feedback to citizens, people, and stakeholders.
- **A**wareness of gaps and remedial actions thereafter.
- **C**ommitment to quality compliance and sustainable planning and development using environmental aesthetics and the Aesthetic Relational Values in Planning and Development Framework (ARVPDF).
- **H**onesty about what must be achieved with a smart nation-building plan between 2020 and 2064, and beyond.

Though coaching is inherent in public administration and management systems and recruitment processes, it is not confined to the performance of the public administration and management system (Kaul, 1996:131-150; Matthew 4:19). In this book, coaching refers to the support given to followers and officials by leaders in respect of technical skills-related learning and growth. In a structured program, a mentor is someone who enjoys developing people and who has the stature, experience, insight, and maturity to be a source of inspiration and influence for a protégé in developing him or her to attain competency. Mentorship and structured coaching programs provide the following benefits for individual members:

- Job enrichment
- Increased self-awareness
- Better organizational communication
- Increased peer recognition and admiration
- Individual growth and development
- Improved networking
- Career advancement

A coach must be an assertive leader. Jude (2006:142) defines assertiveness as an expression of one's needs, desires and feelings in a manner that is honest, open, appropriate and direct. From an organizational development perspective, the use of structured mentorship and coaching results in:

- More skilled, capable and satisfied employees
- New challenges for skilled and experienced employees
- Identification of new talent to fill vacancies
- Improved organizational loyalty and growth in terms of career path development

As may be observed at the end of the nineteenth century, independent schools and churches flourished because of Ntsikana's mentorship and coaching. It can be inductively and deductively argued that he was an extraordinary mentor. Some of his characteristics as a mentor included the following:

- **Supportive** – he supported the needs and aspirations of mentees and encouraged them to accept challenges and to overcome difficulties in, for instance, establishing churches at Mgwalana near Alice, and elsewhere in the Eastern Cape.
- **Patient** – he was patient and willing to provide adequate time to interact with mentees and, for instance, advised mentees on how to cope with anxiety, uncertainties and the trauma of wars and killings among people of God that arose from unethical and immoral behaviors.
- **Respected** – he earned the respect of people within the Imbumba yamaNyama movement, as a result of which others took up the vision and rolled it out to form associations, unions and leagues, where he became an icon and a true role model of how to be a Christian in the nineteenth century.
- **People-oriented** – he was genuinely interested in people and had a desire to help others. He was able to resolve conflict and give appropriate feedback. His intense interest in people and his desire to help others develop and grow, led to him being an advisor and counselor of his country's kings, queens, chiefs and church leaders. As a successful mentor, Ntsikana kaGabha devoted time

to his people using his ethics-based leadership skills, complemented by his communication and interpersonal skills, and knew how to communicate effectively and listen actively. Consequently, his advice regarding the Battle of Amalinde of 1818, and other conflicts, caused him to be regarded as an advisor par excellence, an analyst and a mentor focused on problem-solving and mutual respect among the parties involved.

- **A good motivator** – he needed to be able to motivate mentees through encouraging feedback and challenging portfolios of evidence, for instance, when he mentored his sons in supporting churches and schools for restoring human dignity lost through the endless wars of his time. As an extraordinary mentor, Ntsikana kaGabha was able to stretch his sons' potential, abilities and skills by setting new limits for what they could do to drive God's Kingdom in the Cape Colony in the nineteenth century.
- **Respectful of others** – he showed regard for the wellbeing of others. But everyone, including a mentor, has certain vulnerabilities and imperfections that must be accepted. Ntsikana kaGabha acknowledged the differences between himself and Nxele kaMakhanda in terms of articulating God's Word and spreading the Word to people, without passing judgment. By accepting such differences, Ntsikana as an international coach (as he had received God's revelation) had adopted an open-door policy where he learned from others.
- **An effective teacher** – he helped to manage and guide mentees in their learning. Ntsikana had a thorough understanding of the skills required and motivation required to tap into emotional intelligence as he was competing with a colonial agenda.
- **An achiever** – he set lofty career goals for his sons and other people, continually evaluating them.
- **Secure in his position** – as a secure mentor, Ntsikana was delighted to see his sons and other mentees achieving and making new discoveries. Mentors must appreciate their mentees' developing strengths and abilities, without viewing them as a threat. They must enjoy being part of their mentees' growth and success.

The benefits of Ntsikana kaGabha's mentorship attributes can still be felt, as his coaching and mentorship lessons can assist both individuals and learning organizations to become more productive and innovative, and therefore capable of delivering higher performance. The latter is due to the fact that the outcomes of mentorship and coaching include:

- Improving the performance of individuals as officials and leaders in their organizations;
- Determining smart performance goals;

- Analyzing and understanding the present reality using various tools, such as BOTT, 3Es, 4Es, 5Cs, 3Ps, SWOT analysis, CAR, DISC, STEEPLE, ACES, restoration of PRIDE, and creation of WEALTH;
- Exploring options using creativity, innovation, and ideapreneurship to achieve goals;
- Developing an inclusive sustainable action plan to execute programs and projects in line with the shared vision and strategy between 2020 and 2064;
- Implementing agreed-upon actions (learning); and
- Reviewing progress at the next session (feedback).

It can be seen that aesthetic leadership has been infused into the spiritual and emotional leader in order to achieve self-confidence, commitment, and compassion for citizens of God on earth. In Ntsikana's hymn, the concept of beauty involves the notion of harmony with the environment, rather than prescriptions for reasoning. From Ntsikana kaGabha, and those before him, aesthetic leadership is seen as an effective means for leaders to maintain harmony in their relationships with citizens, followers, managers and officials in various organizations by displaying positive emotions; mastering situations and contexts; being clearly aware of themselves and their context-bound environmental settings; pursuing aesthetic relational values, a shared vision and collective goals under the nation-building plan of their country as part of the global world; and influencing others to practise good-enough governance and authentic judgment in designing, planning and developing in the context of environmental aesthetics.

It is the role of all leaders to take forward the notion of aesthetic leadership to their organizational business plan or country nation-building plan, to design and establish Paradise Cities in harmony with our biodiversity. The Ntsikana Paradise Cities are conceptual models to be explored to reduce rapid urbanization, reduce poverty, and create wealth in partnership with others through the use of integrated infrastructure investment models attuned to specific contexts and associated relational values. We believe that Ntsikana kaGabha Paradise City models are based on planned, designed and development-based aesthetic relational values. I personally believe that such Paradise Cities, as graphically designed in collaboration with the Imbumba yamaNyama Royal Council, the House of Traditional Leaders, Khoisan kingdoms and relevant international stakeholders, will significantly contribute to new Paradise Cities in our fragile world. These cities will be characterized by a productive workforce and authentic, aesthetic leaders in terms of the COP21 Paris resolutions.

3.3 Development in conflict with biodiversity

It is also significant that while the widespread use of the terms *fragile world*, *fragile environment* and *fragile landscape* in the global literature seems to have emerged in the 1970s, in that period these terms were invariably used to refer to changes in international, social, economic and political public administration and management systems. This included issues such as the proliferation of nuclear weapons, growth, inflation, and matters related to international insecurity and decreases in the quality of life. Since the early 1980s, however, the concept *fragile world* has taken on another meaning that is more geocentric in focus. This can be seen in the development of the International Geosphere-Biosphere Programme (IGBP): A Study of Global Change, commissioned in 1986 by the International Council of Scientific Unions (Goudie, 2013:7-8). The IBGP study was aimed at describing and understanding the interactive physical, chemical and biological processes that regulate the total Earth system, the unique environment that it provides for life, the changes that are occurring in the Earth system, and the manner in which they are influenced by human activities. The term *fragile world* has in many senses come to be used synonymously with global warming, climate change, environmental degradation, pollution of water sources, modification of the hydrological cycle, deforestation and desertification.

Recently, Steffen (2010), cited by Goudie (2013:7-8), argued that in the last 300 years environmental development has moved from the Holocene into the Anthropocene. The Anthropocene is a new epoch in Earth's history. This refers to the epoch when human activities have become so dominant and pervasive that they rival or exceed the great forces of nature in influencing the functioning of the Earth system. Stendel (2002:1011), supported by Goudie (2013:6-8), agrees with three stages of the movement from the Holocene into the Anthropocene as follows:

Stage 1: 1800-1945, which refers to the industrial era (Gottschalk, 1945:219).

Stage 2: 1945-2015, which refers to the great acceleration of the Earth's destruction, environmental degradation, pollution, salinization, deforestation and desertification (Goudie, 2013:222-83).

Stage 3: 2015 onwards, which refers to an era in which people are aware of the extent of human impact and the necessity to start a nation-building plan between 2020 and 2064 to restore and maintain aesthetic relational values, or start a stewardship of the Earth system informed by the COP21 Paris resolutions, to drive blue and green city models – especially in Africa's rural communities.

3.4 Historical transformation to a blue and green economy

Historically, if one compares our socio-economic and political phases with those of the United Kingdom (UK), South Africa's transformation of its mining-based economy to a blue and green economy has a long way to go. We still have a number of obstacles to overcome. Gyford (1985:77-97), cited in Tsibani (2014a:100-

3), distinguished five stages in the process of the socio-economic development and politicization of public administration and management systems in the UK, namely:

- Diversity (1835 to 1865)
- Crystallization (1865 to 1890s)
- Realignment (1890s with the rise of the Labour Party to 1945)
- Nationalization (1945 to 1973)
- The current period of re-appraisal (1974 to date)

Indeed, if democratic consolidation is a necessary condition in a country with a long-established public administration and management system, and a generally stable socio-economic and political system, how much more necessary must it be for Third World countries with the hallmarks of imperialism, colonialism, frontier wars, slavery practices, poor bulk infrastructure, collapsed economic and education systems, complex abject poverty, systemic unemployment and increased inequality problems, corruption, and a water-scarce environment characterized by highly skewed water distribution to consumers (Musvoto et al., 2014:1–97; Tsibani, 2014a:70–6; UNEP, 2012b:36)?

3.5 The roles and responsibilities of traditional leaders

The government's response to abject poverty, systemic unemployment, and increased inequalities has not been consistent. The sectoral departments and State-Owned Enterprises (SOEs) have delivered socio-economic impact projects in a piecemeal and poorly aligned manner, as the country did not have an IR and UIIP implementation strategy informed by ARVPDF. In some cases, government and SOEs implemented infrastructure using inherited apartheid institutional arrangements. As infrastructure investment programs are urban-biased, rural people tend to move to informal settlements around big cities and mining towns. These people are often regarded and treated as temporary migrants, instead of permanent citizens with rights to public services. In some cases, big cities and towns, which did not have former homelands, tend to make decisions without consulting traditional leaders. No discussion of the need for socio-economic growth and development and implementation of integrated rural and urban infrastructure investment programs (IR and UIIPs) using an ARVPDF can be complete without the central role of traditional leadership in Africa. This is an indication that the proposed subverting of histories and replacement of pseudo-archaeology in Africa require, inter alia, the restoration of clans and kingdoms lost under imperialism and colonialism. Among other things, such restoration will ensure that defeated clans and kingdoms can be given a voice using the constitution of each African state. It is also crucial to note that a king is born, not made, in terms of the underlying principles of the customary law of succession in most African states. In other words, the king never dies. The law ascribes to the king, in his political capacity, absolute immortality; and immediately upon the decease of the reigning king, the king's dignity, prerogatives, and socio-political capacities, by an act of law, without any interregnum or interval, are vested at once in his successor. In the case of the AmaCirha, Cirha's kingship has been poorly and inaccurately recorded and documented, partly by colonizers in the former Cape Province.

It is significant that the main traditional groupings in South Africa are divided into Nguni, Sotho, Venda, and Tsonga. AmaXhosa falls under the Nguni grouping, which consists of Swazi, Zulu, Ndebele and Xhosa. The colonial influence on African royalty and kingdoms undermined the nature and content of indigenous relationships, and often led to a divide-and-rule type of impact, as was the case with Nkosiyamntu's sons, namely Cirha, Jwarha, Tshawe and Ngqwambe. The Black Administration Act, No. 38 of 1927, adopted this divide-and-rule strategy that was used as part of the British Indirect Rule system. British law made the prime minister a supreme chief of all the black nations in South Africa. The Act was formulated to ensure better control and management of black affairs. This empowered the prime minister to appoint or depose any clan or tribal chief, and delegate responsibilities accordingly. A situation emerged where some traditional leaders or kings were appointed because of their compliance with government policy instead of according to their hereditary status, as happened in the case of the AmaCirha under the AmaXhosa kingdom. Kings were demoted to the status of so-called 'paramount chiefs', senior traditional leaders and some to junior traditional elders or headmen. This was further exploited by the National Party (NP) from 1948 onwards, whereby a cadre of compliant traditional leaders was established as kings, queens and chiefs under the Black Authorities Act of 1951. These traditional leaders were then instrumental in developing former homeland systems (Promotion of Bantu Self-Governing Act of 1959). The British Indirect Rule and Apartheid Bantu Administration systems were inhuman PAM systems. They distorted African governance and undermined legitimate kings and queens, and their moral authority.

In accordance with the principles of democracy, the South African Constitution (Section 211) recognizes the strategic role of traditional leaders. The relevant section reads as follows:

1) The institution, status, and role of traditional leadership, according to customary law, are recognized, subject to the Constitution.
2) A traditional authority that observes a system of customary law may function subject to any applicable legislation and customs, which includes amendments to, or repeal of, that legislation or those customs.
3) The courts must apply customary law when that law is applicable, subject to the Constitution and any legislation that specifically deals with customary law.

The role of traditional leaders in the South African Constitution, Section 212, is defined as follows:

1) National legislation may provide for a role for traditional leadership as an institution at the local level on matters affecting local communities.
2) To deal with matters relating to traditional leadership, the role of traditional leaders, customary law and the customs of communities observing a system of customary law–
   a) national or provincial legislation may provide for the establishment of houses of traditional leaders, and
   b) national legislation may establish a council of traditional leaders. [Yet, a king as a traditional leader always performs his duties on the advice of the people. The rural and urban authorities are therefore structures under the jurisdiction of a king.]

It may be argued that the British policy of Indirect Rule, complemented by apartheid policies, was meant to manage 'black affairs' and create endless claims and disputes about kingdoms and chieftainships in Mother Africa. It is clear that the Constitution has created a framework in South Africa through which various cultures can be promoted, and where clans and kingdoms defeated under repressive and unbearable colonial and apartheid dispensations can be restored. The intention of such an approach is to ensure, inter alia, inclusive social cohesion aimed at restoring human dignity and PRIDE lost after the European invasion of Africa. Under democracy, the role of traditional leaders is more than just symbolic. It is more about a contribution to a nation-building plan in each country, landscape, space, heritage site, town or city in Africa. Citizens can only feel they belong to a city or town if they feel they have the means and space to advance their needs, especially the need to reduce poverty. It is envisaged that through the proposed Nation-Building Plan (2020-2064), new smart or post-colony cities will build a sense of belonging and foster spiritual tolerance.

3.6 Designing Paradise Cities and landscapes

As discussed earlier on, the Home of Legends, in terms of the South African National Heritage Council (NHC), UNESCO and the tourism sector on the frontier war province or 'the combined international heritage' from the pre-colonial era and the current modern blue and green environment under the 'Mandela legacy' and 'social cohesion', has the potential to ensure that 'all people are entitled to take part in the administration of the country' (and its radical economic development goal of a better life for all). In the context of the Eastern Cape, this refers to a blue and green economy in the sense of sustainable planning and development, with Thwathwa as a spiritual retreat – a place of culture, history, justice, healing, attachment and belonging – and Mvezo as a 'historic liberation route' in terms of the 'long walk to freedom,' with the implementation of integrated rural and urban infrastructure investment programs (IR and UIIPs) as part of a nation-building plan. Accordingly, Ixhorha, Jeffrey's Bay, Dr. MWB Rubusana City, Nelson Mandela Bay Metropolitan Municipality, Hondeklip Bay, Springbok, Mossel Bay, Saldana Bay, George, Cape Town and Coffee Bay represent blue coastal cities, while Mvezo, Hankey, Tsitsikamma and Thwathwa represent green cities (see Figure 1.2). A blue and green city model provides an aesthetic local space for inclusive, innovative and interconnected ideas of the landscape that work in harmony to generate a range of benefits for socio-economic growth and development to 2064 and beyond. Many of the goods and services provided by blue and green cities have economic value, such as the production of clean air and water, and carbon sequestration, leading to creative industries and cities in the Home of Legends.

In this blue and green economic model, the Eastern Cape landscape is seen as a Home of Legends, with a beautiful landscape stretching from Mzimvubu via Ixhorha (Hole in the Wall), Coffee Bay, Tsitsikamma, Mvezo (AbaThembu bakaDalinyebo), and from the Great Kei River (Nciba) to the Fish River, up to the Nkonkobe, Bhukazana and Table Mountains in the west.

For this reason, Ntsikana kaGabha Paradise City models, as part of mental reflection and the affirmation of co-creating and coexistence, are not only advancing IR and UIIPs to feed into a nation-building plan (2020-2064), but also maintaining and restoring our aesthetic relational values, as depicted in Figure 3.1.

In a workshop with traditional leaders in Dr. MWB Rubusana City (formerly known as Buffalo City) in 2017, Tsibani (2017) supported by Advocate Mancotywa (2017) argued that Ntsikana kaGabha had a dream of a state of equilibrium that aspired to develop an ecologically, economically, socially, culturally, emotionally, psychologically and spiritually healthy community for the long term, using the Aesthetic Relational Values in Planning and Development Framework (ARVPDF) for sustainability as a guide for an international public environmental commission and the combined heritage of nations. Accordingly, Imbumba yamaNyama members use the Awareness, Baseline, Creating and Developing (ABCD) approach to driving social cohesion and reconciliation between nations, clans and kingdoms. The Imbumba yamaNyama Royal Council adopted a Sustainable Action Plan, which includes, inter alia:

- **A-** Raising **A**wareness about aesthetic relational values in planning and development, read with the graphic design of the Ntsikana kaGabha Paradise City in Figure 1.2. These sustainable planning and development principles in designing new cities and towns – including emotional intelligence and spiritual support to clans, kingdoms, and African states – drive social cohesion and reconciliation.
- **B-** Creating a city- or region-wide **B**aseline of information on water mega nexuses to restore PRIDE and create WEALTH by drawing up an inventory of current and future projections using advanced IT software systems or software-modeling reports for forecasting analysis.

C- **C**reating a compelling future vision by having WEALTH projects and programs to feed into a country nation-building plan.

D- **D**eveloping a sustainable action plan as part of a nation-building plan with SMART deliverables and impact indicators, read with some of the recommendations in section 6.2. This is important for aesthetic leaders to guide, lead and direct their communities, municipalities, districts, provinces, countries, regions and continents. Hereby a common vision will be shared, and communication barriers and conflicts will be reduced as far as possible.

In terms of the ABCD approach, and the associated sustainable action plan and interpretation of Ntsikana's message, it can be argued that Mandela's character from AbaThembu was already prophesied by Ntsikana before 1821. Leaders like Sobukwe, Biko, Hani, Tambo, Sisulu, Mbeki, Mlangeni and Mandela, to mention but a few, reflected their aesthetic context. The process of intellectual reflection revolves around the interplay of aesthetic relational values as part of the learning experience, and reflects the use of Ubuntu principles. 'I am because we are' is a personal reflection of both inner and outer appropriateness of one's actions either to change the world, or to accept that one's nation will perish. Our motto is: *I am a Blue or Green City because the citizens are the city.*

Furthermore, the ABCD approach will add value to the beautiful coastal and inland landscapes, from the Drakensberg to the Nkonkobe Mountains, which provide uniqueness, along with major rivers, such as the Xesi, Tyhume, Bushman's, Sundays, Fish, Kat, Kei, and Mbashe. These rivers, as part of a blue and green economy, add a significant blend of ecosystems and biodiversity, complemented by aesthetic historical sites, churches, schools, colleges, universities, old buildings, forts, monuments, and the artworks of the indigenous people.

It is clear from the description of the Cape provinces' sites – towns and places, both blue and green – that they inform aesthetic relational values in planning, designing and developing cities. In short, a *city* is an inhabited place of greater size or population than a town or village, identified and legislated by an Act of Parliament, and demarcated in its boundaries and public functional areas by a demarcation board. A city is a large and permanent human settlement that is defined as Category A by the Municipal Systems and Structures Acts in South Africa. Although there is no generally accepted agreement on how a city is distinguished from a town in the English language, many cities have a particular administrative, legal or historical status based on local law. In the case of the Eastern Cape, we have Dr. MWB Rubusana City and Nelson Mandela Bay Municipality. These two metropolitan cities have complex systems of sanitation, utilities, land usage, housing, and transportation as compared to the ten district municipalities in the Eastern Cape. Both Dr. MWB Rubusana City and Nelson Mandela Bay Municipality can be seen as global cities and megacities, with prominent centers of trade, banking, finance, innovation, and markets. Yet there is a difference between global cities and megacities. Accordingly, a *global city* is a city with enormous power or influence on **s**ocial, **t**echnical, **e**conomic, **e**cological, **p**olitical, **l**egal and **e**nvironmental (called STEEPLE) factors in the world. In this case, the term *megacity* refers to any city of enormous size, such as the City of Tshwane in Gauteng. Yet Johannesburg, with Sandton and Midrand, is a global economic city seen from business and economic perspectives.

Towns such as Berlin, Stutterheim, Keiskammahoek, Peddie, Middledrift, Alice, Fort Beaufort, Grahamstown, Kenton-on-Sea, Middelburg, Queenstown, Aliwal North, Cradock, Hankey, and so forth, are human settlement areas larger than villages but smaller than Dr. MWB Rubusana City (formerly known as Buffalo City) and Nelson Mandela Bay Municipality (NMBM). The size definition of what constitutes a *town* varies considerably in different parts of the world.

From their inner and outer relational values, aesthetic leaders mentioned in previous chapters took appropriate action to change the world for the better. Their contributions are referred to as encompassing the intellectual and aesthetic qualities of judging and doing what is appropriate to save the world, using Ubuntu relational values to ensure both good governance and harmony with the environment. In Ntsikana's prophetic message rooted in Ubuntu, he focused on collective efforts, leadership, networks and joint actions. The Ubuntu paradigm refers to *I belong therefore I am, and so we become God's children.* Memorials among African people from Cape Town to Cairo are an integral part of heritage resources management and are conceptually reconstructed by Imbumba yamaNyama to honor our great God in Heaven through our historical legacy and sociocultural roots. The envisaged Ntsikana kaGabha Paradise Cities will not only restore aesthetic relational values, but will also add to the spiritual heritage of Christians and African people. According to Swartz (2010), such environmentally aesthetic cities will not only restore Ubuntu principles and aesthetic relational values, but will commemorate land restitution, thereby ensuring integrated planning and development to create Ntsikana Paradise Cities. The Ntsikana Paradise Cities refer to modern cities that are based on Ubuntu and aesthetic relational values as envisaged by Swartz (2010) and Tsibani (2014a). Indeed, the Ntsikana Paradise Cities will be led by aesthetic leaders who are profoundly righteous, as well as those with a heart for matters concerning their nation, and who are proud of their culture, and also willing to obtain aesthetic relational knowledge from the present generation to drive sustainable planning and development in harmony with future generational human and environmental needs (enyanisweni emsulwa engenachaphaza, ubunzulu bobulungisa yincamisa yobom kwabo bantliziyo ibubuncwane belizwe namagugu alo obuntu bethu ngentliziyo elungelele ukwamkela imfundiso yexesha lamandulo kumbo nomxesibe welixesha phantsi kweenjo zokuzisa uzindzo nengcubeko kuluntu).

In his environmental and aesthetic thesis, as may be seen in Figures 1.1.-2.1, Dr. Moshe Ncilashe kaSwartz (2010:448-459), citing King David's reign with reference to Psalm 72, has already warned our leaders to have regard for and apply aesthetic relational values in planning and development. According to Dr. Swartz (2010:449-50), the decline of the Hebrew nation, which is very close to African religious historical presuppositions, began when King Solomon disregarded King David's advice in Psalm 72. Leaders such as the Prophet Ntsikana kaGabha, Commander Nxele Makhanda, His Excellency Mangaliso Sobukwe, the Honourable Steve Biko, Commander and Chief-of-staff Thembisile Chris Hani, former President Nelson Mandela, and many founding members of our Africanist and Ubuntu philosophy derived from aesthetic relational values have issued a warning to us. King Solomon disregarded King David's lofty advice as he turned his back on aesthetic relational values. Consequently, these values were replaced by ethnicity, tribalism, ignorance, greed, cruelty, instability, social ills such as rape, high crime rates and alcohol abuse, kingship and chieftainship abuses, adultery, unfair distribution of resources, cronyism and factionalism, abuse of state power, undermining of Jewish (democratic) rule and constitutionalism, racial tensions and conflicts, and class contradictions and their negative consequences for children, women and people living with disabilities.

The selection of the term 'lofty advice' by Dr. Moshe Ncilashe kaSwartz is significant as it is critical to understand, in this context, that it means that King David was showing the aesthetic importance, dignity, and nobility of decisions, judgments and actions relating to the nation-building plan. Since the time of King David's advice, the socio-economic and historical development of the Jewish people has been characterized by misfortunes, as testified by events such as the Masada massacre and the Holocaust. The entire nation has never known peace to this very day – so concluded Dr. Swartz (2010:449). At the core of aesthetic relational values is the reclaiming and restoring of the purpose of God's creation (UQamata) across nations. We must also restore our ecosystem so that there is mutual respect, harmony, unity, admiration, peace, stability, socio-economic growth and industrial development to eliminate poverty through wealth creation; develop a classless society, replace racism with non-racialism, and abolish slavery systems with humanity, love, good-enough governance and international cooperation in all aspects of life, and sustainable planning and development. This links very well to the cultural competence of the nation-building plan, which is based on the aesthetic relational values called the 'Law of Self-sacrificial Living' represented by King David in Israel, Fyodor Dostoevsky in Russia, Albert Schweitzer in the tropical jungles of Africa, Mahatma Gandhi in India, Martin Luther King Jr in the United States of America, and Nelson Mandela in South Africa. These aesthetic leaders had one thing in common: the vision to inspire people to be committed to aesthetic relational values, high moral norms and standards, and industrial and technologically sustainable planning and development programs to honor God's agape love as a Creator (uQamata). These great men also had a common understanding of one thing: people are part of one another, created by God Almighty (uQamata) to fulfill His agape love on earth as it is in heaven.

Johannes Kepler, Isaac Newton, and Galileo were, by and large, the founders of modern science, and were profoundly spiritual men. They wanted to believe in an impeccable harmony and the principle of beauty, with the universe operating and evolving according to the Law of Cause and Effect. In the absence of knowledge about the origin of the Garden of Eden or Paradise or the Park of Light, the question for science is: How can there be a universe created out of nothing? Why is there something rather than nothing? Johannes Kepler, who discovered the laws that govern the motion of the planets in the seventeenth century, wrote:

> *Great is the God, our Lord is His Power, and*
>
> *there is no end to His Wisdom.*
>
> *Praise Him, and Glorify Him sun and moon, and*
>
> *you planets.*
>
> *For out of Him, through Him, and*
>
> *in Him are all things.*
>
> *Every perception and every knowledge.* (cited in MacLaine, 1989:260)

All in all, creating social cohesion as part of a nation-building plan is not an easy task and cannot be implemented without a concrete reindustrialization program in post-colonial Africa. The need for restoring family and clan PRIDE is central to the stability and growth of African states. The landscape, which may be compared to the Garden of Eden, provides an opportunity for Africa's renaissance, a concept that was first articulated by Cheikh Anta Diop in his capacity as an historian, anthropologist, physicist, and politician. Diop was born in Senegal on 29 December 1923 and died on 7 February 1986. His views, which were set out in a series of essays beginning in 1946, were re-introduced and revised by former President Thabo Mbeki as part of the intellectual agenda of post-colonial Africa. Through Diop's book *Towards the African Renaissance: Essays in culture and development, 1946-1960*, his ideas have influenced African diaspora intellectuals and the forming of the Door of Return as a pan-African initiative by members of the Pan-African Parliament to launch new cooperation between African states and the African diaspora in the twenty-first century. This was further adopted by the United Nations General Assembly in Resolution 68/237 on 23 December 2013 under the theme: The International Decade for People of African Descent, 2015-2024. The strategic aim of the African Renaissance project is to overcome the problems and challenges mentioned above by achieving cultural, scientific, economic and political renewal through exploiting the raw natural resources and human capital of the youthful continent.

3.7 Conclusion

The development framework presents long-term difficulties with regard to the environmental problems outlined in this chapter. Therefore, motivation of the significance of the Earth Movement, as defined by Goudie (2013:3-6), and the understanding of social and economic cohesion and a nation-building plan (Gyford, 1985:7797), require aesthetic and visionary leaders with SPACE competencies who are willing to use the UK's unification political process and democratic consolidation referred to under paragraph 3.4. I am making this comparison because people tend to argue that we should be ready to have social cohesion without taking into account diversity, crystallization, realignment and democratic consolidation processes in a nation-building project (Tsibani, 2014a). Furthermore, South Africans tend to ignore the impact of imperialism, colonialism, and apartheid – including the compromises reached during the negotiated settlement in South Africa and its famous 'sunset clause'.

It can be concluded that silo interventions can be bridged if the developmental state of South Africa can plan ahead by appreciating that different rural and urban landscapes be aligned into an ARVPDF with IR & UIIP, whereby the economic role of heritage sites, secondary towns, and metropolitan cities are planned, taking into account the need for interdependence and synergies between these landscapes. If one can implement IR & UIIP plans using blue and green economic models, it is envisaged that some of the rural and heritage sites and landscapes can help to absorb the rapid urbanization currently facing mining towns, secondary towns and metropolitan cities in South Africa. The latter is due to the argument that the real national purpose of integrated rural and urban infrastructure investment programs (IR and UIIPs) is to eradicate poverty, not to address poverty or deal with some of the manifestations of poverty (e.g. to free family members and clans from the deprivation trap). Given the challenge of bad habits (2 Corinthians 9:8; Romans 12: 9-13); Colossians 3: 12-14) as well as outdated and outmoded cultural practices in a modern democracy and among traditional leaders and various politicians in Africa, the IR and UIIPs must take harsh measures to eradicate current unsustainable practices in order to bring about radical blue and green economy reforms based on environmental aesthetics (UNEP, 2011b:548).

It appears that the National Growth Path (NGP) framework, the Industrial Policy Action Plan (IPAP), the Black Industrialist Programme (BIP), the NDP 2030 vision, and other sectoral programmes by state-owned enterprises (SOEs), development finance institutions (DFIs) and international development agents need inter-ministerial task teams under the custodianship of sectoral departments, the National Heritage Council (NHC) and the South African National Heritage Resources Agency (SANHRA) to implement a sustainable action plan based on an Aesthetic Values in Planning and Development Framework (ARVPDF), as crafted by Dr. Moshe Ncilashe Swartz. This ARVPDF was adopted to dramatically transform and relieve current unbearable living conditions through a radical socio-economic and cultural transformation, using Ntsikana kaGabha's philosophy. As a result, families, clans and nations will have a sustainable action plan based on a nation-building plan between 2020 and 2064. Accordingly, the ARVPDF will empower families, clans, citizens, practitioners and leaders to be practically and mentally linked to Paradise City development models (Korten, 1980:499). Swartz (2010), supported earlier by Korten (1980:499), argues that the ARVPDF provides the principle of 'addictiveness', or predictable routine, in the mindset of both followers and leaders to deal with the complexity of current developments that are in conflict with the environment or biodiversity, whereby traditional and cultural practices that are outdated and outmoded are replaced with environmentally friendly solutions and interventions (UNEP, 2011b:548).

The Ntsikana kaGabha Paradise City model aims to solve social and ecological problems while promoting social efforts, with the help of state institutions, using a public-private partnership (PPP) delivery model for integrated rural and urban infrastructure investment programs (IR and UIIPs). This means that every individual will be an agent for maintaining a quality environment and promoting the acceleration of social and economic cohesion to eradicate poverty, unemployment and inequality within the human race.

It can be concluded that the proposed Nation-Building Plan provides a developmental approach, in contrast to the largely rhetorical and vacuous policy statements that have gone before. It is an argument that can be tested, but its significance in social cohesion focusing on families, clans, and kingdoms (subverting histories as a necessary step for social cohesion, socio-economic growth and development, and a nation-building plan) is that it actually begins to confront tough and previously silenced matters, to make proper investments in our aesthetic landscapes in Mother Africa. The nation-building plan should be the starting point of vigorous public debate about reindustrialization, the restoration of PRIDE and the creation of WEALTH. While governments and international development institutions, including foundations, have made various public statements, the concept of social cohesion in nation-building is taken at face value and adopted by various institutions as part of the policy template. Despite the existence of public debates around social cohesion as part of the nation-building plan by credible national, regional, continental and international foundations and government sectoral departments, African countries are now experiencing a growing gap between rich and poor, racial tensions and xenophobia, class divisions and increased inequalities, as well as a lack of reconciliation between families, clans, tribes and nations. As the case of South Africa has demonstrated, should the nation-building plan be implemented in an unreflective manner, several unintended consequences may be the result, where the defeated and silenced families, clans, kingdoms and race groups will remain historical hostages. Therefore, the proposed Nation-Building Plan lays the groundwork for new thinking and the subverting of distorted histories in order to realize the state of equilibrium envisaged by Paradise City models.

Chapter 4 explains the motivation for and significance of a nation-building plan that uses aesthetic relational values in planning and development.

CHAPTER 4

4 APPLICATION OF A NATION-BUILDING PLAN USING AN AESTHETIC RELATIONAL VALUES IN PLANNING AND DEVELOPMENT FRAMEWORK

4.1 Objectives and outcomes

By the end of this chapter, the reader will be able to:

- Apply the concept of the Home of Legends to any appropriate landscape;
- Understand and apply the Swartzist Framework, or the Aesthetic Relational Values in Planning and Development Framework (ARVPDF) in various settings, situation, and sites using the public administration and management system of governance;
- Apply the ARVPDF in various principles of the Ubuntu paradigm; and
- Apply SPACE competencies in both traditional and elected leadership roles and project management principles in any context, landscape, space, environment or organization.

4.2 The concept of the Home of Legends

> Ingumangaliso Imisebenzi kaThixo
> Hayi ubuhle bendalo yoMdali
> Kwinzonzobila zolwandle
> Ezintabeni emahlathini nasesibhakabhakeni
> Buyabonakala ubuhle bendalo yoMdali
> Kwizinto ezisehlabathini (Ngxokolo)
>
> Oh how beautiful is the Creator's nature
> In the deep of the sea,
> On the mountains, in the forests and the sky.

> The beauty of the Creator's nature is visible
> In all things that are in the world.

The concept of the Home of Legends or Ntsikana Kagabha Paradise City model refers to rich heritage sites, archaeological sites and historical settlements from the pre-colonial era to the current democratic era in Africa, graves and burial grounds of various soldiers and leaders across the globe, and cultural and military objects from the nine frontier wars in the Cape provinces, in the case of South Africa. It is argued that the rich historical heritage of the Cape is based on its intellectuals who played a significant aesthetic leadership role and were responsible for the crafting and design of the current reality of this beautiful landscape, which is geared up for blue and green economic models.[24] Accordingly, green integrated rural and urban infrastructure investment programs (IR and UIIPs) with a bias towards agribusiness, agri-villages, and blue economy concepts (in the coastal towns and cities) have been globally adopted to deal with our fragile environment within the framework of aesthetic relational values. Swartz (2010) has argued that an ARVPDF must be linked to the restoration and maintenance of aesthetic relational values if a sustainable impact is to be achieved, as implicitly and explicitly analyzed in Figure 1.2 and Table 2.1. The ARVPDF is informed by the notion that aesthetic relational values have existed for as long as humankind has lived on earth. The five pillars of the ARVPDF indicate that blue and green city models can generate a multitude of STEEPLE values and benefits up to 2064 and beyond, and may be key to the future resilience and sustainability of Paradise Cities. It is clear that there is a need to cultivate aesthetic leaders to restore and maintain our aesthetic relational values as envisaged by our ancestors and forefathers. We need aesthetic leaders to address the current challenges and problems in our fragile world. Through aesthetic relational values, we will be able to inspire leaders to lead, govern and bring change with good-enough governance in our Paradise City models, as depicted in Figure 1.2 and interpreted in the context of a state of equilibrium in Tables 2.1, 2.2 and 4.1.

According to Swartz (2010), aesthetics can be defined as 'knowing on the basis of sensuous perceptions'. Aesthetics represent a form of emotional, ethical, moral and spiritual knowledge. As was the case with both Ntsikana and Mandela, experience within aesthetic processes permits social, economic, developmental, environmental, cultural, emotional, ethical, spiritual and political reasoning that creates a new sense of reality. The rationale behind these personal and subjective experiences includes an ability to creatively imagine a future different from the reality experienced at present in Thwathwa or Mvezo or Ixhorha. Experience in the context of an aesthetic process is knowledge-producing insofar as it offers a heightened sense of reality pregnant with possibilities and a greater depth of insight, which is achieved through the use of graphic design for the model of a typical Ntsikana kaGabha Paradise City. By means of such models, aesthetics can open our eyes to the beauty beyond our brains and arouse our imaginings of and emotions towards Paradise Cities, inspiring us to respond to new demands and the restoration of aesthetic relational values in property development and in planning, designing and developing modern cities in harmony with the environment. Good-enough governance, as coined by Tsibani (2014), is required to deal with complex sustainable development programs, as depicted in Table 4.1 below.

Table 4.1: Governance and good-enough governance

The current form of governance	The ideal form of good-enough governance
1. Emerging from dual colonialism, neo-liberalism, and apartheid.	1. A sustainable action plan (SAP) is implemented to deal with natural disasters, such as droughts and floods, on one hand, and, on the other hand, the SAP is used to restore and maintain aesthetic relational values by adapting to a blue and green economy as part of a socio-economic transformation agenda by all the organs of state, with art and culture used for inclusive participation and advanced development in paradise and smart cities.
2.1 An unfair agreement between the colonizers and liberation movement negotiators. 2.2 Institutional constraints in a post-war scenario and a new cold war. 2.3 Totalitarian oligarchy (cronies/small cliques, whereby institutions are seen as ceremonial and acclamatory bodies of the cronies).	2.1 Change of government via democratic mechanisms (e.g. ballot box). 2.2. Institutions of governance, such as the Office of the Public Protector, have constitutional powers and human rights bodies that advance good-enough governance and compliance with international norms and standards in planning, development and environmental management policies and regulations. 2.3. Leadership representation based on a vision to respond to current and future demands and needs.
3. Socialism and nationalization policies (homogeneous state authority needs homogeneous state property and communal property).	3. Mixed economies based on the free market system (a mixed economy is the most considered option in Third World countries).
4. A centralized form of governance, where both provincial and local spheres of government are seen as administrative extensions.	4. Interdependence between the three spheres of government – national, provincial and local – as guided by the principle of cooperative governance and statutory clauses or articles (characterized by decentralization and devolution of powers and functions to developmental local government, and a government close to communities and land issues as critical key performance areas for addressing the legacy of colonialism).

Nation Building Plan Between 2020 & 2064

The current form of governance	The ideal form of good-enough governance
5. Economically catastrophic situation/collapse of financial institutions that are dependent on party ideology or considered as instruments for the centralization of economic means.	5. Market conformity subject to direct and open competition with private trade and industry and commercial institutions, based on economic proportionality and not cronyism or the corruption of leaders.
6. Primitive technology and problems of abject poverty, increased inequality, systemic unemployment of vulnerable groups, families and clans trapped in a vicious cycle of deprivation, and deeply rooted corruption in both private and public institutions.	6. Advanced technology taking into account germline modification in science and future technology for biological options and choices among married couples (Revelation 21:5), and a smart Sustainable Action Plan (SAP) to implement and apply IR and UIIPs within the context of an ARVPDF for a nation-building plan.
7. Social Disintegration.	7. Social integration and cohesion using a bottom-up approach for communities and Paradise Cities to advance a blue and green economy.
8. Racist and sexist modes of operation.	8. Non-racist and non-sexist modes of operation.
9. Poor planning.	9. A mixture of settlements with rural, informal, peri-urban and urban characteristics caused not by poor governance, but rather by other influencing factors, such as witnessed during post-colonialism, and a need for a combination of modern cities with indigenous knowledge and aesthetic relational values, as described by Ntsikana in his Gospel Hymn.
10. No elections – 'One president, one country' slogan, or the manipulation of citizens using propaganda and twisted facts, or promoting a syndrome of community dependence on state welfare systems rather than self-reliance.	10. Continuous elections based on four-year terms, including by-elections; yet aesthetic leaders must have a vision of performance measured by infrastructure investment interventions to address abject poverty, systemic unemployment, and increased inequality (PUI) problems, including rooting out corruption in all institutions and instituting good corporate governance in terms of the King IV framework.
11. Poor or no regulations to attract foreign investors.	11. Foreign investment-friendly regulations with a nation-building plan implemented with Ntsikana Paradise Cities rooted in aesthetic relational values and the Ubuntu philosophy in terms of daily business and corporate programs.

The current form of governance	The ideal form of good-enough governance
12. Poor strategies for development.	12. Innovative strategies for development based on aesthetic relational values to feed into a nation-building plan.
13. An unsound system of justice used for centralization by executives elected on the basis of cronyism and cliques.	13. A sound system of justice with reasonably independent committees/portfolios/representatives.
14. Crises, anarchy and atrocities (pessimism).	14. Stable socio-economic, environmental and political development (optimism).
15. No compliance with environmental regulations. Post-extraction mineral landscapes are often unstable and unpredictable toxic wastelands. The industrial-scale destruction and alteration of geological features and vegetation render the surfaces uninhabitable. Mining sites worldwide are similar: places of unusual impoverishment in local populations. The parallel presence of rich resources, in the form of underground mineral wealth, and extreme poverty is called the resource curse, through which indigenous peoples lose arable land and clean water and also suffer other losses and hardships. This leads to more acid drainage and contamination of groundwater, with the poor being on the receiving end.	15. Human and environmental needs comply with blue and green economic projects and programs, which feed into a nation-building plan per country or kingdom. Through Paradise Cities, countries and provinces, such as the Home of Legends, blue and green strategies support, inter alia, the following: ✓ Blue and green economic skills revolution or SPACE skills ✓ Land rehabilitation ✓ Agro-processing industries in cities like Coffee Bay, Ixhorha, Tsitsikamma, Mvezo, Hankey, Dr. MWB Rubusana City, and Thwathwa ✓ Blue and green jobs and entrepreneurship ✓ Self-sufficiency (producing own food, water and energy) ✓ Blue and green reindustrialization ✓ Production of biofuel resources ✓ Promotion of rural and urban agriculture and the establishment of food gardens in various communities, etc. ✓ Acceleration of blue and green programs and projects to adapt to climate change consequences and the implementation of the COP21 Paris resolutions.

The current form of governance	The ideal form of good-enough governance
16. Distorted histories using highly selective colonial and apartheid oral memories, books, poems and myths from early childhood development (ECD) onwards are meant to keep current and future generations in post-colonial Africa hostage, whereby illegitimate clans and kingdoms are rulers. According to Section 4.10 of the White Paper, which preceded the establishment of the Nhlapo Commission, this argument is explained as follows: (Imperial, colonial and apartheid) legislation transferred powers to identify, appoint and/or recognize and depose traditional leaders from traditional institutions to the (colonial and apartheid) government (and their administrators were supported by awards and sponsors on projects that promoted divisions, myths and related fictitious stories, all part of social Darwinism). In the process, the role of customary institutions in the application of customary rules and procedures were/are substantially reduced or completely ignored to date. In some instances, not only were/are illegitimate traditional leaders and authority structures appointed or established by colonial and apartheid governors, administrators and historians, but other legitimate traditional leaders, like Cirha, were/are removed and legitimate authority disestablished, all part of managing black and African affairs during and after the colonial period in Africa. What is also a major concern is that black and African historians are (un)consciously trained to reproduce the same distorted histories to maintain the status quo.	16. Subverting histories as critical projects may assist Africa to achieve reconciliation between clans and kingdoms. This social cohesion may lead to a nation-building plan under the Aesthetic Relational Values in Planning and Development Framework (ARVDPF) of post-colonial Africa, as coined by Swartz (2010). This can be implemented in youthful Africa through integrated rural and urban infrastructure investment programs (IR and UIIPs) to bridge the gap between rural and urban dimensions, using Paradise City models. Unfortunately, the ARVDPF and its implementation vehicle, IR and UIIPs, require aesthetic leaders with SPACE competencies to create WEALTH in Africa and restore our lost PRIDE.

Source: Adapted from Tsibani (2014a).

4.3 Paradise City models require SPACE competencies

It can be deduced from Table 4.1 above that the space for Paradise City models requires aesthetic leaders to have SPACE competencies that can be described as follows:

- **S**ituational analysis of the landscape to implement IR and UIIPs for a blue and green economy through understanding the needs and priorities of the people, as well as a country's top priorities for growth and development. From Ntsikana kaGabha's lofty advice, aesthetic leaders in the Home of Legends (or in this fragile global world) must have the habit of referring all matters to divine guidance for wisdom and impartiality.
- **P**resence, which refers to aesthetic relational values as signals of good personal dignity and a universal presence to influence international politicians and leaders to protect the environment and the planet. This refers to the Holy Spirit guiding leaders to resist, endure and triumph over the tests, trials and temptations of our fragile world.
- **A**uthenticity, which refers to leadership, attributes that cause leaders to be seen as honest, open, moral, ethical and trustworthy to lead a global blue and green economy. Leaders in a Paradise City must have a sense of justice, gratitude, integrity, and goodwill towards both current and future generations, even if the leader should lose benefits and privileges associated with his or her position or occupation in society.
- **C**larity in providing IR and UIIP plans to transform the current mining-based economy into a blue and green economy using a nation-building plan.
- **E**mpathy in terms of compassionate concern about the challenges faced by citizens and future generations and the need for urgency in driving blue and green sustainable programs and projects based on an ARVPDF (2010).

From Figures 1.2 to 1.3 in Chapter 1, and the interpretation of SPACE in Tables 2.1 and 2.2 in Chapter 2, it appears that an ARVPDF refers to a need for aesthetic leaders to analyze both the internal and external environmental aesthetics in the environment in which they operate. One kind of context analysis – called a SWOT analysis – allows a business to gain insight into its **st**rengths and **w**eaknesses and also the **o**pportunities and **t**hreats posed by the market and the metaphysical environment within which it operates. The main goal of context analysis, SWOT or otherwise, is to analyze the environmental driving factors for success in aesthetic leadership in their internal and external relations in order to develop a strategic plan of action for an Ntsikana Paradise City.

4.4 The theoretical framework of African life

The ARVPDF assumes that human beings (*abantu*) are directly linked to their environment. Some clans regard blue cranes (ii*ndwe*), blue duikers or bluebuck (a*maphuthi*), buffalo, blue wildebeest (ii*nkonkoni*), black wildebeest (ii*nqu*), eland (iim*pofu*) and elephant (iin*dlovu*) as part of their heritage and environmental livelihood. The word 'duiker' comes from the Afrikaans word 'duik', or Dutch 'duiken'. This refers to 'dive'. Accordingly, the blue duiker *(iphuthi)*, which is often confused with bluebuck (an extinct antelope) frequently dives into forests and vegetation for cover. In other words, Afrikaners called any of several small African antelopes 'duikers', which can be small grey, red and/or blue bucks. According to Reverend Mbulelo Livingstone Dyibishe (2019) who has worked with the Department of Rural Development and Land Reform (DRD&LR) in the Eastern Cape for more than 30 years, AmaXhosa and AmaCirha, AmaJwarha and AmaTshawe clans claim that iphuthi is the smallest buck amongst other antelopes or 'duikers'. Yet these distinguished animals are non-existent in parts of the Cape provinces, and the bluebuck is now extinct. Restoring and recognizing the beautiful relational values of our environmental creatures and ecosystems may mean restoring and maintaining our heritage and the appreciation of God and His creations. Therefore, an ARVPDF is highly relevant and calls for an urgent intervention by both traditional and elected leaders to 'save our fragile world'. As part of avoiding extinction, we need aesthetic leaders to restore aesthetic relational values to prevent the disappearance of plants and animals through balancing the ecosystem, so that sustainable planning and development can be managed for current and future generational needs in the Home of Legends.

4.5 Five pillars of an ARVPDF by Swartz (2010)

The aesthetic relational values proposition advanced by Swartz (2010) personifies the beliefs, motivations and aspirations of the founding members of Imbumba yamaNyama and those before them, as depicted in Figure 1.3. When we read this together with Figure 1.2 (which depicts the Ntsikana kaGabha Paradise City), it is clear that the Ntsikana kaGabha Paradise City model is rooted in various kingdoms or in a combination of urban and rural livelihoods, with the primary purpose of ensuring public good by applying commercial strategies to maximize improvements in human and environmental wellbeing, rather than maximizing profits for external shareholders (UNEP, 2011b:548). It is apparent that the five pillars of an ARVPDF (Swartz, 2010) are meant to empower people to advance their political, social, cultural, ecological, economic, developmental, spiritual, emotional, environmental and human justice agendas, where the SPACE competencies are used for implementing a blue and green economy.

4.6 Interpretation and analysis of ARVPDF

Globally, Ntsikana paradise societies are attractive places where people live in harmony with the environment. The business model is a combination of modern cities (such as Sandton in Gauteng, South Africa) and the newly emerging cities of Africa, the Middle East, Asia and Latin America within an environmentally aesthetic paradigm.

It is argued that the Ntsikana Paradise City business strategy from 2019 onwards includes the following landscape pillars for sustainable planning and development (see Figure 4.1 and Table 4.1):

- *The sense of justice:* This speaks to upholding and strengthening social justice, democracy, and the rule of law. Like Ntsikana kaGabha in the past, our international icon, Nelson Mandela, the first president of a democratic South Africa, advanced Imbumba yamaNyama founding principles when he said, 'We speak as fellow citizens to heal the wounds of the past with the intent of constructing a new order based on justice for all. This is the challenge that faces all South Africans today, and it is one to which I am certain we will all rise'.
- *The sense of limits:* This refers to building a culture of understanding the limits of natural resources and using them in a way that will not deprive future generations of their benefits, through a policy of replenishing, re-use and renewal.
- *The sense of place:* The phrase 'beauty is in the eye of the beholder' is often quoted to emphasize the subjectivity in determining scenic values.
- *The sense of history:* This includes communities that understand and preserve where we come from and build a heritage worthy of conservation. The Department of Arts and Culture (DAC), SAHRA, UNEP and UNESCO – in partnership with universities and the organs of civil society – must document the frontier wars to include, inter alia, routes, pre-colonial life, the era of conflicts, the missionary education system, the legacy of aesthetic leaders from the frontier war provinces, and the modernization under Nelson Mandela's legacy in our global village.
  - ✓ The Ntaba kaNdoda Mountain near Debe Nek was named after the Khoi chief Ndoda. Ndoda lived in the area during the 1700s. Rharhabe gave Ndoda's wife, Queen Hoho, the mountain behind Pirie Mission near the AmaHleke Kingdom.
  - ✓ As a frontier war province, the Eastern Cape has military forts, such as Fort White (1835), Fort Cox (1835), Fort Peddie (1835), Fort Beaufort or the Watchtower (1822), Milkwood Tree or AmaMfengu aseMngqwasheni eNgqushwa (1838), Fort Hare (1847), Fort Fordyce (1853), Piet Retief Post Fort (1835), Fort Armstrong (1835), Fort Willshire (for commercial trade between the AmaXhosa and Europeans between 1824 and 1830), Eland's Post or Inqaba yaseMpofu

(1830), Fort Michel (post for the 1850-1853 war near Tyume in Alice), and Castle Eyre in Keiskammahoek (1850). In the Western Cape, we have the Castle of Good Hope (1666-1679), Redoubt Dujnhoop (1654), and so forth.
- ✓ The missionary education institutions include Lovedale (1824) near the Incerha River, Healdtown Methodist Missionary School (1855), Philipton Mission School in the Kat River Valley (1830), St. Matthew's Missionary School in Keiskammahoek (1855), Pirie Mission near the Hoho Mountains and the Pirie Dam, Freemantle, St John's, Buntingville, Mfundisweni and others. These missionary education colleges produced African pioneers in an array of fields. The professionals stemming from these institutions included teachers, lawyers, doctors, nurses, journalists, newspaper publishers, authors, church ministers, military commanders and the chiefs of staff in the people's armies, engineers, accountants, and politicians. These educated pioneers led the struggle on various fronts, with education seen as a strategic weapon to articulate the needs and aspirations of the African people and the mobilization of an international community through Imbumba yamaNyama, using peaceful resistance tactics against imperialism, colonialism, and colonialism of a special type under the apartheid system.
- ✓ South Africa has massacre sites, such as that of the Juanasburg massacre near Fort Hare in 1850, Jan Smuts massacre of workers during the 1922 mine strikes, the Sharpeville massacre of 21 March 1960, the Bisho massacre of 1992, and more recently, the massacre related to the Marikana miners' strike (or Lonmin strike), which was a wildcat strike at a mine owned by Lonmin in the Marikana area, close to Rustenburg, in 2012. Unfortunately, the Marikana massacre on the platinum belt represents and signals 'the moment when the revolution eats its own children'. The murder of these striking miners changed public awareness of mining and governance. It is anticipated that this struggle between unions and businesses will result in South Africa mechanizing mining operations in line with international trends, changing the country's historical labor dependency.
- *The sense of emotional attachment:* We have various graves from our combined historical heritage between the pre-colonial and democratic dispensation eras in our blue and green landscape. This refers to the whole process of building, planning and finalization of Paradise Cities to reflect the entire way of life for ensuring good-enough governance and a state of equilibrium (Williams, 1977:108; Gramsci, 1971:328).
- *The sense of craft building:* This refers to using people's skills and capacity to create assets and quality of life, thereby enhancing objects and livelihoods. Universities and historical colleges should be used as centers of excellence (COEs) to produce an industry workforce to exploit the

blue and green economic potential and opportunities in Mother Africa's 55 countries and beyond the African Union Agenda 2063.
- *The sense of nature:* To work with nature and not against it, while using natural resources and beauty to enrich our lives (Manjezi, 2007: DBSA – Sustainable Community Development Model).

In consultation with stakeholders, it was further revealed that a nation-building plan exercise involves developing behaviors, positive attitudes, good practices and aesthetic policies that reflect the integration and transformation of cultural knowledge, skills and awareness about individuals and groups of people into standards, policies, and practices to increase the quality of interactions and outcomes in harmony with the ecosystem. This means that aesthetic leaders must have SPACE competencies to conceptualise and familiarise themselves with cultural characteristics, socio-economic and cultural histories, values and belief systems, and the behaviour of citizens, officials, managers and organisations within the context of an ever-changing metaphysical environment, advanced technology and a world of scientists who have the capabilities and skills to manipulate genes using artificial intelligence, bioinformatics and the design of computer chips.

Ethically, and culturally, these scientists are capable of giving the world not only the language, art, and music that define our humanity and aesthetic relational values, but also the capacity to remake our own form and character. The profound shifts in our lives and values are not some socio-economic and cultural fluke. They are the child of a larger transformation wrought by the diffusion of technology from every corner of the world into virtually every aspect of our daily business and lives, through trade and by the instantaneity of the physical and biological world around us.

The coming challenges of human genetic enhancement are intensifying, whereby humanity is moving out of its childhood and into gawky, stumbling adolescence in which we must learn not only to acknowledge its immense new values and powers, but also figure out how to use them wisely. According to Andile (Aah! Zwelibanzi) kaNobhoma (2014), it has been demonstrated beyond a reasonable doubt that resistance and resilience against imperialism and colonialism could not be have been adopted without unity. With full realization of the divide-and-rule strategy of imperialists and colonialists, Ntsikana kaGabha, before his death in 1821, advocated for zenibe yimbumba yamanyama (unity is a strength). His promotion of unity against evil was a strategic, tactical and operational tool to counter tribal and ethnic wars between indigenous people and their leaders. This is in line with a well-known African ethos of *umanyano ngamandla, sonqoba simunye* (united we stand, divided we fall) in IsiXhosa. On the basis of Advocate Mancotywa's heritage accounts of the frontier wars, and the contemporary relevance of Ntsikana kaGabha in a nation-building plan between 2020 and 2064, it is argued that there is a need for a spiritual heritage site to be designed to honor Ntsikana kaGabha's contribution to packaging a roadmap for unity in diversity, and to combine such an aesthetic national, regional and local heritage site with local values, as depicted in Figures 1.1 to 1.3. It is apparent that the Ntsikana Paradise City is a philosophical and physical model to be crafted by youth and leaders alike to restore and maintain aesthetic relational values under the current extreme weather conditions, and with current development programs and projects being in conflict with the environment and biodiversity. Therefore, the Ntsikana Paradise City model, as depicted in Figure 1.2 – using both North-South and South-South methodologies, oral histories, modern archaeology techniques, workshops, presentations, inputs from experts and mixed methods – can be explained as follows:

- It is a picturesque architectural and graphic design representing more than 136 years of legacy of Imbumba yamaNyama aesthetic leadership beyond the physical features of the tarred Thwathwa road, the blue waterfalls of Coffee Bay, Dr. MWB Rubusana City, Ixhorha, Hankey, Tsitsikamma, Mvezo's Liberation Route, wildlife species on the African continent, Cape Town's fifth-best blue sky in the world, the world's largest underground caves, namely the Cango Caves near Outshoorn in the Western Cape, the oldest previously undiscovered and unknown caves in the mountains in the Cape, home to both the largest land mammal (elephant) and the smallest mammal (shrew), and the highest level of biodiversity worldwide. South Africa's concept of trans-frontier peace parks includes aesthetic relational values as captured in Ntsikana's Gospel Hymn before his death and burial at Thwathwa, 30 km west of Fort Beaufort in the small town of Seymour, close to the Bhukazana and Nkonkobe Mountains. Using a poetic articulation, Ngxokolo in his choral music (kwingoma yakhe) states that 'Ingumangaliso Imisebenzi kaThixo' (God's creation is aesthetically amazing).

> Hayi ubuhle bendalo yoMdali Kwinzonzobila zolwandle
> Ezintabeni emahlathini nasesibhakabhakeni
> Buyabonakala ubuhle bendalo yoMdali
> Kwizinto ezisehlabathini

This can be loosely translated as:

> Oh how beautiful is the Creator's nature
> In the deep of the sea,
> On the mountains, in the forests and the sky.
> The beauty of the Creator's nature is visible
> In all things that are in the world.

- The Ntsikana Paradise City is a great city to live in, now and in the future. Together with the community of the Raymond Mhlaba Local Municipality, the African House of Traditional Leaders, the Eastern Cape House of Traditional Leaders, the Imbumba yamaNyama Royal Council, and Khoisan Associations in the SADC region, it was agreed that an ideal city must work towards the vision of Ntsikana Paradise Cities by striving to be:

    - ✓ An accessible city
    - ✓ An active and healthy city
    - ✓ A city designed for living
    - ✓ A city of inclusive communities
    - ✓ A clean and green city
    - ✓ A clean and blue city
    - ✓ A creative city that leads, as guided by aesthetic leaders
    - ✓ A regional and world city
    - ✓ A smart and prosperous city where leaders 'think globally and act locally' in advancing blue and green programs to eradicate poverty by embracing Ntsikana Paradise City models.

- The Ntsikana Paradise City, or Thwathwa, once a holy city in the nineteenth century, has risen to its present status thanks to trade and commercial and industrial infrastructure investment programs. These should be nurtured and implemented under the Departments of Tourism, Cooperative Governance and Traditional Affairs, and Arts and Culture (DAC), the National Heritage Council (NHC), the South Africa Heritage Resources Agency (SAHRA), and the RSA cabinet economic cluster for industrialisation and enterprise development in partnership with SOEs, DFIs, sectoral departments and international development agencies such as UNEP and UNESCO.
- Blue and green economic cities with features of modern Middle Eastern cities must implement IR and UIIPs facilities whereby centers of excellence would be able to use indigenous knowledge management systems (IKMS) and local materials for socio-economic growth and development, including industrialization of the space occupied by the proposed blue and green city models.

Notwithstanding the aforementioned, the citrus produced here brought riches to the city. In the envisaged scenario for the Ntsikana Paradise City, the Nobhoma Agricultural Research Council's research and development programmes and projects – complemented by universities such as Rhodes, Fort Hare, Walter Sisulu University, Nelson Mandela University, Tshwane University of Technology and Stellenbosch, to mention a few – have successfully produced international ideapreneurs, agriculturalists, engineers, technicians, industrialists, geologists, archaeologists, technicians, economists, planners, artists, and other scarce and critical skills, expertise and specializations. Students from across Africa, and other continents, are drawn to these beautiful university campuses. From a heritage perspective, it is significant that the University of Fort Hare is an alma mater of many African leaders, such as Oliver Reginald Tambo, Robert Sobukwe, Seretse Khama, Robert Mugabe, Mangosuthu Buthelezi, and Nelson Mandela wabaThembu.

It is important that blue and green cities and heritage sites combine various city models using the systematic combination of various scientific paradigms such as paleontology, archaeology, geology, astronomy, cosmology, philology, sociology, anthropology, folkloristics, biology, botany, history, biochemistry, mathematics and engineering. In the Paradise City model these disciplines and methodologies are beautifully packaged to give an aesthetic view of Ntsikana Paradise Cities. In this context, the local site allows for radically new patterns of environmental aesthetics to be based on integrated infrastructure investment programs, with mixtures of modern and indigenous knowledge designs to allow new interactions to emerge. Furthermore, Ntsikana Paradise Cities have the power to open up pathways and breathing space in our rigid world. Through this, integrated rural development and agribusiness companies will be empowered by using agri-village and incubator interventions with relevant sectoral partners through the support of the NHC, SAHRA and the House of Traditional Leaders in various communities, provinces, and regions.

In addition, in the future Paradise City, there are internationally acclaimed research institutions for African music, English and IsiXhosa literary museums, aquatic biodiversity science laboratory centers, botanical gardens, liberation movement archives, and exceptional museums and libraries for the collection of indigenous knowledge management systems as well as modern scientific solutions. In the envisaged scenario, this has supposedly led to Ntsikana kaGabha's Paradise City being seen as a future model of an environmental aesthetic city, receiving international awards in various disciplines from credible international institutions. The Mtiki Forestry or Nobhoma Agricultural Research Council and the Rubusana Centre of Excellence – in partnership with both national and international academic and research institutions – are continuously carrying on these integrated rural and urban infrastructure investment programs. They do so by using modern, state-of-the-art technological designs and systems without conflict with environmental aesthetics (Brandy, 2006).

Artistically created and constructed (drawing on memories, oral stories, and historical connections and symbols), Ntsikana Paradise Cities are a global, environmental, aesthetic public mission of world organizations. These organizations include UNEP, UNESCO, and leaders from all continents. Their aim is to highlight the role played by Ntsikana's vision of Imbumba yamaNyama in the nineteenth century and to combine it with modern aesthetic relational values that are part of an environmental aesthetics paradigm. The Ntsikana Sacred Stone and frontier war monuments in various towns, and three metropolitan cities in the Cape provinces, provide an aesthetic and spiritual panoramic picture, through sight, taste, touch, smell and sound. Features that appeal to the senses include the sweet melody of the towns and cities, attractive landscapes such as the Mtiki indigenous forests, Nobhoma agricultural produce, and mammals and birds.

Attracting tourists, visitors, students, scholars, experts and leaders, the envisaged world-class Ntsikana tourism transport service system has various study tour routes. The unique African heritage and tourism routes offer global treasures and beautiful landscapes that can provide deep enjoyment.

Traveling with the world-class Ntsikana transport services, such as luxury buses, along various liberation routes, such as Mvezo, and to other heritage sites and sacred areas, one would be tempted to think that God was in this part of the world when He said, 'There shall be light'. While one is thinking this, tour guides imaginatively explain to tourists and scholars the local people's significant places, themes, and memories as they move from the oceans to natural veld areas with grasslands and flora comprising dense bush, rocks, natural wells and river valleys formed by the Great Kei and Fish Rivers. The Amatola and Katberg Mountains stretch along the hinterland north of Makhanda (formerly Grahamstown) and King William's Town, west of Stutterheim. The mountain ranges have an alpine character, reaching heights of more than 2 000 meters and, in winter, many peaks are covered in snow. The foothills are covered with open thornveld, interspersed with pine and bluegum plantations.

The varieties of habitat accommodate thousands of plant and animal species. Mountains and rocks along the liberation routes, and the routes to missionary educational centers and forts, are home to many species. The forts and monuments arouse special emotions in those affected, and an appreciation of the richness of Ntsikana's Paradise City and his brave leadership qualities gleaned from both oral history and the realities of Thwathwa. Ntsikana's world-class transport services and study tour routes evoke nostalgia around nineteenth-century life and elicit a deep aesthetic appreciation of nature, while visitors are enjoying luxurious, state-of-the-art services.

Undoubtedly, Ntsikana kaGabha's Paradise City model is a comprehensive exhibition of our humanism and our true aesthetic relational values from Ntsikana in the nineteenth century to AbaThembu in the twenty-first century, under the aesthetic leadership of AbaThembu bakaSabatha Dalindyebo (Ah! Jonguhlanga), AmaBonvane bakaOliver Tambo and, more recently, Rolihlahla (Ah! Dalibunga) kaMandela. Conscious of the rich heritage of the sites, towns, and cities, the Imbumba yamaNyama Royal Council's initiative, in consultation with the House of Traditional Leaders, has been urging the DAC, the NHC, and UNESCO to preserve the sacred city of Ntsikana and its historical, cultural and spiritual buildings. This is in the interest of conserving our combined and shared rich history, and thereby being able to attract new scholars and investors so as to change towards the advanced blue and green economy and environmental aesthetics.

Agricultural industrialists and farmers using Tsibani circumcision schools for boys and Miselwa Angelina kaQwakanisa women's centers of excellence for girls are part of the aim to push back the frontiers of poverty through on-the-job training. The Nobhoma Agricultural Research Council, Rhodes University, Fort Hare University, Nelson Mandela University, Walter Sisulu University of Technology, Stellenbosch University and the Tshwane University of Technology support this initiative in advancing the creative arts. Meanwhile, nearby academic colleges complement the Mtiki Citrus Fruit Factory by linking to other artisanal and scarce skills through various organs of the state. To ensure success, Ntsikana's Paradise City is further conceptualized through IR and UIIPs with the scientific knowledge that women often have a close relationship with environmental resources.

During the Southern African Young African Leaders Initiative Conference at Ekurhuleni Metropolitan City from 17 to 19 May 2015, funded by USAID, and the Pan-African Parliament held in Midrand from 21 to 25 May 2016, African leaders and speakers were inspired by Dr. Nelson Mandela's dream: 'I dream of an Africa which is at peace with itself'. Former President Obama, citing Nelson Mandela, argued that the time for African leaders and Africa's rise in the global economy and in using advanced technology for global competitiveness in this twenty-first century is now. Therefore, an investment in the youth and leadership is pertinent; it is also enshrined in the Constitution (Ngcukaitobi; 2018:1).

As has been mentioned, SPACE competencies are required for designing and implementing Ntsikana kaGabha Paradise City models for climate-change adaptability and accelerating blue and green pro-environment entrepreneurship programs and projects. Ntsikana kaGabha Paradise City models, as a continuation of the SPACE leadership legacy from Ntsikana Cirha Gabha to Nelson Madiba Mandela, were succinctly summarised by the legend himself when he said: 'The time is always right to do right' (Nelson Mandela, 1995). Therefore, ensuring economic opportunities through blue and green economy models for post-colonial smart cities, such as Coffee Bay, Ixhorha, Tsitsikamma, Hankey, Mvezo and Thwathwa, will lead to 'business unusual' approaches to investment. In short, the aesthetic leaders will be able to analyze the Complexities of biodiversity with an understanding of the required Connectedness within organizations (Context) to overcome the identified problems caused by poor decisions or bad management of our fragile world (required Change). These are the 4Cs, as depicted in Figure 4.1 below.

According to Tsibani (2014b:168), the country needs a 'business unusual' paradigm, as climate change is one more layer of concern that has been added to the existing complex capacity constraints (3Cs) between human and biodiversity needs. This highlights the need for appropriately deployed citizens, officials, managers and champions (Heads) who can make reasonable decisions and commitments for the public good (Hearts) by properly managing (Hands) the limited natural resources to advance ecosystems and their related aesthetic relational values to the human and animal world (3Hs). The impact of climate change is potentially disastrous in our fragile world, with the knock-on effects possibly having serious implications for the nation-building plan. The proposed Nation-Building Plan strategy must be complemented with good-enough governance, which refers to competent and skilled citizens, officials and managers who, as local aesthetic leaders, must drive adaptive strategies for our fragile world for the public good, and coexistence with biodiversity and the related aesthetic relational values thereof (1 Corinthians 11:7; see also Figure 4.1 below).

Figure 4.1:4 Cs in advancing WEALTH creation

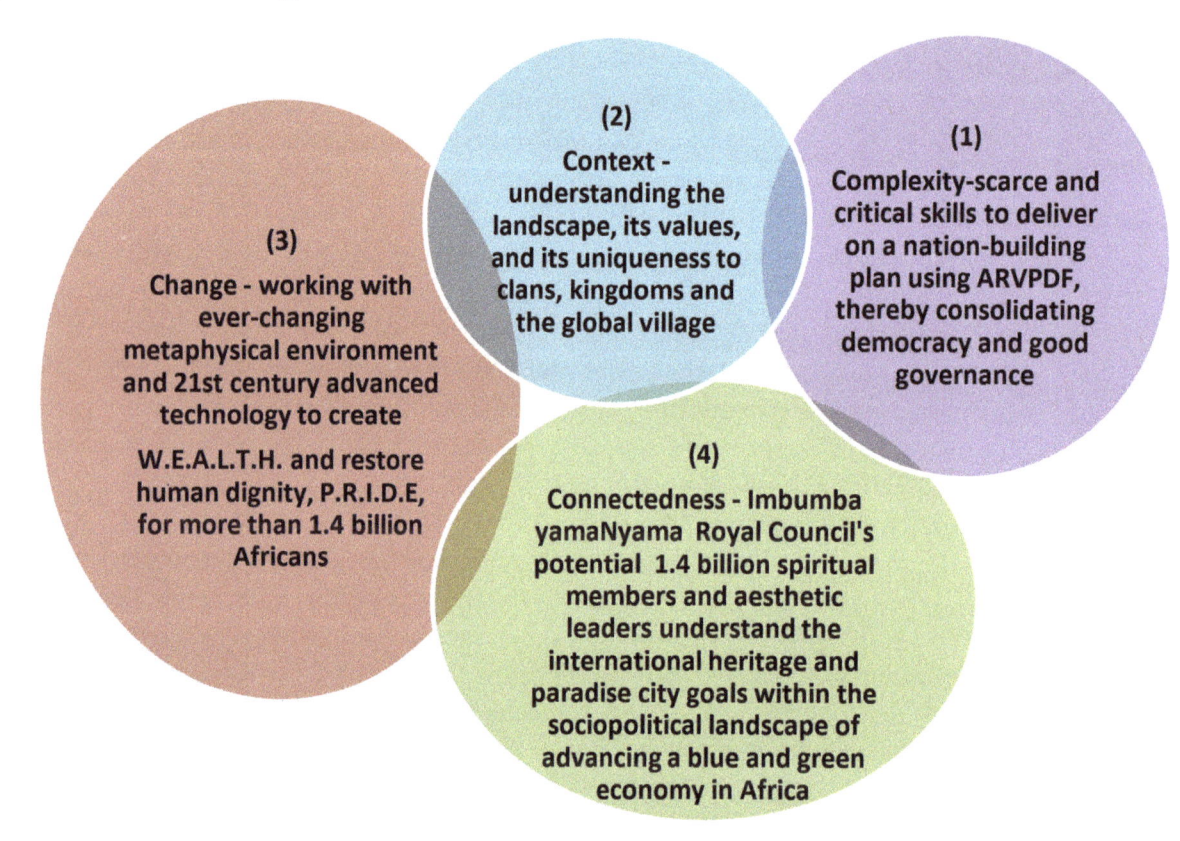

(1) Complexity-scarce and critical skills to deliver on a nation-building plan using ARVPDF, thereby consolidating democracy and good governance

(2) Context - understanding the landscape, its values, and its uniqueness to clans, kingdoms and the global village

(3) Change - working with ever-changing metaphysical environment and 21st century advanced technology to create W.E.A.L.T.H. and restore human dignity, P.R.I.D.E, for more than 1.4 billion Africans

(4) Connectedness - Imbumba yamaNyama Royal Council's potential 1.4 billion spiritual members and aesthetic leaders understand the international heritage and paradise city goals within the sociopolitical landscape of advancing a blue and green economy in Africa

From what is required in terms of the **4Cs**, it is likely that the use of all the twenty-first century's advanced technology has gained much African attention within the context of a global village. Accordingly, WEALTH creation, with the help of advanced technology means, inter alia, that there are new approaches to be followed by aesthetic leaders (3Hs) whereby the human mind (IQ or Head) and machine intelligence (IT or robotics, and highly computerized systems such as mobile phones) are combined to create smart cities or super-intelligent solutions with unpredictable results. It is predicted that in the highly intelligent world of the future, for the purpose of creating blue and green economic models, machines and technology will be used to benefit people. In this less ideological future world or state of equilibrium, scientific solutions and robots will replace human activities. It is argued that all African states as part of the global village must link their socio-economic and political strategies, using the Agenda for Sustainable Development (AfSD), the Sustainable Development Goals (SDGs) and countries' national development plans (NDPs) for adapting to a new world framework or model which is less ideological and more characterized by an era of high competitiveness among nations playing a critical role, with Asian countries already emerging as global leading players.

Governance is generally a means to achieve ends rather than an end in itself. Good-enough governance should use proper ethical and effective twenty-first century technology business intelligence to add value to the lives of citizens, and particularly indigenous people, by providing goods and developmental services while taking into account population growth, as depicted in Figure 4.2 below, as well as related STEEPLE drivers or factors. Blue and green economic models must further take into account the well-known indices compiled by international bodies for comparative purposes. These indices include:

- The Ibrahim Index of African Governance (IIAG);
- The United Nations Development Program (UNDP) Human Development Index (HDI) Report;
- The Transparency International (TI) Index (TII) and Global Corruption Barometer;
- The World Economic Forum (WEF) Global Competitiveness Index (GCI);
- The Gini coefficient on (in)equality; and
- World Bank and the Development Bank of Southern Africa (DBSA) reports.

This means that the Blue and Green Economic Model Appraisal Framework must take into account the indices above. From a native or indigenous person perspective, the designing and planning of paradise or smart cities will be affected by population growth and economic opportunities between countries and regions, BRICS, the G20, the G7, the economic shift to Asia, the Africa link to China and Eastern Europe. Programs and projects must, therefore, take into account related developmental basic services summarised in countries' national development plans, and African Union Agenda 2063 priorities, read with the MDGs and SDGs, using inter-regional and international comparisons vis-à-vis population growth as depicted in Figure 4.2 below.

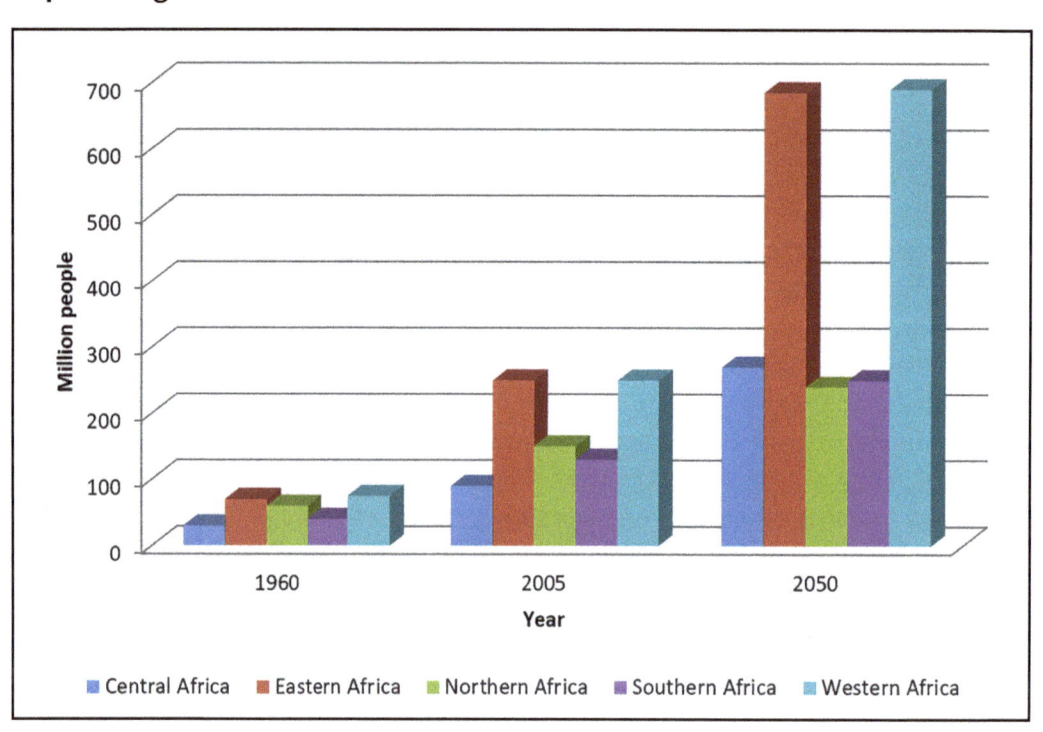

Figure 4.2: Population growth in Northern Africa

In Figure 4.2, above, from the World Bank Report (2018), it can be observed that the human development and population growth in Africa will spill over in important ways into accelerated economic advancement in terms of Maslow's hierarchy of needs vis-à-vis the blue and green economic models of the twenty-first century (depending on the adaptive capacity of African states to respond to climate change and related consequences). From a health perspective, child mortality has significantly declined. Concerning the combating of communicable diseases, the burden of disease is shifting inexorably towards chronic cases. The obesity rate of 10% and abject poverty remain a great concern. Despite health and related uncertainties, exacerbated by climate change, poor farming, political crises, migration of Africans to other continents, and immigration, there are underused resources – arable land, and mineral and natural resources – in African countries. Additionally, energy and other mineral resources are underexplored, including new large oil and gas reserves.

Ntsikana Paradise Cities are complex organizations that have to meet the needs of a great many different, and sometimes competing, stakeholders. To achieve their goals, cities have to adapt and develop new organizational models and incorporate new information and communications technologies to help them lead, guide and manage change effectively. To become high-performing organizations, Ntsikana Paradise Cities must develop, and in some cases transform, their capabilities in line with the dynamic global environment in which they operate. Just how successful they will be in meeting these challenges is largely dependent on how competent they are in aesthetic leadership, guidance and management internally, and in respect of three capital Ps in particular:

a) **P**eople: Without the services of motivated, skilled and well-managed people, Ntsikana Paradise Cities will flounder, regardless of the quality of their vision and ambitions. Good practice in people management includes: people requiring careful management and significant investment in training and development. Ntsikana Paradise Cities need to ensure that employees have the right skills to manage new programs and new ways of delivering services. Without these, people employed by these cities become a 'wasting asset', with dire consequences for city services. It is in this context that efficient human resource (HR) processes are needed to be responsive to new demands and needs.
b) **P**roperty development: In Ntsikana Paradise Cities, land and buildings are arguably the most visible and identifiable aspect of front-line services, and have a major influence on how these cities are perceived. They provide the facilities for conducting business and are essential for supporting the technology, business processes and cultural change required to raise a city's governance performance. They are also inextricably linked with city regeneration. Poor property asset management means:
    - ✓ Significant wasted resources – annual investment in and expenditure on the property is a significant cost for Ntsikana Paradise Cities where land prices are relatively high;
    - ✓ Non-compliance with building regulations and workplace statutory and regulatory codes, such as health and safety;
    - ✓ Disruption to service delivery if the physical infrastructure fails or does not support business processes; and
    - ✓ Staff dissatisfaction, leading to problems with staff retention and recruitment.

Good property asset management and planning in Ntsikana Paradise Cities cut across departmental, administrative and geographic boundaries. Good practice in this regard includes:

- ➤ Strong governance for corporate property asset management, including the active involvement of senior officials and elected members;
- ➤ A corporate asset strategy that responds to the property implications of the corporate vision and sets out coordinated medium- to long-term investment, divestment and management plans;

- The regular challenge of property needs and options for meeting future requirements, together with a transparent framework for prioritizing projects;
- Strong business processes, including supply chain management, customer relationship management, financial management, performance management, data management, program management and risk management; and
- Sourcing the right expertise and capacity to deal with both the strategic and day-to-day management.

c) **Processes**: Ntsikana Paradise Cities need to have efficient and effective processes in place to secure an appropriate return on their investment in people and property. There are a number of particular areas where Ntsikana Paradise Cities should aim to have in place 'best-in-class' processes to get the most out of their assets and to drive and support a culture of continuous improvement. These are:
- Program and project management (PPM) as part of the public administration management system (PAM);
- Performance management;
- Procurement and accountability framework;
- Risk management; and
- Reputation and brand management in terms of corporate governance and the King IV framework.

In this context, the African economy is beginning to take off. Here blue and green economic models must fuel and support a drive to diversify economies from subsistence farming towards reindustrialization, manufacturing and service sectors, with indigenous people being at the center of such investment models. It is significant to note that Africa is one of the continents with high youth numbers and ample natural resources, and should be seen as a 'great unfinished business', as former President Barack Obama could have concluded. Undoubtedly, good infrastructure investment using an ARVPDF is no panacea for sustainable growth and development in Africa, but without a blue and green economy in designing and crafting Ntsikana Paradise City models, sustainable planning and development to restore and maintain our natural beauty may prove to be impossible.

Andile kaMtiki kaNobhoma (*inyathi elusinga yaseCumakala*) succinctly summed up the road ahead with a good communication strategy to get collective support for the nation-building plan, when he said the following:

> Vuthelani amaXilongo sizeke mzekweni
> Yathetha ingwevu yakwaQhanqolo
> Yathi le nto ithi masithandaze
> Yathi le nto makulahlwe inzondo

> Vuthelani amaxilongo mabandla okwewethu
> Kubuyiswe iinkomo zoobawo
> Kubuyiswe umhlaba wookhoko kuzokulinwa, kusengwe and kuvutywe
>
> uQhanqolo watsho mandulo kuthi wathi
> Makulahlwe iibhekile neembharha
> Makulahlwe iintlonti ezimanukunyezi
> Makulahlwe inzondo nentiyo nenkohlakalo
> Makulahlwe umona nekratshi
>
> Misani indlu kaQamata
> Niyeke ubhukuqo lobukumkani bukaThixo
> Misani indlu kaThixo kuthandazwe uThixo wookhoko
> Ezindaba mazibikwe eThwathwa, eMhlangeni,
> eMpofu nangaphaya kweeNtaba, nemilambo, namalwandle
> (Mtiki: 29-12-2014 – SMS unedited to retain authenticity)

It is clear from the words of the late Andile Mtiki kaNobhoma that the prophetic message of Ntsikana requires a spiritual heritage site under the Raymond Mhlaba Local Municipality. Mtiki sent the above SMS to me when he was facing dire health problems. I then communicated it to the elders of the Imbumba yamaNyama Royal Council. I was instructed to coordinate a meeting with the chief executive officer of the National Heritage Council (NHC), Advocate Mancotywa. The meeting was held on 14 March 2017 in the Dr. MWB Rubusana City Council Chambers in honour of Counselor (advisor) Andile Mtiki's efforts and endeavours to reconcile clans and nations, including his struggle to ensure that the AmaCirha claim to the AmaXhosa Kingdom is managed using non-violent methodologies and tactics. As discussed with the mayors of both Dr. MWB Rubusana City (formerly known as Buffalo City) and the Raymond Mhlaba Local Municipality, as well as the CEO of the NHC, it is envisaged that the spiritual heritage site of Ntsikana kaGabha will be designed and constructed at Thwathwa in line with Figure 1.2 in Chapter 1. This was followed by an Imbumba yamanyama Royal Council imbizo with people of eThwathwa and Cirha clans, when a celebration was held on 24 September 2017. According to the CEO of the NHC, Advocate Sonwabile Mancotywa, the Imbumba yamaNyama Royal Council must lead the reconciliation of families and clans in the Cape provinces (14 March 2017, Council Chambers in Dr. MWB Rubusana City) and write the true relevance of Ntsikana kaGabha's prophetic message as part of Nation-Building and social cohesion in post-apartheid democratic South Africa.

In short, the Home of Legends is a global cradle of humankind, indeed. As part of South Africa's cradle of humankind, the Home of Legends can also claim that South Africa is the only country in Africa to house two Nobel Peace Prize winners, namely the first democratically elected president of the Republic of South Africa, Dr. Nelson Rolihlahla Mandela of AbaThembu (Ah! Dalibunga), and Archbishop Emeritus Desmond Mpilo Tutu. They both had houses in Vilakazi Street, Orlando West. In 2005, *Time* magazine hailed former President Thabo Mbeki as the most powerful man in Africa, and in 2007 former union secretary-general, businessperson, current president of the Republic of South Africa and ANC president democratically elected at the 54th ANC National Conference at Nasrec, Comrade Cyril (Silili as he is affectionately known by Nguni-speaking people in southern Africa) Ramaphosa, was included in the annual *Time* list of the 100 most influential people in the world. Moreover, in 2006 the Department of Tourism (DOT) claimed that the number of tourists visiting South Africa had grown by 188% since 1994, with Singita Game Reserve voted as the best hotel in the world by the readers of a leading travel magazine (*Condé Nast Traveler*), and the country housing three of the largest telescopes in the world at Sutherland in the Karoo.

The human rights background of leaders in South Africa is rooted in the concept of unity in diversity, peace and stability, and the national anthem[25] (composed by Dr. Enoch Sontonga). It has been declared that some of the world's most profoundly compassionate philosophies originated in South Africa, e.g. the Ubuntu paradigm (the belief in a universal bond of sharing that connects all humanity in terms of aesthetic relational values and principles of coexistence), and Gandhi's notion of passive or non-violent resistance (Satyagraha) that he developed while living in South Africa. As a sport and recreational country, South Africa became the first country in Africa to host the Soccer World Cup in 2010. This made South Africa one of the few countries to have hosted the President's Golf Cup and the Cricket, Rugby and Soccer World Cups. Economically, South Africa has the Johannesburg Stock Exchange (JSE) that is currently ranked the 19th largest stock exchange in the world by market capitalization, and the largest exchange on the African continent. Given its aforementioned paradigms of Ubuntu and Satyagraha, characterized by a quest for aesthetic governance and leadership, South Africa is the first country in the world to have voluntarily dismantled its nuclear weapons program. The country chose to rather employ its nuclear plant to advance science and technology so as optimally to use WEALTH mega nexuses as part of the Agenda for Sustainable Development (AfSD), subject to availability of funds. In this context, South Africa has an ample number of ports – with Durban having the largest port in Mother Africa. Durban's port is also ranked ninth in the world.

South Africa is also an economic giant, accounting for 20% of the region's gross national income (GNI). With a stable democracy and democratic institutions, South Africa is the second-largest economy in Africa (after Nigeria), although the country is home to only 5.4% of the population of sub-Saharan Africa. This means that the GNP per capita is 3.7 times higher than the regional average (Roux, 2017:188-208). The new socio-economic habits based on our aesthetic relational values and customized services, as depicted in Figure 1.1

and Figure 1.2, may lead to the required growth, development, and performance of managers, politicians and leaders in Mother Africa. According to Roux (2017:38-39), the total production of goods and services in South Africa increased from R317.2 billion in 1946 to R3 055.2 billion in 2015. This translates to an average growth rate of 3.3% per year over a period of 69 years. With her mineral and natural resources – whereby infrastructure investment programs are informed by blue and green economic models, IR and UIIP projects are rooted in tourism, and heritage conservation and the new process of Build Operate Train and Transfer (BOTT) are implemented in building new Paradise Cities – it is envisaged that the rise of GNP per capita on average per year can increase by more than 1.2%. Other driving factors for return on investment include the following:

- BBBEE and black industrialist programs will promote middle-income groups, especially black entrepreneurs and ideapreneurs.
- Blue and green economic models linked with IR and UIIPs using a transnational private-provider funding model may lead to a stable monetary and fiscal environment as tourism will perform better in respect of our heritage sites and aesthetic landscapes in Mother Africa.
- After the 2008/2009 global economic recession, the blue and green economic models, complemented by IR and UIIPs in building environmentally friendly Paradise Cities, may lead to more business confidence and investors willing to add value to humanity.
- Sustained local, regional and global economic growth and development may create global stability and greater competitiveness without instabilities and wars.
- In developing countries, living standards have improved, and people are using new technology skills to advance growth and development in terms of next-generation interests and needs – which is leading to more people being self-employed.

4.7 Conclusion

Economics is the study of humankind in the ordinary business of life.

– Alfred Marshall (cited by Roux, 2017:1)

In Chapter 4, readers are provided with specifications for applying the ARVPDF in their Home of Legends or any other appropriate site. A brief explanation of IR and UIIPs within the application of an Aesthetic Relational Values in Planning and Development Framework (ARVPDF) is provided, whereby public administration and management (PAM) theoretical principles are used to measure or assess the status quo. Furthermore, it is stressed that the differentiation between governance and good-enough governance (Table 4.1) can be used for SWOT analysis and scenario planning by learning organizations or institutions, such as the Imbumba yamaNyama Royal Council, to aid with the drafting of a roadmap for their business plan. Reference is made to the Ubuntu paradigm and required corporate governance to achieve Ubuntu principles. The latter is due to the fact that the principles in the South African Constitution are informed by the Ubuntu paradigm, i.e. a caring government led by servant and aesthetic leaders, as envisaged by Ntsikana kaGabha and those before him.

The notion of citizenship implied in such an inclusive system of governance should not be left as an abstract principle embodied in the Constitution of South Africa; it has to be translated into the daily realities of both rural and urban management systems of smart and Paradise Cities, using blue and green economic investment models. The notion of a nation-building plan (NBP) sets out the broad parameters or vision of what inclusive citizenship will entail in a state of equilibrium, with the adaptive capacity to natural disasters and climate change. As outlined, the readers – as NBP agents – now stand at the point of translating these aspirations into workable programs and projects in various Homes of Legends, heritage sites or Paradise Cities in Africa.

It is becoming clear that addressing the historical exclusion of various families, clans and kingdoms is imperative to achieving social cohesion as part of an NBP. A first step is to identify the institutional barriers that prevent the defeated families, clans, nations and kingdoms – under colonialism and in post-colonial Africa – from accessing the (albeit limited) resources of the state. While there are clear differences in sectors and specific cities, there are general pointers that relate to the social, environmental and economic mandates of aesthetic leaders to prioritize a nation-building plan for socio-economic growth and development using various inclusive programs, such as reindustrialization to restore PRIDE and to create WEALTH.

When one studies the history of civilizations' rise and fall, it appears that monarchies, kingdoms, nations, and states that rejected industrialization, the wellbeing of citizens, and the importance of stable families and clans as fundamental social units, have been unable to survive for a long time. Obviously, one of the reasons for their fall was their failure to acknowledge the centrality of families and clans as essential elements of good-enough governance. As outlined, South Africa's macro-economic environment is stable, and it is clear that investors will be attracted as the security of property rights is constitutionally recognized and protected. Through adopting water mega nexuses linked to rich heritage in South Africa, using blue and green economic models, aesthetic leaders are required to spend more time on focusing on high investment and sustained growth and development, as South Africa managed to record a growth of 5% during the four years preceding the 2008/2009 global financial and economic recession (Roux, 2017:206). This suggests that appropriate investment in exploiting our rich heritage and building Paradise City models will unleash the economy's inherent potential to grow, but at an even higher rate. The leaders can use black industrialist programs and projects and infrastructure investment, as well as modern solutions and technology in terms of the Agenda for Sustainable Development (AfSD, 2030 vision) in African countries. Through blue and green economic models, complemented by the implementation of IR and UIIP initiatives, our country's labor force will be more productive. This is because blue and green economic models, IR and UIIPs, and using water mega nexuses (WEALTH), will promote Build Operate Train and Transfer (BOTT) processes and skills transfer for global competitiveness. To capitalize on this new economic passion based on blue and green economic models to implement IR and UIIPs in building post-colonial paradise or smart cities in Mother Africa, aesthetic leaders and investors must work together to achieve country goals and targets, now subsumed in this book under a Nation-Building Plan between 2020 and 2064.

Chapter 5 provides the conclusion and recommendations that emanate from this study to be considered by decision makers, leaders and practitioners.

Chapter 4: Endnotes

24. Thembinkosi Wakashe, CEO of the Film and Publication Board (FPB), highlighted the importance of social history complemented by oral history and a need to document social history in various creative arts, industries and economies in Africa to build social cohesion and related benefits. An interview with Wakashe on the role of arts and culture in a nation-building plan with social history as one of the pillars to restore a sense of history, identity and belonging was held in April 2015 in Pretoria. He was supported by Ike Motsapi (content developer and communication specialist, Department of Human Settlements, Water and Sanitation (DHSW&S)), who argued that the book is a well-written analogy on how to work together using the simple tried-and-tested past models to bring sanity into our governance structures and approaches, and to bring justice through the alleviation of poverty for all. Ike Motsapi said, 'One gets much inspiration and the will to live through Bible verses that clearly drive the message home' (2015, email sent to the author on 9 July).

25. Based on the influence of Ntsikana kaGabha as the first African prophet in the Cape Colony, Enoch Sontonga's song became a National Anthem of South Africa, Zambia and Tanzania to honour God as a righteous and just God who can create a state of equilibrium and liberate His people from all forms of oppression (Luke 4:18–19).

CHAPTER 5

5 SYNTHESIS, CONCLUSION AND RECOMMENDATIONS

5.1 Conclusion

Hope lies in dreams, in imagination, and in the courage of those who dare to make dreams into reality.

– Jonas Salk (28 October 1914-23 June 1995), American medical researcher and virologist

As the majority of African countries are faced with numerous new and complex challenges, constraints and a lack of aesthetic leadership to guide citizens on the road of change that inevitably lies ahead, delegates in workshops, seminars, indabas, imbizos and conferences have argued that we need well-designed Paradise City models rooted in aesthetic relational values. Delegates have foreseen that this should stimulate (re)industrialization, complemented by tourism, agribusiness programs, farming, a wildlife economy, rural enterprise infrastructure investment programs, and expansion, empowerment and development programs for emerging farmers and rural communities. The new recovery program is based on a nation-building plan (NBP) in each country in Africa. To stimulate growth and development, the use of integrated rural and urban infrastructure investment programs (IR and UIIPs) feed into the nation-building plan, informed by the following global economic facts:

- All **wealthy** countries have cities that are industrialized, complemented by high production in green agriculture and farming sectors, and blue imports and exports of goods and services. Paradise Cities in the Home of Legends, or any other landscape, are seen as drivers of diversified socio-economic growth and development and reduction of unemployment – all part of post-colonial city models. Premature deindustrialization is a threat to low- and middle-income countries, as it shrinks their opportunities for technological development, and their capacity to add value in global value chains and tradable sectors, thereby ultimately reducing their scope for productivity increases. In order to reverse this trend and run the risk of falling behind in the global industrial landscape, appropriate packages of industrial, technological and innovation policies have to be deployed. These are essential economic policy tools for escaping the middle-income trap, increasing domestic value addition and, more critically, reversing the processes of premature deindustrialization. Moreover, trade relationships between South Africa and the new industrial giants have mainly reinforced the ongoing structural processes of premature deindustrialization. Over the past decade, China and India have emerged as the top two destinations of South Africa's intermediate exports, while China became South Africa's largest supplier of imports in 2009. By 2011, imports from China were already above 12% of total imports, and were overwhelmingly of manufactured goods, while South Africa's exports remained mainly composed of natural resources, i.e. mining and basic metals. The effectiveness of industrial policy in addressing premature deindustrialization in South Africa is critical in terms of global industrial performance and competitiveness to achieve the new deal, dawn and socio-economic cohesion between 2020 and 2064. Drawing lessons from Brazil, India, China, South Korea, and Malaysia, it can be concluded that:

➢ First, there are significant opportunities for value addition and technological development in agro-business value chains in South Africa. The industrialization of agriculture opens new venues for increases in productivity, upgrading in global markets and diversification. However, in order to capture these opportunities, public technology intermediaries must provide key technology and product services to reach product quality standards and transform agricultural activities into highly productive industrial processes;

➢ Second, the promotion of technological upgrading in manufacturing industries cannot be done simply by jumping to frontier technologies, i.e. the so-called fourth industrial revolution. The China case study, in particular, emphasizes how the building of a solid productive and technological capability foundation over several years is a precondition for innovation across several industrial fields. The other lesson is that institutions promoting technological innovation will have to change over time to respond to the changing nature of the innovation challenges firms face in the fast-changing global landscape; and

➢ A third policy lesson is that, to increase value addition and value capturing in the domestic economy, countries need to target the development of their local production system. The building of integrated supply chains in the domestic economy gives countries sustained industrial and productivity growth. Therefore, industrial policy focusing on the attraction of a multinational or the setting up of an export-promotion zone must be fully coordinated with other policy measures that induce the real industrialization process in South Africa.

Re-industrialization in South Africa will result from the use of one of these instruments to build the required socio-economic growth and development envisaged under the Presidential Job Summit on the 4-5 October 2018, supported by the Black Business Council (BBC) Job Summit on 28 February 2019 to 01 March 2019. This will lead to development of the local production system as a strategy to move beyond the middle-income trap faced by South Africa and her cities. While manufacturing remains a cornerstone for reindustrialization and technological development in South Africa, new value addition opportunities can be found at the interface of the other economic sectors and the intersection of different technology systems. Well-coordinated and coherent industrial policy packages are critical in shaping this new industrial ecosystem in South Africa and moving the country beyond the middle-income trap.

- Institutions that participate in building and restoring blue and green economies using a **public-private partnership (PPP)** model will emerge through socio-economic progress. It is strongly argued that a credible, inclusive and creative team is required, with the universities championing actionable research, and the required indigenous knowledge management systems (IKMS) being used for skills transfer and further refinement of the nation-building plan.
- Through the use of a **comprehensive nation-building plan and a vision** to foster real blue and green planning and development, it is envisaged that blue and green city models and related business activities will lead to sustainable job creation and the design of large-scale economic interventions to create links between heritage towns and metropolitan cities. The programs and related value-driven projects will create stability, lasting peace and harmony with the environment. Indeed, the best-performing cities excel at creating efficient local links among industrial producers from different sectors.
- **E**fficiency, **e**conomic viability and **e**ffectiveness (**3Es**) must be supported by a vision of a sustainable building environment. The city designs must be energy-efficient (**e4** alternative energy), thereby being able to instill environmental changes creatively.
- The need for co-nurturing and co-creating of local space for governance was succinctly expressed by a former president of the United States of America when he said the following with regard to his own national context:

We here highly resolve that these dead shall not have died in vain; that this nation, under God, shall have a new birth of freedom, and that government of the people, by the people, for the people, shall not perish from the earth. (Abraham Lincoln, Gettysburg Address, 19 November 1863)

Boulding (1966:11) later supported former President Abraham Lincoln (1863) when he argued that:

There is a great deal of historical evidence to suggest that a society which loses its identity with posterity, and which loses its positive image of the future, loses also its capacity to deal with present problems and soon falls apart.

We need to adopt a **C**oncepts, **C**hallenges, **C**ontexts, **C**apabilities, and **C**ompetencies (**5Cs**), and **O**pportunities framework, as we are moving to a technologically advanced world and related technological opportunities for socio-economic growth and development. The 5Cs framework will focus on constructive criticism and innovative sustainable development of new smart cities or Paradise City models, leading to intergenerational equity and integration in local and global communities. This framework is rooted in the argument that blue and green city models are not a luxury, but prerequisites for intergenerational equity and sustainable development. Through applying the 5Cs framework, complemented by IR and UIIPs, it is argued that a meaningful inclusive economy and political transformation to adapt to climate change are urgently needed. Under the notions of self-identity, self-love, and co-creation of governance innovation using IR and UIIPs as part of a nation-building plan, the following can be noted:

> *Inspiring leaders are not just born to the role. They are born, then made, and sometimes unmade, by their own actions. A leader who is not in tune with the followership will become a leader in limbo.* (Khoza, 2011:3)

In short, in our fragile world, technical skills such as ACES and SPACE competencies are not enough to equip leaders to co-create governance innovation and partnerships. The ability to build aesthetic relational values between nations and ecosystems and to influence other leaders, citizens, community champions, managers and officials, are key characteristics and traits of aesthetic and inspiring leaders. From an ARVPDF it appears that the envisaged PPPs have a rich heritage, liberation routes and spiritual attachments for their design as Paradise City models and blue and green city models in global UNESCO and UNEP flagship programs, which will be new cities designed and constructed based on three key economic drivers, namely:

- Productivity
- Inclusivity
- Resilience in democratic (South) Africa

> *We need an economy that is more dynamic, competitive and sustainable, where innovation and productivity lead to better jobs with high wages, and where entry is supported. In order to do this, there needs to be a new vision for reindustrialization under a political settlement which prioritizes long-term investment in productive capacity and rewards effort and creativity rather than incumbency. It requires a broad rethink rather than piecemeal initiatives, in order to place reindustrialization and industrial policies at the center of the country's development strategy.* (Bell et al, 2018:60)

The socio-economic, cultural and political transitions in Africa ushered in not only an era of non-racial and non-sexist democratic administration systems, but also a commitment to social cohesion as part of nation-building plans by the state that would reduce inequality and poverty. In this book, I have argued that much of African history has been told through the eyes of its former colonizers and white scholars who, through self-interest and a lack of cultural understanding of African families, clans, kingdoms and societies, have produced either a one-sided biased account, or fictitious histories to advance and consolidate their colonial and apartheid interests beyond post-colonial scenarios in Africa. These fictitious histories, and highly selective oral memories and myths, such as those of Nongqawuse, the Mfecane, and others, have continued to keep Africa's true histories hostage. African countries were part of global economic models, including trade with the Mediterranean area, the Middle East and Asia, since the seventh century. In other words, in the pre-colonial era, African states were supplying raw materials to Europe and Asia. Unfortunately, the African raw materials and natural resources led to the so-called 'Scramble for Africa' by Europeans.

It is also significant that white sociologists, ethnologists, ethnographers, anthropologists, and academics argued that Africa was a dark or uncivilized continent to justify imperialism and colonialism, partly because of her rich natural resources. Historical evidence indicates that African towns, cities and kingdoms were established in ancient Egypt, and traded with raw materials, minerals and agriculture products (Fage & Tordoff, 2008:103; Van Zyl, 2016:49-50). Historians and sociologists argue that, with wealth and power, African societies in the pre-colonial era had well-established monarchies, traditional governance and well-structured systems of government using the Ubuntu philosophy and their customary norms and standards, which were democratically accepted by families, clans, and kingdoms. In effect, Fage & Tordoff (2008:103), cited in Van Zyl (2016:50) maintain that in the sixteenth and seventeenth centuries, the Europeans' demand for African natural and raw materials began to reconstruct African monarchies, economies, governance structures and systems. This led to slavery being introduced, for converting raw materials and mineral resources such as gold and platinum, in European industrial sites. Consequently, African natural and mineral resources were forcefully taken to Europe for manufacturing purposes.

It is also significant that the Berlin Conference of 1884/1885, hosted by European states, further divided African territory into countries without respecting families, clans and kingdoms, but based on European boundary interests. This further led to African societies being divided, and certain kingdoms erased. The conference ushered in a period of heightened colonial activity by European powers, which eliminated or overrode most existing forms of African autonomy and self-governance. The colonization by European countries was motivated mainly by the desire to take control of the continent's resources and riches, rather than for trading with the African states. It can be argued that, throughout the nineteenth century, European countries took control of all supply chain processes, and distorted African families, clans and kingdoms (Ayittey, 2005:402-403; Prah, 2005:13). By 1902, 90% of all the land that makes up Africa was under European control. A large part of the Sahara was French, while – after the quelling of the Mahdi rebellion and the ending of the Fashoda crisis – Sudan remained firmly under joint British-Egyptian rulership, with Egypt being under British occupation before becoming a British protectorate in 1914. The Boer Republics were conquered by the United Kingdom in the Boer War from 1899 to 1902. Morocco was divided between the French and the Spanish in 1911, and Libya was conquered by Italy in 1912. The official British annexation of Egypt in 1914 ended the colonial division of Africa.

Ultimately, Africa was totally colonized using Berlin Conference principles, which included:

- Creating and establishing new government administration systems in the new settlements;
- Creating colonies by planting a flag;
- Using military force to protect territories or colonies;
- Making use of the colony economically;
- Establishing rights over the land using colonial policies and laws; and
- Signing agreements with monarchies and kingdoms.

Though the list is not exhaustive, the consequences of the Berlin Conference included the following:

- Africa lost her political, social and economic freedom;
- European powers agreed to safeguard and protect Christian missionary education and missionaries;
- Effective occupation of the African continent meant that trade was replaced by unequal exchange and the exploitation of African resources;
- European nations were assured of a maximum supply of raw materials, cheap labor, and markets for their industrial manufactured goods;
- European commercial companies penetrated the interior of Africa, and later trade systems and economic models completely changed; and
- New physical boundaries were drawn during this period, which ignored ethnic origin or kingdoms. They were designed based on divide-and-rule principles, and in some cases even supported illegitimate kingdoms to generate endless conflicts, as witnessed in various wars in this century.

It is also significant that each colonial country had to register its new colonies with the European Committee and Council dealing with African colonialization to avoid illegal trade between European countries, and conflicts, as far as possible. Some scholars have tried to argue that colonialism and slavery systems were not the same between these countries, as in the case of the Dutch and French colonies (Van Zyl, 2016:50-51). For me, colonialism and slavery systems are inhuman wherever they occur. They have similar consequences of injustice, distortion of histories, loss of cultural identities, and loss of land and wealth by African families, clans, and kingdoms, irrespective of the name of the colonizers. It is argued that even the abolishment of the slavery system in the nineteenth century was driven by a need for mechanical skills and competencies rather than the manual labor force of the fifteenth to eighteenth centuries. As a result of mechanization in Europe, artisan skills were required, leading to European countries deciding to abolish the slavery system. Therefore, human rights and moral values did not inform this decision. Paradoxically, European leaders were informed by commercial outputs and profits rather than human rights.

I have tried to provide an account of why social cohesion among Africans has been destroyed by colonialism and neo-colonialism in post-colonial Africa. In other words, defining our rich history and heritage requires careful attention to where development takes place and who has been defeated and excluded under repressive colonial and apartheid laws and associated atrocities. Distorted histories must be reviewed so that the lions can be reflected in their own stories (not in the hunters' self-constructed renditions). We must identify and recognize who is poor and, finally, make sure that the nation-building plan, using IR and UIPPs, eradicates poverty, reduces class inequalities, and supports innovative initiatives to eradicate systemic unemployment among our youth – as Africa is defined as a youthful continent.

Accordingly, urban and rural definitions must be properly conceptualized and contextualized by taking into account imperial, colonial and neo-colonial policy, such as influx policies and related consequences for the urban and rural poor. Implicitly, this means addressing both national and sub-national structures and activities of each state in Africa. Crucially, embracing the notion of a nation-building plan demands that we focus first and foremost on the incomplete transformation of families, clans and kingdoms, and the impact of pseudo-archaeology in writing down oral memories and histories about African societies (Prah, 2005:13). The correcting of histories is meant to ensure inclusivity, achieve social cohesion, and provide an understanding of social, environmental and economic obligations in a manner that builds citizenship and fosters sustainable and equitable growth in Africa up to 2063 and beyond.

While we cannot afford to continue blaming colonialism and apartheid in post-colonial Africa, it must be taken into account that a new culture of social Darwinism was institutionalized through myths, stories, and histories, such as those of Nongqawuse, the battle of Thuthula, Tshawe, and Shaka. These were constructed and sponsored tribal wars among African families and clans. One classic example includes white scholars creating Nongqawuse, Tshawe, and Shaka as warriors for fighting their fellow citizens, whereby these images were appropriated and manipulated to serve various Berlin Conference principles and resolutions. These appropriated and manipulated political images of African leaders were informed by social Darwinism, which held that cultural and economic development and governance of families and clans were based on the survival of the fittest. (This can be seen in the AmaCirha and AmaJwarha vis-à-vis Tshawe constructed discourse, including the well-structured colonial machinery of the 1800s, as well the published story of Shaka recently popularized for self-independence by the Inkatha Freedom Party (IFP).) Under social Darwinism or the 'survival of the fittest' or 'winner-takes-all policy', Ubuntu, trust, cooperation, a mixed and balanced economy rooted in Ubuntu principles and values, and collective and shared leadership, are undermined and suppressed at all costs.

In addition, African poverty and economic stagnation are neither accidental nor entirely self-inflicted. While imperialism, colonialism, and apartheid (in the case of South Africa) are contributory factors in the current socio-economic, ecological, environmental, cultural and political situations, there is also a need to review current leadership policies, plans and strategies being implemented in post-colonial Africa. Literature evidence suggests that African states are still not able to deal effectively with the triple challenges of abject Poverty, systematic Unemployment and increased Inequalities (PUI, as coined by Terreblanche, 2012) and successfully transform their states into Paradise Cities or states of equilibrium envisaged under the struggle for total independence and freedom. Some of the reasons are, inter alia, the following:

- African countries do not have purpose-driven leaders.
- African leaders established more abstract development paradigms, which have often been adopted without adequate adjustments to their own cultural, geographical and physical conditions. Most of the plans adopted are more applicable to the West. These abstract programs are developed by individual experts and organizations that do not understand the cultural or practical nature of life for most Africans (Van Zyl, 2016:57-58).
- African countries adopt ideologies without concrete, practical steps and solutions to adjust them to geographic, topographic and contextual realities of their countries, which are characterized by a racialized capitalist system and the structural impact of colonialism and apartheid in post-colonial Africa.
- Many African countries lack exemplary leaders who continued with revolutionary good intentions and programs in various sectors of governance.
- Infrastructure left by colonial governments was meant only to serve the colonial population and was operated and maintained by colonial and apartheid administrators as part of Berlin Conference solutions and principles.
- African leaders are largely dependent on foreign aid and related assistance, which does not allow for localization and beneficiation in manufacturing and industrialization of products. This results in a tendency for foreign aiders and funders to benefit from the continued marginalization of Africa in terms of the global economy and context.
- Poor governance and corruption, characterized by greed, is a very real cancer of post-colonial Africa if Ntsikana Gabha's prophetic message can be taken into account.

African leaders must think globally and act locally to adjust to and adopt globalization, and use fourth industrial revolution technology to create WEALTH and restore PRIDE. The blue and green economic models using IR and UIIPs to advance an ARVPDF must also take into account disruptive changes due to technology and new sets of skills for technologically advanced societies by the end of the twenty-first century. It is envisaged that by 2030, African states must build new cities, as the world will have advanced robotics and autonomous transport, artificial intelligence and machine learning, advanced materials, biotechnology, and genomics. With the avalanche of new products, new technologies, and new ways of working in a highly global technologically advanced world, workers, managers and leaders will be required to become more creative in dealing with complexity by the end of the twenty-first century. They will need disruptive innovation and problem-solving technology to create wealth.

It can be deduced that social and economic cohesion must be adopted as part of the nation-building plan to change the lives of citizens. Accordingly, achieving this social and economic cohesion between 2020 and 2064 requires aesthetic leaders who have the ability to:

- Listen to citizens, sectors, and stakeholders;
- Build efficacy in themselves and the people, using inclusive socio-economic, cultural and political programs and projects;
- Draw lessons and best practices from other countries by using North-South and South-South methodologies, but these practices must be adapted rather than simply adopted;
- Promote reindustrialization, local beneficiation and manufacturing of natural resources by sending students and scholars to various academic institutions as future champions of growth and development, including manufacturing using state-owned enterprises (SOEs) for the benefit of their countries and regional economic forums;
- Promote accurate histories with the purpose of creating good-enough governance and excellent corporate governance, and marketing of Africa's rich cultural and historical heritage and landscapes, such as paradise sites, towns and cities;
- Implement practical programs and projects to restore aesthetic relational values in planning and development of reindustrialization, local beneficiation, manufacturing and restoration of nearly lost histories and African PRIDE; and
- Make political commitments and develop the will to eradicate poverty and promote the wellbeing of citizens by exploiting Africa's youthfulness, rich natural resources and beautiful landscapes.

There is a consensus among local and global scholars, policymakers and decision-makers that, compared to Asia and the Middle East, socio-economic growth and sustainable development of African states – including

South Africa – over the past six decades have been disappointing. The reasons for this unbearable and undesirable state of affairs are numerous, complex, and often based on imperial, colonial and apartheid regimes. It can be deduced that we must embark on social cohesion as part of nation-building plans informed by blue and green economic models using IR and UIIPs and aesthetic relational values in planning and development between 2020 and 2064. It is concluded that social cohesion, as part of such nation-building plans, will encourage African states to embark on inclusive growth and development, complemented by reindustrialization, to reduce the current reliance on the production and exploitation of raw and unprocessed materials (mineral and natural resources). Instead, African states and nations need to reindustrialize in order to produce well-educated, productive workers informed by highly increased mechanization and twenty-first century technology to create WEALTH and restore PRIDE. The envisaged reindustrialization, based on aesthetic relational values in planning and development, may lead to IR and UIIP programmes and projects, creating reliable and accessible infrastructure and promoting entrepreneurship with a view to using African heritage sites, towns and cities to promote local companies to produce goods and services for local, national, regional, continental and global markets. With Africa as a youthful continent, social cohesion as part of nation-building plans may not only lead to socio-economic growth and development, but may also help bring about a new economic and developmental renaissance, similar to that of Asia.

Despite complex constraints, Africa has a population of 1.4 billion and a combined gross domestic product (GDP) of US$3.5 trillion, which can attract investors and foreign direct investment (FDI) agencies. Moreover, Africa has the highest rate of population growth among major areas of the world, with an estimated urban population of 50% by 2030, up from 36% in 2016. Benefiting from her rich precious resources, economies of scale and socio-economic inclusive transformation, post-colonial or smart or Paradise Cities have to use social cohesion as a strategy to find the best trajectories for socio-economic growth and development, as envisaged in the Agenda for Sustainable Development (AfSD), taking into account city-specific local metaphysical conditions in attracting both private and public investment models. For instance, I have argued in a 2014 DBSA workshop, with the theme *Rapid urbanization in South Africa as part of Africa*, that African countries were institutionally and financially not ready to effectively deal with rapidly advancing and unavoidable urban growth because most countries are deeply rural without transportation infrastructure. The continent has a largely rural-based population, which is a majority. It has mushrooming informal human settlement conditions with less access to urban land for property development. In dealing with these structural realities, African leaders must aesthetically lead to ensure all enjoy the fruits of freedom and civilization. In this context, Nkrumah (1957) summed up the way forward when said

> *We shall measure progress by the improvement in the health of our people, by the number of children in school, by the quality of their education, by the availability of water and electricity in*

our towns and villages, and by the happiness which our people take in being able to manage their own affairs. The welfare of our people is our chief pride, and it is by this that my government will ask to be judged.

Yet, other factors are shaping future Paradise Cities, which include the following:

- There is a growing middle class with high purchasing power driving architectural designs of WEALTH and Paradise Cities in response to global markets.
- Paradise Cities will be architecturally designed for advancing sustainable city models by using advanced technology for connectivity.
- Paradise City models are architectural designs structured for advancing a public-private partnership model, including skills exchange programs and institutional twinning arrangements (Tsibani, 2005).
- Therefore, investing in large infrastructure will address current infrastructure deficits and replace these infrastructure deficits with blue and green investment as part of adaptive capacity to extreme weather conditions or the consequences of climate change.

It is concluded that post-colonial cities, or Paradise Cities, are required in the Home of Legends and elsewhere in Africa to enable the continent to seize a more prominent position in the global economy by enhancing accessibility, connectivity, markets and urban attractiveness using IR and UIPs, thereby being able to create WEALTH. By making use of the Continental Free Trade Agreement (CFTA), reindustrialization and manufacturing supported by agricultural processes and innovative projects, these programs, underpinned by good-enough governance, can generate the highest number of direct jobs. Accordingly, Agriculture as one component of WEALTH creation coincides with investment in technologies, innovation, logistics, and related services in various Paradise Cities. By using water nexuses, Paradise Cities in Africa will be able to be robust and resilient to global market shocks. In the Agriculture and Agro-processing industries, there has been widespread liberalization of markets, except for sugar, which continues to enjoy protection. The resultant restructuring has brought huge job-losses. The fresh fruit sector has emerged as a strong export generator, and has built considerable capabilities to export fruit into international markets. While downstream processing of sugar, dairy and fruit do present opportunities for industrialization, value chain challenges remain. This includes, for instance, continued support for the sugar industry, and raising the price of sugar for downstream producers. The dairy processing sector is concentrated, with the increasing presence of multinationals resulting in significant barriers for new entrants. The retail level of the value chain is also concentrated. It can thus be deduced that economic development requires deliberate industrial policies, which are at the heart of countries' development. Industrial policy plays an important role in coordinating investment in interdependent activities, addressing underinvestment in capability development due to externalities, and dealing with the inherent discrepancies in the ability to deal with risk and uncertainties between individual producers. The lack of an overarching industrial policy in South Africa in the 1990s and early 2000s, and poor commitment across government following the introduction of the National Industrial Policy Framework in 2007, has undermined various industrial policy interventions and limited its impact on industries. Moreover, the failure to manage the commodities boom to ensure the exchange rate was not over-valued and that revenues were saved and invested, exacerbated the hollowing out of industrial capabilities over the 2000s.

It is envisaged that Paradise Cities will continue to perform a quintessential strategic role in the age of globalization and the emerging fourth industrial revolution. Consequently, African leaders must invest in long-term social, cultural, ecological, environmental, economic and developmental goals, as expressed in the National Development Plan (NDP) 2030 vision of the South African government, the African Union Agenda 2063, the United Nations New Urban Agenda, UN-Habitat's State of African Cities reports, and the World Bank's Africa's Cities reports. Therefore, careful policy and infrastructure investment models using public-private partnership models, co-funding, transnational funding, and others, should be followed by aesthetic leaders in pursuit of new post-colonial, smart and Paradise Cities. Such cities would use aesthetic relational values in architectural designs grounded on the optimal use of local materials and resources to bring a sense of history, identity and emotional and spiritual attachment to citizens.

5.2 Recommendations

It is recommended that the SETAs, DAC, DRDLR, DEA, COGTA, DPSA, DHSW&S, DHETS&T DPW, NHC, SAHRA, UNEP, UNESCO, and various other international development agencies, fund the proposed Nation-Building Plan (2020-2064) in South Africa, using IR and UIIPs to restore and maintain aesthetic relational values. Through this nation-building plan and related interventions, it is hoped that the following outputs will be achieved:

5.2.1 Prioritisation of IR and UIIPs for promoting the Home of Legends, heritage sites, and tourism. The Department of Arts and Culture, and its agent SAHRA, will be the custodians of heritage and cultural programs and interventions, informed by intellectual thinking as represented by the Imbumba yamaNyama Royal Council and other African kingdoms, to consolidate the Ntsikana kaGabha legacy with the current modern legacy of our international icons, such as Prixley kaSeme, Albert Luthuli, Mangaliso Sobukwe, Steve Bantubonke Biko, Oliver Tambo, and Nelson Mandela. Given the importance of land to African people, it is envisaged that heritage, indigenous knowledge and traditional governance workshops with international and continental experts on best practices will lead to a Sustainable Action Plan (SAP). These historical and oral memories workshops must be aligned to feasibility studies using sectoral plans, such as Spatial Planning, Water Master Plan, Water Security Framework, Energy and Alternative Renewable Energy Plans, Tourism Master Plan and Heritage Site Integrated Master Plan in a nation-building plan rooted in aesthetic relational values and a blue and green economy.

5.2.2 Best practices from Latin America, Palestine, South Korea, and other African kingdoms on Paradise City models must be documented to feed into the heritage strategy towards social cohesion. In southern Africa we had the old Kingdom of Mapungubwe between 900 and 1300 AD. The remains of this pre-colonial state are located at the confluence of the Shashe and Limpopo Rivers, south of Great Zimbabwe. The kingdom was the first stage in a development that would culminate in the creation of the Kingdom of Zimbabwe in the thirteenth century, with gold-trading links to Rhapta and Kilwa Kisiwani on the African east coast. The Kingdom of Mapungubwe lasted about seventy years and, at its height, comprised about 5 000 people. Additionally, in South Africa, we have strong and well-established kingdoms, such as the Royal Bafokeng Nation at Phokeng, near Rustenburg, under Kgosi (King) Leruo Molotlegi. The Royal Bafokeng Kingdom is a good example of a modern kingdom with advanced infrastructure (such as the FIFA-accredited Royal Bafokeng Stadium) and formal contractual agreements with the platinum mining sector on economic benefits to the kingdom from its natural resources.

5.2.3 The submission of the Ntsikana kaGabha Paradise City as part of the global environmental public commission by the NHC and UNESCO, with the support of sectoral departments such as the DAC, DEA, DRDLR, DPW, COGTA, DHSW&S, LGSETA, DPSA and the Tirelo Bosha Public Service Improvement Facility, the NHC, SAHRA, and the House of Traditional Leaders in Africa under IPAP. This will ensure, inter alia, that the community and citizens in these historical and heritage sites are active participants and ideapreneurs for sustainable job creation, where land is optimally used for production and blue and green economy products.

5.2.4 The Ntsikana Paradise City models and related architectural designs, as part of the United Nations Environment Programme (UNEP) and global environmental public commissions for a blue and green economy, must include towns and cities in the Home of Legends (Eastern, Northern and Western Cape provinces). As part of the smart or Paradise Cities' architectural designs, it is recommended that the NHC, UNESCO and sectoral departments devise a mapping of land, as most of the land might have been stolen using colonial and apartheid mapping exercises.

5.2.5 Workshops with experts to be followed up with sectoral departments and ministries in Africa, SAHRA, the NHC, UNEP, UNESCO, CONTRALESA, the Kingdom of Khoekhoen, the Imbumba yamaNyama Royal

Council, and the House of Traditional Leaders. Plans and priorities need to be finalized to ensure access to land for development and for sanctioning of the Nation-Building Plan (2020-2064) by stakeholders. Co-funding models will be developed and consolidated into a feasibility study. This feasibility study will lead to bankable Paradise City business plans between 2020 and 2064, covering both the frontier war province, metropolitan cities and heritage towns as pilot programs. This must be accompanied by portable skills transfer to local and vulnerable groups using Build, Operate, Own and Transfer (BOOT) strategies and programs to ensure that artisans, miners, industrialists, manufacturers, entrepreneurs and indeapreneurs are co-nurtured and co-created to implement the nation-building plan programs and projects as part of a resource investment model used for reindustrialization in various countries that are now regarded as First World countries.

5.2.6 Workshops with the House of Traditional Leaders, the Imbumba yamaNyama Royal Council, the Kingdom of Khoekhoen, SADC and CONTRALESA on aesthetic planning and development, developing and writing blue and green bankable business plans, and energy, water and agricultural governance, as well as aesthetic leadership short courses, are required. This will lead to a global Ntsikana kaGabha Heritage Festival to be held on 24 September each year. An inter-ministerial task team is required to brand the proposed workshops to ensure the adoption of public-private partnership (PPP) models, using South Africa's experience of hosting international events, such as the Rugby World Cup in 1995 and the Soccer World Cup in 2010. The research to address distorted histories must be funded and conducted using various institutions led by inter-disciplinary and trans-disciplinary teams of experts, specialists and leaders.

5.2.7 Given the use of water mega nexuses (abbreviated as WEALTH creation), it is critical that the planning processes be informed by capacity-building and training programs. Some of the planning and development processes or phases, as adopted from the DBSA (2007), include the following:

- *Conceptual Framework and Planning Workshop* – community and participatory research to inform engineering and technical infrastructure:
    - ✓ Drafting a conceptual and graphic design of a Ntsikana Paradise City;
    - ✓ Training on an Aesthetic Relational Value in Planning and Development Framework and a business plan with stakeholders and Imbumba yamaNyama leaders;
    - ✓ Meeting with the Imbumba yamaNyama Royal Council as custodian of the Ntsikana kaGabha heritage to understand the concept and its value;
    - ✓ Holding a strategic workshop with Imbumba yamaNyama to map the project scope of work;
    - ✓ Holding a workshop with Imbumba yamaNyama leadership and other traditional royal councils;
    - ✓ Holding a workshop with the Imbumba yamaNyama youth forum;

- ✓ Holding a workshop with public institutions and sectoral departments on priorities and mandate areas;
- ✓ Writing a draft sustainable action plan (SAP) and resolutions from the public institution consultative meeting or workshop – project phases and priorities;
- ✓ Holding a consultative workshop with experts in landscape, heritage, and infrastructure;
- ✓ Drafting a proposal and a business case; and
- ✓ Drafting a funding proposal subject to a feasibility study.

- *Land Enabling and Preparation* – optimal use of landscape:

  - ✓ Update pre-feasibility;
  - ✓ Town planning;
  - ✓ Sketch plans;
  - ✓ Rezoning survey;
  - ✓ Infrastructure requirements;
  - ✓ Scoping;
  - ✓ Documentary and technical reports and reviews;
  - ✓ Integration of plans;
  - ✓ Land claims and land availability; and
  - ✓ Preliminary costing.

- *Site Development Planning* – site development plan:

  - ✓ Infrastructure review and site inspection;
  - ✓ Environmental impact assessment (EIA);
  - ✓ Rezoning;
  - ✓ Land consolidation and subdivision;
  - ✓ Infrastructure design;
  - ✓ Property improvement designs; and
  - ✓ Preliminary costing and budgets.

- *Field and Infrastructure Assessments:*

  - ✓ Submissions and compliance with government regulations and norms and standards;

- ✓ Intensive consultation with authorities;
- ✓ Certificates and guidelines compliance; and
- ✓ Approval of plans.

- *Implementing Top Structure, Financing and Development* – business plan (financial models and infrastructure investment plans):

  - ✓ Legal structuring;
  - ✓ Financial arrangements;
  - ✓ Project management;
  - ✓ Bulk and service infrastructure;
  - ✓ Land parcels – specific delivery options;
  - ✓ Undertaking archaeological excavations, especially the Dyibishe human evolution site; and
  - ✓ Commissioning of the scientific work, complemented by engineering infrastructure investment models.

- *Land and Asset Management – a* portfolio of profitable investments:

  - ✓ Land management;
  - ✓ Investment and funding models;
  - ✓ Consultation workshops;
  - ✓ Project management meetings;
  - ✓ Marketing; and
  - ✓ Investor relations and business approval.

- *Deliverables and Outputs:*

  - ✓ Draft graphic design including the picturesqueness of Ntsikana kaGabha city;
  - ✓ Stakeholder reports;
  - ✓ Imbumba yamaNyama and its youth forum report;
  - ✓ Program phases and projects;
  - ✓ Bankable feasibility study reports;
  - ✓ Project funding models;
  - ✓ Business submission to funders;

- ✓ Contracts and project management;
- ✓ Heritage report and documentation of Ntsikana kaGabha tourism routes;
- ✓ Historical documentation of Ntsikana kaGabha Paradise City;
- ✓ Manual on aesthetic leadership in our fragile world;
- ✓ Manual on restoring and holding aesthetic relational values in planning and development;
- ✓ Manual on water governance and leadership innovation;
- ✓ Manual on environmental management and practices;
- ✓ Manual on water and wastewater management;
- ✓ Manual on traditional leadership in a modern democracy; and
- ✓ Training programs to ensure knowledge is applied to carry out the deliverables and outputs of the nation-building plan.

5.2.8 As advised by Ntsikana kaGabha, our unity is our strength; and therefore a synergism between Ntsikana kaGabha Paradise City and the celebration of South Africa's Heritage Day on 24 September each year must be linked to historic liberation routes such as Mvezo (to honour Dr. Nelson Rolihlahla Mandela's legacy) and Hankey to Tsitsikamma (to honour the Khoikhoi and the San) in line with Ntsikana's prophetic message to his followers in the nineteenth century.

5.2.9 Coffee Bay, Dr. MWB Rubusana City, Raymond Mhlaba Local Municipality, Ndlambe, Nelson Mandela Bay Municipality, Hessequa, George, Mossel Bay, Cape Town, and Ixhorha (Hole in the Wall) must be included to represent blue cities in the coastal SPACE or landscape of the Cape provinces.

5.2.10 The Department of Environmental Affairs (DEA), the Department of Arts and Culture (DAC), the Department of Tourism (DOT), the NHC and SAHRA, through their MOUs with various Sector Education and Training Authorities (SETAs), SOEs, DFIs, sectoral departments and international development agencies, can start to fund a youth indaba on blue and green economy models in June of each year, to be held in the Cape provinces as part of the annual Ntsikana kaGabha Global Heritage Festival during the week of 24 September.

5.2.11 The youth indaba must be guided by the House of Traditional Leaders, CONTRALESA, the Kingdom of Khoekhoen, and the Imbumba yamaNyama Royal Council, on aesthetic leadership, and co-create governance innovation programmes in April and May each year to come up with a clear SAP to include best practices from other kingdoms, using North-South and South-South methodologies, as mentioned earlier.

5.2.12 The date 24 September each year is to be used to celebrate Ntsikana kaGabha Paradise City models in partnership with the Office of the Presidency, the African Union (AU), the Pan-African Parliament (PAP), UNEP, UNESCO, the NHC, SAHRA, and relevant ministries in various countries for best-practice purposes.

5.2.13 Through an inter-ministerial task team, an annual communication strategy must be developed by April/May each year to restore aesthetic relational values and implement sustainable programs and projects for socio-economic growth and for restoring and balancing the ecosystem through aesthetic leadership and management.

5.2.14 Leadership programs with both traditional leaders and local champions for the programs are to be implemented, to ensure the readiness and inclusive participation of communities. This means that each city, town, fort, heritage site, and ward committee must identify blue and green programs and projects to be incorporated into the Home of Legends business concept, to make the Cape provinces better places for business investment.

5.2.15 Researchers must focus on the required emotional intelligence for delivering sustainable infrastructure programs and projects within the context of increased global competitiveness.

5.2.16 Should African states want to reduce disparities between rural and urban development by 2030 and onward, it appears that IR and UIIPs must be adopted by all states, including a new curriculum in schools, colleges and universities using advanced technological intelligence.

5.2.17 The proposed blue and green economic models to build new post-colonial cities in Africa will not be realized unless indigenous people that faced all sorts of atrocities and violence by the colonial regimes are recognized in Traditional Houses by the Pan-African Parliament (PAP), and a PAP Traditional Leadership Framework must be approved to guide social cohesion and a nation-building plan in each state in Africa. For instance, at the time of writing this book, the statutory recognition of AmaCirha, AmaJwarha, AmaNdwandwe, Khoi and San groupings in South Africa into the existing houses of traditional leadership is crucial to addressing justice and human rights for all indigenous people of South Africa. As the South African Parliament is informed by Ubuntu principles, the existing South African Traditional Leadership and Governance Frameworks (2003) must be replaced with an inclusive South African Traditional Leadership and Governance Framework (2019 onwards) to enhance social cohesion and advance the idea of a united South African society as envisaged in the Preamble of the Constitution of the Republic of South Africa.

5.2.18 SOEs and African companies must be ready for global investment models. Evidence-based policies and strategies must be proactively developed not only for individual countries, but also across regions or economic blocs, and possibly the entire continent. The proposed African Investment Policies to support African reindustrialization and manufacturing should be considered by Heads of State in Africa, whereby Paradise Cities should do the following:

5.2.18.1 Adopt economic diversity to increase resilience against economic shocks, as witnessed in 2008. This implies that blue and green economic diversification should go hand in hand with continental and regional specialization and the skilling of youth as future leaders to drive the Nation-Building Plan beyond 2064.

5.2.18.2 Invest in inclusive economic, social and environmental development in addressing food security.

5.2.18.3 Design local technological hubs for high-tech corporate companies, to increase municipalities' absorptive capacity and capabilities.

5.2.18.4 Focus on embracing new technologies to produce advanced high-tech manufacturing whereby domestic products are locally manufactured and produce robust local markets as far as possible. This implies that Paradise Cities should integrate all different modalities and functions through ICT solutions. In other words, ICT will improve accessibility between rural and urban human settlements as the infrastructure connects all types of human settlements. If local people are empowered through ICT and the digital revolution, the population pressure on cities can be progressively reduced, as employers will be spread to heritage sites, villages, and small and medium-sized towns. This ICT economy and related knowledge will prepare cities and their inhabitants to adjust to fourth industrial revolution requirements.

5.2.18.5 Capacitate their public administration and management directorates by investing in infrastructure and public transportation systems, such as the envisaged Ntsikana kaGabha high-speed train from Seymour to Cape Town, and from Seymour to Johannesburg via East London, Durban, Nelspruit, and Polokwane.

5.2.18.6 Africa's economic blocs to promote heritage and tourism flagship programs and projects in advancing aesthetic and architectural designs of post-colonial cities and towns beyond 2064.

The next section, Chapter 6, provides detailed definitions of terms used throughout this book using social anthropology and ethnographic interpretation grounded in discourse analysis, to enrich a comprehension of the subject, and empower the reader about the book's in-depth message.

CHAPTER 6

6 DEFINITION OF TERMS

It is clear from Chapters 1 to 5 that the social cohesion roadmap, as part of the Nation-Building Plan between 2020 and 2064 requires every person to contribute for the sake of humanity. Those that are historians, ethnologists, ethnographers, experts, specialists, managers, practitioners, politicians, chiefs, queens and kings of various parts of our aesthetic landscape of Africa have to work with various credible institutions and partners to drive the Nation-Building Plan and related programmes and projects to reindustrialize Africa and restore our PRIDE by, on the one hand, creating WEALTH by means of various funding models, including green and blue economic models. On the other hand, credible institutions and partners have to work with families, clans and kingdoms who were defeated under imperialism, colonialism, and apartheid to bring about social, economic, political and cultural reconciliation as part of a new growth path framework under the proposed Nation-Building Plan.

As some of the terms and concepts are unpacked, the reader is exposed to how facts were twisted to suit imperial and colonial ideologies. Moreover, illegitimate leaders and colonizers replaced legitimate and aesthetic leaders. Using methods outside scientific research, colonizers sponsored writers and authors to write fictitious stories as part of colonial constructs and discourse. In addition, a major concern is that the current advisors, experts, specialists, historians, ethnologists, anthropologists, ethnographers, managers, politicians and leaders in various parts of Africa have opted to ignore these distorted histories in post-colonial Africa. The concepts and terms used to explain some of the ideas and decisions that are a barrier to fairness, justice and the application of constitutional customary norms and standards are unpacked. While some have been explained in previous chapters, the concepts and terms below are unpacked in detail to support academic research by students and scholars aimed at reviewing the current colonial and apartheid histories to advance social cohesion as part of a nation-building plan between 2020 and 2064. These highly selective historical distortions come to the fore in the quest to build a state of equilibrium and post-colonial Paradise City models. These concepts and terms are explained to demythicize hidden agendas and colonial discourses so that new cultural habits of blue and green city models can be adopted for restoring PRIDE and creating conducive environments for reconciliation between clans and kingdoms of Mother Africa.

Furthermore, historians and writers do not have a copyright on concepts they use. For this reason, these terms are written and interpreted using the 5Cs (concepts, challenges, context, capabilities and competencies) to stimulate the reader's ideas, views and opinions and, perhaps, solutions to drive our new roadmap of unity in diversity, through which families, clans and kingdoms would be reconciled. As the journey to the nation-building plan is a difficult one, it cannot be implemented in post-colonial Africa without the strategic and customary roles and responsibilities of traditional leaders. By unpacking these terms or concepts, the book attempts to create a synergy between oral memories and historical stories vis-à-vis the constructed historical stories, images, myths and oral memories that have served imperial and colonial agendas. Therefore, the use of the 5Cs to discuss our journey to social cohesion as part of the Nation-Building Plan between 2020 and 2064, based on appreciating the past and current realities in order to determine a future state of equilibrium, means that our rich historical heritage is too important to be left as an unfinished post-colonial African scenario. The meaning and applications of the 5Cs to create space for growth and development requires being realistic about the negative effects of distorted histories for families, clans, nations and kingdoms that have been defeated. Undoubtedly, it is useful, for the purpose of clarification, to define some of the terms used in this book.

6.1 Vision

Vision refers to a declaration or statement that answers the question of what someone or an organization wants to create or achieve, for instance, in a learning organization or in a Home of Legends. Vision statements explain where organizations or leaders want to go and how they intend to get there. According to Lewis (1997:9), supported by Lennon & Wollin (2001:410) and Senge (2006:192), an effective vision, as extracted from Microsoft and Ernst & Young, must be realistic in terms of time span, be simple and doable, be challenging, and be reflective of organizational aspirations. It must be endorsed and frequently communicated to the operational level by top management, or leaders, as the case may be. Thus, a shared vision unites the organization and ensures that all energies are directed towards achieving the stated goals, as recently witnessed in the case of the Ntsikana Paradise City Models, championed by the Imbumba yamaNyama executive board members and leaders, to feed into the country's nation-building plan.

Furthermore, aesthetic leadership increases the meaningfulness of the goals of a nation-building plan and its related actions by showing how these goals are consistent with the collective past, present and future – using, in this case, Swartz's Aesthetic Relational Values in Planning and Development Framework (ARVPDF), and thus creating a sense of evolving – which is central for self-consistency and a sense of meaningfulness, accountability and responsiveness (Malachi 2:10; Psalm 133:1). In addition, aesthetic leadership stresses the importance of the goal as a basis for group identity and nation-building, and for distinguishing the group (or collective) from other groups. This brings meaning to the lives and efforts of followers, officials and managers by connecting them to larger entities, and to concerns that transcend their own limited existence. By these leadership actions, certain identities are evoked and made more salient, and are therefore more likely to be involved in the action.

6.2 State building and nation-building plan

To understand the concept of nation-building, and the related plan, one needs to have some definition of what a nation is. The Department of Arts and Culture (DAC) defines nation-building (in South Africa) as a process whereby a society with diverse origins, histories, languages, cultures, and religions comes together within the boundaries of a sovereign state with a unified constitutional and legal dispensation, a national public education system, an integrated national economy, and shared symbols and values, as equals, to work towards eradicating the divisions and injustices of the past, to foster unity, and to promote a countrywide conscious sense of being proudly South African, committed to the country, and open to the continent and the world.

Nation-building, in this sense, and in the context of South Africa, cannot be the perpetuation of hierarchies of the past, based on pre-given or ethnically engineered and imposed divisions of people rooted in prejudice, discrimination and exclusion. It calls for something else; that is, a rethinking, in South African terms, of what socio-economic cohesion, linked to a nation-building plan (2020-2064), should be. Accordingly, a nation is conceived as a social formation based on the unity and equality of its members, consisting of the following shared and recognized attributes:

- Shared origin and history
- An internationally recognized territory
- A unitary sovereign state
- A single judicial system
- Single public education system
- Nationally recognized languages
- Nationally recognized cultures
- Nationally recognized religions
- Shared values
- Shared symbols
- A shared national consciousness

Inductively, a *nation* refers to a large body of people united by common descent, history, culture or language, inhabiting a particular state or territory or kingdom. The people of a nation generally share a common national identity, and part of *nation-building* is the building of that common identity. The notion of identity, or sameness, is something explorers, ethnologists, anthropologists, ethnographers, sociologists, historians, and economic and political scientists have invented to conceptualize scattered ideas implicitly held by families, clans, and kingdoms – in this instance in pre-colonial Africa, or elsewhere. It helps to unscramble what people mean when they say they belong to clans or kingdoms, i.e. defining themselves as a group or community, as the case may be. It has cultural content as the salient feature. Further, it has personal psychological meaning that surfaces when that identity is under threat. It is associated with an anthropological or sociological mechanism that permits the group to imagine itself as a translocal community. According to identity theory in sociology, the self is composed of a series of identities, each of which corresponds to a role played by an individual. Identities form a salient hierarchy, with the most salient being those to whom the individual is most committed. A recent study on local identities in a 'globalized world' has shown that when great structures change, and cultural knowledge changes in our time, this produces great changes in people's lives. Anthony Cohen (1982) says that ethnographic studies of the locality should 'provide an account of how people experience and express their difference from others, and of how their sense of difference becomes incorporated into and informs the nature of their social organization and process' in daily life.

Significantly, academic literature reveals that there are various dimensions to identity. The first identity can be associated with the clan, ward, local municipality, national state, region, religion, sport and recreation, and so forth. The second identity can be associated with multiple identities related to a range of sociocultural, economic, environmental and political practices. These multiple identities are, on the one hand, further linked to individual and organizational structures, such as Imbumba yamaNyama. On the other hand, they may also refer to structures of class, ethnicity or grouping (e.g. AmaNguni), race (African), and gender (masculine or feminine). As defined in this book, there has been a fusion of identities (Nguni with Khoisan, African with European diaspora) leading to new identities, commonly known as hybridity of cultural identities (e.g. AmaGqunukwebe, AmaSukwini, AmaMfengu and AmaHlubi among the AmaXhosa, to mention but a few hybrid cultural identities). The identities are not pure, but the product of mixing, fusion, and creolization, whereby mixing and movement of cultures has been developed in a particular site or settlement. For instance, AmaMfengu brought African beer from the Cape to the AmaXhosa who were using sour milk for their ceremonies. Traditional ceremonies have thus become fused with assimilated and adopted global practices, or modern cultural, religious and political practices. Therefore, modern societies are a product of the assimilation of one or more cultural practices or traditions of another culture. For instance, the cultural identity of diasporic identities, such as African Americans, Jews, and the Afrikaners in Africa are classic examples.

In the case of Ntsikana kaGabha's imagined identity, it can be argued that he changed from a traditional African culture, where he identified himself as being of a Cirha-type clan, and turned into a global icon and visionary leader for a state of equilibrium, and for one universal religion, which is Christianity, as summarised in his Gospel Hymn. In short, Ntsikana kaGabha is a hybrid product influenced by the Holy Spirit, who moved out of being a Cirha or Xhosa person to becoming a prophet of God. As a person, he saw himself as born again (wahlamba imbola), having gone through the Holy Spirit baptism, and took up the commandment to save God's people from all forms of slavery, both known (external suffering or psychological deafness to God's will on earth) and unknown (internal suffering or spiritual deprivation).

As Carneiro (1970:733-8), supported by Fukuyama (1996:185), argues, nation-building is the creation of a sense of national identity to which citizens and individuals are loyal – an identity that supersedes their loyalty to clans, tribes, ethnicities, villages, ward committees, municipal boundaries and regional or provincial constituencies. Nation-building requires the creation of intangible things, like national traditions, heritage, symbols, and shared historical memories, and tangible common socio-economic, cultural, emotional, psychological, environmental, developmental and spiritual points of reference, like Freedom Park in Pretoria, and other heritage sites or historical settlements, such as Thwathwa in the Eastern Cape as a Home of Legends. National identities can be created by states through acts of parliament, which are the spine of a developmental state or nation-building plan. These acts of parliament are followed by policies on languages, religion and education, using archaeological and paleontological sites, historical settlements, graves and burial grounds, books, documents, and cultural and military objects, to mention but a few. In the case of Africa, traditional and cultural poets, philosophers, aesthetic leaders from all disciplines, novelists, musicians, and political leaders often complement these national identities as part of nation-building.

Some distinguish between an ethnic nation, based on (the social construction of) race or ethnicity, and a civic nation, based on a common identity and loyalty to a set of political ideals and institutions and the linkage of citizenship to nationality. Today the word *nation* is often used synonymously with the *state*, as in the United Nations. Nevertheless, a state is more properly the governmental apparatus by which a nation rules itself. Fukuyama (1996:185) defines *state-building* as the 'creation of tangible institutions – armies, police, bureaucracies, ministers, and the like. Hiring staff, training officials, giving them offices, providing them with budgets, and passing laws and directives' to accomplish it.

This means that the term *nation-building* is often used interchangeably with state-building, democratization, modernization, political development, post-conflict reconstruction, economic development, and growth path frameworks, a balance between human and aesthetic values, peacebuilding, and living in harmony with the environment. Through the process of globalization of nation states and advanced technology in terms of communication, networks, businesses and collaboration between countries and regional economic powerhouses, one has a global, spiritual, cultural, aesthetic and social culture – a world culture based on advanced technology, the spirit of science, a rational view of life, a secular approach to social relations, a feeling for justice in public affairs and, above all else, the acceptance in the political realm that the prime unit of the polity should be the nation-state.

Nation-building plans are critical for global harmony, a secure world, and ecosystems being sensitively managed and supported for maintaining harmony between human wellbeing and biodiversity needs. It is proposed that a nation-building plan is designed as a purposeful action to develop the capacity, institutions, and legitimacy of the state in relation to effective economic, social, developmental, emotional, historical, political and spiritual processes for negotiating the mutual demands between state and societal groups in harmony with the environment. Legitimacy will be a principal outcome of the effectiveness of such a process over time, although legitimacy may also be embedded in historical identities, a combined heritage, and the experiences of individual members and learning organizations. Together, capacity, resources, learning organizations, such as Imbumba yamaNyama, legitimacy, and effective socio-economic, cultural, spiritual, environmental and political processes combine to produce resilience. Successful nation-building plans will usually be the product of domestic actions, but they can be significantly enabled by well-targeted and responsive partnership programs and projects based on environmental aesthetics that feed into the plan.

6.3 Innovation

Innovation refers to the process whereby a newly perceived or real benefit or added value for a customer, employee or shareholder is created. The benefit ranges across functional, psychological, emotional and financial aspects. Innovation may be understood as an idea applied to initiate or improve a product, process or service. Professor E Schwella (2008) stressed in a lecture that 'innovation is no longer a strategic decision or choice by organizations, but a business necessity for the companies and organizations to be competitive in the context of increased international competitiveness and supply and demand'. Accordingly, Schwella notes, 'innovation is the art of making new connections, and continuously challenging the status quo'. A term very close to *innovation* is *creativity*. According to the *Oxford English Dictionary*, creativity refers to 'the use of the imagination or original ideas in order to create something'. Creativity and innovation go hand in hand. To be innovative, one has to be original; one must not fall back on the conventional, and one has to think of dealing with the fragile world in a new way. Creativity provides one of the tools and techniques to think differently. In the end, creativity is an experience, a lifelong process of changing the way one looks at one's life, ambitions and goals, as well as one's organization, business or world.

6.4 Capability

Capability refers to organizational collective skills, abilities and expertise vested in employees as ideapreneurs beyond the twenty-first century. Capability is maintained and developed through various human resource practices, including job design, training, rewards, recognition, and career path development. Everybody is born to be a leader. However, each of us must go through a process to understand leadership values and principles.

6.5 Competencies

At the organizational level, *competencies* are typically the things that the organization excels at. Competency is an abstract concept embedded in the unique application of resources and capabilities. From a human resource perspective, competencies are viewed as personal characteristics related to effective job performance.

6.6 Change management

Change management refers to the process of managing change and reforms. In other words, change refers to a shift in thinking or action by organizations, in order to embark on a change management process as a journey towards ideapreneurship for learning organizations. In this book, associated terms with change management include *restructuring* and *re-engineering*. In the case of re-engineering, the term is used to mean a radical redesign of an organization's processes, institutions, and culture to enhance the required organizational performance, with simultaneous improvements in profit-making and customer services (Schwella, 2012). The word *restructuring* is often confused and used interchangeably with re-engineering, but I believe that there is a clear difference: restructuring refers only to a change in the structure or organizational design (Robbins, 2011:453). *Change* can mean an alteration or a reform of activities within organizations in terms of structures, tasks, the introduction of new products, new services, new processes or new attitudes and cultures (Lewis, 1998:381). Therefore, throughout this book, the terms re-engineering, change and reform are used interchangeably.

6.7 Leadership

A leader is defined by the Collins English Dictionary as

> *a person who rules, guides or inspires others while leading [and] entails the process of showing the way by going with, or ahead … to serve as the means of reaching a place or goals.*

Arguably, leadership has to do with the process of inspiring and influencing others to work hard to accomplish important tasks, activities and targets. Leadership must always inspire and foster positive change, whereby Paradise City models, in this instance, can be built for the public good. Leadership is associated with a clear vision to transform structural problems and complex challenges, to bring them a clear sense of future, and steps to achieve the future. In order to transform complex societal challenges, aesthetic leadership is imperative. *Leadership* is linked to the ability to lead effectively under conditions of a rapid information explosion and natural changes, and the high complexity of organizations and the world (Schwella, 2008). For leaders to be effective in learning organizations, they must have great abilities to respond effectively to change and complexity in the business environment – acting as experts, achievers, catalysts, coordinators, co-creators, and synergists in accordance with what Quatro, Waldman & Galvin (2007) call the ACES domains of leadership. ACES is an acronym for encompassing the **a**nalytical, **c**onceptual, **e**motional and **s**piritual aspects of effective leadership in modern organizations (see also Adair, 2005:20; Tsibani, 2014a). Whatever the qualities and characteristics of a leader/manager, the job of a leader is to get the required results by employing the three key areas of leadership, as depicted in Figure 6.1 below.

Figure 6.1: Three key areas of leadership

• *Achieving the task* using a sense of urgency to mobilize resources and trigger an SAP for implementation of IR and UIIPs using an ARVPDF as part of a country's nation-building plan. • *Building the team* by creating a shared vision using marketing and communication strategies, including branding the concept of Paradise City models as a response to our fragile world, using a blue and green economy model. • *Developing individuals* using both short-term wins and structured mentorship and coaching programs to empower others, whereby the Paradise City models based on an ARVPDF are institutionalized in organizational performance and a country's state of the nation address (SONA) every year; and each financial year is used to review and affirm commitments to IR and UIIPs, to advance a blue and green economy, and consolidate the nation-building plan by using Paradise City models or modernization of cities to proactively design and plan for sustainable development, without compromising future generational needs or allowing our demands to threaten our fragile world and precipitate the negative consequences of climate change.

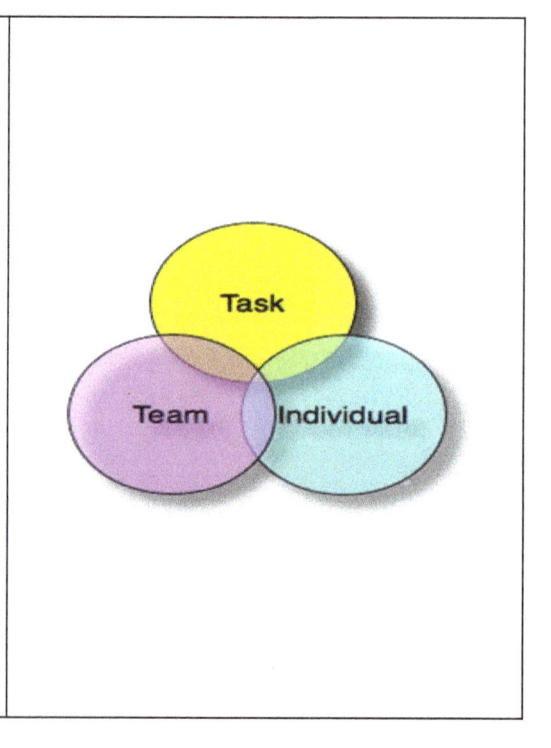

Leaders' skills in achieving the required results through the group are matched by their skills in managing the hostilities and anxieties of the individuals, and of the group as a whole.

6.8 Learning organizations

Learning organizations are able to tap their inherent capacity to self-organize to ever-higher orders of complexity and coherence, as required by the business environment from time to time (Lennon & Wollin, 2001:410; Senge, 2005:2). In other words, learning organizations are able to thrive in conditions of turbulence and rapid change as they tend to have self-organization, self-reference and self-transcendence. In this book, organizational learning is defined as 'a system of actions, actors, symbols and processes that enables an organization to transform information into valued knowledge, which in turn increases its long-run adaptive capacity' (Schwandt & Marquardt, 2000:43).

6.9 Strategy

Strategy refers to a complex web of thoughts, ideas, insights, experiences, goals, memories, perceptions and expectations that provide guidance to *ideapreneurship*, whereby strategy implementation difficulties are addressed (Tsibani 2014a).

6.10 Pilgrimage

It is critical to define and differentiate between *pilgrimage* and *paradise*. Literature reveals that a pilgrimage to a holy land is a spiritual journey rooted in moral and aesthetic relational values. Thwathwa, for instance, is a place of spiritual attachment for more than 1.4 billion potential spiritual members of Imbumba yamaNyama. It is believed that uQamata is omniscient, omnipotent and omnipresent, as defined in the Ntsikana hymn. As a pilgrimage destination, Thwathwa is a temple of God for spiritual retreat and revival. In this context, a visiting person or member of the Imbumba yamaNyama Royal Council is called a pilgrim. As part of a green pilgrimage destination, the Holy Land of Thwathwa is to be planned and designed to comply with environmental management guidelines and policies under the stewardship of Imbumba yamaNyama. Pilgrims to the Holy Land of Ntsikana kaGabha believe the following:

- A person is saved through acceptance of Christ and baptism in the name of the Father, the Son and the Holy Spirit (Christian Bible, Matthew 28:19).
- A person prays to God (uQamata) in the name of Jesus Christ.
- We are all created by God.
- The purification of sins is obtained through confession, repentance and prayer.

- The spiritual leaders of the Ntsikana Church preach the Gospel of Jesus Christ as laid out in the Holy Bible.
- The Ntsikana Church congregation believes in prophets and prophecy.

6.11 The similarity between pilgrimage and paradise

Paradise is a religious or metaphysical term for Thwathwa, in which Ntsikana kaGabha was a prophet, and able to ensure harmonious aesthetic relational values and the liberation of people to accept salvation for eternal life (John 3:14-17). The Ntsikana Paradise City is a spiritual, emotional, social, economic, developmental and political place characterized by peace, prosperity, good-enough governance, accountability, responsibility, integrity, honesty, responsiveness and happiness. Thwathwa is regarded by Imbumba yamaNyama and the Ntsikana Church as the holiest place, where children of God or the heroic and righteous dead hope to spend eternity. As a paradise, it is associated with the Garden of Eden – that is, the perfect state of the world prior to the fall from grace, and the perfect state that will be restored in the world to come (2 Corinthians 12:4; Genesis 2:8; Haggai 2:23; Jeremiah 22:24; Luke 23:43; Revelation 2:7).

6.12 Ntsikana Paradise City landscape

The individual elements of the Ntsikana Paradise City are many, and it may take years to design them graphically. They make up the beautiful landscape, including prominent or eye-catching features, such as the Bhukazana and Nkonkobe Mountains, the hills, rivers, valleys, savannah, olive trees (iminquma), Katberg, the Kat River Dam, the Amatola Mountains and related catchment management areas, forts and academic buildings, and the Thwathwa road as a link between households and their immediate environment. Through a feasibility study, these elements could be quantified and easily described and interpreted. The Ntsikana Paradise City is a landscape that is characterized by various environmental patterns, resulting from particular combinations of natural (physical and biological) and cultural (land use) factors, and how people perceive these features as part of a global combined heritage site. From the graphic design of the Ntsikana Paradise City (see Figure 1.2), it is clear that the visual dimension of the landscape is a reflection of the way in which these factors create repetitive groupings and interact to create areas that have a specific visual identity. The process of assessing the character of the landscape could increase the appreciation of what makes this landscape distinctive, and what is important about this area. The description of the character of the landscape thus should focus on the nature of the land, rather than the response to it by Imbumba yamaNyama and stakeholders, as part of a global heritage site.

6.13 Clan

A clan is a unilineal kin group, as depicted in Figure 6.2, which is usually exogamous (customary norms and standards of marriage outside a community or clan). In some cases, particularly in a modern society where youth and couples lack cultural and clan identity, customary regulations are applied – such as claiming descent from a common ancestor, and representation by a totem. In the case of AmaCirha kaNkosiyamntu, kaMalangana, kaXhosa, kaNguni and kaNtu, the bluebuck (iPhuthi) and elephant (iNdlovu) are classic examples of associated totems, and were in the nineteenth century associated with Thwathwa for spiritual ceremonies to praise Great God in Heaven (UThixo omkhulu oseZulwini) and the King of kings (uKumkani wookumkani). Accordingly, Ubuntu has its origins in the African conception of a 'supernatural being' that is Umvelinqangi (isiZulu), Uqamatha (isiXhosa), Nkhubyani (Xitsonga), and so forth.

It appears from literature evidence that the word *clan* refers to a unit of social organization, or a collective of people (abantu bakaQamata), such as AmaCirha, AmaJwarha and AmaTshawe. It is the oldest societal structure in the region, other than family and direct lineage. As opposed to matricians (lineages from the mother), African clans, like Cirha, Jwarha, and Tshawe, have patrilineal descent (related to the father Nkosiyamntu kaMalangana kaXhosa or descent through the male lineages). AmaXhosa clan names (iziduko) are family names that are considered more important than surnames among Nguni people. Clan names are used to trace family history back to a specific male ancestor or stock. Mentioning the clan name of someone you want to thank is the highest form of respect, and it is considered polite to enquire after people's clan names when meeting them. Members of that clan sometimes also use the clan name as an exclamation. Accordingly, when a woman marries, she may take her husband's surname, but she always keeps her own clan name, adding the prefix 'Ma-' to it. As in the Bible, 'Ma' (isini sobufazi, or female gender representative) stands for *wo* (man) when God created a partner for Adam (man).

The definition of 'sex' is annotated as different from 'gender' in the *Oxford English Dictionary*, which determines that sex 'tends now to refer to biological differences, while [gender] often refers to cultural or social ones'. The *American Heritage Dictionary*, however, lists 'sex' as both 'either of the two divisions, designated female and male, by which most organisms are classified on the basis of their reproductive organs and functions', and 'one's identity as either female or male', among other definitions. It also refers to a usage note associated with the gender entry. A working definition in use by the World Health Organisation (WHO) for its work is that 'sex refers to the biological and physiological characteristics that define men and women' and that 'male' and 'female' are sex categories used especially in succession plans among African kingdoms. The structure is found in modern-day Ntu within the sub-group Nguni languages. The people of the area use a variety of vernacular terms to describe this concept.

Clan membership is a loose concept, with a correlation to lineage based more on oral tradition and personal belief than on concrete evidence. In the case of the Nguni group, its clans and members have dispersed over time, and are no longer associated with particular regions in central Africa. Clans differ somewhat in their nature, depending on their region, country, province, district and locality. This is owing to the fact that a clan is a very structured unit with common cultural and ritual activities and functions. The AmaXhosa further subdivide the clans into sub-clans. Clans in indigenous societies are likely to be exogamous, meaning that their members cannot marry one another. In other words, a man and a woman who have the same clan name (for instance, AmaTshawe, and AmaNgconde, AmaCirha and AmaJwarha, AmaQwambe kaNkosiyamntu, kaMalangana, kaXhosa, kaNguni, kaNtu) may not marry, as they are considered to be related. Clans preceded more centralized forms of community organizations, such as Imbumba yamaNyama (1882), the House of Traditional Leaders in Southern Africa and the Pan-African Parliament (PAP) to protect their land, people and communities against enemies or military attack. The lineage of the AmaXhosa Kingdom is depicted in Figure 6.2. to Figure 6.5. respectively.

Nation Building Plan Between 2020 & 2064

Figure 6.2: The history of Abantu

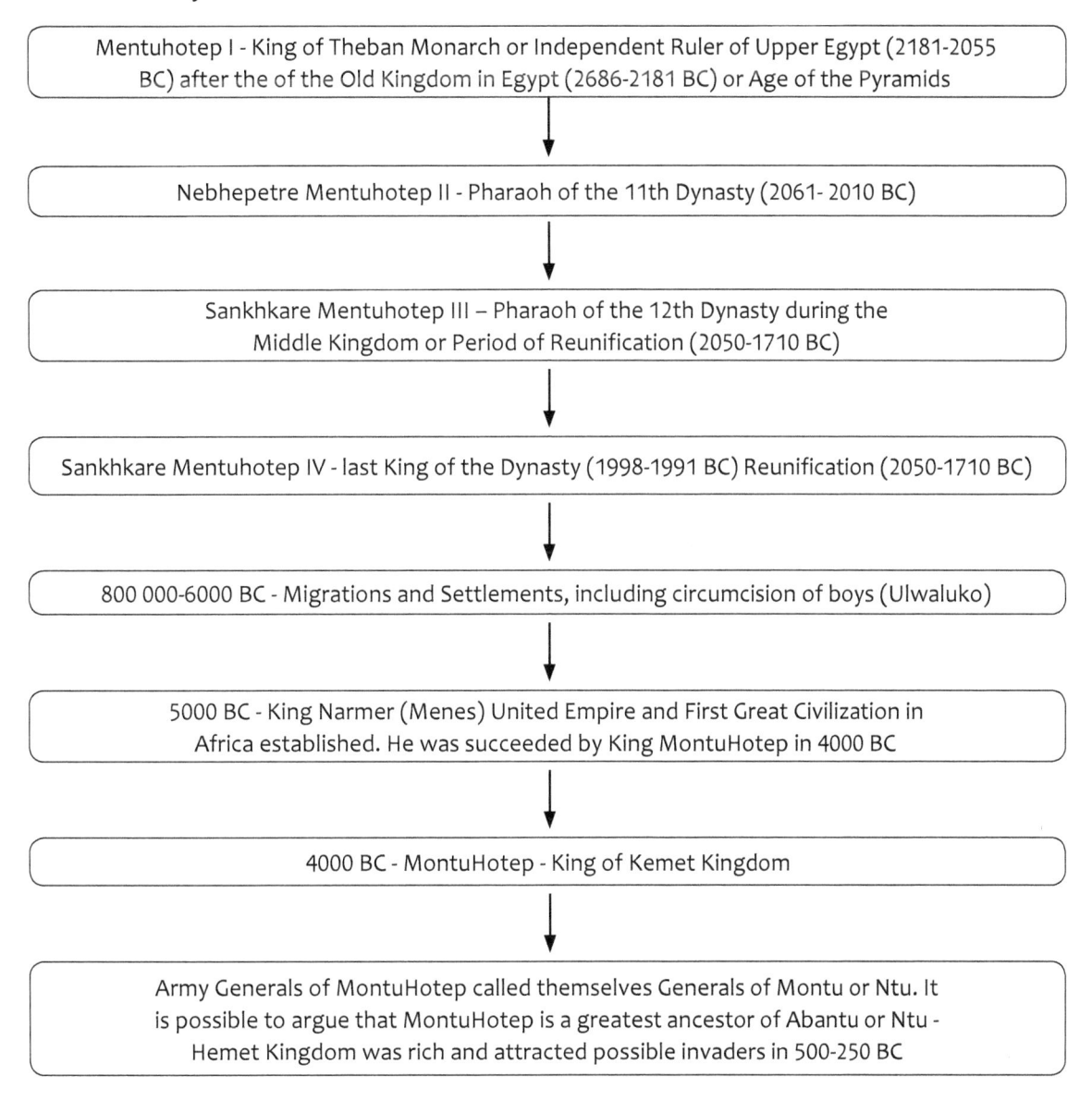

```
┌─────────────────────────────────────────────────────────────────┐
│ Mentuhotep I - King of Theban Monarch or Independent Ruler of   │
│ Upper Egypt (2181-2055 BC) after the of the Old Kingdom in      │
│ Egypt (2686-2181 BC) or Age of the Pyramids                     │
└─────────────────────────────────────────────────────────────────┘
                                 ↓
┌─────────────────────────────────────────────────────────────────┐
│ Nebhepetre Mentuhotep II - Pharaoh of the 11th Dynasty          │
│ (2061- 2010 BC)                                                 │
└─────────────────────────────────────────────────────────────────┘
                                 ↓
┌─────────────────────────────────────────────────────────────────┐
│ Sankhkare Mentuhotep III – Pharaoh of the 12th Dynasty during   │
│ the Middle Kingdom or Period of Reunification (2050-1710 BC)    │
└─────────────────────────────────────────────────────────────────┘
                                 ↓
┌─────────────────────────────────────────────────────────────────┐
│ Sankhkare Mentuhotep IV - last King of the Dynasty (1998-1991   │
│ BC) Reunification (2050-1710 BC)                                │
└─────────────────────────────────────────────────────────────────┘
                                 ↓
┌─────────────────────────────────────────────────────────────────┐
│ 800 000-6000 BC - Migrations and Settlements, including         │
│ circumcision of boys (Ulwaluko)                                 │
└─────────────────────────────────────────────────────────────────┘
                                 ↓
┌─────────────────────────────────────────────────────────────────┐
│ 5000 BC - King Narmer (Menes) United Empire and First Great     │
│ Civilization in Africa established. He was succeeded by King    │
│ MontuHotep in 4000 BC                                           │
└─────────────────────────────────────────────────────────────────┘
                                 ↓
┌─────────────────────────────────────────────────────────────────┐
│ 4000 BC - MontuHotep - King of Kemet Kingdom                    │
└─────────────────────────────────────────────────────────────────┘
                                 ↓
┌─────────────────────────────────────────────────────────────────┐
│ Army Generals of MontuHotep called themselves Generals of Montu │
│ or Ntu. It is possible to argue that MontuHotep is a greatest   │
│ ancestor of Abantu or Ntu - Hemet Kingdom was rich and          │
│ attracted possible invaders in 500-250 BC                       │
└─────────────────────────────────────────────────────────────────┘
```

continuation of figure 6.2: The history of Abantu

```
┌─────────────────────────────────────────────────────────────────────┐
│ 3600 BC - Asians invaded the rich Hemet Kingdom but King            │
│ Ahmose I restored order and defeated Asians                         │
└─────────────────────────────────────────────────────────────────────┘
                                    ↓
┌─────────────────────────────────────────────────────────────────────┐
│ 2500 BC - Persian - Asians followed by Europeans and later Romans   │
│ invade Kemet Kingdom leading to a period of African Dark Ages or    │
│ Great Migrations                                                    │
└─────────────────────────────────────────────────────────────────────┘
                                    ↓
┌─────────────────────────────────────────────────────────────────────┐
│ 2000-1500 BC - Abantu were discovered in the Great Lakes Regions    │
│ and southern Africa subject to discovery by European colonialists   │
│ and writers                                                         │
└─────────────────────────────────────────────────────────────────────┘
                                    ↓
┌─────────────────────────────────────────────────────────────────────┐
│ Kingdoms were not known. It is believed that ancestors of Africans  │
│ lived in the Omo River region in the present day Ethiopia           │
│ (200 000 BC)                                                        │
└─────────────────────────────────────────────────────────────────────┘
                                    ↓
┌─────────────────────────────────────────────────────────────────────┐
│ 17 000-40 000 BC - Foundation of Culture common amongst African     │
│ groups using Imbola (red ochre), which Ntsikana kaGabha washed in   │
│ 1790 when he received the Holy Spirit from God (uQamata)            │
└─────────────────────────────────────────────────────────────────────┘
```

Nation Building Plan Between 2020 & 2064

Figure 6.3: The sub-clans that form the Ntu clan

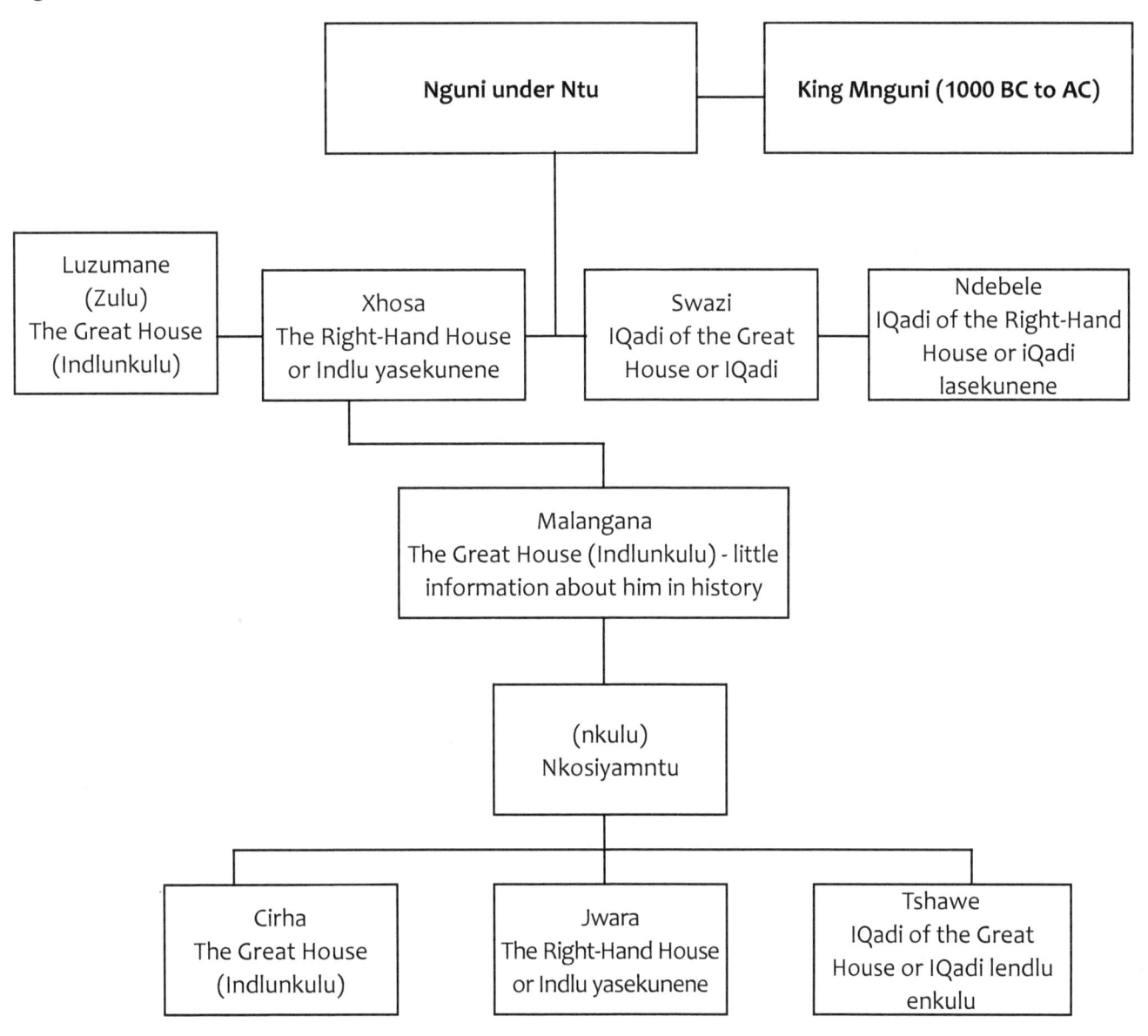

```
                    ┌─────────────────────┐     ┌─────────────────────────┐
                    │   Nguni under Ntu   │─────│ King Mnguni (1000 BC to AC) │
                    └──────────┬──────────┘     └─────────────────────────┘
                               │
   ┌──────────────┐  ┌─────────┴────────┐  ┌──────────────────┐  ┌──────────────────┐
   │  Luzumane    │  │     Xhosa        │  │      Swazi       │  │    Ndebele       │
   │   (Zulu)     │  │ The Right-Hand   │  │ IQadi of the     │  │ IQadi of the     │
   │ The Great    │──│ House or Indlu   │──│ Great House or   │──│ Right-Hand House │
   │   House      │  │ yasekunene       │  │ IQadi            │  │ or iQadi         │
   │ (Indlunkulu) │  │                  │  │                  │  │ lasekunene       │
   └──────────────┘  └────────┬─────────┘  └──────────────────┘  └──────────────────┘
                              │
                    ┌─────────┴──────────────────────────┐
                    │            Malangana               │
                    │ The Great House (Indlunkulu) -     │
                    │ little information about him in    │
                    │ history                            │
                    └─────────────┬──────────────────────┘
                                  │
                         ┌────────┴─────────┐
                         │    (nkulu)       │
                         │  Nkosiyamntu     │
                         └────────┬─────────┘
                                  │
         ┌────────────────────────┼────────────────────────┐
   ┌─────┴──────┐          ┌──────┴──────┐          ┌──────┴──────┐
   │   Cirha    │          │    Jwara    │          │   Tshawe    │
   │ The Great  │          │ The Right-  │          │ IQadi of    │
   │   House    │          │ Hand House  │          │ the Great   │
   │(Indlunkulu)│          │ or Indlu    │          │ House or    │
   │            │          │ yasekunene  │          │ IQadi lendlu│
   │            │          │             │          │ enkulu      │
   └────────────┘          └─────────────┘          └─────────────┘
```

Fumene George Tsibani

Figure 6.4A: The History of AmaCirha

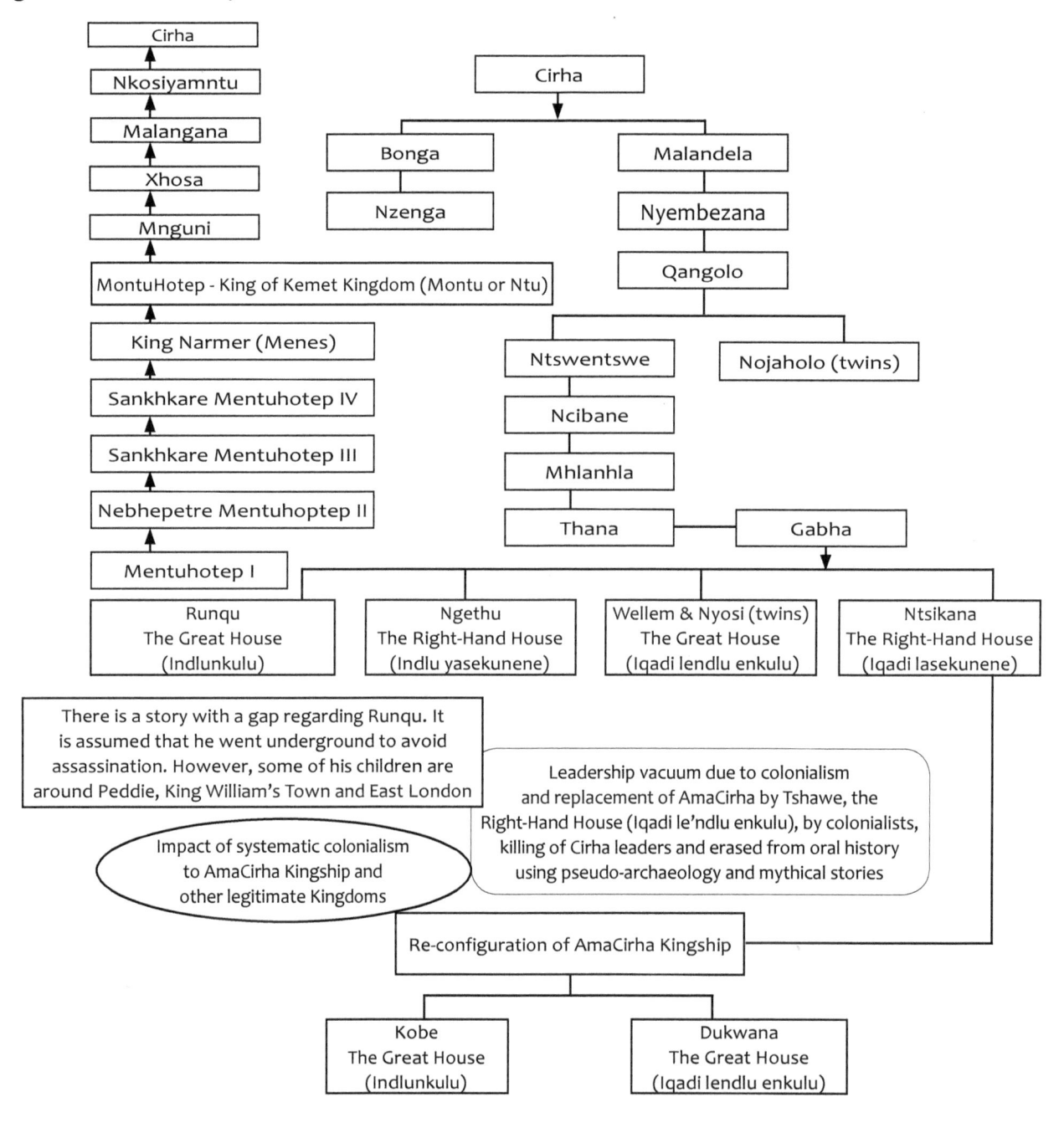

Left lineage (bottom to top):
- Cirha
- Nkosiyamntu
- Malangana
- Xhosa
- Mnguni
- MontuHotep – King of Kemet Kingdom (Montu or Ntu)
- King Narmer (Menes)
- Sankhkare Mentuhotep IV
- Sankhkare Mentuhotep III
- Nebhepetre Mentuhoptep II
- Mentuhotep I

Right lineage (from Cirha):
- Cirha
  - Bonga
    - Nzenga
  - Malandela
    - Nyembezana
      - Qangolo
        - Ntswentswe
          - Ncibane
            - Mhlanhla
              - Thana
        - Nojaholo (twins)
  - Gabha

Houses:
- Runqu — The Great House (Indlunkulu)
- Ngethu — The Right-Hand House (Indlu yasekunene)
- Wellem & Nyosi (twins) — The Great House (Iqadi lendlu enkulu)
- Ntsikana — The Right-Hand House (Iqadi lasekunene)

Notes:
- There is a story with a gap regarding Runqu. It is assumed that he went underground to avoid assassination. However, some of his children are around Peddie, King William's Town and East London
- Impact of systematic colonialism to AmaCirha Kingship and other legitimate Kingdoms
- Leadership vacuum due to colonialism and replacement of AmaCirha by Tshawe, the Right-Hand House (Iqadi le'ndlu enkulu), by colonialists, killing of Cirha leaders and erased from oral history using pseudo-archaeology and mythical stories

Re-configuration of AmaCirha Kingship:
- Kobe — The Great House (Indlunkulu)
- Dukwana — The Great House (Iqadi lendlu enkulu)

Nation Building Plan Between 2020 & 2064

Figure 6.4B Lineage of Tsibani Family

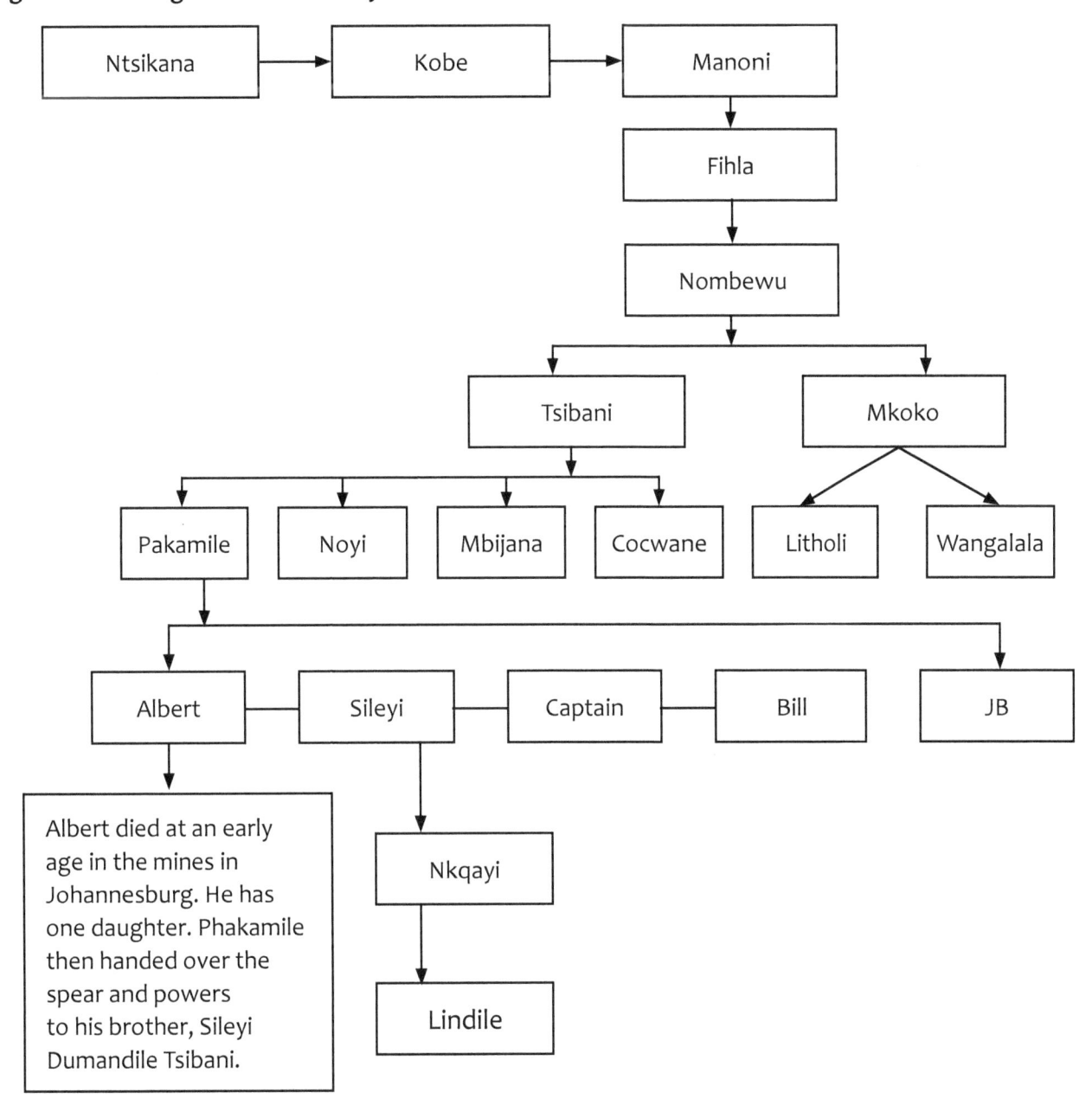

Ntsikana → Kobe → Manoni → Fihla → Nombewu

Nombewu → Tsibani, Mkoko

Tsibani → Pakamile, Noyi, Mbijana, Cocwane

Mkoko → Litholi, Wangalala

Pakamile → Albert, Sileyi, Captain, Bill, JB

Sileyi → Nkqayi → Lindile

Albert died at an early age in the mines in Johannesburg. He has one daughter. Phakamile then handed over the spear and powers to his brother, Sileyi Dumandile Tsibani.

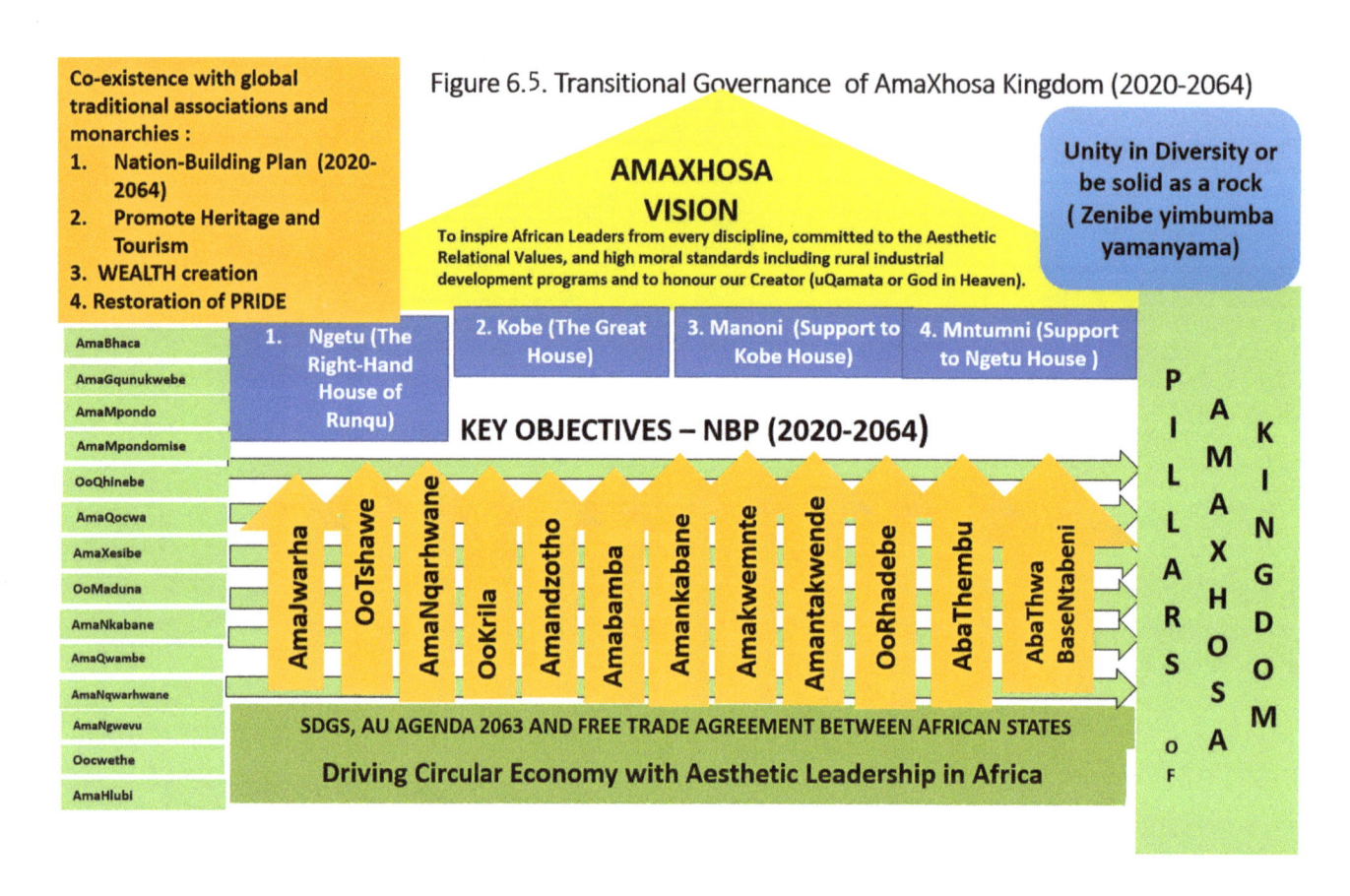

Figure 6.5. Transitional Governance of AmaXhosa Kingdom (2020-2064)

Co-existence with global traditional associations and monarchies:
1. Nation-Building Plan (2020-2064)
2. Promote Heritage and Tourism
3. WEALTH creation
4. Restoration of PRIDE

AMAXHOSA VISION
To inspire African Leaders from every discipline, committed to the Aesthetic Relational Values, and high moral standards including rural industrial development programs and to honour our Creator (uQamata or God in Heaven).

Unity in Diversity or be solid as a rock (Zenibe yimbumba yamanyama)

AmaBhaca, AmaGqunukwebe, AmaMpondo, AmaMpondomise, OoQhinebe, AmaQocwa, AmaXesibe, OoMaduna, AmaNkabane, AmaQwambe, AmaNqwarhwane, AmaNgwevu, Oocwethe, AmaHlubi

1. Ngetu (The Right-Hand House of Runqu)
2. Kobe (The Great House)
3. Manoni (Support to Kobe House)
4. Mntumni (Support to Ngetu House)

KEY OBJECTIVES – NBP (2020-2064)

AmaJwarha, OoTshawe, AmaNqarhwane, OoKrila, Amandzotho, Amabamba, Amankabane, Amakwemnte, Amantakwende, OoRhadebe, AbaThembu, AbaThwa BaseNtabeni

PILLARS OF AMAXHOSA KINGDOM

SDGS, AU AGENDA 2063 AND FREE TRADE AGREEMENT BETWEEN AFRICAN STATES

Driving Circular Economy with Aesthetic Leadership in Africa

It has been argued that the history of the AmaXhosa as part of the Nguni grouping starts with Mentuhotep I – King or Theban Monarch or Independent Ruler of Upper Egypt (2181-2055 BC) after the Old Kingdom in Egypt (2686-2181), or 'Age of the Pyramids' to the Ntu groupings in northeast Africa. Ntu groupings moved in all directions – some to the rich Great Lakes. Mnguni, the son Ntu begot four sons, namely Luzumane (Zulu), Xhosa, Swazi and Ndebele, as depicted in Figure 6.3 above. I have argued that Cirha is the first son of Nkosiyamntu (the Great House or Indlunkulu in terms of African Traditional Governance and Kingdom succession plans). There is limited historical literature evidence about Ndebele kaNguni. Yet, I have included Ndebele, as informed by Mzilikazi's movement to Zimbabwe. Mzilikazi was born in 1770 and died on 9 September 1868 at Ingama village, about 20 km southwest of Bulawayo. With regard to AmaNdebele in South Africa, most are found in the Lowveld or Mpumalanga, and they are regarded as AmaHlubi in some historical books. Also, if one considers the similarity between the languages of AmaNdebele of

Zimbabwe and AmaZulu, they are the same, except for a few dialectical differences or words. Compared with AmaNdebele of South Africa, the Ndebele language is slightly different, as informed by the context and interaction between the Zulu, Pedi, Swati, and Tswana languages, which resulted in a unique language being established. It is in this context that some historical books refer to AmaNdebele as AmaHlubi (this interesting history falls outside the scope of this book).

The recent Ph.D. thesis by Hleze Welsh Kunju at Rhodes University further supports a need by the NHC and UNESCO to invest money into proper research on Ntu groupings in Africa. Dr. Kunju found a linkage between the AmaXhosa in the Cape provinces and a community of over 200 000 others living in Mbembesi in Zimbabwe. Using ethnographic methodology in the absence of prior studies, he found that this group of AmaXhosa has preserved their culture while living alongside the Shona and AmaNdebele kaMzilikazi in Zimbabwe. This is partly due to the fact that the Zimbabwean Constitution of 2013 allowed for the preservation of cultural identity, including circumcision, or the sacred rite of passage, of boys to manhood. Although Dr. Kunju's topic was on curriculum development of IsiXhosa in the SADC region, the bigger picture of Nguni languages (similar to Tanzania's language revolution led by Julius Nyerere to fight imperial and colonial tribalism) will be critical for social and economic cohesion as part of the Nation-Building Plan. The study must also be contextualized: colonial demands for labor in terms of developments in South Africa at the time must be considered, especially after most AmaXhosa lost their livestock during the playing out of the Nongqawuse myth. Due to labor demands in Zimbabwe, some AmaXhosa moved to Zimbabwe as farm workers. Dr. Kunju's study (2017) further demonstrates beyond any reasonable doubt that the scientific application of ethnographic methods and oral histories can reveal true histories and oral memories, and provide presently unknown, but possible, explanations as to why the AmaXhosa still salute 'AmaCirha' as the original kings of the AmaXhosa (Iikumkani zomthonyama), despite all the aggressive propaganda machinery of colonialism and its neo-colonial public administration and management (PAM) systems to date.

It is significant that the Ntu people inhabit a geographical area stretching east- and southward from central Africa, across the Great Lakes Region, down to the Southern African Development Community (SADC) countries. Ntu is a major branch of the Niger-Congo language family spoken by most populations in sub-Saharan Africa. Individual Ntu groups today often number millions of people, who include the Luba of the Democratic Republic of Congo, the Zulu, Xhosa, Swazi, and Ndebele (who form the Nguni group in South Africa), and the Kikuyu of Kenya, among others. Based on oral narratives, and historical and written sources, the Luzumane (Zulu), Xhosa, Swazi and Ndebele, as depicted in Figure 6.2, which is an oral diagram open to historical criticism, settled in KwaZulu-Natal, Mpumalanga and the Cape provinces.

Under the democratic administration of South Africa, the present Eastern Cape, Northern Cape, and Western Cape represent the erstwhile Cape Province. It is unfortunate that the democratic administration in South Africa, and states elsewhere in Africa, tend to ignore the rich histories of the African clans and kingdoms in antiquity, and rather focus on Eurocentric historical narratives, voyages of discovery, and wars of Africans as recorded by European settlers, colonizers and administrators. For instance, in paragraph 4 of the Nhlapo Commission Report, it is stated that the AmaXhosa moved from northeast Africa and settled on the land between the uMzimkhulu and the then Cape Colony in about 1525. Accordingly, Malangana and Nkosiyamntu (Soga, 1930a:81; Wilson, 1982:88; Balfour-Noyi; 2017:25-174) succeeded Xhosa. King Nkosiyamntu fathered Cirha from *indlunkulu* (Great House), Jwarha from *indlu yasekunene* (Right-Hand House), and Tshawe, the son of *Iqadi* (Supporting House). This historical narrative by the Nhlapo Commission ignored more than 17000 years of South African social history dating back to Mentuhotep I, as outlined in Chapter 1.

The decision by the Nhlapo Commission to investigate various claims made by African kingdoms about their kingship status, especially by the AmaXhosa, dating back to September 1927, remains unresolved, as those claims, as interpreted by the Nhlapo Commission, were not informed by the social history of the Khoi and the San people, which dates back thousands of years, nor the rich anthropological history of African kingdoms, supported by the argument of the cradle of humankind, dating back to Mentuhotep I. Furthermore, the Nhlapo Commission did not take into account the land dispossession wars, often referred to as frontier wars. The nine frontier wars and the pre-imperial and pre-colonial presupposition about South African kingdoms could have provided the country with a reasonable conclusion to achieve social cohesion and value for money. Traditional leaders around the country, emanating from the manipulation of traditional systems by imperial, colonial and apartheid public administration and management systems and related governors, as well as imperial and colonial governments, set the dispute against the backdrop of contestations in relation to various kingships. The colonial authorities had exploited the institutions of traditional leadership to control Africans and traditional leaders, and to compel their dependence on the state as their authority, and for their financial security. Those who were perceived as uncooperative, such as AmaCirha and AmaJwarha of Nkosiyamntu and kaMalangana kaXhosa, were replaced with conformists by means of various pseudo-archaeological strategies and tactics and military interventions. By the dawn of democracy, many illegitimate leaders were entrenched as traditional leaders, and the Nhlapo Commission supported what can be called a crossover of a colonial and Apartheid Traditional Framework and protection of status quo of beneficiaries of past legacies, to a post-colonial South African Traditional Leadership and Governance Framework.

In section 4.10 of the White Paper on Traditional Leadership and Governance, which preceded the establishment of the Nhlapo Commission, it is argued that imperial and colonial legislation transferred powers to identify, appoint and/or recognize and depose traditional leaders from traditional institutions to the imperial, colonial and apartheid government. In the process, the role of customary institutions in the application of customary rules and procedures was substantially reduced. In some instances, illegitimate traditional leaders were appointed, and illegitimate authority structures established. Moreover, some legitimate traditional leaders were removed and legitimate authority disestablished, in cases such as the Kingdom of AmaCirha among the AmaXhosa.

It is also significant to observe that, in an attempt to resolve these historical distortions, the Nhlapo Commission was established in 2004 in terms of section 22 of the Traditional Leadership and Governance Framework Act (2003, Old Act). The Nhlapo Commission had a lifespan of five years. Its tasks included the investigation and resolution of traditional leadership claims and disputes within the Republic of South Africa, including the AmaCirha kingship claim. In terms of section 28(7) of the Old Act, it had to investigate the positions of paramountcies and paramount chiefs that had been established and recognized and were still in existence when that Act came into effect. It had the authority to investigate and determine, among other things, whether the paramountcies qualified to be recognized as kingships. It had to determine the identity of the legitimate kings in respect of the kingships in terms of section 26(2). The decision of the Commission had to be conveyed to the president within two weeks of it being taken, or immediate implementation was required in accordance with section 9 or section 10, where the position of a king or queen was affected by such a decision.

As the Nhlapo Commission's work was not completed within its lifespan, on 22 October 2009 the Commission was extended, in terms of section 25(5) of the Old Act, to 31 January 2010. Accordingly, the Old Act was amended extensively in terms of the Traditional Leadership and Governance Framework Amendment Act 23 of 2009 (the New Act). Of significance under the New Act is that the powers of the Commission regarding the resolution of traditional leadership disputes and claims were altered, so that it could only make recommendations on the resolution of the disputes, as opposed to making decisions in respect thereof. The New Act provides that the recommendation of the Commission must be conveyed to the president within two weeks of having been made for him to make a decision thereon within 60 days. A further relevant change brought about by the New Act is a deeming provision, section 28(8), in terms of which an incumbent paramount chief, at the time of coming into effect of the New Act, is deemed to be a king subject to the investigation and recommendation of the Commission in terms of section 25(2).

It is significant that the AmaCirha Kingdom submissions were not considered, while reliance was rather placed on historians, colonial and apartheid administrators, and those who had been beneficiaries of distorted histories of replaced legitimate kingdoms. There was no meeting held officially with AmaCirha and AmaJwarha by Nhlapo Commission experts and lawyers in terms of section 25(2)(a)(i) of the New Act, which provides that the Commission has the authority to investigate and make recommendations on a case where there is doubt as to whether a kingship was established in accordance with customary law and customs. This should have been followed by section 26 of the New Act, which deals with the recommendations of the Commission.

AmaXhosa kingship, as part of entire African kingdoms, has always been governed by the principle of male primogeniture. In its pure form, the custom was that the leader of the AmaXhosa or king (Ikumkani) would marry several wives. The great wife's (indlunkulu) son would be the preferred successor of Nkosiyamntu, kaMalangana, kaXhosa. In terms of AmaXhosa customary laws, norms and standards, the son of the right-hand wife (ikunene), being the first wife, would not succeed the father (Jwarha), but could establish a semi-independent community. The eldest sons of the consorts (AmaQadi (singular iqadi)), who supported the two main wives, would step in as a successor if the Great Wife had no male issue. The Iqadi (Tshawe) among the AmaXhosa cannot be a legitimate king of the AmaXhosa unless the African customary laws, norms, and standards are replaced by British Indirect Rule, and by the Bantu Administration Act through which imperialists, colonialists, and apartheid governors and administrators wanted to enforce conformist behavior, using the well-known strategy of divide-and-rule, as well as socio-economic Darwinism, coded as 'survival of the fittest'.

Given that Parliament, in 2004, as well as statutory acts of Parliament, including the White Paper on Traditional Leadership and Governance, acknowledged the distorted histories, as mentioned earlier by the state, the Nhlapo Commission (if it had not been captured by beneficiaries of the colonial and apartheid establishment) would have had a session with AmaCirha and AmaJwarha elders, stalwarts and leaders, who have the socio-economic, political and governance interests of the nation-building plan and social cohesion between nations at heart, as well as reconciliation between clans that 'ukuthelekiswa nguMlungu' (were divided by whites) or misled by beneficiaries of the colonial and apartheid administrative systems. As the case of the AmaCirha and AmaJwarha clans is not disputed by all nations, such as AmaMpondo, AmaHlubi, AmaZulu and so forth, it is difficult to comprehend why the Nhlapo Commission declared 'iqadi' house – against AmaNguni and AmaXhosa customary norms and standards – king of AmaXhosa – unless the experts and lawyers were captured or misdirected beyond reasonable doubt on the clear lineage of AmaXhosa kaNkosiyamntu, kaMalangana, kaXhosa, kaMnguni, kaNtu, kaMuntu and so forth.

As cited in the Nhlapo Commission, Cirha clans are direct descendants of the Great House of Nkosiyamntu, and direct descendants in the male line of Malangana and his predecessor, Xhosa. Since membership of the clan (isiduko) passes directly in the male line from father to son and so on, a man would have to acquire a social status of some significance in the group and, more importantly, have male descendants, before his name could be transmitted as the patronymic of the clan. For other logical arguments beyond AmaXhosa customary laws, norms and standards, the same Nhlapo Commission announced and recommended the King of AmaXhosa from Tshawe descendants.

The Nhlapo Commission was commissioned to restore true histories, but the following steps were not followed in terms of section 9(1) of the Traditional Leadership and Governance Framework Amendment Act 23 of 2009 (the New Act). Accordingly, in the recognition of kings and queens in accordance with section 9 (1) of the New Act, whenever the position of a king or queen is to be filled, the following process must be followed:

a. The royal family, including the direct descendants of the Great House of Nkosiyamntu (Cirha) must, within a reasonable time after the need arises for the position of a king or a queen to be filled, and with due regard to applicable customary law (i) identify a person who qualifies in terms of customary law to assume the position of a king or a queen, as the case may be, after taking into account whether any of the grounds referred to in section 10(1)(a), (b) and (d) apply to that person; and (ii) through the relevant customary structure of AmaXhosa as a sub-group of AmaNguni (aa) inform the President, the Premier of the province concerned, and the Minister, of the particulars of the person so identified to fill the position of a king or a queen; (bb) provide the President with the reasons for identification of that person as a king or a queen; and (cc) give written confirmation to the President that the Premier of the province concerned, and the Minister, have been informed accordingly.
b. The President must, subject to subsection (3), recognise a person so identified in terms of paragraph (a)(i) as a king or a queen taking into account (i) the need to establish uniformity in the Republic in respect of the status afforded to a king or a queen; (ii) whether a recognised kingship exists; (aa) that comprises the areas of jurisdiction of a substantial number of senior traditional leaders that fall under the authority of such king or queen; (bb) in terms of which the king or queen is regarded and recognized in terms of customary law and customs as a traditional leader of higher status than the senior traditional leaders referred to in subparagraph (aa); and (cc) where the king or queen has a customary structure to represent the traditional councils and senior traditional leaders that fall under the authority of the king or queen; and (iii) the functions that will be performed by the king or queen. (2) The recognition of a person as a king or a queen in terms of subsection (1)(b) must be done by way of (a) a notice in the Gazette recognizing the person identified as king or queen, and (b) the issuing of a certificate of recognition to the identified person. Where there is evidence of an allegation that the identification of a person referred to in subsection (1) was not done in accordance with customary law, customs or processes, the President (a) may refer the matter to the National House of Traditional Leaders for its recommendation; or (b) may refuse to issue a certificate of recognition; and (c) must refer the matter back to the royal family for reconsideration and resolution where the certificate of recognition has been refused.
c. It is further argued that the Nhlapo Commission neglected the AmaCirha claim to the kingship of AmaXhosa, whereby the responsible MEC and premier in the Eastern Province failed to follow the prescripts of the Constitution and the interests of AmaCirha vested, under customary law, with the power to identify and appoint a traditional leader for the community. Given the years of rule of AmaXhosa by Tshawe dynasties, including the institutionalization of this dynasty in oral memories and history books, an appropriate interpretation of the provisions of both the Old and the New Acts

means that the Nhlapo Commission, the Eastern Cape premiers, and the President of the country should have considered the AmaCirha claim to achieve the founding principles of the Constitution of the Republic of South Africa. Reference is made to subsection (3), which relates to instances where there is evidence or allegations that the identification of a person as a king or a queen of AmaXhosa was not done in accordance with customary law, customs or processes. Rather, this was done to continue colonial and apartheid laws, rules and policies under the supremacy of the Constitution, especially Chapter 12. Sections 211 and 212 of the Constitution provide, inter alia, for recognition of the institution and role of traditional leadership, and for the application of customary law and customs of communities in dealing with matters of traditional leadership. These sections apply especially to the well-known case of the AmaCirha Kingdom. Given this historical fact, AmaCirha and AmaJwarha have clearly been excluded from the democratic State in South Africa, the Eastern Province administration, and benefits of kingships.

The fact that the AmaCirha and AmaJwarha are still prominent clans among the AmaXhosa today suggests that, at the very least, their founding fathers or elders not only survived the succession dispute to tell the tale, but also had male descendants to transmit their clan names down to the present. In this book, the clan is seen as a critical pillar for a nation-building plan to correct a historical distortion in order to build sustainable community models and combine their heritage to advance a blue and green economy and the prosperity of our nation. In doing this, a clan would use a nation-building plan that is guided, commissioned and envisaged by the Imbumba yamaNyama Royal Council, Eastern Cape House of Traditional Leaders, and other kingdoms in Africa.

Like any other clan, the Cirha clan is a group of people united by actual or perceived kinship to, and descent from, an ancestor, who in their case is Xhosa. The Cirha clans, by customary law and traditional community genealogy norms and standards in Africa, are supposedly the kings of the AmaXhosa – if imperialism and colonialism had not distorted the facts, for obvious reasons. Even if lineage details are unknown and have been distorted from the 1500s to the present, Cirha clan members may be organized around the founding members of Imbumba yamaNyama and around Ntsikana kaGabha as a prophet for all nations. The kinship-based bonds may be symbolical, whereby the clan shares a 'stipulated' common ancestor (Prophet Ntsikana kaGabha), who is a symbol of the clan's unity backed by the first national liberation organization in Africa's resistance against imperialism and colonialism, known as Imbumba yamaNyama. When these 'ancestors' are non-humans, they are often referred to as totems, such as *iNdlovu* (elephant) and *iPhuthi* (blue duiker or bluebuck) by Cirha clans. Clans can most easily be described as a nation, or sub-groups of a nation in the case of South Africa. For instance, Cirha, Jwarha, and Tshawe are brothers who fall under the societal definition of AmaXhosa. AmaXhosa, who are a sub-group of Nguni or AmaNguni kaNtu or Abantu, have various kingdoms.

In different cultures and situations, a clan may mean the same thing as other kin-based groups, such as castes and bands. Often, the distinguishing factor is that a clan is a smaller part of a larger society, such as a nation of the AmaXhosa, a chiefdom, or a state. Nations such as the AmaXhosa – particularly owing to wars, colonialization, and various battles in the case of the AmaXhosa – refer to territorial and political units in Africa. These African clans, sub-groupings, or nations are not necessarily kin, as they serve only as a geopolitical unit. The Cirha clan is a sub-group of the AmaXhosa grouping as a socially constructed part of AmaNguni under the major group of Ntu or Abantu, whose roots, boundaries, origins, and ancestors can only be traced in Africa, which also applies to the Khoisan groupings. AmaXhosa and Khoisan groupings' citizenship in South Africa and/or anywhere in Africa cannot be defined based on discovery concepts conceived by imperialists and colonialists. It is my submission that AmaXhosa and Khoisan groupings are Africans. It is, unfortunately, the case that land dispossession wars, or frontier wars, as they are often referred to, were documented by the same imperialists and colonialists with the agenda to ensure endless conflicts when it comes to restoring land to its rightful owners who are Africans. As colonialists have adopted a social and economic Darwinism framework, they have employed administrators and governors, as well as researchers, to advance any form of divide-and-rule, including defining 'first people' in particular areas between various groupings of Africans.

It is significant that AmaXhosa is composed of several numbers of clans and kingships which have bands (Iziduko, https://iziduko.wordpress.com/, accessed 22 May 2019; Icamagu, 2019). AmaXhosa clan names (*isiduko* (singular.), *iziduko* (plural.) in isiXhosa) are family names, which are considered more important than surnames among AmaXhosa people. Much like the clan system of ancient African kingdoms in the pre-colonial era, each Xhosa person can trace their family history back to a specific male ancestor or lineage, except those who have been erased in history as part of colonial agendas. Based on oral history and Icamagu (2019) a few clan names of AmaXhosa and related ethnic groups include:

- **Bhayi** (Khetshe, Mkhumbeni, Msuthu – they belong to the amaVundle people)
- **Bhele** (divides into several sub-clan groups: Dongo, Langa, etc.)
- **Bhukhwana** (ooMbara, Mtshobo, Phaphulengonyama, Into ezingaphathwa mntu ngoba zizinkosi ngokwazo)
- **Cirha** (Malangana, Nkosiyamntu, Ncibane, Nojaholo, Ntswentswe, Qhanqolo, Gabha, hlomla lidala lineempondo, Rhunqu, Mabhalarhana, Gabha, Ntsikana, Manoni, Makeke, Fihla, Rhubusana, Nombewu, Dyibishe, Tsibani, Mkoko, Mdlankomo, Hlalatu, Mhlophe, Ngetu, Nobhoma, Somazembe, Mntumni, Mtiki , etc.)
- **Debeza** (OoDebeza, ngoJebe, Nonyanya, Nongoqo, Mbeka Ntshiyini Bathi uqumbile, Khonkcoshe Mbokodo engava mkwetsho – these are royalty in the Amampondomse group)

- **Dlamini** (or Zizi, Jama kaSjadu, Mabetshe, Bhanise, Ngxib'inoboya, Fakade – the clan name of Thabo Mbeki, khatsini, mtikitiki, nomana ndab'azithethwa intsuku ngentsuku, bhengu, nonyathi – an Mfengu sub-group)
- **Dlomo** (different lines, Thembu or Hlubi sub-groups) (Dlomo, Madiba, Yem-Yem, Zondwa, Sophitsho, Ngqolomsila, Vela bambhentsele, Tubhana, Qhumpase, Tande, MThembu, Ncikoza, Mtshikilana, Malangana, oZondwa zintshaba ezingasoze zimenzele nto)
- **Dontsa** (oNoDlidlu, oNoDlabathi, oSwahla, oMntungwa uNdukuMkhonto, uShembe, bath' uDontsa akananyongo kant' abay'bon' uba igqunywe ngesbhadlalala so mhlehlo (Hlubi clan))
- **Faku** (Nyawuza, Thahla, Ndayeni, Mpondo, Hlamba ngobubend'amanz'ekhona)
- **Gaba** (Mngqosini, Mjobi, Thithiba, Cihoshe, Nozinga, Mnt'womlambo, Thikoloshe, Ndoko, Mbokodw'emnyama Kahili, Msuthu)
- **Gampu** (Memela, Msuthu Nontuli, Ngwekazi)
- **Gatyeni** (Mamali, ndondela, nkomo zibomvu, nywabe, indoda uyivumi nepokoto, ocubungu)
- **Gqwarhu** (omhlophe, Khawu, Ntenge, Mtabasa ka Dingana, Jalamba)
- **Gxarha** (Cwerha, Vambane, Mahlahla, Mlawu, Potwana – Mpodomise sub-group clan name)
- **Jola** (SingaMampondomse ngohlanga, ooJola, ooJoliNkomo, ooMphaNkomo, ooQengeba, nomakhala, njuza, sthukuthezi, sithandwa mhla kukubi, hoshode, hakaha, mfaz' obele 'nye omabele made, oncancisa naphesheya komlambo)
- **Jwarha** (Mtika, Mazaleni, Jotela, Khatiti, Mnangwe, Mayarha, Mbelu, Ndabase, Bantw'abahle noba bapheth' izikhali, ndlu yasekunene kaCirha, Nkosiyamntu, Malangana)
- **Khiwa** (Qwebeda) (Khonjwayo, Ngcekula, Ndzondela, Hlaka, Ngetu, Phoswa, Silwanyana, Makalanyana, Sikhehlana – a Pondo clan)
- **Khwemte** (Dabane, Gqabaza, Sgadi, Mekhi, Ntswentswe, Fulashe, Nojaholo, Ncibane, Qhanqolo, Ntlokwenyathi, Ngququ, venge)
- **Krila** (Mbamba, Thangana, Bodlinja, Mbamba, Krila, Rhaso, Mbombo, Gcaleka, Nkomo zibomvu namathol'azo, Nqele, Bhurhu, Mayisithe, Nomazele, Gobingca, bhukuxa umthondo uwujongise emntwini)
- **Kwayi** (Ngconde, Togu, Ubulawi, Ngcond'oneentshaba, etc.)
- **Madiba** (the clan name of Nelson Mandela, a Thembu. Important rulers and chiefs include Mthikrakra, Ngangelizwe, Dalindyebo, Joyi, Jumba, Sabatha, Buyelekhaya)
  - Dlomo
  - Madiba
  - Yem-Yem
  - Zondwa

Nation Building Plan Between 2020 & 2064

- Sophitsho
- Ngqolomsila
- Vela bambhentsele
- Tubhana
- Qhumpase
- Tande
- MThembu
- Ncikoza
- Mtshikilana
- Malangana
- oZondwa
- Zintshaba
- Ezingasoze
- Zimenzele nto

- **Maduna** (Maduna – Nokhala, Msuthu, Gubevu, Jiyane, Mpungushe, Mandl'amakhulu, Sivunguvung' esawis' indoda emahlangeni, imamba kandidini ngoba ngimesabile, uNokhala owawela ngempalazo eyaphalazwa ngamadoda, Maduna omuhle ngekhala lakhe, isilo esinamadevu emlonyeni, Ngaculende emabalabala njenge ngwe, iinkomo ezingqukuva azibuyi emzini xa bekulotyolwe ngazo)
- **Mambi** (Nxontsa ka Xesibe, uBhulingwe kuvele imamba, uNtabazikude zikuMganu, Mntshontsho uSabela uyabizwa emazibukweni)
- **Manci** (Mbali, Wabane, Tshitshis'intaba, Mdludla ka Bekiso, Zinde Zinde Zinemiqala)
- **Maya** (omaya oyem yem osophitsho, omagwa, ongqolomsila, obhomoyi)
- **Mahlangu**
- **Matshaya** (Mbathane)
- **Mdlane** (Tutuse, Mdimba)
- **Mdlangathi** (Mome mome Sirhama Somntwana, Juta)
- **Mfene** (Lisa, Jambase, Hlathi, Buswayo, Canzi, Sanzanza)
- **Mhaga** (noSabe, Amawel'ukuzana, uQwetha no Gqubushe)
- **Miya** (Gcwanini, Sibewu, Sijekula, Salakulandelwa)
- **Mjoli** (Qubulashe, Wushe, Nonina)
- **Mkhwemte** (Dabane Sgadi Mekhi Ntswentswe Fulashe Nojaholo Ncibane Qhanqolo Ntlokwenyathi Ngququ venge)
- **Mpangela** (Mvinjwa, Rhoshana, Ndlazi, Dlomo, Sibetho, Magwala, Gwadzi elisilika bubuhle)

Fumene George Tsibani

- **Mpehle** (Mpodomise – sub-group clan name)
- **Mpemvu** (uJali ,uJuda, uNtlotshane, Bumela, uNgciva – a Thembu clan name)
- **Mpinga** (Mbetshane, Hlahla lamsik' umntu es*ndeni, ngceza, Sintila, Nyaw' zinoshukela, mzukulu kaSityulu, kheth 'omthandayo, Mawawa) – the clan of Enoch Sontonga, author of 'Nkosi Sikelel' iAfrika', part of National Anthem of Republic of South Africa
- **Mtakwenda** (Leta, Libele, Tyebelendle, Ngcwadi, Kwangeshe, Mentuko, Mboyi, Solizembe)
- **Mthunzi** (Nyukwana, Homposhe, Njifile, Ntibane, Pepepe, Thambo lihlab'elimzondayo, Qabel'eliweni)
- **Mvulane** (Ncilashe, Msuthu – they belong to the amaVundle people)
- **Mweli** (Jili, Msingawuthi, Ngqambela, Sibakhulu, Ntlangwini's enebathat yaseMakhuzeni)
- **Myirha** (Mzondi, Sampu, Ziyeka (Ithambo lenyoka lihlaba elimzondayo))
- **Nala** (Mpembe, uNdokose, Nokhay'ehlungwini, uNgquma, uNojakadelana, uSbheku-bhekuza, uMpondo zihlanjiwe, uJiba isihlobo sikaDzangwe, uHlubi) – Originally from amaHlubi and abaThembu tribe.
- **Ndaba** (Tshibase, Bhadela, Mntungwa, Nonunu, Nomangcangca, Nogubela)
- **Ndala** (Ndala ka Momamana, uMncotshe, Msunu Sdumbu, Thole, Ngxunga Smukumuku, Ndithinina)
- **Ndlovu** (Mntungwa, Gengesi, Malunga, Mancoba (zidlekhaya ngokuswela umalusi))
- **Ndzaba** (Msuthu, Bhili, Mancoba, Gase, Mwelase, into ezehla ezintabeni/ezinkahlambeni zishubele ngenqatha lehashe)
- **Nkabane** (Majeke, Mayeye)
- **Nkomo** (Mntungwa, Khumalo), who were amaMfengu. They are originally Ndebele from Natal and arrived as refugees in Thembuland in 1828 during the time of the Mfecane wars.
- **Nkwali** (Mfengu/Hlubi clan name: Bhukula, Mkhwanazi, Nkwali ye Nkosi). The Nkwalis were born ebukhosini (kingdom) buka Ndwandwe and they were famous during the rule of Dlomo the Thembu king. Nkwali originates from Mkhwanazi ka Ndwandwe. Nkwali joined the amaHlubi tribe and gave birth to Mlabatheki who gave birth to Bukula. Like Bukula, Maphela also comes from Nkwali.
- **Nompunzi** ((thole lempunzi), Gcodi, Lusalu, Catala ka Qoyi, mbumbulu inye zingabambini ziyadubulana)
- **Nozulu** (Kheswa, Mpafane, Mchumane, Mpangazitha, Macocobela, Mbanguba, Thukela)
- **Nqarhwane** (ooZduli, ooHintsabe, ooMaqhula, ooHlabilawu)
- **Nxuba** (Mduma, Rhudulu)
- **Nyawuza** (Faku, Mpondo)

- **Mqadi** (Ngqwili Nondlobe, Ngcwina)
- **Qhinebe** (Gqugqugqu, Zithonga-zthathu, Haha, Mlunjwa, Mkhomanzi, Duka namahlathi, konjanémnyama idlalémafini)
- **Qocwa** (Zikhali Mazembe, Jojo, Tiyeka, Butsolo Beentonga Mbizana, Mabombo)
- **Qoma** (Qomukuyitya, Nyoyela, Nwaba ndikwenze, Singqu, Sisiqobo eso)
- **Qithi** (Ndinga, Nkomo ayizali izala ngokuzaliswa, Yem-yem, Sopitsho, Ngqolomsila, Velabembhentsele, Zondwa, Thembu)
- **Thwane** (Fulela wanetha, Mfazi olivila, Mpemvu, Sabelo, Wuwu)
- **Mqwambi**, Holomi
- **Qwathi** (Iinkomo zikaXesibe, zikaJojo, zikaMtshutshumbe, ogqaz'indlel'ebhek'ebuNguni) It is also argued that the amaQwathi are not a clan, but an independent nation founded by Mtshutshumbe kaMthetho, who split from the amaXesibe nation and settled in the Mqanduli area in Thembuland some 350 years ago.
- **Rhadebe** (Bhungane, Mthimkhulu, Ndlebentle'zombini, Makhulukhulu, Mafuz' afulele njengelifu lemvula, Mashwabada owashwabadel' inkomo nempondo zayo, Mbucwa, Zikode (amaHlubi))
- **Sithathu** (means 'third' – the third Khoi-khoi ancestry clan) (oChisana, Khopoyi, Ndebe, Hasa, Lawu)
- **Skhosana** (Novaphi, Mntungwa, Ntuthwana, msikamhlanga, uNtuthu uyeaqhuma zonke izizwe zabikelana zathi ngabakwaSkhosana. Dunga) by Onesimo Langeni
- **Skhoji** (A group of Xhosa speaking people who mainly occupy the small town called Tsolo on the Tsitsa valley. They are the direct descendants of a Scottish man by the name of William Saunders who befriended a Xhosa girl (Icamagu, 2019))
- **Sukwini** (with Khoi-khoi ancestry) (Chwama, Dibashe, Lawu'ndini, Nja-bomvu, Sandlala-ngca, Ithole loMthwakazi, Tiki ayivumi napokotho, unnqayi linqindi, imvaba yiketile)
- **Thangana** (Krila, Mtengwana, Rhaso, M'bamba, Bodlinja, Gobingca)
- **Thole** (Gqagqane, Buzini, Ndlangisa, Mzimshe, Lwandle)
- **Tolo** (Hlubi clan name) (Dlangamandla, Mchenge, Mabhanekazi, Zulu, Vumbalempongo liyanuka)
- **Tshangisa** (Zulu, Skhomo, Mhlatyana, Rhudulu, Nxuba, Mngwevu)
- **Tshawe** (Mdange, Tshiwo, Ngcwangu, Phalo, Hintsa, Sigcawu, Sarhili, Xolilizwe, qadi likaCirha, kaNkosiyamntu, kaMalangana, kaXhosa.)
- **Tshezi** (the ruling Bomvana clan of the Jalamba-Gambushe line, with European shipwreck ancestry)
- **Tshomane** (with shipwreck ancestry, split from the ruling Nyawuza clan of the Mpondo)
- **Tshonyane** (The clan name of Chris Hani) (aphuma kubelungu abatyekezwa yinqanawe), (Chungwa, Dikiza, Sawu, Tota, Simnke, Khwane, Hani, Zulu, Mth'uzimele, Gqunukhwebe, Nkomo z'bomvu)

- **Xesibe** (AmaXesibe are a nation made up of several clans and tribes, but their history is not well-documented. Common clan names are Nondzaba, Mbathane, Tshomela ka Matsho)
- **Xhamela** (they are also called amaGcina, found in Thembuland)
- **Yeka** (uMyeka, umThembu, unoYhila, umNgqavu, uMvela, uMjuku … njalo njalo)
- **Zangwa** (Khwalo, Ncuthu, Sohobese, Oonkuma – amaMpondo)
- **Zima** (Ceduma, Sopitsho, Bhomoyi, Vela bembhentsele) (AmaZima yinzala ka Zima. Imbali ithi uZima ngumntakwabo Ntade. uNzima wayemdala ngokweminyaka kodwa ezalwa kwindlu yasekunene, uNtande ezalwa nguNdlunkulu (Great House). Siqikelela ukuba bobabini bangoonyana bakaToyi kaCeduma ka Dunakazi ka Bhomoyi ka Thembu ka Ntongakazi ka Malandela ka Njanye ka Sibiside)
- **Zulu** (Ntombhela, Mahlahlula emaduneni, Tshaka)

Dr. Luvuyo Dondolo, in his presentation of AmaXhosa Complexities during the celebration of Ntsikana kaGabha Legacy in the Eastern Cape, Seymour at Thwathwa in 2018, funded by the Department of Eastern Cape Sport, Recreation, Art and Culture (SRAC), National Heritage Council (NHC), Imbumba yamaNyama Royal Council and Mthengenya and Associates (Pty) Ltd, explained that not all AmaXhosa-speaking people belong to the AmaXhosa nation, whose rulership descends from Mnguni, Xhosa, Malangana and Nkosiyamntu. Nkosiyamntu had four wives, who gave birth to Cirha, Jwarha and Tshawe, with Qwambe being Iqadi of Jwarha. As part of British Indirect Rule, Tshawe took over the Kingdom of AmaXhosa from Cirha in the early 1400s. During the years of apartheid, it is unfortunate that the Tshawe lineage was used to establish Bantustans, namely the Transkei (the AmaGcaleka Kingdom) and the Ciskei (AmaRharhabe Kingdom). Even though Tshawe's sons fought bitter battles against colonialism and apartheid, including against land dispossession, wherein Cirha and Jwarha acted as military advisors, counselors and councilors of various AmaTshawe kings, it can be observed that there has been a silent agreement amongst archaeologists, anthropologists, writers and historians to erase the strategic role of AmaCirha in history, and related heritage activities, at the time of writing this book. I have noticed further that the AmaXhosa nation is often, unfortunately, referred to as the descendants of the line of Tshiwo to Phalo who begot Gcaleka and Rharhabe. Some people make the mistake of saying all AmaXhosa speakers are 'Umzi kaPhalo', i.e. house of iqadi (support house) (see the Recognition of Customary Marriages Act 120 of 1998). The House of Phalo split into the AmaGcaleka and AmaRharhabe, and the Kingdom of AmaXhosa was won by Iqadi of Gcaleka, and not necessarily Cirha, the Great House, as known in African Traditional Governance, Norms and Standards. Dr. Dondolo (2018), supported by Dr. FG Tsibani (2018), concluded that the complexities of the AmaXhosa Kingdom remain unresolved, and the story still has gaps. It is in this historical context that the Imbumba yamaNyama Royal Council and National Heritage Council, in partnership with academic research institutions, are expected to conduct historical research to advance reconciliation, and unity in diversity, as was championed by Ntsikana kaGabha in the nineteenth century, and Nelson Mandela, who put in place the Truth and Reconciliation Commission to restore the pride of all South Africans, and ensure that an appropriate reconciliation strategy was implemented. This was meant to ensure that in post-democracy South Africa all state organs developed their programs and projects with the aim of social and economic cohesion to meet the long-term strategy goals for Africa, for youth and other vulnerable groups. It is inductively and deductively concluded that not all Xhosa speaking people belong to the AmaXhosa nation whose rulership descends from the AmaCirha kingdom. The Cirha kingdom comes from the descendants of the line of Nkosiyamntu borne by Malangana and direct firstborn male of Xhosa. Whilst submissions were made in terms of Cirha claims to the AmaXhosa Kingdom, these felt on the deaf ears and AmaXhosa kingdom remains unresolved in a supposedly democratic South Africa.

Furthermore, some of the nations which were forcefully grouped under AmaXhosa include:

- **AmaBhaca** (descended from Madzikane, chief of the amaNgwane, killed during the invasion of Thembuland in 1828)
- **AmaMfengu** (amaHlubi, amaBhele, amaZizi, amaNgwane, etc.)
- **AmaMpondo** (Pondoland; their kingdom is in dispute, like that of the amaXhosa)
- **AmaMpondomise** (their kingdom was destroyed by British colonists in revenge for the killing of magistrate Christopher Hope by Mhlontlo's forces during the Anti-Colonial Revolt of 1880. The revolt was led by Mhlontlo of the amaMpondomise, together with Gecelo of the amaGcina, Dalasile, and Stokwe of the amaQwathi, and Squngathi of the abaThembu)
- **AmaQwathi** (Qwathiland)
- **AbaThembu** (their kingdom is in dispute between the Matanzima and Dalindyebo descendants; Dalindyebo descendants are regarded as the rightful Kings of Thembu)
- **AmaXesibe** include big clans like AbaThembu. These clans include:
  - **Xesibe** – Nxanda kaXesibe, Mnune Mkhuma, Nondzaba, Mbathane, Nondize, Bhelesi, Matshaya ngenqaw'ende abanye betshaya ngezimfutshane, Nxele, Bhimbi, Khandanyawana, Mayitshin'eyibheka njengomntwana, Mantsaka, Mganu. Nondzaba, Mbathane, Tshomela ka Matsho
  - **Qwathi** – Dikela, Noni, Noqaz' indlela. Iinkomo zikaXesibe, zikaJojo, zikaMtshutshumbe, ogqaz'indlel'ebhek'ebuNguni. KumaQwathi kukho amaDikela, amaTshaba, ooSdindi, ooBhlangwe, ooBhose, amaNzolo, imiNcayi, amaNtondo, amaKhombayo, ooMkhondweni, amaVumbe, ooKhebesi, amaBangula, amaDumba, ooMhotho, ooCakeni, ooBhabha, amaMvala, amaDabisa, ooS'ximba, etc.

- **Mambi** – Nxontsa ka Xesibe, uBhulingwe kuvele imamba, uNtabazikude zikuMganu, Mntshontsho, uSabela uyabizwa emazibukweni)
- **Matshaya** – Mbathane

Similarly, AbaThembu have big clans in Southern Africa countries like AmaXesibe. Some of the AbaThembu clans include:

- **Madiba** – Dlomo, Madiba, Yem-Yem, Vela bambhentsele, Sophitsho, Ngqolomsila, Tubhana, Qhumpase, Ntande, MThembu, Ncikoza, Mtshikilana, Malangana, Bhomoyi
- **AmaNtande** – Dlomo, Sopitsho, Ngqolomsila, Zondwa ziintshaba
- **Qithi** – Ndinga, Nkomo ayizali izala ngokuzaliswa, uRhadu, uNomsobodwana, uSopitsho uNgqolomsila uYemyem uVela bembhentsele, Zondwa, MThembu)
- **Ndungwana** – u Bhejula uDiya uMaqath' alukhuni, uVelabembhentsele uHala.
- **AmaNgxongo** – oontsundu, bhomoyi zondwa zintshaba, osophitsho.
- **AmaGcina** – Xhamela, Helushe, Ncancashe, Magwebulikhula, Malambedlile, Nokwindla, Thyopho ka Phato owathyaphakela eXonxa , Gabul' ikhula, Malamb'ayendle aty' igusha athi ziz' duli zethafa, Nxego, Butsolo beentonga, Dlelanga, Ntlonipho (Bahamba bepheth'isali – ihashe bakulifuman'emlungwini, izinto zabantu abazibi koko bayazigcini, bathi iigusha zizaduli zentaba)
- **Qhudeni** – UMthembu, uThukela, uQhudeni, uMkhubukeni, uGoza, uMpafane, uMthembu obhuzuzu, odla amathibane az 'indlala iwile.
- **Maya** – oMaya, oYem Yem oSophitsho, oMagwa, oNgqolomsila, oBhomoyi
- **Mpangela** -Mvinjwa, Rhoshana, Ndlazi, Dlomo, Sibetho, Magwala, Gwadzi elisilika bubuhle.
- **Mpemvu** – uJali ,uJuda, uNtlotshane, Bumela, uNgciva
- **Ndala** – Ndala ka Momamana, uMncotshe, Msunu Sdumbu, Thole, Ngxunga Smukumuku, Ndithinina)
- **Zima** – Ceduma, Sopitsho, Bhomoyi, Vela bembhentsele. (AmaZima yinzala ka Zima. Imbali ithi uZima ngumntakwabo Ntade. uNzima wayemdala ngokweminyaka kodwa ezalwa kwindlu yasekunene, uNtande ezalwa nguNdlunkulu (Great House). Siqikelela ukuba bobabini bangoonyana bakaToyi kaCeduma ka Dunakazi ka Bhomoyi ka Thembu ka Ntongakazi ka Malandela ka Njanye ka Sibiside)

Yet, partly due to nomadic lives, the movements of clans and tribes for greener pastures, wars, and need for human settlements, some nations or group of clans joined AmaXhosa. These include AmaBhaca, AmaGqunukhweba, AmaHlubi, AmaRigwa, AmaHigwa, AbaThwa (Khoisan or AmaSukwini), AmaMfengu, AmaMpondo, AmaMpondomise, AmaBomvana, AmaFingo, AmaXesibe, AmaHegebe kaHolomisa, AmaQadi,

AmaFengu, etc. For instance, it is argued that AmaMpondo has a separate lineage that is traceable from Sibiside to Dlemini to Njanya, to Mpondo and Mpondomise (twins) and Xesibe. In some historical books, authors have argued that AmaXesibe are believed to have had independent chieftaincy amongst the AbaThembu, which they lost during wars, and started to pay allegiance to the Xhosa Kings. AmaXesibe is a nation made up of several clans and tribes, but their history is not well documented and is significantly inconclusive. Yet, common clan names are Nondzaba, Mbathane, Tshomela ka Matsho, Matshaya, Makhuma Sandlala, and so forth. The descendants of Mpondo are Santsabe, Sukude, Msiza, Ncindise, Cabe, Gangata, Bhala, Chithwayo, Khonjwayo, Ngcoya, Hlamandana, Tahle, Nyawuza, and many others. The descendants of Xesibe are Ntozabantu to Ndzuza to Miyana to Bimbi to Nondzaba who begot Hlabe, to Mthetho to Mtshutshumbe, who founded the amaQwathi nation. Mtshutshumbe begot Mndwana begot Ncobe begot Nkovane begot Ntswayibana begot Dikela. The AmaMpondo, AmaMpondomise, AmaXesibe and amaQwathi nations are related, but the amaQwathi settled in Thembuland more than 350 years ago and, as a result, Qwathi chiefdom is more AbaThembu in culture and political association. Swartz (2010) argued that these nations are often distinguished by language dialect, distinct language and culture, most having clans and bands as the basic kinship organizations. Therefore, proper documentation and historical analysis of AmaXhosa and their positive impact through combined heritage are outside the scope of this book. The latter is due to the fact that imperialism, and systematic colonialism using discriminatory policies such as the Black Administration Act 38 of 1927, created not only a significant distortion of the history of the Nguni and Ntu groups, but also created pseudo-archeology, with Cirha clans being on the receiving end of these inhuman systems.

The list became endless as other African groupings and clans joined the AmaXhosa to defend the country against imperialists, colonialists, and neo-liberal colonialists, as well as associated tendencies, approaches and strategies. It is also significant that the AmaSukwini are a separate nation with a different kingdom from that of the AmaXhosa kaCirha. Some of the groups, such as the Hoho clans, are Khoisan descendants. The AmaSukwini, for example, have direct Khoikhoi ancestry. Their clan names include the Chwama, Deyi, Dibashe, Lawu, Lubisi, Ndlela, Ndlakhwe, Sandlala-ngca, Nja-bomvu, Somchiza, Somda and Ithole loMthwakazi.

In our discussions with Chief Mwelo Nonkonyane, Khoekhoen Royal Kingdom, and Imbumba yamaManyama Royal Council elders, AmaXhosa have inter-marriages with Khoisan groupings, especially in the area of Adelaide, Seymour, Fort Beaufort and Alice leading to a formation of a Khoisan grouping called amaGqunukhwebe. The clans include:

- AmaGiqwa – Mvamba, Jingqi, Jikijwa
- OoSithathu – Chisana, Ndebe, Hase
- AmaNqarhwane – Ziduli, Hintsabe
- AmaSukwini – Dibashe, Lawu

- Tshonyane, Chungwa, Dikiza, Sawu, Tota, Simke, Khwane, Hani, Zulu, Mthuzimele, Gqunukhwebe, Nkomo z'bomvu .
- Cethe – Chizama, Mlanjana, Bhurhuma, Ncenceza, Mbambo zinomongo, yint'ety'inyama ekrwada, uHani, malahl'aluthuthu ayatshisa wawanyathela ungafa
- Gqunu
- amaGqwashu
- Sithathu

Furthermore, it is significant that not all Xhosa-speaking people belong to the AmaXhosa nation, whose rulership descends from the AmaCirha Kingdom. The Cirha Kingdom comes from the descendants of the line of Nkosiyamntu, born of Malangana and a direct firstborn male of Xhosa. While submissions were made in terms of Cirha claims to the AmaXhosa Kingdom, these were ignored, and the inheritance of the AmaXhosa Kingdom remains unresolved despite the new democratic South Africa and its supreme Constitution.

6.14 Pseudo-archaeology and pseudo-history

Pseudo-archaeology refers to deliberate interpretations of the past from outside of the academic archaeological community, which typically also rejects the accepted scientific and analytical methods of the discipline. A related term is pseudo-history, which, according to Wikipedia is a form of pseudo-scholarship that attempts to distort or misrepresent the historical records based, in this context, on colonial and apartheid archives. In this book, my use of the term pseudo-archaeology should be understood as also including pseudo-history.

The adoption of pseudo-archaeology to construct theories about the past that differ radically from those of mainstream academic archaeology, is in order to supplement new historical claims with evidence for both imperial and colonial reasons. This means that kings and queens were established and documented outside of the customary laws and traditional council systems. In terms of pseudo-archaeology or pseudo-history, kings and queens were established to institutionalize imperialism, colonialism, and colonialism of a special type including, more recently, the former homeland system in South Africa. In most cases to date, pseudo-archaeology has been motivated by racism, xenophobia and anti-Semitism and it has reduced indigenous intellectual knowledge to clan lineages in Africa (Harinck, 1969:154-155; Theal, 1897:111-112). Using oral interviews with Cirha and Khoekhoen elders, stalwarts and leaders between 2000-2018, there was a succession of at least five kings – Malangana, Nkosiyamntu, Tshawe, Ngcwangu and Sikhomo – within the AmaXhosa kingdoms. In terms of this example, the reader is unfortunately misled into thinking that these were actual kings or chiefs of the AmaXhosa based on African customary norms and standards and lineage.

Another major concern is that even African historians, scholars and writers are trained to reproduce these distorted histories, which is an embarrassment to democratic academic institutions. These writers have failed to transcend colonial and apartheid legacies, claiming to be experts on 'us'. Military killings and genocides, especially in southern Australia, New Zealand and some parts of Africa, have often followed the use of pseudo-archaeology and commissions that have provided states with legal justification for their actions, based on a Whip framework or liberal ideology founded on the Westminster system of governance. Genocide refers to the systematic slaughtering of large numbers of innocent people by a military power to achieve capital interests. Genocide is often perpetrated by imperial and colonial empires or states committed to notions of racism, ethnicity, and tribalism. Accordingly, African intellectuals and mature SPACE leaders have been assassinated, suppressed, detained without trial, or poisoned to ensure that original pre-imperial and pre-colonial societal structures, clans, and kingdoms are completely destroyed or replaced with new histories to advance colonial interests in post-colonial Africa.

Aligned with this, there appears to be a collective effort to ensure that the erosion of the AmaCirha Kingdom and its history is achieved. The latter argument is based on another misleading website publication, which requires, inter alia, an intervention by the House of Traditional Leadership, COGTA and the National Heritage Council as a custodian of our historical heritage. The publication is titled *AmaXhosa Kingdom – A History (Part 1)* (XhosaCulture, http://xhosaculture.co.za/amaxhosa-kingdom-history-part-1/). This document provides information on the historical journey of Abantu, especially of the Nguni grouping, from Ethiopia to southern Africa. Once again, this account provides a distorted representation of Nguni genealogy with a bias towards the Tshawe Kingdom, whereby defeated and suppressed kingdoms and clans, that were further suppressed by the inhuman system of colonialism and the apartheid Bantu Administration and Homeland system, are not acknowledged. According to this compilation of AmaXhosa Kingdom discourse, the rise of Tshawe was based on political maneuvers and support from other clans and kingdoms to undermine African traditional governance and leadership. It appears that the history of the AmaXhosa Kingdom continues to be written to reflect colonial and apartheid administration systems. Less qualified African historians and writers have been used to re-write African histories using highly selective knowledge by white scholars. In this historical account of the AmaXhosa Kingdom, the reader is not provided with the complexity of historical realities, like the scramble for land by European countries, frontier wars, and conflicts between the imperialists, colonialists, neo-colonialists and legitimate traditional leaders that led to legitimate AmaXhosa kingdoms being replaced with illegitimate kingdoms. In a similar vein as this colonial and apartheid-constructed discourse, Theal (1897:111) provided the following fictitious speculations about the defeat of AmaCirha and AmaJwarha by Tshawe:

- Tshawe and his followers owed their victory to the fact that they were better armed with iron-tipped spears and javelins (imikhonto) than their adversaries.
- Cirha had no retinue (isihlwele) of male followers of his own, who are usually selected from the youths circumcised with the future traditional leader.
- As frequently happened historically in the succession of traditional leaders among the AmaXhosa, it is possible that Cirha had not been circumcised at the time Tshawe contested his political authority by defeating Jwarha, and was considered an infant or minor.
- Because battles were largely fought over questions of political supremacy, and because victory was easily computed in terms of cattle captured, pre-colonial wars among the southern Nguni tended to be relatively bloodless.

Surely, African people have provided history writers with the true history of the AmaXhosa Kingdom. Unfortunately, colonial and apartheid administrators were paid to distort history and provide fictitious justifications outside of African kingdom norms and standards of governance.

The fictitious explanations reflected above were an attempt to erode the AmaCirha claim to the kingdom of the AmaXhosa, despite there being no evidence for a legitimate counter-argument. White scholars tried also to undermine African governance systems, as well as their African norms and standards, by providing explanations that leave the reader with a notion that they were either stupid or unreasonable. This was all part of the colonial and apartheid-constructed discourse. What is clear is that the AmaCirha and AmaJwarha clans were popular because they were able to adapt and adjust to psychological war games and use appropriate political tactics to resist colonialism and apartheid. In other words, as Dyibishe & Mtiki (2014) argued, the elders told them that they must resist colonialism and apartheid rather than focus on tribal, clan and family wars, citing the case of other African states in the Congo River region. By participating in frontier wars, AmaCirha and AmaJwarha earned credibility, legitimacy, trust, and leadership among families and clans of the AmaXhosa. With leaders like Nxele kaMakhanda, Ntsikana kaGabha, and Dr. MWB Rubusana, to mention but a few, it was difficult for the enemy to make them focus on their claim to a kingdom, as the notion of 'zenibe yimbumba yamanyama' was critical to protect the land from settlers. AmaCirha ancestors, elders, and stalwarts saw land not just as a commodity, but rather as a means to an economic end. For AmaCirha leaders, the land was about dignity and identity. They connected land to 'being', and to their forebears. The AmaCirha and AmaJwarha clans saw the call of 'zenibe yimbumba yamanyama' as a priority to liberate all Africans first. Therefore, AmaCirha and AmaJwarha assumed African leadership above a narrow ethnic-separatist approach written by white scholars, and more recently by Africans who are beneficiaries of African kingdoms established by either colonial or apartheid administration systems, or by both.

It is possible that colonial and apartheid administrators did not support AmaCirha and AmaJwarha because they did not cooperate with these regimes and their repressive laws. As Peter Childs & Patrick Williams (1997:123) suggest:

> *Colonial rule is necessarily enmeshed with a system of representation and, as an apparatus of power, its discourse constructs a knowledge of 'subject peoples' through which it variously authorizes that rule, installs racial differences, and produces the colonized as entirely knowable.*

After imperialism, colonialism and apartheid, attitudes and perceptions espoused in these regimes persisted, with the consequence that African writers have reproduced the same histories, myths and fictitious stories, such as those about Shaka, the Thuthula Battle, Nongqawuse, and the Mfecane (Difaqane or Lifaqane) that were introduced as part of African languages and stories from early childhood development (ECD) onwards. It can be argued that there are very few monographs written by Africans that are unique and provide an in-depth analysis of pre-imperial and pre-colonial discourse about 'us' without re-packaging already highly selective imperial and colonial histories or monographs. In other words, these myths and fictitious histories were and still are meant to institutionalize colonial and apartheid-constructed discourse from one generation to the next. In this way, colonized people are often used to reproduce those distorted histories using oral memories, drama, poems, and other platforms, such as iimbizo or iindaba, meetings, councils, summits and conferences (Brown, 1998:10; Balfour-Noyi, 2017:28-31). Those who have been made beneficiaries of colonial and apartheid-era kingdoms are then sponsored to rewrite their histories to reflect highly selective knowledge and oral memories, which are then used to erase legitimate kingdoms and leaders from memory. Through these highly selective histories and oral memories, socio-economic, cultural and political myths are composed in poems, which eventually become acceptable to leaders and representatives of the colonized. These false texts are used to convey greetings, such as 'Mzi kaPhalo', when opening important occasions such as iimbizo or iindaba, meetings, councils, summits, conferences, events and occasions (Wright, 1989:272-291). This is one of the impacts of a book titled *The House of Phalo* by Jeff Peires (1981, 2003), which has been used in history courses or as a prescribed text in various academic institutions, and has overshadowed other histories, such as that of AmaCirha kaNkosiyamntu, to name but one instance.

It can be deduced that there are various accounts regarding the origin and existence of the AmaXhosa characterized by inconsistency. The meaning of the term 'Xhosa' itself has been given implausible connotations by non-African scholars. Swartz (2010:226-237) adds that the Kingdom of AmaCirha is the 'oldest historically' among the AmaXhosa (Mostert, 1992:462), thus making that of Tshawe, who supposedly defeated his brother Cirha, the second-oldest kingdom. By sharp contrast, reading Peires, it would appear that the installation of the AmaTshawe as the Royal Family of the AmaXhosa was the earliest historical occurrence specific to the AmaXhosa (Peires, 1982:13). According to Swartz (2010:227), supported by Dyibishe and Mtiki (2014), it appears that the oral history of the AmaXhosa, however, does not accept the version of Professor Jeff Peires. The traditional version was recorded by Rubusana in 1906 (thus making it older by at least thirty years than that of JH Soga, upon which Peires bases his 1980 dissertation). It is significant that Peires and other European scholars had difficulty in tracing the genealogy of the AmaXhosa, at least up to Xhosa, whose existence Peires rejects rather prejudicially without sufficient reason (Swartz, 2010:227). It requires a certain level of cultural grounding and access into the tacit side of African cultural knowledge to be able to weave one's intellectual way through and within its life-world. Being able to do this through the beautiful simplicity of those Nguni clans, such as AbaThembu, AmaMpondo, AmaMpondomise, AmaZulu and AmaJwarha, in the language isiXhosa, makes it easier to embrace the assertion made not only by Rubusana, but also by other scholars, elders and traditional leaders, including writers like JJR Jolobe (1958), who said that these people 'baphuma sinqeni sinye' (are from the same ancient source). Even when writing about the Cirha Kingdom, most authors use the term 'AmaCirha chieftaincy' to undermine the indigenous authority of African kingdoms, as they are fully aware that the power of African societies is centralized in the king (Ikumkani) and queen (Indlovukazi).

As suggested by the arguments of Brown (1998) and Wright (1989) about the sociocultural and political methodologies used by colonizers, the histories of the AmaXhosa Kingdom, and Africa, continue to reflect ethnic conflict rather than social cohesion and the good traditional leadership qualities of our ancestors. It is in this context of subverting histories that the AmaXhosa Kingdom should be contextualized within the context of the colonial and apartheid periods. There is a clear attempt by authors to support created myths and colonial constructs, which state that Africans are from Ethiopia, Khoisan people are the 'first people' of South Africa, and KwaZulu-Natal is a land of Zulu people, created, discovered and established in 1843. The short-lived Boer Republic of Natalia was annexed by the British government in 1843 and became the Colony of Natal, which led to the migration of Afrikaners to the Transvaal (Gauteng) and Orange Free State (Free State). In 1849, Theophilus Shepstone introduced a policy aimed at reserving large tracts of land for Africans. Land of Nguni leaders such as Dingiswayo (1807-1817), Shaka (1817-1828) and Dingane (1828–1840) was forcefully included in the Natal Colony in 1879, after a bloody war, and an area of Zululand was formally annexed in 1887; while self-administration of the Natal Colony was granted by Britain in 1893. It is also significant that the black reserves under the Native Land Trust of 1864 were used to establish the homeland administration system of KwaZulu. In the late 1980s and early 1990s, with the release of political leaders in South Africa, Natal and KwaZulu became the scene of political violence – mainly between the African National Congress (ANC) and the Inkatha Freedom Party (IFP). It is also significant that the histories of other kingdoms, such as the Ndwandwe, which are situated in the same region, were not accounted for (Buthelezi, 2004:1-103).

The historical truth is that customary law and traditional African norms and standards dictate that the AmaXhosa Kingdom must come from the AmaXhosa King Nkosiyamntu, who fathered Cirha from indlu enkulu (Great House), Jwarha from indlu yasekunene (Right-Hand House), and Tshawe, the son of iqadi (Supporting House). In short, colonialists should have restored the AmaXhosa Kingdom to its legitimate traditional leadership under the Cirha clan (Great House, or indlu enkulu), rather than relying on the constructed pseudo-archaeological justifications, historical distortions, fictions, myths and apartheid-constructed histories provided by white administrators and academics. Martin Luther King Jr., cited by Dr. Myles Munroe (2014:135), warned us that

> ... if we are to go forward, we must go back and rediscover these precious values – that all reality hinges on moral foundations and that all reality has spiritual control.

Most texts about the AmaXhosa Kingdom are often based on oral testimonies of which the authenticity is unknown. It is significant to note that this distorted situation continues at this time, and may affect land claims. It is also significant that oral histories recorded by white scholars, anthropologists and administrators claim to provide accurate historical accounts of African people, societies and histories. Yet, these texts bear the imprint of colonial and apartheid ideological reworking of events over time, from their occurrence to the present democratic administration system. These oral sources are part of hegemonic discourses, which are often based on colonial and apartheid administration systems and are characterized by embarrassingly inaccurate and illogical historical arguments and articulations – especially in the case of the AmaCirha Kingdom. It is also significant that there are more accurate historical versions from white scholars, administrators, and writers, such as Mostert and Theal. Yet, all of them have common oral memories and histories, which tend to be understood differently by the defeated families, clans and kingdoms. Buthelezi (2004:102-103), writing about a similar construction of colonial and apartheid kingdoms in present-day KwaZulu-Natal, concluded that it is legitimate to claim that justice should be dispensed to those – or their families – who were displaced and violated under colonial and apartheid rule. The same argument holds for the AmaXhosa Kingdom, under which individuals, families, and clans were subjected to violence and dispossession of land.

As I discussed with the Imbumba yamaNyama Royal Council and the National Heritage Council on 14 March 2017, there is a need for a series of recriminations for events which took place in the past and present to erase AmaCirha claims to their legitimate AmaXhosa Kingdom, in order to expose the fallacies on which some of the self-assured versions of the history of the AmaXhosa Kingdoms are built (Buthelezi, 2004:103). Accordingly, Dyibishe & Mtiki (2014) concluded that Africans, and South African families and clans, must know that there are histories beyond colonial and apartheid-constructed discourses, which run concurrently with those that have been authorized through colonial and apartheid administration systems in various oral memories, stories, publications and museums. Along with social cohesion as part of the nation-building plan, and correcting the histories of African kingdoms in the Home of Legends, there is a need for the voiceless to tell their own histories and stories, and provide accurate historical accounts in order to create a conducive environment for social cohesion. This will replace pseudo-archaeology in our oral memories and histories. This will enable African kingdoms to follow the example of the AmaCirha Kingdom, to enter into a critical and self-reflective dialogue with one another, as Africans, while trying to establish new post-colonial modes of relating to and interacting with one another, without continuing to be held hostage by 'historical facts' of dubious provenance (Buthelezi, 2004:103).

As mentioned, the Eastern Cape, as part of the Cape provinces, may be represented with reference to land dispossession and frontier wars. The frontier wars started in the 1770s when the AmaXhosa and whites clashed at the Fish River. Historically, the first two frontier wars took place during the time of the Dutch-East India Company (VOC) that ruled the Cape from 1652 to 1795, and the third during the period of the first British occupation of the Cape, that lasted from 1795 to 1803. These three wars are briefly outlined as follows:

- The First Frontier War broke out in December 1779. Adriaan van Jaarsveld captured a large number of cattle from the AmaXhosa. Van Jaarsveld justified his war by claiming that he had driven the AmaXhosa out of the Zuurveld by July 1781 (Moodie, 1860:18).
- The Second Frontier War lasted from 1789 to 1793. It was a continuation of the First Frontier War that broke out in 1779. The AmaGqunukwebe clan began revenge attacks and attempted to reconquer the lost land of the Zuurveld (an area between the Great Fish and the Sundays rivers). Ndlambe, of the AmaTshawe dynasty, formed an alliance with white farmers and trekboers to defeat the AmaGqunukwebe.
- The Third Frontier War lasted from 1799 to 1803 and was a continuation of the First and Second Frontier Wars. The Khoisan revolted and joined the AmaXhosa in fighting General TP Vandeleur. The Khoisan started attacking white farmers and trekboers in July 1799. After the general uprising of Khoisan and AmaXhosa, a peace agreement was reached in February 1803, leaving the AmaXhosa in the Zuurveld.

After the British re-occupied the Cape in 1806, these three wars were followed by an additional six other frontier wars:

- The Fourth Frontier War lasted from 1811 to 1812. This was the beginning of the forced removal of approximately 20 000 AmaXhosa. The AmaXhosa were driven back across the Fish River, away from the Zuurveld. The towns of Grahamstown and Cradock were established as permanent barracks or military forts, and the area was renamed Albany. The white farmers and trekboers had given the area the name of Zuurveld because of the quality of grazing. It was 'zuur' (Dutch-Afrikaans word for 'sour' or 'acidic'), and suitable for trekboers' cattle and sheep grazing throughout the year. The AmaXhosa had been staying in this area for generations before the trekboers and white farmers arrived. It is significant that between the Fourth and Fifth Frontier Wars, the Battle of Amalinde broke out between Ndlambe and Ngqika, around 1818, against the lofty advice by Ntsikana kaGabha.

- The Fifth Frontier War lasted from 1819 to 1820. In 1820, approximately 4 000 British immigrants arrived, who were supported by Cape Governor Lord Charles Somerset. The British settlers were seen as a buffer between the AmaXhosa and the trekboers on the eastern frontier.
- The Sixth Frontier War lasted from 1834 to 1835. It is reported that the AmaXhosa drove off an estimated 250 000 head of cattle and sheep and burned over 450 homesteads in the Albany district. During this event, a substantial number of traders and farmers were killed. The British troops declared the Sixth Frontier War, during which Ngcaleka's grandson Hintsa was killed. His head was cut off and sent to England. As part of the colonization of the land, Sir Benjamin D'Urban created the province of Queen Adelaide (Khobonqaba) for white settlement. This province covered land east of the Fish River and between the Kei and Keiskamma rivers.
- The Seventh Frontier War lasted from 1846 to 1847. It was known as the War of the Axe, or the Amatola War, as it was alleged that Tsili had stolen an axe from a trader in Fort Beaufort in March 1846. Taking part in this frontier war were Khoisan, Fengus, British settlers, Boer commanders, and imperial British troops from London sent to fight Ngqika, assisted by Ndlambe and AbaThembu. It was a bloody war in which scorched-earth military tactics and strategies were used. This refers to an act of destroying the food, livestock (cattle and sheep) and water supply of the civilian population. In the twentieth century, this tactic was banned under Article 54 of Protocol 1 of the 1977 Geneva Convention. It is assumed that scorched-earth military tactics were very popular in this war, to the extent that the 1856-1857 Nongqawuse story (the AmaXhosa cattle-killing) was constructed as a continuation of the Seventh Frontier War tactics. It is also significant that Sir George Grey, governor of the Cape Colony from 1854 to 1861, and an anthropologist and ethnologist, had spent time among the AmaXhosa and understood their cultural beliefs, which could have been exploited as a grand scorched-earth strategy whereby moral reasoning was used for colonial purposes. Although there are various accounts of the Nongqawuse cattle-killing event by different authors, such as Gqoba (1888:22-23), Jordan (1973:111-116) and more recently Peires (2003:35-40), it is assumed that Sir George Grey used and manipulated the beliefs of the AmaXhosa. There is, however, no evidence that he promoted Nongqawuse's prophetic message among the AmaXhosa. Sir George Grey

stockpiled food before the incident. He then gave food to starving people on the condition that they committed to supporting British Colony policies and worked as ordinary laborers. This incident led to widespread famine, and more than a third of the AmaXhosa died of starvation. It is also significant that Sir Harry Smith (British governor, 1 December 1847 to March 1852) was believed to be behind the extermination of the AmaXhosa. Sir Harry Smith, a former governor of Australia and New Zealand, where the Aborigines were killed between 1824 and 1831, makes it possible to assume that a similar strategy was considered in the Cape Colony against both the AmaXhosa and Khoisan groupings. Sir George Grey, a governor of southern Australia (1841-1845) and governor of New Zealand (1845-1853), who had been militarily trained in Ireland, was interested in studying the cultures of indigenous people. In 1840, he wrote a paper on the racial assimilation of indigenous people, and was then appointed as governor of New Zealand in 1845 to deal with racial challenges. He instructed his lieutenant, Donald McLean, to purchase land from the Maori, and to kidnap and imprison without charge Ngati Toa chief Te Rauparaha. As a result, European settlers to New Zealand increased rapidly. He was then instrumental in drafting and finalizing the New Zealand Constitution of 1852 for both the provincial and national spheres of government. A number of Aboriginal massacres are documented in Australia, including on 29 November 1847, when poisoned flour was given to Aboriginals. In southern Australia, there were various other massacres, including approximately 40 people who were massacred at Rufus River (27 August 1841), 100 Bundjalung that died at Evans Head (1842), and 15 people that were massacred in the Djangadi area (1841-1851) under the watchful eye of Governor Sir George Grey. Grey left New Zealand in 1853 to become governor of the Cape Colony, just after the Eighth Frontier War. With his military experience of genocide as governor of southern Australia and New Zealand, and as an ethnologist, anthropologist and ethnographer, Grey studied the cultures of the Maori, Aborigines, Khoisan and AmaXhosa people to advance colonial oppression and create a pool of laborers for white settlements in the aforementioned three countries, by using various military tactics. His academic disciplines and governorships provided him with the ability to learn about indigenous people in terms of their families, clans, formations, compositions, settlements, social welfare characteristics, materiality, spirituality, and ethnogenesis. This included an analysis of the terrain, their adaptive strategies to climate change, cultural activities, habits, and beliefs. Grey was able to observe the cultural behaviors and the socio-economic life of indigenous people, and the meaning of symbolism, within clans and tribes. The AmaXhosa, for instance, believed in ancestors, namely an acceptance that ancestors appear to family or clan members without proof. As Mhlakaza (uncle to Nongqawuse) was an advisor to the chief, Sir George Grey might have manipulated Nongqawuse using ethnographic simulations, which were introduced to her. Given the fact that Grey had been trained in Ireland using sophisticated war machinery and advanced technology of the time, he exploited AmaXhosa beliefs as part of military strategy. From an ethnogenesis (formation of clans and nations) perspective, in the eyes of an internationally experienced military explorer, ethnologist, anthropologist, ethnographer and governor of the Cape Colony, the killing of cattle ensured a systematic execution of the self-determination and self-identity of blacks, and AmaXhosa in particular, through an indirect approach, and as a means of creating a labor force for white settlers and trekboers. Other contributory factors to the AmaXhosa famine included natural disasters, such as epidemic cattle disease, drought, and severe winter weather. Consequently, there was a shortage of food, and suffering. The poet JJR Jolobe succinctly captured the situation in his poem 'Ukwenziwa komkhonzi' (the making of a servant or laborer).

Fumene George Tsibani

Ukwenziwa Komkhonzi	**The making of a servant**
Andisenakubuza ndisithi kunjani na!	I can no longer ask how it is
Ukukhanywa yintambo yedyokhwe emqaleni	To be strangulated around the neck by the Strop
Kuba ndizibonele kwinkabi yomqokozo,	Because I have witnessed this in the inspanned ox,
Ubumfama bamehlo busukile ndagqala	Blindness of the eyes was cleared and I gained understanding
Kuba ndikubonile ukwenziwa komkhonzi	For I have witnessed the making of a servant,
Kwinkatyana yedyokhwe.	In the young yoke ox.
Ndiyibone inyuka iminqantsa women do	I saw it going up steep roads
Ithwele imithwalo enzima ixelenga,	Carrying heavy luggage working hard,
Iludaka kubila ingenisela omnye.	Muddy and sweating for someone else's profits.
yomsebenzi yinxaxheba kuvuno.	Sharing in the profits makes one enjoy working
Kuba ndikubonile ukwenziwa komkhonzi	Because I have witnessed the making of a servant
Kwinkatyana yedyokhwe.	In the young yoke ox.
Ndiyibon' ilambile ngaphantsi kwaloo mbuso	I saw it hungry under that rule
Iliso liinyembezi umxhel' ujaceklle,	Tears dripping from the eye, spirit dejected
Ibe ingasakwazi nokuchasa imbuna,	No longer able to resist, tame.
Ithemba yimigudu ezond' inkululeko	The hope being the success of the struggle for liberation
Kuba ndikubonile ukwenziwa komkhonzi	For I have seen the making of a servant
Kwinkatyana yedyokhwe.	In the young yoke ox.

The poem above refers to Sir George Grey as governor of the Cape Colony whose plan was to pacify the AmaXhosa and assimilate them into the European way of living – a man who had already succeeded in such a task with the Aborigines of Australia between 1837 and 1843, and with the Maori of New Zealand from 1845 to 1853, before he was brought to the Cape Colony. Rutherford (1961:53) argues that, from an economic perspective, the plan entailed that the government and colonists should offer the aborigines (Africans or blacks) regular employment as laborers, farm hands and servants, and thus draw them into association with Europeans (Swartz, 2010:336). The shortage of labor for the Cape Colony was huge. Although there is no literature evidence regarding scorched-earth military tactics (genocide similar to that in Australia and New Zealand against indigenous people) by Sir

Harry Smith who preceded Grey as governor of the Cape Colony, it is also possible to argue that there was a synergy between these two tactics and the abuse of AmaXhosa beliefs by Sir George Grey. Soon after his arrival in the Cape Colony to take up his post as governor in early 1855, Grey received a letter from his friend George Barrow in London (quoted in Gump, 1998:89). It challenged him to accomplish at the Cape what he had done among the Maori: 'If you succeed with the Natives there in any degree approaching what you have achieved in New Zealand, what a glorious triumph it will be after all that has been said of the impossibility of doing anything with them' (Swartz, 2010:368). This reflects the notion that ethnogenesis could be used to include and exclude any ethnic group or clan in the Cape Colony at the time. As blacks were historically called 'Caffers' (unbelievers), or 'barbarians', it is possible that the killing of cattle was further used to 'change their behaviors', in partnership with missionary schools and scholars. Under starvation, AmaXhosa and Khoisan groupings were ungraciously forced to adjust to the language and labor conditions of the oppressors, i.e. the colonialists. Consequently, a new formation of starving blacks, as a group without identity and livestock, became a new force to serve labor demands. Etymologically, this type of poor nation of AmaXhosa and Khoisan groupings in the Cape provinces were defeated to serve the colonizers' strategic goals (Rutherford, 1961: 273; Gump, 1998:36).

- The Eighth Frontier War lasted from 1850 to 1853. Notwithstanding what had happened up to this time, it can be inductively and deductively argued that the AmaXhosa were totally defeated and forced to adopt Western norms, standards and lifestyles. Sir Harry Smith conquered the Orange Free State and alienated trekboers in the Cape Colony; he also instructed his military forces to displace the AmaXhosa from the Kat River region. This Eighth Frontier War, called 'Mlanjeni's War', was named after the AmaXhosa prophet Mlanjeni who rose from the homeless and displaced AmaXhosa, and predicted that no guns would kill the AmaXhosa. This created a psychological and mental readiness to fight the colonialists, leading to the outbreak of the Mlanjeni War in December 1850. Although the AmaXhosa kaMlanjeni had some successes, they suffered military setbacks in January 1851. They were attacked by British soldiers and trained Khoisan gunmen, allowing the British to take offensive action against the AmaXhosa. Towns like Fort Cox, Fort Beaufort, Fort Hare and Fort Armstrong were used to defeat the AmaXhosa. Chief Maqoma used his military base on Mount Misery between the Waterkloof Forests and Harry's Kloof to score victories in areas such as Fort Fordyce. Legassick (2010:1-4) adds that even distinguished and honorable historians in Africa have tried to avoid the term 'genocide' to describe the deliberate extermination against the Khoisan groupings in general and the AmaXhosa in particular during this time. He argues that, by the mid-nineteenth century, one of the new strategy concepts that had become popularized by colonists was the extermination of the AmaXhosa, and governor Sir Harry Smith meant to convey the message of the killing of the Khoisan groupings and AmaXhosa to the colonialists – that even appeared on a banner carried by British settlers in the period 1850-1853 – who were invited to come and shoot the 'Caffers' without mercy, using the same genocide tactics applied in North America, New Zealand and Australia. This period towards the end of the Seventh Frontier War (1846-1847) was harsh and led to the Eighth Frontier War (1850-1853), which can be termed a genocide war against blacks by Sir Harry Smith. It can be argued that the idea of extermination among whites was further supported by evolutionary pseudo-science in terms of social and economic Darwinism.

- The Ninth Frontier War lasted from 1877 to 1879, also called the Ngcayechibi War or AmamFengu-Gcaleka War. Given the blow suffered as a result of the Nongqawuse incident, the AmaXhosa were converted into workers and laborers. Some of the people were recruited by the trekboers, AmaMfengu as Mngqwashini, Khoisan and British settler frontier people. The Eighth Frontier War, and other unrecorded wars, including the killing of cattle, reportedly affected the AmaGcaleka. In addition to the negative impact of the frontier wars on the AmaXhosa, the drought of 1875 triggered war between Ngcaleka and the multiracial group of AmaMfengu and British troops. Accordingly, in September 1877, Ngcaleka attacked the Cape Colony police made up of AmaMfengu, Boers, AbaThembu and AmaMfengu, deployed by Cape Prime Minister John Molteno. Ngcaleka was defeated. This was followed by the disarmament of all black people in the Cape Colony, leading to a revolt by black soldiers against Prime Minister Molteno. Using the Amatola mountain range as their hideout, the AmaXhosa fought, but were defeated by the British soldiers when they entered the Amatola range. The Ngcaleka's land was annexed by the British. It is reported that both the AmaXhosa and the British governor wanted peace, as they were exhausted by the series of wars. This frontier war was the most bitter and brutal of all, as it lasted for two years and subjugated the AmaXhosa to poor-quality land areas, like the former Ciskei area.

The concept of extermination was further entrenched by declaring South Africa a white man's country, and from 1844 onwards it was used for the purpose of rural development of white South Africans. Land and labor were acquired from the indigenous people by military means. This new rural capitalism, as prophesied by Ntsikana kaGabha, gave rise to a new racist discourse framework. As Ntsikana kaGabha prophesied for the nineteenth century, whites introduced radical and exploitative capitalism, with indigenous people being their main labor force. Colonialism, separate development, and later apartheid public administration and management systems systematically controlled land and created two worlds in South Africa:

- A social Darwinism country dominated by whites as masters and owners of the land. Social and economic Darwinism meant that Europeans used racism or subhuman methods to control vast regions and countries in terms of land acquisition by means of brutality, genocide, and military strategies, including sophisticated divide-and-rule techniques and laws. According to Swartz (2010:ii), 'the colonial forces that burst into Africa with violence from minds bent on foreign conquest were primarily driven by an ethos of covetousness that has come to characterize the existing international order. Stealing, not only of natural resources has continued side by side with the denuding of the very souls of people – as has happened so successfully in Africa – of their humanity'.

- Land dispossession in a society dominated by Africans meant that evil had arrived in Africa. The frontier wars were seen as evil, and lives lived in poverty were viewed as a clear assault on the humanity, dignity and free souls of Africans. Therefore, the creation of a dual economy based on social and economic Darwinism to promote imperialism and colonialism meant the AmaXhosa and Khoisan groupings were extremely deprived, and European countries and settlers weakened their resistance to British colonization in the nineteenth century.

Since these frontier wars, Africans were controlled by a system of colonialism and separation whereby they were limited to certain colonial boundaries. African people were grouped into a single tribe irrespective of their history or clan as an identity. This was followed by military interventions to force clans to affirm approved leaders of colonial or apartheid public administration and management systems, leading to the systematic formulation of Bantustanization or former homeland systems. It is also significant that the United Kingdom (UK) institutionalized its monarchy system in the ranks of Africans. This was done through the institutionalization of kings and queens and chieftainship leaders to serve rural white capitalism in South Africa. The institutionalization of traditional leadership as representing communities helped the colonial and apartheid public administration and management systems to deal with a single structure in traditional community affairs. Kings, queens and chiefs were then declared custodians of customary law, in respect of which the colonial or apartheid administrators had veto powers to replace kings, queens and chiefs who were not cooperating with the system. This led to broken relationships between the kings, queens and chiefs and their communities.

To add insult to injury, Western law or legal systems always superseded customary law or traditional succession. The application of Western legal systems was only limited to internal administrative affairs of rural African communities and former homelands. This led to the promulgation of the Black Administration Act 38 of 1927, to formalize the customary laws by promoting tribalism or laws per tribe. This Act gave rise to a greater negative impact on Africans and leadership rooted in Ubuntu principles. Some of the negative consequences of the Western legal systems using the Black Administration Act include the following:

- Legitimate traditional leaders were often replaced by those who would serve the commercial and market interests of colonizers and apartheid planners;
- The rich local variety of customary laws was disregarded and replaced by a uniform Black Administration System;
- State-dominated kings, queens, and chiefs abused their powers and functions to serve their masters rather than their subjects or followers. Those who represented their communities were either eliminated or prosecuted, or the colonizers combined their forces to defeat the legitimate and aesthetic leaders; and
- Clans lost their social and cultural fabrics; some nations' histories and kingships were deliberately left undocumented to ensure that kingdom and leadership issues remained unresolved beyond the lifespan of colonialism and the apartheid system.

This book argues for an inclusive social cohesion to enhance socio-economic, cultural and political relationships between people, and foster what Udenta (1993:22), supported by Swartz (2010:4-32), called 'revolutionary aesthetics' to advance truthful histories. In accordance with this, aesthetic leaders must focus on restoring aesthetic relational values in any planning and development that promotes myths and distorted histories.

With critical consideration of historical hindsight, it is clear that the Rharhabe and Ngcaleka assisted with the establishment of the apartheid homeland system, which enabled the imperialists and colonialists to exploit the division of Africans (AmaXhosa nations or Khoisan groupings or battles between Africans) to the detriment of a nation-building plan (Nhlapo Commission, paragraphs 9.3.1-9.3.19). If one reads paragraph 10.2.5, one would assume that the Nhlapo Commission concludes that, in terms of customary law and the Traditional Leadership and the Governance Framework Act, the AmaRharhabe paramountcy is not a kingship. This is a fallacy, as both AmaGcaleka and AmaRharhabe are, by customary law, traditional and community procedures and geographical background, born from iqadi (Supporting House). Section 211(1) of the Constitution of South Africa further confirms this premise. Thus, the Tshawe Kingdom continued to rule and to be subjected to apartheid laws and systems, including the further division of Tshawe into Rharhabe (Ciskei) and Ngcaleka (Transkei) as part of the homeland. Read with the Nhlapo Commission report, paragraph 9.3.1(c)(d), it is alleged that some kings complied with colonial and apartheid laws to apply to be kings and be approved by the Commissioner of the Bantu Authorities Act. It is significant that in some cases kings and paramount chiefs agreed to work under the Bantu Administration Authorities, which led to the formation of former homeland systems. This co-existence and conspiracy allowed both parties to make use of customary laws, supported by the Bantu Administration Act. This was contrary to, and in contravention of, the established customary laws common to most indigenous people in Africa, including the AmaXhosa genealogy, which is traceable to Cirha as a king of the AmaXhosa.

Consequently, Africans' social and cultural fabrics were mostly eliminated and destroyed through colonial and apartheid violence, ethnocide and land dispossession. They were pushed into increasingly dry and marginal lands in the former homelands, and into the deserts of southern Africa in the case of Khoi and San groupings. Under apartheid, the Khoi and San groupings were not even recognized as distinct cultural groupings. Instead, they were assumed to have become 'extinct'. Accordingly, many people of Khoi and San ancestry were simply assimilated into the apartheid category of 'colored'. They were generally the poorest segment of the South African population and eked out an existence as laborers on commercial farms, especially in the Northern Cape in South Africa.

It appears, therefore, that colonialism was used to create a division between Khoisan and AmaXhosa, on the one hand. On the other hand, clans and kingdoms were established using the divide-and-rule strategy. It was not until 1891 that a formidable resistance and collective political strategy was planned against the Cape Colony with the formation of Imbumba yamaNyama. Legassick (2010:110) concludes that, despite the mineral revolution and segregation, inclusive industrialisation, apartheid and Bantustanization (all pseudo-states to consolidate the regionalization of tribalism and apartheid institutionalization per region, tribe and clan), which undermined it economically and politically, the efforts of colonialism to destroy the cultural roots of the African people in our society have not succeeded to this day. This is to a large extent due to endless collective efforts and the strategic leadership and guidance of Imbumba yamaNyama from 1891 onwards. Instead, the Africans, including AmaXhosa and Khoisan groupings, have argued that the issue of land reform has reached the point of no return. This must be linked to

> *a nation-building plan and associated nation strategy for building capabilities [that] must bring together technology, policy, investment and industry incentives to present a coherent path for firms in various heritage sites, small towns, and cities between 2020 and 2064.* (Tsibani, 2017)

What is required is for aesthetic leaders to join hands to address land reform, including understanding the impact of a negotiated settlement, the use of distorted histories under a democratic administration, the lack of reconciliation between races, and further division under a racialized dual economy with increased inequalities between the 'haves' and the 'have nots'. The Pan-African Parliament (PAP), and country parliaments, must promote the recognition of indigenous groupings that have been suppressed and excluded in the legislative framework of post-colonial Africa, such as AmaCirha, AmaJwarha, Khoi and San people, in the case of South Africa.

As the land question in Africa has emotional and ancestry values, it will be critical for aesthetic leaders to develop an archipelago, chains, and connections of blue and green economic programs and projects to restore the quality of life of Africans, and restore human dignity, lost through wars of land dispossession. The land ownership programs and projects should be supported by engineering and technical value-generating support tools and resources linked to African free trade agreements. South Africa, as part of Africa, faces a time in the history of socio-economic development to mobilize global resources and focus at all levels of human settlements to guide land reforms towards the water mega nexuses, using integrated rural and urban infrastructure investment programmes (IR and UIIPs) to build smart, post-colonial Paradise Cities informed by an Aesthetic Relational Values in Planning and Development Framework (ARVPDF) as part of the Agenda for Sustainable Development (AfSD) by 2030. It is possible to argue that

> *A city is not gauged by its length and width, but by the broadness of its vision and the height of its dreams.* (Herb Caen, American journalist (1916-1997))

A reorientation of macroeconomic policy is required to ensure the long-term management of natural resource earnings, consider the appropriate exchange rate, take into account the causes of inflation and dis-incentivize volatile capital flows. Fiscal policies need to prioritize longer-term investment at various Paradise Cities in the Home of Legends or other landscapes in Mother Africa. The new dawn or 'social pact', or new deal to restore PRIDE through WEALTH, is to mobilize heritage sites, towns and cities through effective skills upgrading and investment, and productive ideapreneuers and entrepreneurs through opening up economic opportunities. The new dawn or social pact or contract must speak to community aspirations where industrial agglomerations are built. It must reach and sustain a shared and binding commitment which, through shared growth and investment, will lead to a reversal of the growing inequality in WEALTH. The notion of Paradise City models needs agreement around the expectations for large firms, rewarding long-term domestic fixed investment, innovation and dynamic competitive rivalry with effective developmental state-integrated rural and urban infrastructure investment policies, strategies and plans regarding infrastructure, procurement, skills development, technology, and opening regional and international markets. It must be captured in a socio-economic nation-building plan, which is designed and delivered locally, where people have a strong sense of identity, culture, belonging, history, and spiritual values, and a stake in the outcomes of a nation-building plan between 2020 and 2064.

REFERENCES

Adair, J. (2005). *How to grow leaders: The seven key principles of effective leadership development.* London: Kogan Page.

African National Congress. (2007). *Building a national democratic society: Strategy and tactics of the ANC discussion document.* [Online] Available: http://.www.anc.org.za/show.php?id=227. Accessed: 26 March 2017.

Althusser, L. (1965). *For Marx.* London: Verso.

Althusser, L. (1971). *Essays on ideology.* London: Verso.

Althusser, L. & Balibar, E. (1970). *Reading capital.* London: Redwood Burn Limited.

Amathole Museum. *AmaCirha chieftainship: Fact or fiction.* [Online] Available: http://www.museum.za.net/index.php/imvubu-newsletter/81-the-amacirha-chiefdom-fact-or-fiction. Accessed: 1 January 2018.

Ayittey, G.B.N. (2005). *Africa unchained: The blueprint for Africa's future.* New York: Palgrave Macmillan.

Balfour-Noyi, V. (2017). *The constitutional revolution of AmaKwayi-AmaNgconde.* East London: Harry's Printers.

Bokwe, J.K. (1914). *Ntsikana.* Alice: Lovedale Press.

Boulding, K. (1966). The economics of the coming spaceship earth. In Jarrett, H. *Environmental quality in a growing economy.* Baltimore: Johns Hopkins University Press.

Brandy, E. (2006). Aesthetics in practice: Valuing the natural world. *Environmental Values,* **15**: 277-291.

Brown, D. (1998). *Voicing the text: South African oral poetry and performance.* Cape Town: Oxford University Press.

Brown, J.T. (1925). *Among the Bantu nomads.* London: Seeley, Service, and Co.

Brown, L. (2006). *Plan B 2.0: Rescuing a planet under stress and a civilization in trouble.* New York: Norton and Co.

Brownlee, C.P. (1896). *Reminiscences of Kaffir life and history, and other papers.* Alice: Lovedale Mission Press.

Brownlee, C.P. (1916/1977). *Reminiscences of Kaffir life and history, and other papers.* Pietermaritzburg: University of Natal Press.

Buthelezi, M. (2004). *'Kof' Abantu, Kosal' Izibongo?' Contested histories of Shaka, Phungashe, and Zwide in Izibongo and Izithakazelo.* Master of Arts thesis in the Programme of English Studies. Pietermaritzburg: University of KwaZulu-Natal.

Cabral, A. (1973). *Return to the source: Selected speeches of Amilcar Cabral.* New York: Monthly Review Press.

Cabral, A. (1980). *Unity and struggle.* London: Heinemann.

Carneiro, R.I. (1970). A theory of the origin of the state. *Science,* **169**: 733-738.

Carter, G. (undated). *A narrative of the loss of the Grosvenor upon the coast of Caffraria on 4 August 1782.* London: Minerva Press.

Carter, W.G. (2008). *Individual expertise profile.* [Online] Available: http://myprofile.cos.com/carterw73. Accessed: 20 January 2018.

Casper, G. (2000). The United States at the end of the 'American Century'. *Journal of Law & Policy,* **4**. Washington: Washington University.

Chambers, R. (1983). *Rural development: Putting the last first.* Essex: Longman.

Childs, P. & Williams, P. (1997). *An introduction to post-colonial theory.* Harlow: Longman.

Clapham, N.J. (1996). *Case studies in war-to-peace transition.* Washington: World Bank.

Cloete, E. (2013). *Everyone's right to clean water*. Stellenbosch University. [Online] Available: http://www.infrastructurene.ws/2013/03/13/stellenbosch-university-walks-for-everyones-right-to-clean-water/. Accessed: 20 January 2018.

Cobbing, J. (1988). The Mfecane as an alibi. *Journal of African History*, **29**: 487-489.

Cohen, A.P. (1982). The symbolic construction of community. In Hamilton, P. (ed.) *Key ideas*. Milton Keynes: The Open University.

Cope, T. (ed.) (1968). *Izibongo: Zulu praise poetry*. London: Clarendon Press.

Currie, G. (2006). Reluctant but resourceful middle managers: The case of nurses in the NHS. *Journal of Nursing Management*, **14**: 14-15.

De Kock, L. (1996). *Civilizing barbarians*. Johannesburg: Witwatersrand University Press.

Dinh, J.E., Lord, R.G., Gardner, W.L., Meuser, J.D., Liden, R.C. & Hu, J. (2014). Leadership theory and research in the new millennium: Current theoretical trends and changing perspectives. *Leadership Quarterly*, **25**: 36-62.

Ditshego, S. (2018). Rubbing salt in African wounds. Racist societies don't regard a black person as human, as highlighted in Triumph's latest verbiage. *The Sunday Independent*, 21 January: 17.

Dondolo, L (2018). Complexity of AmaXhosa Nation. Seymour, 09 November 2018.

Duka, M.M.M. (2011). *Canon James Arthur Calata*. Queenstown: Khoi Publishers.

Dyibishe, M.L. & Mtiki, A. (2014). The *AmaCirha Kingdom. Suppressed voices and histories of the AmaXhosa Kingdom*. Interviews with Imbumba yamaNyama Royal Council. East London.

Fage, J.D. & Tordoff, W. (2008). *History of Africa in two volumes*. London: The Folio Society.

FAO. (2012). *Greening the economy with agriculture (GEA): Taking stock of potential, options and prospective challenges*. Concept Note. [Online] Available: http://www.fao.org/fileadmin/user_upload/suistainability/docs/GEA__concept_note_3March_references_01.pdf. Accessed: 18 January 2018.

Ferguson, N. (1999). *The house of Rothschild: Volume 2: The world's banker, 1849-1999.* London: Viking.

Finnegan, R. (1988). *Literacy and orality.* Oxford: Basil Blackwell.

Fukuyama, F. (1996). *Political order and political decay: From the industrial revolution to the globalization of democracy.* London: Profile Papers Publishers.

Giliomee, H. & Schlemmer, L. (1989). *From apartheid to nation-building.* Cape Town: Oxford University Press.

Goleman, D. (1998). *Emotional intelligence.* New York: Bantam Books.

Goleman, D. (2013). *Focus: The hidden driver of excellence.* London: Bloomsbury Publishing Pic.

Gottschalk, L.C. (1945). Effects of soil erosion on navigation in Upper Chesapeake Bay. *Geographical Review,* **35**: 219-238.

Goudie, A. (2013). *The human impact on the natural environment: Past, present, and future.* Wiley Blackwell: John Wiley & Sons.

Gqoba, W. (1888). *Isizathu sokuxhwelwa kwenkomo ngoNongqawuse.* Isigidimi samaXhosa, 22-23.

Gramsci, A. (1971). *Selections from the prison notebooks.* London: Lawrence and Wishart.

Gramsci, A. (1973). *Letters from prison.* London: Jonathan Cape.

Gramsci, A. (1978). *Selections from political writings 1921-1926.* London: Lawrence and Wishart.

Gramsci, A. (1988). *Selections from political writings 1910-1920.* London: Lawrence and Wishart.

Greenleaf, R. (1977). *The power of servant leadership.* San Francisco: Berrett-Koehler Publishers.

Gribble, J. & Scott, G. (2017). *We die like brothers: The sinking of the SS Mendi.* London: Historical England.

Gumede, W.M. (2005). *Thabo Mbeki and the battle for the soul of the ANC.* Cape Town: Zebra Press.

Gump, J. (1998). The imperialism of cultural assimilation: Sir George Grey's encounter with the Maori and the Xhosa, 1845-1868. *Journal of World History*, **9**(1): 89-108.

Guy, J. (1979). The British invasion of Zululand: Some thoughts for the centenary year. *Reality: A Journal of Liberal and Radical Opinion*, **2**(1): 1-33.

Hamilton, C. (1992). The character and objects of Shaka: A reconsideration of the making of Shaka as Mfecane motor. *Journal of African History*, **33**: 33-45.

Hirsch, A.O. (1976). *Social limits to growth*. Cambridge: Harvard University Press.

Jaggi, M. (1994). Crossing the river: Caryl Phillips talks to Maya Jaggi. *Wasafiri*, **20**: 25-29.

Jolobe. J.J.R. (1940). *AMAVO*. Johannesburg: Educum Publishers.

Jolobe, J.J.R. (1946). Thuthula. In *Poems of an African*. Alice: Lovedale Press.

Jolobe, J.J.R. (1958). *Elundini loThukela*. Afrikaanse Pers Booksellers.

Jordan, A.C. (1973). The tale of Nongqawuse. In Jordan, A.C. (ed.) *Towards an African literature: The emergence of literary form in [isi]Xhosa*. Berkeley: University of California Press.

Karis, T. & Carter, G.M. (eds) (1972). *From protest to challenge: Documentary history of African politics in South Africa, 1882-1964*. Vol. 1: Protest and hope, 1882-1934. Stanford: Hoover Institute Press.

Karis, T. & Carter, G. (eds) (1973). *From protest to challenge: A documentary history of African policies in South Africa, 1882-1964*. Vol. 2: Hope and challenge, 1935-1952. Stanford: Hoover Institute Press.

Kaschula, R.H. (ed.) (1993). *Foundations in southern African oral literature*. Johannesburg: Witwatersrand University Press.

Kaul, M. (1996). Civil service reforms: Learning from Commonwealth experience. *Public Administration and Development*, **16**(2): 131-150.

Khoza, R.J. (2005). *Let Africa lead*. Johannesburg: Vezabuntu Publishing.

Khoza, R.J. (2011). *Attuned leadership: African humanism as a compass*. South Africa: Penguin Books.

Kok, P., O'Donovan, M., Bouare, O. & Van Zyl, J. (2003). *Post-apartheid patterns of internal migration*. Cape Town: HSRC Press.

Korten, D. (1980). *Community organization and rural development: A learning process approach*. New Jersey: Blackwell Publishing.

Kouzes, J.M. & Posner, B.Z. (1995). *The leadership challenge: How to keep getting extraordinary things done in organizations*. California: Jossey-Bass.

Kunju, H.W. (2017). *IsiXhosa ulwimi lwabantu abangesosinzi eZwimbabwe: Ukuphila nokulondolozwa kwaso*. Ph.D. thesis, Faculty of Humanities, School of Languages. Grahamstown: Rhodes University Press.

Kuse, W.F. (1977). *The form of Mqhayi's poetry and prose*. Unpublished Ph.D. thesis. Madison: University of Wisconsin.

Kwetana, W.M. (2000). *A critical exposition of historicism and implicit activism in Elundini Lothukela*. Ph.D. thesis in Literature in the Department of African Languages and Literature, Faculty of Arts. Cape Town: University of Cape Town.

Legassick, M. (2010). *The politics of a South African frontier: The Griqua, the Sotho-Tswana and the missionaries, 1780-1840*. Basel: Basler Afrika Bibliography.

Lennon, A. & Wollin, A. (2001). Learning organizations: Empirically investigating metaphors. *Journal of Intellectual Capital*, **2**(4): 410-422. [Online] Available: https://doi.org/10.1108/14691930110409697. Accessed: 5 August 2018.

Lewis, C.S. (1997). *Christian apologetics: Pro and Con*. Bassham, G. (ed.). Boston: Brill Rodopi.

Makeba, M. (1962). Umqoko Obomvu endawushiywa ngubaba. [Online] Available: https://www.youtube.co/watch?v=ZmlDdacs2Uq. Accessed: 19 January 2018.

Mancham, J.R. (2015). *Nation*. [Online] Available: http://sirop-cdu-alliance-snm.blogspot.co.za. /2015/09/sir-James-Mancha M-argument-in-nation.html. Accessed: 20 January 2018.

Mancotywa, S. (2017). *The role of Imbumba yamaNyama Royal Council in contemporary democracy. Restoring dignity and reconciliation amongst clans, kingdoms, and nations using Ntsikana's prophetic message*: 14 March NHC and Imbumba yamaNyama Royal Council dialogue. Presentation in the Dr. MBW Rubusana (formerly known as Buffalo City) Council Chambers funded by Mthengenya and Associates (Pty) Ltd and the National Heritage Council.

Mandela, N.R. (1995). *Long walk to freedom*. London: Abacus.

Mandela, N.R. (2001). *Indlela ende eya enkululekweni* [Long walk to freedom]. Translated by P. Mtuze. Johannesburg: Vivilia.

Masualle, P.G. (2015). State of the Province Address (SOPA). Delivered in Bisho, 20 February, 1-41.

Mbiti, J.S. (1969). *African religions and philosophy*. London: Heinemann.

Mbiti, J.S. (1970). *Concepts of God in Africa*. London: SPCK.

Mbembe, A. (2000). Social sciences and institutional cultures. *CODESRIA Bulletin*, **2, 3 & 4**: 78.

Mbembe, A. (2002). African modes of self-writing. *Public Culture*, **4**(1): 239-274.

Mbembe, A. (2003). On the post-colony. *African Affairs*, April, **102**(402).

Mbukushe, F.D. (2003). *A study of JJR Jolobe's selected children's rhymes*. MA thesis in Arts. Stellenbosch: Stellenbosch University.

Mcebisi, J. (2019). After Dawn : Hope after State Capture. Picador Africa. Johannesburg.

McNally, D. (1988). *Political economy and the rise of capitalism: A Reinterpretation*. Berkeley: University of California Press.

Mdaka, S.S. (1992). *Images of Africa: A selective comparison and contrast of themes and preoccupations between Xhosa and other African writers*. MA thesis. Alice: University of Fort Hare.

Mona, G.V. (2014). *A century of IsiXhosa written poetry and the ideological context in South Africa*. Ph.D. thesis. Grahamstown: Rhodes University Publication.

Monare, M. (2006). SACP slams Mbeki. *The Star*, 18 May.

Moodie, D. (1860). *The record, or a series of official papers relative to the condition and treatment of the native tribes of South Africa*. Cape Town: AA Balkema.

Mostert, N. (1992). *Frontiers: The Epic of South Africa's creation and the tragedy of the Xhosa people*. London: Pimlico.

Motsapi, I. (2015). Email comments on the book. 10 July.

Mqhayi, S.E.K. (undated). *A! Silimela*. Colombia AE61: WEN 1826. Record available at SABC Archives in Port Elizabeth.

Mtiki, A. (2016). *Ntsikana kaGabha communication strategy from Thwathwa to various mountains and rivers*. Text message (SMS) citing oral themes sent to Dr. G. Tsibani on 24 December 2016.

Mtiki, A. (2014). *Ntsikana Gabha, a true prophet: From oral tradition to modernity*. Poem recited at the Great Place on the occasion of Ph.D. graduation on 3 May, Mngqesha District, King William's Town.

Mugovhani, N.G. & Ruyembe, C. (2014). *The power of character in leadership*. New Kensington: Whitaker House Publishers.

Musvoto, C., Nahman, A., Nortje, K., De Wet, B. & Mahumani, B. (2014). *Agriculture and the green economy in South Africa: A CSIR analysis*. Pretoria: CSIR.

Myataza, B.B. (2012). 27 January 1912-30 October 1986. He composed a number of songs and was an extraordinary choirmaster.

Nattrass, G. (2010). Transformation in southern Africa in the 19th century: Colonialisation, migration, and war. HSY2603. Department of History: UNISA.

Netshitenzhe, J. (2013). *The vision of Seme 107 years on: Is civilization still a dream and is the regeneration of Africa possible?* [Online] Available: http://www.ias.columbia.edu/blog/vision-seme-107-years-civilization-still-dream-and-regeneration-africa-possible. Accessed: 11 January 2019.

Ngcukaitobi, T. (2018). *The land is ours: South Africa's first black lawyers and the birth of constitutionalism.* Cape Town: Penguin Random House South Africa.

Ngoma, W.Y. (2007). *Complexities of organizational change: The case of the Eastern Cape Department of Education.* Unpublished Ph.D. thesis. Johannesburg: University of the Witwatersrand.

Nkrumah, K. (1957). Broadcast to the Nation, 24 December 1957.

Nkrumah, K.(1965). Address to the National Assembly of Ghana, 26 March 1965.

Ntsikana, W.K. (1906). Imfazwe kaThuthula. In: Rubusana, M.W.B. (ed.) *Zemk' iinkomo Magwalandini.* London: Butler and Tanner.

Nyembezi, C.L.S. (1982, 1958). *Izibongo Zamakhosi.* Pietermaritzburg: Shuter and Shooter.

Opland, J. (1977). Two unpublished poems by S.E.K. Mqhayi. In: *Research in African Literatures,* Spring **8**(1): 27-53.

Opland, J. (2009). *Abantu Besizwe: Historical and biographical writings, 1902-1944 – S.E.K. Mqhayi.* Johannesburg: Wits University Press.

Opland, J. & Mtuze, P.T. (1994). *Izwi labantu.* Cape Town: Oxford University Press.

Opland, J. & Nyamende, A. (eds) (2008). *Isaac William Wauchope: Selected writings 1874-1916.* Cape Town: Van Riebeeck Society.

Parnell, S. (2004). Constructing a development nation: The challenge of including the poor in the post-apartheid city. Paper presented at the conference, *Overcoming Underdevelopment in South Africa's Second Economy*. Organized by the Development Bank of Southern Africa, Pretoria, 28-29 October.

Peires, J.B. (1981). *The House of Phalo: A history of the Xhosa people in the days of their independence.* Johannesburg: Ravan Press.

Peires, J.B. (2003). *The House of Phalo: A history of the Xhosa people in the days of their independence.* Johannesburg: Jonathan Ball.

Peires, J.B (2003). *The dead will arise: Nongqawuse and the great Xhosa cattle-killing movement of 1856-7.* Johannesburg: Jonathan Ball.

Peires, J.B (2014). *Ntsikana kaGabha history.* An input of Ntsikana kaGabha Paradise City models preliminary planning workshop, East London, Premier Hotel Regent, Terrance Conference Centre on 17-18 November 2014, hosted by the Imbumba yamaNyama Royal Council, funded by Mthengenya and Associates (Pty) Ltd and HHO Africa.

Plateau, J.P. (1994). Behind the market stage, where real societies exist – Part 2: The role of moral norms. *The Journal of Development Studies,* **30**(3): 753-817.

Poland, J. (2009). *Abantu beSiswe: Historical and biographical writings of S.E.K. Mqhayi 1902-1944.* Johannesburg: Wits University Press.

Prah, K.K. (2005). Catch as catch can: Obstacles of sustainable development in Africa. In Ukaga, O. & Afoaku, O. (eds) *Sustainable development in Africa.* Trenton: Africa World Press.

Qangule, Z.S. (1979). *A study of theme and technique in the creative works of S.E.K. Mqhayi.* D. Litt. thesis. Cape Town: University of Cape Town.

Quatro, S., Waldman, D. & Galvin, B. (2007). Developing holistic leaders: Four domains for leadership development and practice. *Human Resource Management Review,* **17**: 427-441.

Rotberg, R.I. (1988). *The founder: Cecil Rhodes and the pursuit of power.* Oxford: Oxford University Press.

Rotberg, R.I. (2014). Did Cecil Rhodes really try to control the world? *The Journal of Imperial and Commonwealth History,* **42**(3): 551-567. [Online] Available: doi:10.1080/03086534.2014.934000.

Roux. A. 2017. *Everyone's guide to the South African economy.* 12th edition. Cape Town: Zebra Press.

Rubusana, M.W.B. (1906). *Zemnk' iinkomo magwalandini*. Alice: Lovedale Press.

Rutherford, J. (1961). *Sir George Grey*. London: Cassell.

Sachs, J.D. (2002). *The end of poverty*. New York: Penguin.

Saunders, A.N.W. (1970). *Greek political oratory*. Harmondsworth: Penguin Books.

Schwandt, D.R. & Marquardt, M.J. (2000). *Organizational learning: From excellent theories to global best practices*. Boca Raton, Fla: St. Lucie Press.

Schwella, E. (2008). Administrative reform as an adaptive challenge: Selected public leadership implications. *Politeia*, **27**(2): 25-50.

Senge, P.M. (2006). *The fifth discipline: The art and practice of the learning organization*. Toronto: Doubleday.

Senge, S., Scharmer, C.O., Jaworski, J. & Flowers, B.S. (2004). *Presence: Human purpose and the field of the future*. New York: Doubleday.

Sheppard, A. (1987). *Aesthetics: An introduction to the philosophy of art*. Oxford: Oxford University Press.

Silke, D. (2011). *Tracking the future: Top trends that will shape South Africa and the world*. Cape Town: Tafelberg Publishers.

Sirayi, G.T. (1985). *A study of some aspects of J.J.R. Jolobe's poetry*. Master's thesis. Alice: University of Fort Hare.

Sirayi, G.T. (2015). Role of TUT in creative art using modern technology. A meeting and interview with Professor Mzo Sirayi, 9 April 2015. TUT Arts and Dean's Office, Room 5, Pretoria.

Siwundla, K.P. (1993). *Sicaphula kwintsukaphi kaXhosa*. Umthatha: Shuter and Shooter.

Soga, J.H. (1930a). *The Southeastern Bantu*. Johannesburg: Witwatersrand University Press.

Soga, T. (1930b). *Sales of Goods Act.* Central Government Act. [Online] Available: https://indiankanoon.org/doc/651105/.

Soyinka, W. (1999). *The burden of memory, the muse of forgiveness.* New York: Oxford University Press.

Stern, P.C., Dietz, T., Guagnano, G. & Kalof, L. (1995). Values, beliefs, and emergent social objects: The social-psychological construction of support for the environmental movement. *Journal of Applied Social Psychology,* **25**: 611-636.

Stone, W. (2001). *Measuring social capital: Towards a theoretically informed measurement framework for researching social capital in family and community life.* Research Paper No. 24. Melbourne: Australian Institute of Family Studies.

Stone, M.K. & Barlow, Z. (eds) (2005). *Ecological literacy: Educating our children for a sustainable world.* San Francisco: Sierra Club.

Sugerman, J., Scullard, M. & Wilhelm, E. (2011). *The eight dimensions of leadership: DiSC strategies for becoming a better leader.* San Francisco: Berrett-Koehler Publishers.

Swartz, M.E.N. (2010). *Restoring and holding on to beauty: The role of aesthetic relational values in sustainable development.* Ph.D. thesis. Stellenbosch: University of Stellenbosch.

Terreblanche, S.J. (2002). *The history of inequality in South Africa: 1652-2002.* Pietermaritzburg: University of Natal Press.

Terreblanche, S.J. (2012). *Lost in transformation: South Africa's search for a new future since 1986.* Johannesburg: KMM Review Publishing Company.

Theal, G.M. (1897). *History of South Africa under the administration of the Dutch East India Company (1652-1795),* Vol. 2. London: Swan Sonnenschein & Co.

Tsibani, F.G. (2005). A literature review of the twinning approach in supporting developmental water services by water services institutions (WSIs) and water services authorities (WSAs) in South Africa. *Water Research Commission Journal,* **31**(3): 333-376.

Tsibani, F.G. (2014a). *The graphic design of Ntsikana paradise city as part of the NBP*. Presentation at the preliminary planning workshop of Imbumba yamaNyama in East London, Premier Hotel Regent, Terrance Ocean Conference, 17-18 November 2014, slides 1-166.

Tsibani, F.G. (2014b). *Water services education and training needs of councillors in the local government development agenda (LGDA)*. Ph.D. thesis. Stellenbosch: University of Stellenbosch.

Tsibani, F.G. (2017). Ukuvuthwa kwegaqa lePesika by J.J.R. Jolobe. Unpublished paper presented at the issuing of certificates to 193 Traditional Leaders by LGSETA in East London, 11 May 2017, 1-58.

Udenta, O.U. (1993). *Revolutionary aesthetics and the African literary process*. Enugu: Fourth Dimension Publishing.

Umteteli waBantu, 30 June 1928 and 11 August 1928; 9 July 1932.

UNEP (United Nations Environment Programme). (2012a). *Principles of a green, fair and inclusive economy, Version 3*. [Online] Available: http://www.unep.org/greeneeconomy/portals/88/documents/GEI%20Higlights/Principles%200f%20a%20a%20economy.pdf. Accessed: 19 June 2017.

UNEP (United Nations Environment Programme). (2012b). *Global environment outlook 5 (GEO-5): Environment for the future we want*. 36. [Online] Available: http://unep.org/geo/pdfs/geo5/GEO5_report_full_en.pdf. Accessed: 20 April 2018.

UNEP (United Nations Environment Programme). (2011b). *Towards a green economy: Agriculture – Investing in natural capital*. New York: United Nations.

UNEP (United Nations Environment Programme). (2011c). *Enabling conditions supporting the transition to a global green economy*. [Online] Available: 20 January 2019.

Van Wart, M. (2011). *Dynamics of leadership in public service: Theory and practice*. New York: ME Sharpe.

Van Zyl, E. (ed.) (2016). *Leadership in the African context*. 2nd edition. Lansdowne: Juta.

Wakashe, T.P. (2015). *Draft: A Revised white paper on arts, culture, and heritage*. The government of South Africa: Department of Arts and Culture.

Wilford, R. (1998). Women, ethnicity, and nationalism: surveying the ground. In: Willard, R. and Miller, R. (eds.) *Women, ethnicity, and nationalism: The politics of transition.* London: Routledge.

Williams, R. (1977). *Marxism and literacy.* Oxford: Oxford University Press.

Wilson, B. (1982). *Songwriter 1962-1969: Exploring Brian's muse in a decade of dreams.* Double DVD Video Boxset.

World Bank (2000-2017). *World development report: Equity and development.* The World Bank. New York: Oxford University Press.

Worldwatch Institute (2008). *The state of the world: Innovations for a sustainable economy.* Washington: Worldwatch Institute.

Wright, J.B. (1978). Pre-Shaka age group formation among the Northern Nguni. *Natalia,* **8:** 22-28.

Wright, J.B. (1989). Political mythology and the making of Natal's Mfecane. *Canadian Journal of African Studies,* **22**(2): 272-291.

Wright, J.B. (1994). *If we can't call it the Mfecane, what then can we call it? Moving the debate forward.* Seminar paper, University of the Witwatersrand Institute for Advanced Social Research, 29 August.

Xhosa Culture. *AmaXhosa Kingdom – A history. Part 1.* 16 June 2016. [Online] Available: http://xhosaculture.co.za/amaxhosa-kingdom-history-part-1/ Accessed: 1 January 2018.

Young, J.T. (1992). Natural morality and the ideal impartial spectator in Adam Smith. *International Journal of Social Economics,* **19**(10/11/12): 71-82.

Yancey, P. (1995). *The Jesus I never knew.* Grand Rapids, Michigan: Zondervan.

Zenkovsky, V.V. (1962). Dostoevsky: Religious and philosophical views. In: Wellek, R. (ed.). *Dostoevsky: A collection of critical essays.* Englewood Cliffs, NJ: Prentice-Hall.

APPENDICES

APPENDIX: MESSAGE OF SUPPORT FOR THE NATION-BUILDING PLAN

<u>*KINGDOM OF THE KHOEKHOEN*</u>

<u>*HANCUMQUA ROYAL HOUSE*</u>

<u>*SOUTH AFRICA*</u>

29 October 2019

DR GEORGE TSIBANI (MD)
MTHENGENYA AND ASSOCIATES (PTY) LTD
PRETORIA
0001

Dear Dr. Tsibani

Greetings unto you in the matchless name of our Lord and Saviour.

RE.: SUPPORT FOR THE NATION BUILDING PLAN BY OUR ROYAL COUNCIL MEMBERS AND TRADITIONAL LEADERS

We, the above Royal Council, with blessings and approval from our King, Professor Daniel D.W. Brown, undertake to honor our agreement with you to advance unity in diversity. Our King is a member of the Cirha clan and direct descendant of Queen Hoho and Ndoda near Pirie Mission in King William's Town.

Fumene George Tsibani

Our duty is to advance restoration of Khoisan dignity by advancing a new civilization under your Nation Building Plan between 2018 and 2063 as part of our common identity with Imbumba yamaNyama.

As discussed with Imbumba yamaNyama on 23-25 October 2015 at Pirie Mission: Ntsikana kaGabha Ceremony, our Kingdom and its Royal Council would like to advance aesthetic relational values beyond African boundaries in order to declare Jesus Christ as King of kings, Lord of lords in the international community. Your book is more relevant now.

Yours sincerely
PROF DANIEL DW BROWN
KING – ROYAL COUNCIL

APPENDIX: MESSAGE FROM IMBUMBA YAMANYAMA ROYAL COUNCIL

Imbumba yamaNyama Royal Council

CSIR Campus, Building 10F / Lower Ground Floor / Meiring Naude Road
Brummeria, Pretoria, City of Tshwane
Tel: +27 12 349 1152 / Mobile: 082 809 2162 / Email: tsibanig@mthengenya.co.za

28 October 2019

The book has identified causes of lack of social and economic cohesion in Africa. It refers to some nations, clans or kingdoms to illustrate these social and political realities in various cases in South Africa using ethnographic studies. The book provides definitions of terms using an essay type approach to make known some historical realities, especially in Chapter 6. As the author has consulted with most of our members and various Houses of Traditional Leaders in South Africa, Kenya, Tanzania, South Sudan, Namibia, Zimbabwe, and Malawi, including experts in various institutions between 2004 and 2017 (see acknowledgments), Imbumba yamaNyama Royal Council assumes that the book will add value to the strategic role of aesthetic leadership in planning and development between 2018 and 2064 as our rich historical heritage is too important to be left to historians. This book has provided readers with an African-based interpretation of leadership using some of the African intellectuals of the 19th century such as Ntsikana kaGabha.

The book seeks to reject pseudo-archaeology and advances the notion of correcting our distorted histories in order to create required reconciliations between nations and kingdoms. The book does so by taking into account the vision of unity in diversity (zenibe yimbumba yamanyama) rooted in the internationally adopted paradigm of Ubuntu, developed in South Africa. By looking at various historical writings of African writers vis-à-vis required SPACE competencies to drive a nation-building plan (2020-2064) using blue and green economic models, the book provides a theoretical framework of Aesthetic Relational Values in Planning and Development framework (ARVPDF) and designs an implementation program called Integrated Rural and Urban Infrastructure Investment Program (IR & UIIP) to achieve a state of equilibrium and/or paradise or smart cities in post-colonial Africa. The book further argues that Africa requires aesthetic leaders to implement African solutions in Africa rather than using plans, strategies, and programs outside the realities of African communities and heritage sites.

It is our understanding that this book is written to provoke managers and politicians to be aesthetic leaders by defining differences between managers, politicians, and leaders complemented by typical skills demonstrated by Ntsikana kaGabha in the 19th century including his philosophy of unity in diversity.

Yours sincerely
Rev. Mbulelo Livingstone (Ah! Ngubesilo) Dyibishe – Secretary General of Imbumba yamaNyama Royal Council

ABOUT THE AUTHOR

Dr. Fumene George Tsibani holds a Ph.D., MA, B.Ed, HDE, and BA, and has more than twenty-nine years of experience in capacity building, training and development, complemented by program evaluation and research in public policy and management. He has worked in these areas with various sectoral departments, state-owned enterprises (SOEs), development finance institutions (DFIs) such as the Development Bank of South Africa, and international development agencies such as GIZ, DANIDA, DFID, and USAID. He was instrumental in facilitating the Community Water Supply and Sanitation Services Programmes (CWSSP) in the early 1990s as part of Operation Hunger (an NGO) in the Eastern Cape and advancing the skills revolution within the Sector Education and Education Training Authority (SETA) system.

He is a member of the Water Institute of Southern Africa (WISA), Black Business Council (BBC): chairing Infrastructure: Water and Sanitation Work Stream; and Black Business Council in the Built Environment (BBCBE) as a Corporate Member.

This book reflects his personal observations, interpretations and in-depth analysis of a nation-building plan (NBP), applying Ntsikana kaGabha's prophesies and lofty advice since the launch of Imbumba yamaNyama in 1891 in Port Elizabeth (Nelson Mandela Bay Municipality). Given the new, complex capability constraints in Mother Africa and the need for (re)industrialization in Africa using the blue and green economy infrastructure investment model, Dr. Tsibani argues that our heritage and culture can add more value to creative cities and industries, in accordance with the African Union (AU) 2063 agenda.

You may send your comments to him through the following contact details:

Telephone number	+27 (0)82 809 2162
Postal address	PO Box 4129 The Reeds, Centurion City of Tshwane 0158, Gauteng Republic of South Africa
Email	**tsibanig@mthengenya.co.za** **lindo.tsibani@gmail.com**

CPSIA information can be obtained
at www.ICGtesting.com
Printed in the USA
LVHW010229090623
749128LV00009B/62

9 781647 532468